Critical Studies of Education

Volume 10

Series Editor
Shirley R. Steinberg, University of Calgary, Alberta, Canada

Editorial Board
Rochelle Brock, University of North Carolina, Greensboro, USA
Annette Coburn, University of the West of Scotland, UK
Barry Down, Murdoch University, Australia
Henry A. Giroux, McMaster University, Ontario, Canada
Bronwen Low, McGill University, Montreal, Canada
Tanya Merriman, University of Southern California, USA
Marta Soler, University of Barcelona, Spain
John Willinsky, Stanford University, USA

We live in an era where forms of education designed to win the consent of students, teachers, and the public to the inevitability of a neo-liberal, market-driven process of globalization are being developed around the world. In these hegemonic modes of pedagogy questions about issues of race, class, gender, sexuality, colonialism, religion, and other social dynamics are simply not asked. Indeed, questions about the social spaces where pedagogy takes place—in schools, media, corporate think tanks, etc.—are not raised. When these concerns are connected with queries such as the following, we begin to move into a serious study of pedagogy: What knowledge is of the most worth? Whose knowledge should be taught? What role does power play in the educational process? How are new media re-shaping as well as perpetuating what happens in education? How is knowledge produced in a corporatized politics of knowledge? What socio-political role do schools play in the twenty-first century? What is an educated person? What is intelligence? How important are socio-cultural contextual factors in shaping what goes on in education? Can schools be more than a tool of the new American (and its Western allies') twenty-first century empire? How do we educate well-informed, creative teachers? What roles should schools play in a democratic society? What roles should media play in a democratic society? Is education in a democratic society different than in a totalitarian society? What is a democratic society? How is globalization affecting education? How does our view of mind shape the way we think of education? How does affect and emotion shape the educational process? What are the forces that shape educational purpose in different societies? These, of course, are just a few examples of the questions that need to be asked in relation to our exploration of educational purpose. This series of books can help establish a renewed interest in such questions and their centrality in the larger study of education and the preparation of teachers and other educational professionals.

More information about this series at http://www.springer.com/series/13431

Eugenia Smyrnova-Trybulska • Piet Kommers
Nataliia Morze • Josef Malach
Editors

Universities in the Networked Society

Cultural Diversity and Digital Competences in Learning Communities

Editors
Eugenia Smyrnova-Trybulska
University of Silesia in Katowice
Katowice, Poland

Nataliia Morze
Borys Grinchenko University in Kyiv
Kyiv, Ukraine

Piet Kommers
Department of Media,
Communication & Organization
University of Twente
Enschede, Overijssel, The Netherlands

Josef Malach
Pedagogical Faculty
University of Ostrava
Ostrava, Czech Republic

Critical Studies of Education
ISBN 978-3-030-05025-2   ISBN 978-3-030-05026-9 (eBook)
https://doi.org/10.1007/978-3-030-05026-9

Library of Congress Control Number: 2019930833

© Springer Nature Switzerland AG 2019
This work is subject to copyright. All rights are reserved by the Publisher, whether the whole or part of the material is concerned, specifically the rights of translation, reprinting, reuse of illustrations, recitation, broadcasting, reproduction on microfilms or in any other physical way, and transmission or information storage and retrieval, electronic adaptation, computer software, or by similar or dissimilar methodology now known or hereafter developed.
The use of general descriptive names, registered names, trademarks, service marks, etc. in this publication does not imply, even in the absence of a specific statement, that such names are exempt from the relevant protective laws and regulations and therefore free for general use.
The publisher, the authors, and the editors are safe to assume that the advice and information in this book are believed to be true and accurate at the date of publication. Neither the publisher nor the authors or the editors give a warranty, express or implied, with respect to the material contained herein or for any errors or omissions that may have been made. The publisher remains neutral with regard to jurisdictional claims in published maps and institutional affiliations.

This Springer imprint is published by the registered company Springer Nature Switzerland AG.
The registered company address is: Gewerbestrasse 11, 6330 Cham, Switzerland

Introduction to This Book

The integration of Information and Communication Technologies in Higher Education just started by allowing students and teachers to interact via Web-based electronic support systems. However, a much wider impact of ICT has been signaled and demonstrated in the underlying European IRNet project. Its consortium from Eastern and Western European countries and Australia illustrates that international student exchange, Massive Open Online Courses (MOOCs), and enabling mutual learning among teachers and university policy-makers are needed further and also need strategic investments in order to climb on the ladder of benchmarking and thus to attract the better students. The chapters in the book before you show that building internationally intertwined consortia is no longer a cosmetic aspect; it has become a vital attractor for students and staff with higher ambitions. The next cascade of recent and future evolutions in Higher Education can be sketched:

1. ICT for storing, transferring, sharing, and refining learning materials (2002–2010)
2. Social media for connecting students, teachers, employers, and domain experts (2010–2019)
3. Mobile learning via apps for gaming, simulations, and collaborative learning projects (2012–2020)
4. Web-based communities for improving teachers' professional development (2016–2022)
5. Learning analytics for tracing, diagnosing, and predicting student profiles based upon the many big data streams that become available (2018–2025)
6. Immersive 3D virtual reality for ubiquitous connectivity with stereoptic and haptic experiences (2020–2030)

It may be clear that ICT technologies develop quickly and unstoppable. More delicate is the question if universities change its policies and business models. So far we can see that each of the six evolutionary dimensions above has mainly triggered cosmetic trends; essentially each of the technologies has been adopted in order to emulate the traditional functions of last-century education:

1. Transferring information from the expert (teacher) to the novice (student)
2. Emulating teacher-student dialogues via man-machine interaction
3. Testing student knowledge and skills via computer-based assessment
4. Supporting student projects via Web-based task support systems and repositories, etc.

What can we expect to happen in the coming years to Higher Education?

(a) First of all we will see universities to cope with many more training providers like virtual enterprises that let students to develop rather unique (authentic) skills, personalities, and problem-solving styles and allow employers to scout, select, and test new colleagues even during their study.
(b) Secondly, universities will only excel if they offer competitive programs that rest upon the highest quality of MOOCs from around the world. University teachers will spend less time in the actual lecturing, tutoring, and testing; they will become mentors and personal consultants for students who will go through a much more unique learning process.
(c) Thirdly, universities will coach their students to become unique lifelong learners. Future universities will not only transfer the knowledge and expertise to the students via curricula and tests; future universities will motivate students to develop new problem-solving skills and find new solutions to technical and societal challenges.

What is the consequence for future universities?

Universities will rely less and less upon their reputation of "centers of excellence"; universities will become laboratories/ateliers for developing youngsters' talents through special design and problem-solving tasks, revealing real solutions for real problems. Master students will undertake assignments, experiments, designs, and theses, compared to what PhD students achieve nowadays. PhD students will shift toward unique boundary-cutting research instead of performing research that has been prompted by the professor.

What is the role for internationalization in Higher Education in the coming decade?

First of all, internationalization will no longer be a cosmetic feature for students to prove that they can survive in foreign countries. Internationalization will be needed in order to prepare for international careers. This process is illustrated in the way enterprises develop toward multinationals; young talents will join international interdisciplinary teams and demonstrate that they arrive with better solutions than experts who were trained one decade before. In other words, universities will need to know the new type of jobs and explicitly foster the needed skills and competences for students in order to compete students from less-advanced institutes.

This book contains some important research results received in framework European Union Project IRNet (www.irnet.us.edu.pl):

– Nowadays, we can observe a rapid transition of the knowledge society to the "society of global competence," in which both the global economy and the education systems are undergoing changes.

Introduction to This Book

- It is evident that without an active implementation of innovative forms and effective methods of education and, above all, distance learning at all levels of education, these objectives cannot be successfully achieved.
- However, we can identify an existing problem that ICT techniques and e-learning methodology are not fully developed yet either within the EU or in Australia, Ukraine, and Russia.

In this situation, an implementation of the system designed to develop ICT competences of contemporary specialists, in particular current and future teachers, based on the systematic use of selected Internet technologies such as

- Some LMS systems (Moodle, Blackboard, etc.)
- Massive Open Online Courses (MOOCs)
- Virtual classroom technology
- Social media
- Other selected Web 2.0 and Web 3.0 technology

will positively contribute to the development of skills in the area of ICT and intercultural competences.

Additionally, one of the chapters is devoted to the innovative MA program "E-learning in Cultural Diversity," prepared by international team of authors.

As extrapolation of the underlying IRNet project, we may expect that the next-generation ICT applications and infrastructures will be catalytic rather than emulative. Learning analytics, learning games, and immersive 3D virtual reality will not only be offered to the students in order to learn the traditional goals easier and quicker; the new ICT tools will be chosen by the students themselves in order to build their own unique learning process. University professors will not just be the deliverers of expertise; they will be coaches for students who go in diverse directions, depending on the job and career they have in mind.

It implies that the follow-up projects of IRNet need to help universities around the globe to develop unique ways of teaching and mentoring. It will not be easy to find "silver bullets" for developing these requested future universities. Professors, deans, and rectors from now on face the need to encourage prestigious faculty for building unique learning communities for students in international contexts. Progress will only emerge if staff and students want to take risk and "learn to learn."

May the succeeding chapters of this book motivate you to get inspired and make up your mind for imagining your own role in it. Open a discourse with your colleagues in order to create awareness and feel urgency for the larger trends in Higher Education that you may expect now.

Enschede, The Netherlands	Piet Kommers
Katowice, Poland	Eugenia Smyrnova-Trybulska
Kyiv, Ukraine	Nataliia Morze

Contents

1. **Innovative MA Programme "E-Learning in Cultural Diversity"** 1
   Eugenia Smyrnova-Trybulska and Nataliia Morze

2. **Digital Competencies of University Teachers** 19
   Nataliia Morze and Oksana Buinytska

3. **Professional Training: Challenges in the Digital Economy Context** 39
   Tatiana Noskova, Tatiana Pavlova, and Olga Yakovleva

4. **Formation of Computing and Coding Competences of Computer Science Teachers in Ukraine** 49
   Nataliia Morze and Mariia Umryk

5. **Networking Through Scholarly Communication: Case IRNet Project** 71
   Eugenia Smyrnova-Trybulska, Nataliia Morze, and Olena Kuzminska

6. **Report Writing Assessment for Postgraduate Students: Lecturer's Perspective** 89
   Tomayess Issa and Theodora Issa

7. **Develop and Implement MOOCs Unit: A Pedagogical Instruction for Academics, Case Study** 103
   Eugenia Smyrnova-Trybulska, Elspeth McKay, Nataliia Morze, Olga Yakovleva, Tomayess Issa, and Theodora Issa

8. **Synchronous Virtual Classrooms in Problem-Based Learning to Mentor and Monitor Students in Higher Education** 133
   Juan Arías Masa, Rafael Martín Espada, Prudencia Gutiérrez-Esteban, Gemma Delicado Puerto, Sixto Cubo Delgado, Laura Alonso-Díaz, and Rocío Yuste Tosina

9	Multilevel Study of the Higher Education Challenges Caused by the Migration Crisis in Turkey	155
	Iryna Sekret and Darco Jansen	
10	From Face-to-Face Teaching to Online Tutoring: Challenges, Solutions and Perspectives	171
	Iryna Sekret, Soner Durmus, Melih Derya Gurer, and Orhan Curaoglu	
11	E-learning Competencies for University and College Staff	185
	Magdalena Roszak, Iwona Mokwa-Tarnowska, and Barbara Kołodziejczak	
12	Approaches to the Development of the ICT Competence Standard in the System of Research-Based Training for the Future Specialist of Social Sphere in Ukraine	201
	Roman O. Pavliuk and Tetiana L. Liakh	
13	Modernization of Environmental Education with the Use of Project-Based Learning, Outdoor Education, and Mobile Learning Supported by Information and Communication Technology	223
	Imrich Jakab, Martina Zigová, and Zuzana Pucherová	
14	Collaborative Learning as Learning Based on Cooperation with the Use of New Technologies	249
	Jolanta Szulc	
15	Possible Cultural Diversity and Digital Competences: Retrospection from Mathematical Textbooks for Lower Secondary Level	261
	Ján Gunčaga, Matthias Brandl, and Péter Körtesi	
16	Reinforcement of Logical and Mathematical Competences Using a Didactic Aid Based on the Theory of Constructivism	283
	Tomasz Kopczyński and Anna Gałuszka	

Author Index 295

Subject Index 299

Chapter 1
Innovative MA Programme "E-Learning in Cultural Diversity"

Eugenia Smyrnova-Trybulska and Nataliia Morze

1.1 Introduction

The two main recent trends in higher education during the last two decades have been the integration of ICT and the growing momentum of internationalisation. One underlying factor can be seen as growing mobility and growing connectivity as well. The IRNet project accepts this status and faces the new challenges that will need more and more attention in the coming years as otherwise the ambition for internationalisation will fade away quickly. The problem can be characterised as follows. About 20–30% of university students have a natural tendency to study abroad. In this mood they are quite open to meet a different culture. However local students do not necessarily have the needed exotic mindset to assimilate inbound students in their local study arrangements. In other words, the effort to acculturate foreign students is only one aspect; even more crucial is the question if and how local students want to benefit from the multicultural situation that has arisen at that very moment. This article attempts to clarify this fundamental deficit in ongoing practice of international student exchange. The crucial enabler in this process will be Web 2.0 infrastructures, such as social media and social networking, both for students and teachers (Kommers et al. 2015).

E. Smyrnova-Trybulska (✉)
University of Silesia in Katowice, Katowice, Poland
e-mail: esmyrnova@us.edu.pl

N. Morze
Borys Grinchenko University in Kyiv, Kyiv, Ukraine
e-mail: n.morze@kubg.edu.ua

1.2 Causes and Conditioning of Innovative MA Programme "E-learning in Cultural Diversity"

Developing the innovative MA Programme "E-learning in Cultural Diversity" has several causes and conditioning factors (Fig. 1.1).

1.2.1 Expectations of the Labour Market

The Digital Agenda for Europe 2013–2014 (https://ec.europa.eu/digital-agenda/en/news/digital-do-list-new-digital-priorities-2013-2014) analyses and describes in particular 5 entrepreneurship and digital jobs and skills, and in this document it is stressed that "A coalition is needed to take practical steps to avoid one million ICT jobs going unfilled by 2015 because of lack of skilled personnel". Additional action is needed to boost the overall number and the employability and mobility of ICT experts. Therefore the Commission will launch a "Grand Coalition on Digital Skills and Jobs". In Cedefop (2016) Figure 1 shows the level of ICT skills needed to do the job, adult employees, 2014, EU-28.

The European Commission has published the results of the 2018 Digital Economy and Society Index (DESI), a tool which monitors the performance of Member States in digital connectivity, digital skills online activity, the digitisation of businesses and digital public services (https://ec.europa.eu/digital-single-market/en/news/

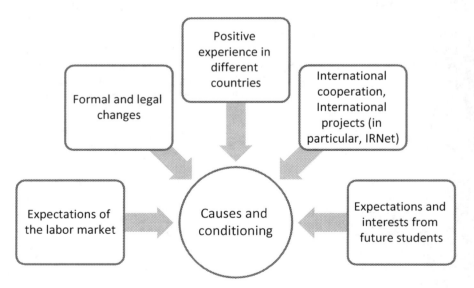

Fig. 1.1 Causes and conditioning of innovative MA Programme "E-learning in Cultural Diversity". (Source: Own work)

1   Innovative MA Programme "E-Learning in Cultural Diversity"   3

how-digital-your-country-europe-needs-digital-single-market-boost-its-digital-performance).

The EU has more digital specialists than before, but skills gaps remain.

The EU has improved very little in the number of Science, Technology, Engineering and Mathematics (STEM) graduates (19.1 graduates per 1000 people aged 20–29 years old in 2015, compared to 18.4. in 2013);

43% of Europeans still do not have basic digital skills (44% last year).

Alongside the Digital Skills and Jobs Coalition, the Commission has launched the Digital Opportunity Traineeships to tackle the digital skills gap in Europe. The pilot initiative will provide digital traineeships for up to 6000 students and recent graduates until 2020 in another EU country (http://europa.eu/rapid/press-release_IP-18-3742_en.htm).

1.2.2 Formal and Legal Changes

Thanks to such features as flexibility, availability, worldwideness, system base, modularity, low costs and new role of the student and the tutor in the education process, distance education is becoming one of major, most popular and effective methods, forms and technologies of teaching and learning. This form and method of teaching is implemented practically at all Polish universities as well as all over the world. Proper level and technical conditions for holding distance classes at the University of Silesia are ensured by the Education Centre. The formal and legal conditions are provided by Regulation No. 66/22 of the Rector of the University of Silesia on principles of teaching didactic classes at the University of Silesia with the use of distance education methods and techniques, dated of 3 July 2012.

§ 1 of the Regulation provides as follows:

1. The didactic classes in full-time and extramural studies taught at the University of Silesia with the use of distance education methods and techniques, hereinafter referred to as distance classes, shall be realised with the use of the University distance teaching platforms or of the platforms made available for the University by other entities, including foreign ones, under partner agreements.
2. The Manager of the Distance Education Centre at the University of Silesia shall be responsible for proper operation of the University distance education platform and for making it available.

In § 2, it has been emphasised that the fundamental condition of realisation of this type of classes "1. […] shall be completion of a special training course organised by the Distance Education Centre at the University of Silesia".

In point 5 of the document, the most important conditions for conducting distance classes have been indicated:

The academic teacher conducting distance classes:

1. shall make available on the platform the syllabus of the subject, the necessary elements of which are: the plan indicating the dates, on which the classes will be conducted in a traditional way as well as online; description of the classes together with the number of

ECTS scores; the manner of verification of the assumed education effects, the assessment criteria; the form of contact with the students, together with the contact address,
2. shall make available on the platform the relevant materials allowing for acquisition of educational content, doing auto-evaluation tests in the network as well as contact with the tutor in the form adjusted to the requirements of the IT systems operating at the University of Silesia,
3. shall provide the students with the possibility of personal consultations in the amount of at least 1.5 clock hours once a week,
4. shall verify the education effects (knowledge, skills and social competences of the students), while completion of the subject and module as well as the examinations may take place solely in the premises of the University.

In § 4, it has been pointed out that "The maximum number of hours of distance classes may not exceed 60% of the total number of hours of the didactic classes determined in the curriculum".

The materials provided on the distance education platforms of the University of Silesia shall be subject to protection in compliance with the Act on Copyright and Related Rights dated of 04 February 1994.

The standards relating to development of an e-learning course are described in detail in a document made available on the website of the Distance Education Centre of the University of Silesia (http://www.cko.us.edu.pl/standardy-e-kursu.html).

Distance classes within the field of study e-learning in culturally diversified environment have been planned in compliance with the requirements determined above, on the basis of Regulation No. 66/2012. The use of the distance education platform of the Faculty of Ethnology and Educational Science of the University of Silesia, based on MOODLE system, has been planned for their practical realisation; the platform shall be used for:

1. Didactic support for courses of curriculum subjects (Fig. 1.2) run as a full-time and extramural course (blended learning)
2. Preparation of future teachers in the field of distance education for the use of e-learning in their professional work as well as for performance of the function of the tutor
3. Conducting pedagogical research and experiments
4. Strengthening international cooperation in the field of e-learning and creation of regional and global educational and information European space

At the University of Silesia, Poland, for example, Decree No. 66/2012 formally allows one to teach up to 60% of classes in the remote mode. Proper operation of university distance learning platforms and their availability is coordinated by the Director of the Distance Learning Centre (DLC) at the University of Silesia. A prerequisite for an academic teacher of distance-mode classes is to undergo special training, organised by the DLC at the University of Silesia (5 h for lecturers and 20 h for authors). The Dean may exempt an academic teacher who has experience in the methods and techniques of distance education from the educational training. Field activities, workshops and laboratories are not carried out in the remote mode.

An academic teacher can teach classes in the distance mode during the academic year for no more than 50% of the hours of their normal working hours (Decree No. 66). The number of hours in remote mode does not exceed 60% of the total number

University of Silesia in Katowice
Faculty of Ethnology and Educational Sciences

Attachment no. 3

1.	**Field of study**	**E-learning in Cultural Diversity**
2.	Academic year of entry	2018/2019 (winter term)
3.	Academic year for which the revised course structure applies	—
4.	Level of qualifications/degree	second degree studies
5.	Degree profile	general academic
6.	Mode of study	full-time
7.	ISCED code	0111 (Education science)

Basic and special subjec

			form of teaching				year 1						year 2					
							semester 1			semester 2			semester 3			semester 4		
No.	Module	E/C	Total	L	O	Total ECTS	L	O	E	L	O	E	L	O	E	L	O	E
1	Intercultural environment *(see description below)	*	60	30	30	10	30	30	10									
2	Theoretical, methodological and practical aspects of e-learning	E	60	30	30	3	30	30	3									
3	Theory and Practi: effective use ICT-tools in e-learning	E	60	30	30	3	30	30	3									
4	E-learning in Cultural Diversity - technology *(see description below)	*	90	45	45	15				45	45	15						
5	E-learning in Cultural Diversity - theoretical and methodological basic *(see description below)	*	90	45	45	15				45	45	15						
6	Quality management in e-education	E	30	15	15	2				15	15	2						
7	Statistical methods in social studies	E	30	15	15	2				15	15	2						
8	E-learning management in enterprises, firms, company	E	30	15	15	5							15	15	5			
9	E-learning management in educational institutions	E	30	15	15	5							15	15	5			
10	Specialist seminar	Z	60		60	10								60	10			
11	Master's seminar	Z	60		60	30											60	30
	TOTAL Basic and special subjec:		600	240	360	100	90	90	16	120	120	34	30	90	20	0	60	30

Internships and field work

			form of teaching				year 1						year 2					
							semester 1			semester 2			semester 3			semester 4		
No.	Module	E/C	Total	L	O	Total ECTS	L	O	E	L	O	E	L	O	E	L	O	E
1	Professional Practice	Z	180		180	10								180	10			
	TOTAL Internships and field work:		180	0	180	10	0	0	0	0	0	0	0	180	10	0	0	0

Other requirements

			form of teaching				year 1						year 2					
							semester 1			semester 2			semester 3			semester 4		
No.	Module	E/C	Total	L	O	Total ECTS	L	O	E	L	O	E	L	O	E	L	O	E
1	English of e-communication	Z	60		60	3		60	3									
2	Practical English	E	90		90	4		90	4									
3	Social science/E-learning vs. social and ethical determinants	E	30	30		3	30		3									
	TOTAL Other requirements:		180	30	150	10	30	150	10	0	0	0	0	0	0	0	0	0
	TOTAL (A+B+C):		940	270	670	120	360		26	240		34	280		30	60		30
	TOTAL						940											

Studia kończą się nadaniem tytułu zawodowego magistra na kierunku E-learning in Cultural Diversity.

*** Groups of modules**

Intercultural environment

Description:				
a student choses two obligatory subjects from A1-A5; receives 10 ECTS				
Modules:	E/C	L	O	ECTS
A1. Theoretical and practical foundations of intercultural education	C	15	15	5
A2. Shaping intercultural competences	C	15	15	5
A3. Intercultural communication in research and educational practice	C	15	15	5
A4. E-learning and lifelong education in the prevention and solving of social problems	C	15	15	5
A5. Identity in the culturally diverse environment	C	15	15	5

E-learning in Cultural Diversity - theoretical and methodological basic

Description:				
a student chooses two obligatory subjects from B1-B4, receives 10 ECTS				
Modules:	E/C	L	O	ECTS
B1. Psychological aspects of e-learning management	C	15	15	5
B2. Adaptive learning	C	15	15	5
B3. Coachning and tutoring in e-learning	C	15	15	5
B4. Innovation processes in education. Innovation methods and e-learning/Multimedia and allied information technology	C	15	15	5

E-learning in Cultural Diversity - technology

Description:				
student wybiera obligatoryjnie dwa przedmioty z C1-C5, uzyskuje 10 ECTS				
Modules:	E/C	L	O	ECTS
C1. Modern programming technologies and computer network configuration	C	15	15	5
C2. Modelling ICT and e-learning technology selection in an educational environment	C	15	15	5
C3. Contemporary Information Educational Environment (IEE). Expertise	C	15	15	5
C4. Social media for flexible online learning	C	15	15	5
Modern programming technologies and configuration of computer networks	C	15	15	5

Legend
Each semester consists of 15 weeks
E/C - examination/course work
E - ECTS
L - lecture, O - all forms of teaching excluding lecture (practical classes, laboratory classes, discussion classes, seminar, proseminar, language classes, field practice, workshop, internship, tutoring)

Fig. 1.2 Curriculum of the MA Programme "E-learning in Cultural Diversity". (Source: Own elaboration)

of hours of classes (Regulation of the Minister of Science and Higher Education of 9 May 2008). The number of ECTS points that can be obtained as part of education using distance learning methods and techniques cannot exceed 50% of the overall number of ECTS points (Journal of Laws of the Republic of Poland, 28 September 2018, item 1861 - Regulation of the Minister of Science and Higher Education1) of September 27, 2018 on Higher Education Studies).

In Ukraine the Regulation of the Minister of Science and Higher Education of 30 April 2013 is applicable. The Regulation defines the distance form similar to the remote form. The Regulation does not detail the time which can be used by teachers of the University to conduct classes online.

The Resolution (authorization) on the implementation of distance education, as a separate form of student training, can be granted to universities by the Ministry of Education and Science in respect of the structural units that are geographically distant from the head office of the University. The University is not allowed to freely choose and implement such learning. On 1 July 2014, the Ministry of Education and Science allowed only 15 universities to implement distance education officially. All the other universities have to conduct blended learning.

Since 2013, the indicators of the universities rating conducted by Ministry of Education and Science and public organisations indicators have been supplemented by indicators that are connected with the presence of university resources in the Internet – webometrics indicators.

Such indicators are an incentive for the heads of universities to implement distance learning and expand e-resources that are part of the electronic learning environment of the University. The formal and legal aspects of the implementation of e-learning at BGKU, Ukraine) have been addressed through the enactment of the following regulations, in particular: regulation on e-learning courses in LMS Moodle and special requirements for e-learning courses certification, 2012; the concept of e-dean in LMS Moodle and its use in the educational process of the University, № 329\2013; regulations on the DL at the University, 2014; regulations on the use of DT in a part-time form of study, according to which in the intersession period (80% of teaching time), in LMS Moodle, containing certified e-learning courses for students, is mandatory, 2014 (Kommers et al. 2015).

1.2.3 Positive Experience in Different Countries

E-learning managers already prepared in some countries within the framework of different specialisations. Presented below are several examples of positive experience in the UK, the USA, Canada, Israel and Ukraine.

According to the concept of e-learning manager preparation in the UK, you can distinguish the following main roles:

- The organiser of e-learning responsible for creating e-learning strategies and for managing individual projects:
  - Strategist
  - Learning analyst
  - Project manager
  - Marketer
- Programmer responsible for developing e-learning programmes and structuring content:
  - Instructional designer

- Writer
- Graphic designer
- Programmer
- Audio-visual specialist
- Tester

– E-tutor or mentor responsible for consulting in the process of training listeners online:

- Administrator
- Coach
- Subject-matter expert
- Assessor

Directions of preparing e-learning managers (Israel):

– Technologies, databases and programming
– Design, user interfaces, graphics and video
– Psychology, working with people, presentation and providing information (didactic) materials

In Canada, to create e-learning projects in practice requires a degree of bachelor in communication, information technology and education. Besides, experience in teaching is needed (E-learning Ontario – http://www.edu.gov.on.ca/elearning/strategy.html).

The diagram "Related Job Salaries" shows the most popular skills for work manager of e-learning and the corresponding salary in the USA (Source: E-Learning Specialist Salary, 2015 (http://www.payscale.com/research/US/Job=E-Learning_Specialist/Salary2015).

Main goals of American e-learning managers are defined as follows:

– Establishment and support of a database for analysing the participants' learning outcomes, their responses and the ability to resolve technical issues
– Coordination and support of e-learning, marketing and technical infrastructure offers
– Developing new online courses and converting existing courses into an e-learning format, from curriculum analysis to final evaluation
– Recommendation and searching for special computer programmes and network services, creating content and interactive media

The chart "Popular Skills for E-Learning Specialist" shows the most popular skills for this job and what effect each skill has on pay (Source: E-Learning Specialist Salary, 2015 (http://www.payscale.com/research/US/Job=E-Learning_Specialist/Salary2015).

E-Learning Specialists report using a diverse set of skills on the job. Most notably, skills in Articulate – E-Learning Software, Course Design, Training Program Development, and Video Editing are correlated to pay that is above average, with boosts between 6 percent and 11 percent. At the other end of the pay range are skills like Adobe Photoshop. Training

Program Development is a skill commonly found among those who know Articulate E-Learning Software. (http://www.payscale.com/research/US/Job=E-Learning_Specialist/Salary2015)

The eLearning Guild has released the 2015 Global eLearning Salary & Compensation Report. Based on data received from more than 5000 Guild members, the average base salary of an eLearning employee increased to $78,310 for the year 2014, which is up 2.5% from 2013. The report, free to Guild members at all levels from Associate to Premium, provides an in-depth analysis of trends in the industry and the multitude of factors that determine a person's salary. (https://www.learningsolutionsmag.com/articles/1625/the-elearning-guild-releases-2015-global-elearning-salary--compensation-report)

The Ukrainian experience of the possibility of training e-learning specialists to manage the IT infrastructure of educational institutions is described in Morze et al. (2017). The contents and results of professional competencies, skills and soft skills formation in the course of "Managing the IT infrastructure of an educational institutions" are studied. The authors stressed that "Training specialists in e-learning is considered for the most part as training an expert who has to pick up the tools for e-learning and is able to design an e-environment, but the manager needs an active stance, a holistic perception of ICT in the educational institution, and should define IT policy and its consequences, pick, design, and build an IT infrastructure depending on the educational process objectives. These requirements necessitated the study of the 'Managing the IT infrastructure of educational institutions' course by pedagogy students in preparing them to be managers of e-learning".

1.2.4 International Cooperation, International Projects (Including IRNet)

One of the goals and expected results of international project IRNet (www.irnet.us.edu.pl) is the development and implementation of an interdisciplinary programme supporting the development of the modern tools and methods in the field of the information and communication technology (ICT) in pedagogic science and distance education as well as development of pedagogy in the context of intercultural competences in the countries of the European Union and in Australia, Russia and Ukraine.

IRNet scientific network:

1. Beneficiary 1: The University of Silesia in Katowice (US), Poland
2. Beneficiary 2: The University of Twente (UT), Netherlands
3. Beneficiary 3: The University of Extremadura (UEx), Spain
4. Beneficiary 4: The University of Constantine the Philosopher in Nitra (UKF), Slovak Republic
5. Beneficiary 5: The Lusíada University in Lisbon (LU), Portugal
6. Beneficiary 6: The University of Ostrava (OU), Czech Republic
7. Partner 1: The Curtin University in Perth (CU), Australia

8. Partner 2: The Borys Grinchenko Kyiv University (BGKU), Ukraine
9. Partner 3: The Dneprodzerzhinsk State Technical University (DSTU), Ukraine
10. Partner 4: The Herzen State Pedagogical University of Russia, St. Petersburg (HSPU), Russian Federation

Strengthening of cooperation among higher education institutions of EU **and non-EU countries** through **mobility and secondment of researchers.**

5. The **goal** of the project is the **assessment of competences** in the field of ICT and e-learning as well as development of effective strategies of implementation of the innovative tools in the educational activity in the context of education **globalisation** through:

   (a) Examination of the **education performance indicators** in the EU and in the non-EU states participating in the project
   (b) Analysis and assessment of **competences** in the field of the use of innovative education forms and proposing of effective strategies of implementation of the innovative ICT strategies in the educational process
   (c) Analysis and **assessment of the social, ethical, scientific, economic, technical and humanist aspects** of the use of ICT and e-learning as well as justification of the proposed innovative **methods** and **models** developed in Europe and in partner non-European countries
   (d) Assessment of **effectiveness of the existing models/methods** aimed at ensuring of the development of the e-learning techniques as well as enhancement of the intercultural awareness
   (e) Development of the **new distance education model** as well as shaping of the intercultural competences based on the existing models/methodology and literature
   (f) Assessment and presentation of the new models/methods of effective distance work in the field of cooperation and improvement of information technologies in higher education in the EU and in other countries
   (g) **Transfer of knowledge** in order to generate strategic effects in the scope of the area of the research
   (h) Promotion of the **scientific discussion** on **integrity and compatibility of education systems**, with emphasis put on the special role of the **competence** issues in the context of **globalisation** and **internationalisation** of higher education and other

1.2.5 Expectations and Interest from Future Students

Evaluation survey for students, teachers, employees of companies, public institutions and nonpublic institutions

The survey conducted in the years 2014–2015 included a description of the proposal of a new field of study. The survey was conducted in three voivodeships:

Silesian Voivodeship, Opole Voivodeship and Lesser Poland Voivodeship. The majority of the respondents – 70 persons – expressed a positive opinion and showed interest in participation in such studies.

1.3 Programme of Study

Connection between a field of study and a university development strategy, including the university mission
The development strategy for the E-learning in Cultural Diversity field of studies fulfils the development vision of the University of Silesia.

The development area of the field includes the key tasks, strategic and operational objectives and activities set forth in the University of Silesia in Katowice – development strategy 2012–2020. Therefore, it will contribute to the sustainable development of the field at the University of Silesia. E-learning in Cultural Diversity, as a multinational course, includes information on ICT, e-learning, pedagogy, psychology of multicultural education and practical knowledge based on social practice. The key tasks include four strategic objectives of the University:

1. Attention to the level of scientific research and strong research teams
2. Increase and improvement of innovative and modern education forms and the teaching offer
3. Intensification and expansion of cooperation with the environment and with foreign universities
4. System management of the course on the division level, in line with the system management of the University

The implementation of those objectives will enable to boost creativity among employees and students, create possibly the best environment to study and carry out research and open to the needs of the University and external units it cooperates with. Areas of activities within the E-learning in Cultural Diversity course are based on the following rules: openness, modernity and creativity. Shaping civic behaviour and prosocial attitudes will significantly influence the broadly understood socio-economic environment.

The development strategies of E-learning in Cultural Diversity, in respect to the strategic objectives of the University of Silesia, include the following:

- Strategic Objective 1: Strong research teams and research projects on international level consist in, i.a., providing support in educational development of the employees, implementing an internal quality control system of research, creating conditions and opportunities for possibly best scientific development of the educational establishments.
- Strategic Objective 2: Innovative education and modern teaching offer consist in, i.a., implementing the idea of lifelong and innovative learning towards students; providing students with knowledge and specialised skills compatible with the

1 Innovative MA Programme "E-Learning in Cultural Diversity"

field of studies and the possibility for further education; implementing the field in line with the organisational and programme rules of the Polish Qualification Framework; employing modern technologies in the education process; ensuring high level of education; providing substantive, psychological and social support to students; and adjusting educational conditions to the needs of disabled people.
– Strategic Objective 3: Active cooperation between the University and the environment consists in, i.a., cooperating with schools and other care and nurture institutions, self-government units, cultural establishments and institutions, cultural and educational companies and other companies, with cooperation and activities coordinating business together with external partners in order to popularise and employ a practical outcome of scientific research; offering patronage and honorary patronage over undertakings carried out in the region and country; ongoing cooperation with institutions and associations on the regional, national and international level; and creating positive image of the field of studied and its brand in media and in the external environment.
– Strategic Objective 4: System management of the University consists in, i.a., long- and short-time planning of the field development; obtaining grants for development of the field activities and their efficient implementation; making sure the organisational culture in the field, at the Department and University, is on high level; increasing self-efficiency of candidates, students and employees aided by services available online; and preparing development and modernisation plan of the camp for better realisation of the teaching aims.

Number of semesters – 4. Graduates are awarded the degree of magister (Master's Degree).

The Area (or areas – for joint or interdisciplinary studies) of education to which the programme is assigned and the leading discipline of art or science for the POL-on system, which is an integrated information system providing information on science and higher education.

Areas and disciplines of art or science to which the learning outcomes of the field of study are related indicate the respective percentage shares: • humanistic studies • humanities – 16%; • management • social studies • social studies – 84%; and • education • psychology • sociology.

The number of ECTS credits required to achieve the qualification equivalent to the level of study is 120.

Percentages of the ECTS credits for each of the areas to which the learning outcomes are related to the total number of ECTS credits are the following:

– Humanistic studies – 16%
– Social studies – 84%

Percentage of the ECTS credits for optional modules in relation to the total number of ECTS credits is 30%.

Total number of ECTS credits that a student must obtain in the modules taught is 110.

The number of ECTS credits that a student must obtain in modules from humanities or social science areas of education (not less than 5 ECTS) – in the case of fields of study assigned to areas other than, respectively, the humanistic or social studies 120.

The diploma-obtaining process in the Faculty of Ethnology and Educational Science for the field of study "E-learning in Cultural Diversity" is organised according to Chapters VI and VII of the Regulations of Studies at the University of Silesia in Katowice.

The diploma-obtaining process in the Faculty of Ethnology and Educational Science for the field of study E-learning in Cultural Diversity is organised and runs according to relevant provision of Chapters VI and VII of the Regulations of Studies at the University of Silesia in Katowice.

1. The student shall select the seminar and the supervisor from the list of the reported diploma seminars in the given academic year. The diploma seminar shall last three semesters.
2. The student shall determine the topic of the diploma paper and the course of the process of its realisation together with the supervisor.
3. The student shall file an application to the Faculty Council/Institute Council for approval of the topic of the diploma paper after its approval by the supervisor – Appendix 1 to Regulation 16 of the Rector of the University of Silesia in Katowice dated of 28 January 2015.
4. The student shall submit the diploma paper in USOS system (https://apd.us.edu.pl/) according to the principles and schedule of archiving of diploma papers of the University of Silesia in Katowice – Regulation 16 of the Rector of the University of Silesia in Katowice dated of 28 January 2015 on implementation of the procedure for submission and archiving of written diploma papers.
5. The student shall submit the diploma paper in printed and electronic version together with the set of documents not later than to 25 September.
6. The diploma paper should be prepared in a language being compliant with selection of the language version of the curriculum, according to the guidelines and recommendations relating to organisation of the diploma-obtaining process and preparation of diploma papers in the Faculty of Ethnology and Educational Science of the University of Silesia in Katowice, inserted on the website: www.weinoe.us.edu.pl.
7. After acceptance of the diploma paper by the supervisor, the Dean shall refer it for two reviews.
8. The Dean shall accept the reviews of the diploma paper and shall potentially (in case of a negative grade of the reviewer) appoint another reviewer; if another reviewer assesses the paper negatively, it may not be the basis for completion of the studies.
9. The Dean shall admit the student to the diploma examination after realisation of the plan of studies and education effects provided for by the curriculum as well as after obtaining of positive grade of the diploma paper.
10. The Dean shall appoint a commission conducting the diploma examination.

11. The Dean shall set the anticipated date of the diploma examination not later than within 6 months from the date determined in point 5.
12. The commission shall conduct an oral diploma examination.
13. The Dean shall set the date of the resit diploma examination not earlier than before expiry of 1 month and not later than after expiry of 3 months from the date of the first examination. The Dean may set the ultimate additional date of the examination in case when the student obtains unsatisfactory grade on the second resit date of the examination; in case of obtaining of the unsatisfactory grade from this examination on the final date, the Dean shall issue a decision on deletion of the student from the list of students.
14. The examination commission shall calculate the final result of the studies on the basis of the diploma examination protocol in compliance with § 34 points 2 and 3 of the Regulations of Studies at the University of Silesia in Katowice, subject to § 34 point 4.
15. The graduate shall obtain higher education diploma of the relevant degree.

24. Internships (hours and conditions) in the case of practical programmes and in general university programme – if such requires internship

I. Characteristics of the apprenticeship

Number of hours: 160 hours
Forms of getting of the credit: ECTS scores with a grade; 3 (semester 3)

II. Objectives of the apprenticeship

1. Acquisition of professional readiness for independent work of the project manager of e-learning in intercultural environment
2. Shaping of own pedagogic skills and skills in the field of e-learning in intercultural environment on the basis of observation and work in natural conditions
3. Ability to apply the acquired theoretical knowledge in practical activities of the student
4. Development of interests and shaping of proper attitudes in the pedagogic work of the project manager of e-learning in an intercultural environment
5. Inspiration for self-assessment and recognition of one's own professional predispositions by the student in various fields and scopes of activity within e-learning in an intercultural environment

III. Tasks to be realised
  1. Acquaintance with the tasks resulting from the organisational regulations (statute) and the regulations of work of the given institution
  2. Acquaintance of the student with the framework schedule of the day of work of the institution, in which they realise the apprenticeship, its internal organisation and plan of work
  3. Acquaintance with the conditions and with the specificity of the work of the teams working in the institution: internal structure and division of competences, specialist personnel and kept documentation
  4. Acquaintance with the work of the project team dealing with implementation of e-learning in the given institution, authors of e-learning trainings, multimedia didacticians and distance education methodologists
  5. Realisation of the statutory objectives of the centre during the apprenticeship
  6. Engagement in the works of the given institution
  7. Observance of classes/training courses realised with the use of the e-learning platform of the given institution, conducting of selected trainings

IV. Lists of institutions in which the students of the field of study E-learning in Intercultural Environment may realise the apprenticeship
  - Educational institutions (schools, education offices, teacher excellence centres)
  - Distance education centres of public and nonpublic universities
  - State or private companies rendering educational and consulting services
  - Training departments of various business sectors
  - Training departments of public administration institutions
  - Companies dealing with development of distance courses

1.3.1 Learning Outcomes

1.3.1.1 Knowledge

The Graduate
K_W01 has in-depth knowledge on the principles of operation of distance education institutions and systems, has ordered knowledge on participants of the distance education as well as on the methods of diagnosing of their needs and expectations, is familiar with their communication capabilities and is able to establish cooperation in diversified educational environment (P7S_WG (hum. sc.), P7S_WG (social sc.), P7S_WK (hum. sc.)).

K_W02 has extended knowledge on the principles, standards and tools for designing of courses as well as on innovative methods of teaching in distance education and the information and communication technology (ICT), applies the principles for management of educational projects and the principles for their evaluation and understands the conditions relating to copyright and intellectual property (P7S_WG (hum. sc.), P7S_WG (social sc.), P7S_WK (hum. sc.), P7S_WK (social sc.)).

K_W03 has thorough knowledge on the types of computer networks and programming technologies and on the principles of their functioning and application in the methodology of distance teaching, knows the principles of safety in the cyberspace and has extended knowledge on the ethical principles and standards in distance education (P7S_WG (social sc.)).

K_W04 has in-depth knowledge on the issues in the field of theory and methodology of multi- and intercultural education; has exhaustive knowledge on the diversified environments, their specificity, phenomena and processes occurring therein; and has thorough knowledge on the cultural conditions of the educational processes (P7S_WG (social sc.)).

K_W05 has ordered knowledge on the processes of communication, establishment of relations and relationships between individuals, groups and organisations in an environment being diversified in terms of religion and nationality as well as in economic, social and cultural terms (P7S_WG (hum. sc.), P7S_WG (social sc.) P7S_WG (social sc.))

K_W06 has ordered and extended knowledge on the methodological standpoints in social science and humanities – knows research orientations, strategies, quantitative and qualitative research methods and techniques (P7S_WG (hum. sc.), P7S_WG (social sc.))

1.3.1.2 Skills

K_U01 can diagnose the conditions of the process of distance education, analyse the needs and expectations of the participants of the distance education process and perform evaluation of the education process (P7S_UW (hum. sc.), P7S_UW (social sc.)).

K_U02 can select the teaching methods and the didactic means in the process of distance education and can select and apply the information and communication technology tools for creation of e-learning courses and platforms (P7S_UW (social sc.)).

K_U03 can initiate new projects connected with distance education, determine principles of cooperation and use IT applications for creation of documents as well as cooperation and communication tools (P7S_UW (hum. sc.), P7S_UW (social sc.)).

K_U04 analyses the cultural phenomena as well as the scientific problems relating to intercultural pedagogy and distance education in a critical and reflexive way and is able to use the normative systems in relation to the social bond and social standards in the course of solving of the theoretical and practical problems (P7S_UW (hum. sc.), P7S_UW (social sc.)).

K_U05 has in-depth research skills; formulates research problems; properly selects methods and techniques for them as well as constructs adequate research tools; interprets the data and draws conclusions; observes, diagnoses and reasonably assesses educational situations and social phenomena of various nature; analyses the reasons; and displays of human behaviour (P7S_UW (hum. sc.), P7S_UW (social sc.)).

K_U06 communicates in a foreign language, using the communication linguistic competences on advanced level, and has the reading comprehension skill in relation to complicated scientific texts and in-depth skill relating to preparation of various written papers (including research ones) as well as speeches relating to the detailed issues from the scope of the given field in a foreign language (P7S_UK (hum. sc.), P7S_UK (social sc.)).

1.3.1.3 Social Competences

K_K01 recognises the significance of knowledge in educational processes as well as in solving of research and social problems; is characterised by striving for deepening of knowledge, development and observance of professional ethics; and understands the need of continuous personal and professional development (P7S_KR (hum. sc.)).

K_K02 is characterised by responsibility in the scope of professional activities as well as in the scope management of e-learning in the intercultural environment (P7S_KR (hum. sc.)).

K_K03 as a participant of the cultural life notices social, cultural and individual differences, notices educational and auto-educational processes and demonstrates responsibility in self-improvement and in acting to the benefit of the natural environment (P7S_KR (hum. sc.)).

1.3.2 Tracking Career Paths of Graduates of the Field of Study

The system of graduate career tracking at the Faculty of Ethnology and Sciences of Education has been in operation for a number of years. Tracking the careers of graduates of the field of study *E-learning in Cultural Diversity* will be carried out by, among other things, the career office and by means of personal surveys and graduates' associations. A graduate database will be set up helping to maintain contact with students who have completed their studies. This will allow for monitoring their career development and creativity. In addition, with regard to tasks carried out by the Field of Study Education Quality Assurance Teams and the Departmental Education Quality Assurance Team, specified in the resolution of the Council of the Faculty of Ethnology and Sciences of Education concerning the adoption of a document entitled *Internal Education Quality Assurance System for Ethnology and Sciences of Education:*

- A specimen questionnaire will be prepared to survey satisfaction levels of students graduating from the field of study *E-learning in Cultural Diversity*.
- Monitoring will be carried out of the education effects achieved in particular modules planned to be offered as part of the field of study.
- Measures will be put in place to monitor education effects achieved during student practicums.
- An analysis will be carried out of results of a study into graduates' career paths and an analysis of compatibility between expected education effects and labour market requirements.

In addition, student career tracking will also be based on experience to date gained in offering the field of study referred to as *E-learning in Cultural Diversity*.

1.4 Conclusions

This chapter describes the innovative MA Programme "E-learning in Cultural Diversity" within the framework of the European research IRNet project (www.irnet.us.edu.pl) in conditions of strengthening international cooperation in internalisation of higher education, digitalisation and global competences. The causes and conditioning factors are presented of innovative MA Programme such as expectations of the labour market; formal and legal bases and changes; positive experience in different countries; international cooperation, international projects (in particular IRNet); and expectations and interest from future students. Additionally, a description is provided of the plan and programme of the MA course, effects of teaching, main modules and tracking career paths of graduates of the field of study.

In February 2018 Erasmus Mundus EMJMD application proposals were submitted with participation of 5 and 9 associated partners. In June we expect positive evaluation and results for our project proposal. A new grant will be a new important stage and support for implementation of the innovative MA Programme *E-learning in Cultural Diversity*. On the other hand, new support and conditions are expected to be provided for development and strengthening international cooperation in internalisation of higher education, digitalisation and global competences.

Acknowledgements The research leading to these results has received, within the framework of the IRNet project, funding from the People Programme (Marie Curie Actions) of the European Union's Seventh Framework Programme FP7/2007-2013/under REA grant agreement No: PIRSES-GA-2013-612536.

References

Cedefop. (2016). The great divide: Digitalisation and digital skill gaps in the EU workforce. *#ESJsurvey Insights, 9*. Thessaloniki: Greece.

E-learning Ontario available online at: http://www.edu.gov.on.ca/elearning/strategy.html. Accessed 31 May 2018.

E-Learning Specialist Salary available online at: http://www.payscale.com/research/US/Job=ELearning_Specialist/Salary 2015. Accessed 31 May 2018.

Kommers, P., Smyrnova-Trybulska, E., Morze, N., Issa, T., & Issa, T. (2015). Conceptual aspects: analyses law, ethical, human, technical, social factors of development ICT, e-Learning and intercultural development in different countries setting out the previous new theoretical model and preliminary findings. *International Journal Continuing Engineering Education and Life-Long Learning, 25*(4), 365–393. ISSN 1560-4624.

Morze, N., Vorotnykova, I., & Makhachashvili, R. (2017). E-learning specialists training for IT infrastructure of an educational institution management. *International Journal of Research in E-learning, 3*(1), 11–26. ISSN 2451-2583 (print edition) ISSN 2543-6155 (digital edition).

Shepherd Clive. Skilling up – learning about e-learning, available online at: http://www.fastrak-consulting.co.uk/tactix/Features/skillingup.htm

Skills Learning Professional available online at: http://www.lifelonglearning.co.uk/links1.htm. Accessed 31 May 2018.

Treser, M. Training and preparation of E-Learning specialists, available online at http://armikael.com/-elearning/elearning-specialist-education.html. Accessed 31 May 2018.

Chapter 2
Digital Competencies of University Teachers

Nataliia Morze and Oksana Buinytska

2.1 Introduction

During the time of economic development, fast changes of technologies, and new quality of society, modern education is based on high-tech means of education, characterized by great mobility, flexibility, and fundamentality. World science requires scientists capable of solving global scientific problems and developing general scientific theories. The international labor market requires skilled professionals with a flexible and operational knowledge system with the possibility of their application in related industries, able to quickly adapt to technological changes, be able to use all new emerging in science and practice, adapt to market transformations and improve own qualification.

Information and communication technologies (ICTs) play an increasingly important role in our professional and private lives, and digital competence is becoming increasingly important for everyone. Almost all jobs require specialists who have a sufficient level of digital competence.

2.2 Digital Competence as One of the Fundamental Competencies of the Modern Competitiveness Expert

The qualifications report for the digital world (Kiss 2017), the Organization for Economic Cooperation and Development (OECD), highlights four types of ICT-related skills that are needed by a modern specialist in the workplace. These include:

N. Morze (✉) · O. Buinytska
Borys Grinchenko University in Kyiv, Kyiv, Ukraine
e-mail: n.morze@kubg.edu.ua; o.buinytska@kubg.edu.ua

© Springer Nature Switzerland AG 2019
E. Smyrnova-Trybulska et al. (eds.), *Universities in the Networked Society*,
Critical Studies of Education 10, https://doi.org/10.1007/978-3-030-05026-9_2

- General ICT skills related to the use of digital technologies for professional purposes, such as access to information on the Internet or with the help of specialized software
- Professional ICT skills needed to create information technology products and services (e.g., programming, application development, network management, etc.)
- Additional ICT skills requiring ICT-related tasks (e.g., information processing, problem-solving, and communication)
- Fundamental skills (digital literacy, emotional and social skills that allow the use of digital technologies)

Digital competence includes not only digital skills but a set of skills, knowledge, views on the nature and role of information technology, and the opportunities that they offer in everyday situations, as well as relevant legal and ethical principles.

"Digital competence is competence, which involves confident, critical, responsible use and interaction with digital technologies for learning, work, participation in society. It includes: information and literacy in digital data, communication and collaboration, digital content creation, security and problem-solving ("Proposal for a council recommendation on key competences for lifelong learning" 2018).

Key components of digital competence are presented in Fig. 2.1.

The component "Information and Literacy in Digital Data" includes:

- Viewing, searching, filtering data, information, and digital content, in particular, formulating the information needs, organizing and accessing the digital environment, and creating a personalized search strategy
- Evaluation of data, information, and digital content (analysis, comparison, critical evaluation of the reliability of digital content sources, analysis and interpretation of digital content)
- Data, information, and digital content management (organization, storage, and acquisition of data in digital environments, data processing, and organization in a structured digital environment)

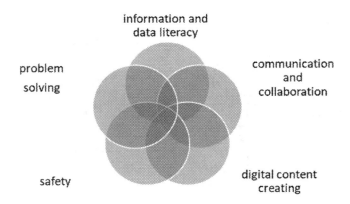

Fig. 2.1 Components of digital competence

Communication and collaboration include interoperability through digital technology with understanding of digital communications for specific content; the sharing of digital technologies (the exchange of digital content through various digital technologies); digital technology collaboration with the use of digital tools and technologies for collaborative activities, processes, resources, and new knowledge; Netiquette (knowledge of norms and know-how in the use of digital technologies, interactions in digital environments, adaptation of communication strategies for certain generations and in certain digital environments); and digital identity management with the ability to protect your own reputation.

Creating digital content consists of creating and editing digital content in various formats; integration and conversion of digital content in order to create original, new content; understanding and knowledge of the distribution of copyright and licenses applicable to digital content; and programming.

Safety includes device protection; protection of personal data and privacy; protection of health and well-being in the use of digital technologies; and protection of the environment from the impact and use of digital technologies.

Problem-solving is the identification and resolution of technical issues, identifying needs and seeking and making technological solutions, including setting up digital environments for personal needs (such as availability); creating use of digital technologies for the creation of knowledge and innovation, both collectively and individually in digital environments; and identifying gaps in digital competence to improve and update them, looking for ways and opportunities for self-development. The DigComp 2.0, a conceptual model updated in 2016, explains some of the areas of digital competence and most of the descriptors relevant to each of the areas ("DigComp 2.0: The Digital Competence Framework for Citizens. Update Phase 1: the Conceptual Reference Model" 2016).

In 2017, for the conceptual model of digital competency of citizens, levels of ownership and examples of knowledge, skills, and competencies were developed for each of the competencies ("DigComp 2.1 The Digital Competence Framework for Citizens" 2017). If DigComp 1.0 has defined four main levels of ownership, then in DigComp 2.1, there are already eight:

- 1st Foundation allows solving simple tasks with the help of acquired knowledge.
- 2nd Foundation allows to solve clearly defined routine tasks and direct tasks not only through the acquired knowledge but also understanding the essence of the task.
- 3rd Intermediate is characterized by the implementation of clearly defined tasks and problems due to the understanding of the situation.
- 4th Intermediate is solving problems in different ways, depending on the application.
- 5th Advanced is solving the most appropriate tasks through assessment of the situation.
- 6th Advanced is solving complex problems with limited solutions, thanks to the ability to create knowledge.

- 7th Highly specialized is solving complex problems with many interacting factors at the level of knowledge creation.
- The 8th Highly specialized creates a solution for solving the problem and offers new ideas, processes, etc.

Considering the European Digital Competence of Educators ("European Framework for the Digital Competence of Educators: DigCompEdu" 2017), we see that the authors distinguish six levels of ownership (Fig. 2.2).

- Newcomer (A1) knows about digital technologies but could not use it and needs manager and support.
- Explorer (A2) knows the potential of digital technologies, began to partially use, but needs encouragement, understanding, and inspiration.
- Integrator (B1) creatively uses and tries to expand the practice but at the level of understanding.
- Expert (B2) is widely used confidently, creatively, and critically, trying to experiment, open to new ideas.
- Leader (C1) has a certain approach, constantly thinks, develops in practice, and exchanges experience with colleagues but worries about disadvantages.
- Pioneer (C2) develops new approaches and methods, introduces innovations, and experiments with innovations.

Modern teachers and future specialists must have digital competence, which today is part of the professional competence of a specialist of any profile. Teachers of higher education institutions need not only to know how to use technology but also to be able to develop training strategies that include methods of influence for gaining knowledge of new technologies. To ensure a high level of educational services provision, the reincarnation of higher education institutions for training in digital age, and the creation of innovative learning environments, the International Society for Technology in Education (ISTE) has developed appropriate standards.

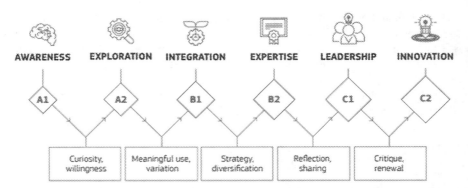

Fig. 2.2 The European Framework for Digital Competence of Educators: ("European Framework for the Digital Competence of Educators: DigCompEdu" 2017)

The ISTE standards ("ISTE standards" 2017) are in fact a road map for courageous, innovative instructors and administration that will enable substantially and effectively integrate technology into the educational process, make it innovative, accessible, and open.

The basic conditions for ISTE are 14 critical elements (Fig. 2.3) that are necessary for the effective use of innovative technologies in education ("Essential conditions" 2015).

According to the ISTE standards, the teacher should combine learner, leader, citizen, collaborator, designer, facilitator, and analyst.

As a leader, the instructor must constantly look for leadership opportunities to support students, their success, and better teaching and initiates and implements digital educational technology to meet the needs of all students.

As a citizen – inspiring students for a positive contribution and responsibility in the digital world – is a mentor for the critical use of digital tools and online resources.

As a collaborator – devotes his time to collaborate with colleagues and students, improve their practices, acquire new knowledge of technology, and use collaborative tools to expand their experience at different levels.

As a designer – develops educational resources and learning environments for quality, maximally effective, active, and in-depth learning, using the principles of curriculum design, digital tools, and resources.

As a facilitator – facilitates technology education to support student achievement of professional competencies, manages the use of technologies and strategies for student learning on digital platforms, virtual environments and models, and develops creativity to share ideas and knowledge.

As an analyst, you must understand and use the data to manage the student's educational process, provide them with alternative ways to demonstrate technical competence, manage progress, and communicate with students and business partners.

And, most importantly, to be constantly learner – to improve their own practice, to study the best practices using innovative technologies, to keep abreast of all innovations, to ensure their development through network education, and to make effective use of all the knowledge gained.

Borys Grinchenko Kyiv University has developed corporate standards for digital competence of all participants in the educational process. However, since the first option was developed in 2013–2014, then it was not about digital competency but about IC competence, which was seen as the ability to effectively use ICT in teaching, research, and everyday activities to address information and professional issues ("On Approval of the State Standard for Basic and Complete Secondary Education" 2011).

By developing a standard for IC competencies, we have been guided by the UNESCO competencies that are defined within the framework of ICT competence for teachers (ICT Competency Framework for Teachers) ("Structure of ICT competence of teachers. UNESCO Recommendations" 2011).

Standard	Description
Common vision	It is a proactive leadership in developing a common vision, building a strategy for introducing technologies into the educational process. It is the driving force behind the technology implementation plan, but it is not formulated or extended from the top
Authorized Leaders	Changes require leaders who have the right to experiment, make critical decisions, take risks, help solve problems, implement changes from within
Implementation planning	This is the basis for technology implementation, which includes a detailed roadmap to reach critical stages of the initiative, with short-term and long-term goals, critical points and timelines, responsibilities and resources sharing.
Consistent and adequate funding	Means the development of a strategic plan for obtaining financing in which the ongoing maintenance, updating, maintenance and development of the infrastructure are transferred, while providing professional training of the staff for its maximum possible use in the educational process.
Valid access	Reliable and equal access to new technologies and resources with the ability to connect all participants in the educational process
Qualified staff	Those who are able to select and effectively use modern digital resources and innovative technologies to increase the efficiency and quality of the educational process, which are constantly self-improving and self-learning, help others point out the importance of technological skills
Constant professional training	Teachers need constant education to be aware of the rapid changes in educational technologies, they must assimilate their knowledge, practice new skills, learn and work together.
Support	This is a guarantee that the technology continues to function, remains relevant and accessible
Educational programs and plans	Technology standards must inform and support educational programs, penetrate them, be part of the educational goal itself, and not a means to achieve it.
Student study	It directs students to be non-passive recipients of knowledge, but to be active participants, to study constantly. The training should be student-centered and practical oriented, promote the development of digital competenciSupport for initiatives at the national and local levels promote the use of innovative technologies in accordance with educational standards.es
Quality assessment	The assessment of the use of technology helps to track the progress of the system to ensure quality, which forms a coherent picture of the quality of education
Collaboration with partners and business structures	cooperation with partners contributes to the competitiveness of the institution, its recognition in society. They understand the role of technology in education, are ready to cooperate, be the bases of practice, lectures and conduct practical classes.
Support policy	Necessary for effective work and introduction of innovative technologies, helps to optimize the process of integration of technologies and their use for specific educational needs.
Supporting external context	Support for initiatives at the national and local levels promote the use of innovative technologies in accordance with educational standards.

Fig. 2.3 Basic standards of ISTE

The main tasks in this case were the creation of an appropriate model of IC competence (for students and teachers) taking into account the standards of ISTE and UNESCO, determining the levels of their formation and appropriate monitoring tools for their formation.

UNESCO's recommendations emphasize that for a modern specialist, it is not enough to be informationally literate and to be able to form technological skills.

Modern teachers should be able to help students use ICTs to successfully cooperate, solve emerging tasks, and master the twenty-first-century skills.

When constructing the model of IC competence of a scientific and pedagogical employee, the main three approaches to the activities of the teacher are distinguished; in fact there are three levels (basic (minimal), advanced (average), professional (high)).

The first approach – "technical literacy" – requires the teacher to help students use ICT to increase the efficiency of academic and research work.

The second – "deepening of knowledge" – requires teachers to be able to help students deep-seated the content of the curriculum, applying the knowledge gained to solving complex problems that occur in the modern world, in particular on the basis of modern ICT.

The third – "creating knowledge" – requires teachers to be able to help students using modern ICTs to produce new knowledge, skills that modern employers require.

To familiarize yourself with the model of the corporate standard of IC competence of a teacher of the Borys Grinchenko Kyiv University in the context of its main aspects of activity, understanding of the role of ICT and their application in educational, scientific activities and qualifications can be found on the official portal of the Borys Grinchenko Kyiv University (http://kubg.edu.ua) ("Corporate standard of ICT competence of the teacher (model). Tools for measuring the formation of ICT competencies" 2014).

Due to the rapid change of technologies and the development of the digital society, the existing model needs to be rethought and refined, taking into account innovations in education and training and the formation of new skills – digital competencies.

Comparing the European Framework for the Digital Competence of Educators and the ICT Competency Framework for Teachers at UNESCO, we see that UNESCO's areas of IC expertise are only superficially covering the first three areas of DigComp's digital competencies, namely, digital literacy and digital literacy, communication and collaboration, and digital content creation. Therefore, for updating, more precisely, the creation of a teacher's digital competency model focused on DigCompEdu and the ISTE standards.

We highlight the main levels of the current teacher (analyst, integrator, expert, leader, innovator) and activities (use of digital resources, educational activities, research, professional interaction and collaboration, self-improvement, and continuous development) (Table 2.1).

Table 2.1 The model of the corporate standard of digital competence of the teacher

Activity	R.1 Analyst	P.2 Integrator	R.3 Expert	P.4 Leader	P.5 Innovator
Using digital resources	Studying digital resources, understanding how to use and trying to use	Experimenting with digital resources for different purposes and for various tasks	Purposefully selects for specific situations, finds the advantages and disadvantages of using it	Uses consistently and comprehensively, sharing experiences	Creates new resources, introduces innovations
Educational activity	Plans and uses to improve the quality of learning activities	Thoroughly integrates digital resources for meaningful learning	Purposefully and critically used to stimulate learning	Evaluates application, reflects on improvement	Introduces new resources to improve quality, experiments
Research activity	Fragmentation use and analysis	Extends research opportunities, scientific communication through the integration of digital resources	Experiments on the implementation of digital resources in research	Effectively and holistically uses digital resources in research	Uses innovative formats for organizing and conducting research
Professional interaction and collaboration	Optional use of digital resources	Expansion and improvement of professional approaches	Discussion of opportunities for interaction and cooperation and their improvement	It uniquely expands the possibilities of cooperation and interaction	It offers new ways and resources for joint e-interaction
Self-improvement and constant development	Increase the use of digital resources	Expand opportunities for awareness	Effective use of tools for expanding capabilities	Constant updating of professional practice	Continuous self-development through digital resources

The definition of the level of formation of the digital competence of the teacher at the University is carried out in three stages: self-diagnosis, conduct of the online survey, and openness of all types of teacher's activity and their analytics, thanks to the developed and the system "e-portfolio." (Morze et al. 2016)

For conducting self-diagnosis, teachers are encouraged to go through a digital online competency-based digital competence test ("Digital competences self-diagnosis test" 2015). This online tool was developed in 2014 in Spain.

In personal reports, the results are visualized (Fig. 2.4), and detailed recommendations are given to increase the level of personal digital competence, and the explanations for convenience for each competency are presented by the discriminators (Table 2.2).

Let's look more detailed tools for evaluating the teacher's digital competency, the introduction of which was created at the University.

A key tool for evaluating digital competency in learning activities is the development, use, and certification of e-learning courses in disciplines that are hosted in the e-learning system (http://e-learning.kubg.edu.ua/), which works on the Moodle distance learning platform.

The tool for measuring the use of digital competence in research activities is the university's institutional repository http://elibrary.kubg.edu.ua/, in which each teacher can independently place his full-text scientific research and scientific and methodological work during the period of activity at the University.

In general, an open indicator of the level of formation of a teacher's digital competence is his e-portfolio. Since e-portfolio is a tool for measuring the results of a teacher's professional activity, it should reflect all aspects of the activities specified in the Corporate Digital Competency Standard and the Corporate Standard of Scientific Activity and accordingly affect the overall representation of the University and its competitiveness and visibility in the educational space.

The quantitative indicators of the quality of educational activity of the teacher are the average score of students' teaching activity, printed and electronic scientific

Fig. 2.4 Example of presentation of personal results of self-diagnosis (According to the results of the test by the author of the article Buinytska O)

Table 2.2 Digital competency discriminators based on the DigComp model

Area	Competence	Description
Information	Browsing, searching and filtering information	To access and search for online information, to articulate information needs, to find relevant information, to select resources effectively, to navigate between online sources, to create personal information strategies
Information	Evaluating information	To gather, process, understand and critically evaluate information
Information	Storing and retrieving	To manipulate and store information and content for easier retrieval, to organise information and data
Communication	Interacting through technologies	To interact through a variety of digital devices and applications, to understand how digital communication is distributed, displayed and managed, to understand appropriate ways of communicating through digital means, to refer to different communication formats, to adapt communication modes and strategies to the specific audience
Communication	Sharing information and content	To share with others the location and content of information found, to be willing and able to share knowledge, content and resources, to act as an intermediary, to be proactive in the spreading of news, content and resources, to know about citation practices and to integrate new information into an existing body of knowledge
Communication	Engaging in online citizenship	To participate in society through online engagement, to seek opportunities for self-development and empowerment in using technologies and digital environments, to be aware of the potential of technologies for citizen participation
Communication	Collaborating through digital channels	To use technologies and media for team work, collaborative processes and co-construction and co-creation of resources, knowledge and content
Communication	Netiquette	To have the knowledge and know-how of behavioural norms in online/virtual interactions, to be aware of cultural diversity aspects, to be able to protect self and others from possible online dangers (e.g. cyber bullying), to develop active strategies to discover inappropriate behaviour
Communication	Managing digital identity	To create, adapt and manage one or multiple digital identities, to be able to protect one's e-reputation, to deal with the data that one produces through several accounts and applications
Content creation	Developing content	To create content in different formats including multimedia, to edit and improve content that s/he has created or that others have created, to express creatively through digital media and technologies
Content creation	Integrating and re-elaborating	To modify, refine and mash-up existing resources to create new, original and relevant content and knowledge
Content creation	Copyright and Licences	To understand how copyright and licences apply to information and content
Content creation	Programming	To apply settings, programme modification, programme applications, software, devices, to understand the principles of programming, to understand what is behind a programme

Area	Competence	Description
Safety	Protecting devices	To protect own devices and to understand online risks and threats, to know about safety and security measures
Safety	Protecting personal data	To understand common terms of service, active protection of personal data, understanding other people privacy, to protect self from online fraud and threats and cyber bullying
Safety	Protecting health	To avoid health-risks related with the use of technology in terms of threats to physical and psychological well-being
Safety	Protecting the environment	To be aware of the impact of ICT on the environment
Problem solving	Solving technical problems	To identify possible problems and solve them (from trouble-shooting to solving more complex problems) with the help of digital means
Problem solving	Identifying needs and technological responses	To assess own needs in terms of resources, tools and competence development, to match needs with possible solutions, adapting tools to personal needs, to critically evaluate possible solutions and digital tools
Problem solving	Innovating and creatively using technology	To innovate with technology, to actively participate in collaborative digital and multimedia production, to express oneself creatively through digital media and technologies, to create knowledge and solve conceptual problems with the support of digital tools
Problem solving	Identifying digital competence gaps	To understand where own competence needs to be improved or updated, to support others in the development of their digital competence, to keep up-to-date with new developments

publications, participation in international and state research projects, scientific conferences, receiving individual mobility grants, management of postgraduate students and defense of dissertation research, preparation of students for effective participation in subject Olympiads and international competitions, creation of electronic training courses and their certification, etc. Qualitative indicators have been selected: professional training, advanced training, a school of science, colleagues' feedback, the use of certified electronic training courses, etc. (Morze and Varchenko-Trotsenko, 2016).

In order to reflect the trustworthy information teacher's portfolio, all information in the system is entered either from the institutional repository (publication activity) http://elibrary.kubg.edu.ua/ or from the registries of the University's activity database http://rg.kubg.edu.ua/ (Fig. 2.5), downloaded by the responsible persons appointed by the order.

To display a coherent picture of the activity of a teacher at the Borys Grinchenko Kyiv University, an e-portfolio system (http://eportfolio.kubg.edu.ua/) was developed that is open access and allows not only the formation of an e-portfolio of the teacher (Fig. 2.6) but also to form rating tables of the indicators of evaluation of the main types of activity of each teacher and all departments with the aim of objective analysis of the quality of staffing of professional activities and the quality of higher education. (Morze et al. 2016)

According to the results of the rating, the teacher determines the level of his professional activity in the position (in general and by type of activity) and can be recognized as high, sufficient, or low.

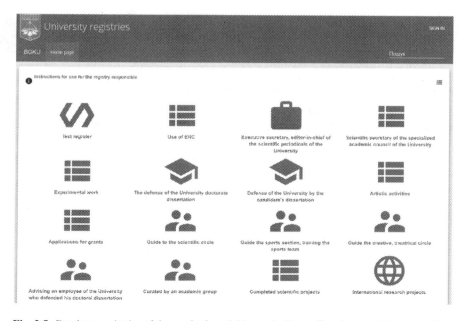

Fig. 2.5 Database registries of the teacher's activities at the Borys Grinchenko Kyiv University

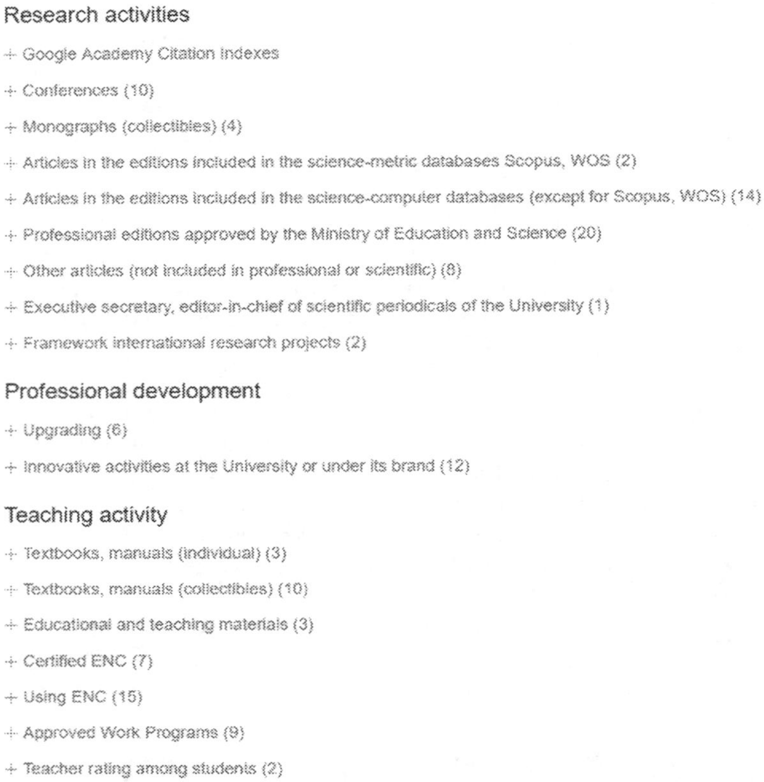

Research activities

- Google Academy Citation Indexes
- Conferences (10)
- Monographs (collectibles) (4)
- Articles in the editions included in the science-metric databases Scopus, WOS (2)
- Articles in the editions included in the science-computer databases (except for Scopus, WOS) (14)
- Professional editions approved by the Ministry of Education and Science (20)
- Other articles (not included in professional or scientific) (8)
- Executive secretary, editor-in-chief of scientific periodicals of the University (1)
- Framework international research projects (2)

Professional development

- Upgrading (6)
- Innovative activities at the University or under its brand (12)

Teaching activity

- Textbooks, manuals (individual) (3)
- Textbooks, manuals (collectibles) (10)
- Educational and teaching materials (3)
- Certified ENC (7)
- Using ENC (15)
- Approved Work Programs (9)
- Teacher rating among students (2)

Fig. 2.6 The page of the teacher's e-portfolio (Buinytska O)

The main tasks of the rating implementation are: to develop the leadership potential of teachers, to increase the efficiency and effectiveness of their activities, formation of high-quality scientific and pedagogical composition of the university; enhancing motivation for innovation and improving the quality of academic and professional activities in the digital world.

In order to carry out an analysis of the activity of teachers, structural subdivisions, and the university as a whole, the main types of statistical reports are implemented in the system – according to the rating points of employees (in terms of positions, degrees, units, etc.) – by structural subdivisions, on the rating indicators of the main types of activity, separately for each of the weights for which the ratings are calculated.

2 Digital Competencies of University Teachers

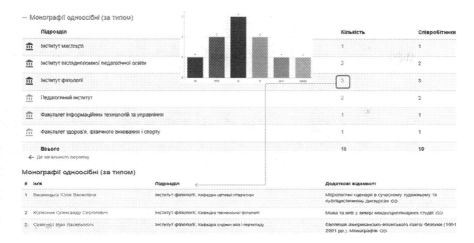

Fig. 2.7 Statistical data "by rule – single monographs"

An example of statistical data according to one of the rules, namely, the writing of monographs during the year, is shown in Fig. 2.7. The specified type of statistics allows you to analyze the number of monographs published by each structural unit of the university (institute/faculty), see the teacher of the department publish a monograph, and get acquainted with the electronic version of the monograph, which is located in the institutional repository.

Statistical data "by ratings" allows us to form rating lists of teachers for a certain type of activity, departments, and elected positions (Fig. 2.6), which undoubtedly motivates teachers to obtain the highest possible rating points and, accordingly, professional development.

For a holistic analysis of university activities, it is advisable to get acquainted with the indicators of rating points in selected areas of activity. The system of indexes of ratings should be used as an indicator of the level of development and efficiency of teachers and activities of the university as a whole. And the annual comparison of performance indicators should be taken into account when determining the quality of educational services and the competitiveness of the university.

Thanks to an online survey conducted to determine the level of the formation of digital competence (Fig. 2.8), the teacher sees its increase, as well as learn more about the needs of teachers to improve their skills and, accordingly, organize and conduct appropriate trainings, seminars, and bar camps under the program "Raising the qualification of scientific and pedagogical staff on ICT issues" (Fig. 2.9).

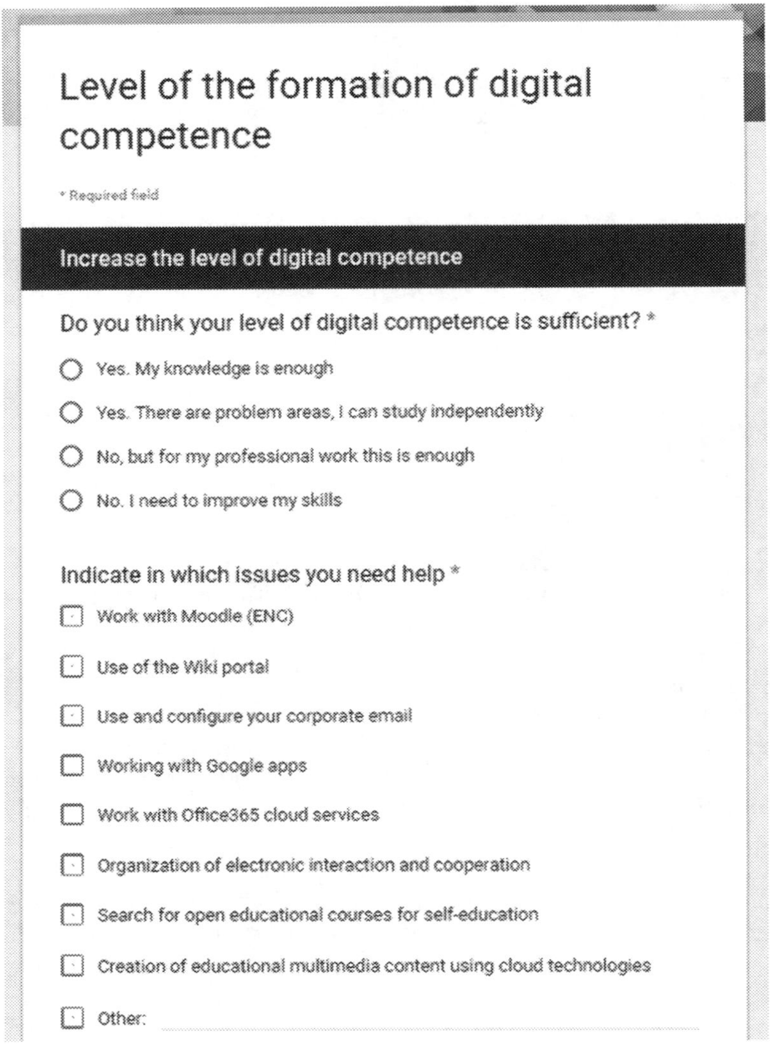

Level of the formation of digital competence

* Required field

Increase the level of digital competence

Do you think your level of digital competence is sufficient? *

- ○ Yes. My knowledge is enough
- ○ Yes. There are problem areas, I can study independently
- ○ No, but for my professional work this is enough
- ○ No. I need to improve my skills

Indicate in which issues you need help *

- ☐ Work with Moodle (ENC)
- ☐ Use of the Wiki portal
- ☐ Use and configure your corporate email
- ☐ Working with Google apps
- ☐ Work with Office365 cloud services
- ☐ Organization of electronic interaction and cooperation
- ☐ Search for open educational courses for self-education
- ☐ Creation of educational multimedia content using cloud technologies
- ☐ Other:

Fig. 2.8 Online survey form on the level of the formation of digital competence

2.3 Organization of the Qualification and Improvement System for Scientific and Pedagogical Staff in the Borys Grinchenko Kyiv University

The main principles of professional development of scientific and pedagogical workers (SPS) at the Borys Grinchenko Kyiv University in order to increase the digital level and be compliance with European and corporate standards of quality of

2 Digital Competencies of University Teachers

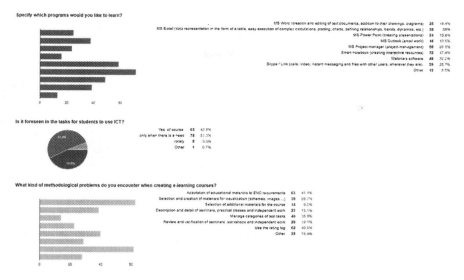

Fig. 2.9 Results of the teacher's questionnaire on digital competency formation

education are: scientific, systematic, innovative; integration, continuity; individualization and differentiation; self-organization and self-control.

The qualification improvement is a long-term process, takes place during the duration of the SPS contract, and lasts annually during the school year. The training program of the Improvement System for Scientific and Pedagogical Staff includes obligatory and variable components. Mandatory part is aimed at the development of key competencies: professional, didactic, research, leadership, and digital; variable involves the development of other competencies, which are chosen by their own desired SPS.

Professional development in a professional module can take place in such types as internship, training in professional programs of the PC, in institutions licensed to carry out such activity, defense of the thesis. The other four modules are provided by the University.

The program of the content module "Information and communication technologies" is an applied program with the professional orientation of in-service training of teachers. It provides the use of training methods based on the use of a project methodology, formative evaluation, the result of which should be the creation of own curriculum on a specific topic (lecture) in teaching disciplines, or a project of the future e-learning course according to the specified standard, which is protected by certain criteria with the participation of two opponents.

The programmatic result of studying on the CM "ICT" is the formation and development of digital competency of the scientific and pedagogical staff of the university.

The objectives of the advanced training program for this module are:

- Develop general ideas about ways and perspectives of digital education

- Develop the ability and sense of the need for continuous self-education and self-improvement and the use of innovative pedagogical and digital technologies and services in the educational process

Teaching SPS is carried out at two levels – basic and creative (high).

The result of training is the formation of program competencies – general and professional (Fig. 2.9) (Morze and Buinytska, 2017a, b).

To general competencies include decision-making, teamwork, ability to communicate with nonprofessional industry, and ability to work autonomously. Among professionals, we distinguish the ability to work in a team of different specialists, ability to work in an international context, project development and management and quality assurance.

Studying a high-level program will ensure the formation of a teacher's digital competence:

- The ability to evaluate the quality of the use of innovative pedagogical and digital technologies in the informal and informal learning.
- The ability to describe and predict educational trends, depending on the development of ICT.
- The ability to identify and compare paths and methods of using digital technologies depending on educational tasks.
- The ability to design educational policy of a modern educational institution based on a systematic approach to the use of digital technologies.
- The ability to effectively apply innovative pedagogical and digital technologies in the educational process.
- The ability to design a system of organization of independent work of students, in particular on the basis of digital technologies.
- The ability to create educational e-resources of different formats and the ability to argue ways and methods of their use depending on the educational goal.
- The ability to integrate digital technologies into the educational process
- The ability to design criteria for assessing the quality of the created educational e-resources of different formats.
- The ability to combine the features of modern LMS and modern Web 2.0–3.0 services to create e-learning resources, depending on the peculiarities of students' learning styles.
- The ability to use various Internet services for effective communication and cooperation.
- The ability to use Internet services to solve problems of effective communication and cooperation in mixed learning.
- The ability to use Internet services to solve molding tasks in mixed learning.

The main approaches to learning in the CM "ICT" are training with the help of master classes and the use of training methods, project methodology, molding evaluation, mixed learning technologies, and the "flipped" class and self-study. The assessment system includes practice, self-evaluation, evaluation of the results of the project activity, sections for evaluating all components of the educational process, and defense of the training project with the participation of the opponents.

The programmatic learning outcomes for the basic and creative levels are: readiness to conduct lectures, seminars, practical, and laboratory lessons on the basis of a combination of innovative pedagogical and digital technologies, mixed learning, and "flipped class" technologies; the ability to organize effective independent work of students, in particular on the basis of the use of information and communication technologies and services Web 2.0, project design and 21st century skills, and "flipped class" technologies; the ability to find forms, methods, and tools for evaluating students' academic achievements; readiness to develop open educational e-resources; and the ability to integrate information and communication technologies into the educational process.

Teaching IC "ICT" is provided by modern technical means of training, which are built on modern digital technologies.

During the mixed learning, educational e-resources are used to the module, and a fully fledged certified ENC is developed on the subject of the module (http://e-learning.kubg.edu.ua/course/view.php?id=2596).

E-learning course "ICT" content modul" that was developed in e-learning system of Borys Grinchenko Kyiv University, implemented by LMS MOODLE.

The development and protection of a final training project for a specific topic (lecture) or a future ENC project was evaluated at 60 points, according to the number of points allocated to the final control. The total number of points scored for the module is 100 points.

During the module, participants at the courses had the opportunity to get acquainted with worldwide educational trends, including 3D printing, embedded systems, and robotics, introduced at Borys Grinchenko Kyiv University (Morze et al. 2015). An overview of the resources for creating e-content included special aspects of the use of virtual boards, services for creating infographics, mental maps, preparation of didactic materials, presentations, publications, etc. During the studies Internet Services and IC Technologies for Effective Communication and Collaboration, Blogger, Skype, Hangouts, Google Classes, Google, Google Docs, Webinars, Wikipedia, Social Networks, and others, which are quite popular today, were reviewed. Particular attention was paid to monitoring the results of learning, which is necessary component of the educational process, in particular the use of molding evaluation. Participants were offered modern assessment tools that help teachers to formulate educational tasks clearly, to organize their work according to these tasks, and to make the student a subject of education and evaluation activity.

The results of the training of teachers for the CM "ICT" indicate the high interest of the SPS material content module and the desire to master them and increase the level of formation of their own IC competence.

An online survey was done to receive feedback from participants and to improve the CM "ICT."

Forty percent of respondents indicated that they should spend more time on practical tasks, because it is difficult to deal with new services and technologies. At the same time, 71% recommend this module to pass on to their colleagues, as it is useful and contains important material.

The most important topics participants defined are:

- Resources for organization of effective cooperation – 77%
- Resources for organization of effective communication – 74%
- Resources for creating e-content – 63%
- Instruments for the implementation of the methods and means of forming assessment – 62%
- Development of the skills of the twenty-first century, use of project activity, and implementation of the distance learning system – 40%

Participants of the "ICT' content module" noted its relevance, expediency, noted that the module's passing contributed to increase their level of IC competence by 35–55%.

Also, in order to increase the IC-competence, teachers are constantly encouraged to register and to attend mass open online courses, to find out about new electronic resources and their use in the University's information and education environment, including the specially developed website "Increasing of IC -Competence" (http://cikt.kubg.edu.ua/).

2.4 Conclusions

As a result of the existing qualification programs at the university, developed of e-resources that are located in the information and educational environment of the university are the formation and development of digital competencies of the university staff, through which the teachers are trained to conduct lectures, seminars, and practical, laboratory classes based on a combination of innovative pedagogical and IC-technologies; have the opportunity to use models of mixed learning and technology "flipped class"; to organize an effective independent student's work, in particular using ICT and design methodology; to develop 21st century skills; to adopt forms, methods, and tools for assessing academic achievement of students; develop open educational e-resources, etc., which is a prerequisite for a university in the digital world.

References

Corporate standard of ICT competence of the teacher (model). Tools for measuring the formation of ICT competencies (2014). Borys Grinchenko Kyiv University. Retrieved April 20, 2018, from http://kubg.edu.ua/images/stories/Departaments/ndl.io/corp_standart_vykla dach.pdf

DigComp 2.0: The Digital Competence Framework for Citizens. Update Phase 1: the Conceptual Reference Model. (2016). *EU science hub. The European Commission's science and knowledge service*. Retrieved July 15, 2017, from https://ec.europa.eu/jrc/en/publication/eur-scientific-

and-technical-research-reports/digcomp-20-digital-competence-framework-citizens-update-phase-1-conceptual-reference-model

DigComp 2.1 The Digital Competence Framework for Citizens. (2017). *EU science hub. The European Commission's science and knowledge service*. Retrieved March 04, 2018, from http://publications.jrc.ec.europa.eu/repository/bitstream/JRC106281/web-digcomp2.1pdf_ (online).pdf

Digital competences self-diagnosis test. (2015). Retrieved April 25, 2017, from http://ikanos.encuesta.euskadi.net/index.php/566697/lang-en

Essential conditions. (2015). Retrieved April 10, 2017, from http://www.iste.org/standards/essential-conditions

European Framework for the Digital Competence of Educators: DigCompEdu. (2017). *EU science hub. The European Commission's science and knowledge service*. Retrieved March 04, 2018, from https://ec.europa.eu/jrc/en/publication/eur-scientific-and-technical-research-reports/european-framework-digital-competence-educators-digcompedu

ISTE standards. (2017). Retrieved April 10, 2017, from https://www.iste.org/standards

Kiss, M. (2017). *Digital skills in the EU labour market*. In-depth analysis, European Parliamentary Research Service.

Morze, N., & Buinytska, O. (2017a). Increasing the level of information and communication competence of scientific and pedagogical workers – a key requirement of the quality of the educational process. *Information Technology and Learning Tools, 59*(3), 189–200.

Morze, N., & Buinytska, O. (2017b). The system of rating indicators for assessing the performance of teachers of modern universities. *Scientific Journal NPU im. M.P. Drahomanova, 19*(26), 2.

Morze, N., & Varchenko-Trotsenko, L. (2016). E-portfolio as a tool of transparency and openness of modern education university. *Information Technology and Learning Tools, 52*, 62–80.

Morze, N., Buinytska, O., & Kocharian, A. (2015). *IC-competence of teachers and students as a way to form the university's informational and educational environment competency-oriented education: Qualitative measurements* (pp. 151–195). Kyiv: Borys Grinchenko Kyiv University.

Morze, N, Buinytska, O., & Varchenko-Trotsenko, L. (2016). *Creating a modern e-course in Moodle* (232 p). Kamianets-Podilskyi: PP Buinytskyi.

On Approval of the State Standard for Basic and Complete Secondary Education. (2011). Decisions of the Cabinet of Ministers of Ukraine, №1392. Retrieved November 23, 2011, from http://zakon2.rada.gov.ua/laws/show/1392-2011-%D0%BF

Proposal for a council recommendation on key competences for lifelong learning. (2018). Brussels. Retrieved January 17, 2018, from http://eur-lex.europa.eu/legal-content/EN/TXT/HTML/?uri=CELEX:52018DC0024&rid=2

Structure of ICT competence of teachers. UNESCO Recommendations. (2011). Retrieved April 23, 2018, from https://iite.unesco.org/pics/publications/ru/files/3214694.pdf

Chapter 3
Professional Training: Challenges in the Digital Economy Context

Tatiana Noskova, Tatiana Pavlova, and Olga Yakovleva

3.1 Introduction

Computer systems and technologies significantly change our society. These changes are interrelated both with social and production spheres. The concept of "digital economy," introduced by Nicholas Negroponte in 1995 (Negroponte 1999), defined the name of the State Program of the Russian Federation, drawing out the prospective until 2024 in such areas as legislation, human resources and education, research competences and technical facilities, information infrastructure, and information security (On the Strategy for the Development of the Information Society in the Russian Federation for 2017–2030, 2017).

Innovative digital technologies have a huge impact on the labor market and professional activities, contributing to their transfer into an electronic environment.

When using digital technologies, modern people set new goals and meet the challenges, with the increasing speed of problem-solving, benefitting from the possibilities of joint distributed actions within networks. In this regard, new competencies of specialists are in a demand.

There are several main questions to be answered: What are the manifestations of professional activity specificity in digital environment? What are the new professional training requirements for a digital economy?

3.2 Changes of Professional Activity in a Digital Environment

The digital environment transforms life and activities of a modern person. To assess the degree of digital technologies penetration to person's life, the project "Ivanov Digital Index" was launched last year in Russia. Ivanov is an average Russian aged 14–64 who lives in a city with a population of more than 100,000 people. The first value of the "Ivanov Digital Index" is 51%. Sberbank Investment Research believes that this indicator reflects a turning point in the penetration of digital technologies into the lives of Russians: on the one hand, many Russians have the technical capabilities to use certain digital products; on the other hand, there is a great potential for further growth and expansion of technology. This index is quantitative but inconsistently reflects qualitative changes in the daily and professional activity of citizens. According to analysts, one of the catalysts for the growth of this index will be the increasing intensity of mobile Internet and mobile services use, as well as the gradual transition of various daily activities to online and more active life online with increasing confidence in digital environment (TASS 2017).

The other important indicator of country digitalization is e-government implementation degree, periodically measured by United Nations experts with special rating – E-government Readiness Index (Ecquaria 2018). An E-government promotes the delivery of essential services with the use of information technologies at different levels: digital interactions between a citizen and a government (C2G), between a government and other agencies (G2G), between government and citizen (G2C), between a government and an employee (G2E), and between a government and business/commerce (G2B) (Jeong 2007).

The data of these ratings allow us to approve that informatization is a new sociohistorical stage of human activity in technical and social aspects. On the technical side, considering informatization as the use of ICT tools for collecting, storing, transforming, and transmitting information, professional activities in digital environment can be interpreted as a change of intellectual tools (Noskova 2015). The transition from "manual work" to digital technologies changes professional activity radically.

According to the psychological theory of activity, the following elements are distinguished: means (conditions), goals, and motives (Leontiev 1975). Sociohistorical change of tools transforms all these interrelated elements. To achieve a new quality of professional activity, first, objectives must be reconsidered. Without stating new goals and tasks, it is impossible to reach a new level of achievements.

Informatization opens the wide information access for every person. However, such remote access becomes relevant only with appropriate personal needs and motivations to extract knowledge from extensive digital resources. Therefore, the principles of new goals and tasks implementation and shaping special personal competencies are gaining importance in conditions of digital professional environment.

New professional goals require new knowledge and skills. ICT competence is extremely demanded in almost all spheres of human activity, but can't guarantee the transition to a new level of achieved results. Specialists should be motivated to explore fundamentally new ways of solving professional problems to reveal the potential of digital technologies.

A modern person acquires an opportunity to solve professional problems, previously unavailable, with the support of information systems, modeling tools, and automated translation systems. From the standpoint of the cultural and historical concept (Vygotsky 1982), this symbolizes the transition to a new stage in human development. Tikhomirov, O.K. specified the expansion of computer devices in human activities as a switch "from the use of signs to the use of sign systems" (Tikhomirov 1984).

3.3 Digital Labor Market: New Demands for Specialists

Because of digital tools and technologies improvement, the labor market is dynamically changing. New industries are being formed and new types of professional activity are emerging; new specialties appear that could not have existed in the last century.

The demand for specialists who are competent in the field of big data processing and analysis, computer modeling, neural network, artificial intelligence, virtual reality, digital platforms, and cybersecurity is expected to grow. Significant changes are expected in industry, medicine, social services, urban environment, and agrarian sector in the near future. The relevance of such concepts as "smart city" and "Internet of things" (IoT) increases rapidly. In the agrarian sector, the digital economy assumes the development of sustainable agriculture and precision livestock farming (PLF) based on GPS (Global Positioning System), GIS (geographic information systems), yield monitor technologies, Variable Rate Technology, etc.; new materials; augmented reality; additive technologies; self-driving transportation devices with elements of artificial intelligence; advanced robotics; cloud computing and data storage technologies; big data and machine learning; and many others – all these phenomena have one common essence: the pervasive ICT scope (Digital Economy of the Russian Federation 2017).

In turn, this causes the growth of high-productivity jobs, the redistribution of human resources, and new demands for professional training and indicates the necessity of significant education quality improvements. Consequently, in professional training, digital environment must be considered as a new comprehensive environment for learning activities, professional activities, and continuous professional development.

3.4 Actual Changes in Professional Training for Expanding Digital Economy

In context of digital economy, new classes of tasks, related to digital technologies, appear for a prevailing number of traditional jobs. Required competencies should be shaped at different stages of training: vocational secondary and high school and advanced training and retraining.

The important trend for all training levels is upgrading of digital educational environment and increasing of e-learning. A process of shaping competencies should be organized in a digital environment.

Annually, the ratings of the most popular ICT tools for education are compiled (e.g., Top 200 Tools for Learning 2017 (Top 200 Tools for Learning 2017)). Learning Management Systems (LMS), Learning Content Management Systems (LCMS), e-learning platforms, electronic libraries, and repositories constitute the technological basis for distance learning technologies and e-learning. In certain cases computer simulators, virtual laboratories, virtual reality systems, etc. are applicable for skills development in e-environments. Learning practices in social networks are explored, and web 3.0 opportunities for education are comprehended (Noskov and Laptev 2016).

Remote access to digital resources provides possibilities to expand the information field of learning by taking advantages of digital portals, databases of publishing houses, scientific databases, and digital knowledge bases. The competition of knowledge is intensifying, because universities and scientific organizations contribute to the global information environment. Universities are evaluated by open resources representation in the Internet (publications, citation, impact factor, etc. (Drlik et al. 2016; Labrosse 2013).

Leading universities by offering their MOOCs provide learning for thousands of people simultaneously. In Russia, a national Open Education Platform was created (https://openedu.ru/) for offering online courses studied at Russian universities.

Thus, professional training in digital environment is carried through the use of new resources, tools, and technologies and therefore requires new methods and pedagogical practices for shaping new competences.

Not only technological innovations are of great importance but also profound psychological changes in training process. In conditions of technological upgrading, formation of digital economy, and uncertainty and dynamics of the labor market, teachers have to direct students to responsibility for active self-improvement. The support of initiative, creativity, and self-realization in learning together with a consideration of personal learning demands and strategies are especially important.

The leading part of students should be oriented to a breakthrough, advanced exploring of new approaches to learning and solving professional problems.

A high potential of an enriched and expanded digital environment is opening an access to unlimited resources in native and foreign languages and achievements of science and culture. Advanced technologies require new personal characteristics in educational and professional activities. Goals of new computer-based cognition methods acquisition become the priorities. Student's ability to select necessary information, learning techniques, and methods contributes to new personal semantic reality and opens new ways for extracting knowledge and training new skills. The free choice of learning activities acquires special significance.

A teacher should understand the diversity of expanded learning opportunities provided for a student. Personal learning environments and training plans become the subject for a joint analysis of a teacher and a student. The implementation of nonlinear educational practices and learning strategies in digital space allows to realize the personal potential in the context of professional interests and life plans (Noskova and Laptev 2016). The center of professional training should be a student as an active learner, as a person of potential professional activity in digital environment.

In recent years, the situation and attitude to ICT in education have changed significantly. A considerable contribution to the changes was provided not only by the growth of the ICT equipment status for educational institutions and students but also by the new target orientations of education. When analyzing pedagogical activity in terms of a degree of digital technologies penetration, it is important to reveal not only quantitative characteristics but also their influence on learning conditions and results, on changing the learning content and teaching methods that ensure the professional competence shaping.

Nonlinear educational practices require changes in the pedagogical design of an electronic environment. A new way to understand these changes is the psychodidactic approach to educational interaction in a digital space. This approach involves an allocation of three general scientific concepts, based on pedagogy, psychology, and informatics: information (digital educational resources), communication (network educational communication), and management of educational interactions (Noskova 2007). To achieve a new quality of the educational process, it is required to coordinate transformations of these basic components of an e-environment. At the same time, a psychological plan of activity in a digital environment acquires of special significance from a pedagogical support point of view. A teacher should explore what are learners' personal goals, internal motives, attitudes, and action methods in the new information conditions. A problem of the correspondence between the educational opportunities provided by a teacher to a student and the potential of the digital educational environment is expanding.

A promising trend is the digital educational environment impact on students' self-development, initiative, leadership, and self-realization in learning and research activities.

The means of the digital environment make it possible setting learning tasks in a new way and to create innovative conditions for shaping students' readiness:

- To act within the framework of corporate information systems, cloud offices, which are the attributes of professional activity in any sphere
- To carry out self-study and professional self-development in open information environment

- To interact effectively with partners within teamwork in the remote mode
- To strive for innovation and assimilation of new means and situations in professional activity

3.5 Experimental Data on the Use of Digital Environment Potential in Pedagogical Activity

According to "Ivanov Digital Index" an average Russian has already crossed the threshold of 50% entry into the digital environment. But can we confirm that situation is the same in pedagogical activities? To draw such conclusion, it is important to find an evidence of an efficient digital technologies application that empowers professional training.

In order to form the relevant set of learning conditions in digital space, it is necessary to correlate an expanded range of educational goals, students' needs and preferences, an appropriate training methodology and teaching methods, and an IT infrastructure of the educational institution. This is the essence of the new pedagogical competencies and attitudes.

For this purpose, a survey was conducted among the academic teachers in order to determine how they use the potential of digital educational environment. Teachers were invited to mark what opportunities they provide to students in e-environment and what ICT tools they use.

The survey involved 120 people with sufficient experience in teaching with ICT (5 years or more). This respondents' selection criterion responds to the fact that the study was supposed to rely on proven experience and methods of ICT application in the educational process.

In accordance with student-centered approach, questions for academic teachers were formulated in context of providing extended learning opportunities in an e-environment. The questions were divided into three categories:

- Acquisition of learning content
- Network communication with learning goals
- Self-organization, self-management, self-realization in learning activity

Survey participants were asked to relate to a 5-point scale their professional activity concerning the diversity of ICT tools and special learning conditions provided for students in an e-environment.

According to the received data, the normalized ICT tools variety index was calculated. It integrates the contribution of different types of ICT tools in pedagogical activity. The obtained value of this index is only 3.24.

Detailed data analysis approved that in their practice, academic teachers predominantly use ICT tools, which are now perceived as traditional and ensure the convenience of interaction between a teacher and students in the remote mode (presentation technologies, 4.68; educational sites, 3.88; computer testing programs, 3.45).

The degree of information systems (LMS, LCMS) application is only 3.14, mobile devices and applications – 2.7.

Experimental data characterizing educational opportunities that educators perceive and provide students in e-environment is much more informative. It directly correlates with shaping of important professional competencies.

The values of indices reflecting conditions for learning content assimilation are presented in Table 3.1:

The value of normalized learning content assimilation conditions index is 3.4. It allows detecting that academic teachers apply interactive and multimedia capabilities of digital learning environment fragmentary, but the environmental potential is much richer.

Data obtained on the second group of questions related to network interaction are presented in Table 3.2.

The value of normalized communication conditions index is 3.79. Data in the table show that to some extent the indicated possibilities of network communication are involved in learning process. Nevertheless, among teachers with considerable experience of professional activity in e-environment, the values of the indices do not reach 4. Thus, the potential of the digital communication environment is not adequately disclosed in pedagogical activity.

Specificity of pedagogical activity in the remote mode is determined by minimized role of direct communication. Learning activities management is based on remote support of students' self-organization and self-management.

Data obtained on the issues referred to the mediated management of learning interaction are presented in the Table 3.3.

The value of normalized self-organization and self-management conditions index is only 3.3. It is the lowest index in three groups of learning conditions that teachers provide in e-environment. Many teachers still prefer to use traditional pedagogical management methods.

Table 3.1 Data reflecting conditions facilitating digital learning content assimilation

Index name	Index value
Individualized content selection (content redundancy, navigation on educational content, foreign language resources, opens online courses, etc.)	3.77
Selection of the preferred learning content formats (text, audio, video)	3.75
Contextual help and tips	3.35
Automated self-monitoring and control of content assimilation	3.32
Learning motivation support (motivating resources, video sequences, examples, real situations, etc.)	3.55
Practical assimilation of learning with the use of digital tools (cognitive map, annotation, abstracting, presentation of the results of mastering the content in a given format)	3.29
Interactive actions with digital learning objects (training programs, virtual tours, virtual laboratories, virtual educational environments, including game environments)	2.75

Table 3.2 Data reflecting conditions referred to network interaction, contributing to shaping social professionally significant competencies

Index name	Index value
Personal communication support (counseling, correction)	3.94
Practical training (discussion, expression of opinions, joint activities with learning partners)	3.86
Learning motivation and reflective learning position support	3.85
Shaping soft skills (responsibility, discipline, teamwork, leadership, etc.)	3.66
Self-realization support (network initiatives, events, competitions, external professional communities, etc.)	3.64

Table 3.3 Data reflecting conditions for self-organization and self-management in learning interaction

Index name	Index value
Personal learning activity planning (digital calendars, organizers, road maps, etc.)	3.37
Identifying personal needs and preferences (online questionnaires, surveys, discussions, etc.)	3.16
Automated control and self-control	3.77
Feedback in learning activities (discussion, online questionnaires, voting, etc.)	3.14
Self-evaluation in learning activities (evaluation criteria)	3.83
Reflective position support (ratings, reflexive questionnaires, self-evaluation, peer evaluation, e-portfolio, etc.)	3.25
Learning activities monitoring (e-grading journals, progress scales, task completion markers, etc.)	3.91

Taking into account that data was obtained only for teachers who have experience in e-environment, we assume that the indicators for an ordinary teacher will be lower.

Still by the analogy with the "Ivanov digital index," which exceeded the middle barrier, the values of indices obtained by described diagnostic tool also indicate a turning point in the penetration of digital technologies in professional training.

There is a real prospect for professional experience and knowledge dissemination, and these indicators will have a positive trend in the near future.

3.6 Conclusions

From a psychological standpoint, informatization transforms all main components of professional activity: goals, conditions, and motives. Activity, including professional, is the active interaction of a person with the environment when he achieves a consciously set goal that arises as a result of the appearance of a certain need for him and the emergence of a motive. Operational and motivational aspects are closely intertwined in human activity.

A new quality of professional results can be achieved only with setting new goals and solving new tasks, which meets the challenges of a changing digital labor market, the emergence of new areas of activity, and the transformation of existing ones.

Therefore, in professional training, along with the use of information systems and digital technologies to solve traditional learning tasks, it is necessary to set new goals and create conditions to support motives reflecting the trends of the digital economy. To ensure prospective specialists training, internal psychological changes must occur in educational interaction.

Academic teachers who participated in the study did not give the high evaluation to the level of educational opportunities that they provide to students in e-environment.

A rich and diverse innovation potential of e-environment should be more fully used in professional training to shape new professional thinking, an open vision of problems and a readiness to new trends apperception. Therefore, not only external changes in the technological plan are important in educational interaction but also deep psychological interpersonal processes within a student's conscious – an adoption of new goals, motivations, and aspirations should be considered in pedagogical support.

In the process of professional training, it is necessary to form a special set of digital learning conditions in e-environment that promotes the active study of new knowledge areas, self-realization, and self-development in a rapidly changing professional environment.

Acknowledgments The research leading to these results has received, within the framework of the IRNet project, funding from the People Programme (Marie Curie Actions) of the European Union's Seventh Framework Programme FP7/2007-2013/ under REA grant agreement No: PIRSES-GA-2013-612536.

References

Decree No. 203 of the President of the Russian Federation of 09.05.2017 "On the Strategy for the Development of the Information Society in the Russian Federation for 2017–2030". http://kremlin.ru/acts/bank/41919. Assessed 6 Aug 2018.
Drlik, M., Morze, N., Noskova, T., Pavlova, T., & Yakovleva, O. (2016). Quality features of university information environment in its external indicators. *International Journal of Continuing Engineering Education and Life-Long Learning., 26*(2), 196–216.
Jeong Chun Hai @ Ibrahim: Fundamental of Development Administration. (2007). Selangor: Scholar Press.
Leontiev, A. N. (1975). *Activity, consciousness, personality*. Moscow: A.N. Leontiev.
Negroponte, N. (1999). *Being Digital*. New York: Knopf.
Noskova, T. N. (2007). *Psychodactics of e-environment*. St. Petersburg.
Noskova, T. N. (2015). *Pedagogy of the knowledge society*. St. Petersburg.
Noskova, T. N., & Laptev, V. V. (2016). Pedagogical activity in the electronic environment: Prospects for a new quality. *Pedagogika*. 10.
Program "Digital Economy of the Russian Federation" Order of July 28, 2017 No. 1632-r, Moscow. http://government.ru/rugovclassifier/614/events/23.01.18. Assessed 6 Aug 2018.

Sberbank began to calculate the level of penetration of digital technologies into the lives of Russians. TASS. 2017. http://tass.ru/ekonomika/4191181. Assessed 6 Aug 2018.

Scientific Output and Collaboration of European Universities / Labrosse I. et. al. (2013).

Tikhomirov, O. K. (1984). *Psychology of thinking*. Moscow.

Top 200 Tools for Learning. (2017). http://c4lpt.co.uk/top100tools Assessed 6 Aug 2018.

UN E-Gov Ranking. Ecquaria. http://www.ecquaria.com/un-e-gov-ranking/#UN-EGov-Development-Index. Assessed 6 Aug 2018.

Vygotsky, L. S. (1982). *Collection of works: In 6 vol. T. 2: Problems of general psychology*. Moscow: Pedagogika.

Chapter 4
Formation of Computing and Coding Competences of Computer Science Teachers in Ukraine

Nataliia Morze and Mariia Umryk

4.1 Introduction

2014 was a year of momentum for coding in schools (Balanskat et al. 2015). In this year the European Commission launched the Code Week with events all around Europe.

> EU Code Week is a grass-roots movement that celebrates creating with code. The idea is to make programming more visible, to show young, adults and elderly how you bring ideas to life with code, to demystify these skills and bring motivated people together to learn. The initiative was launched in 2013 by the Young Advisors for the Digital Agenda Europe. (Bogliolo 2013)

Coding in schools continues to be an increasing world trend.

England was one of the first countries that presented computer programming in its primary and secondary education in state-maintained schools. This will be described in more detail below.

Another initiative belongs to Americans. Former US President Obama stated that Everybody's Got to Learn How to Code. The result was creating and financing of such famous events as Code.org and the "Hour of Code".

According to the Ukrainian educational programmes, informatics became one of the leaders among the disciplines. Informatics (or Computer Science) in the Ukrainian schools is number three after mathematics and the Ukrainian language in hours. And this is an urgent requirement of modern life. Taking this into account the

---

N. Morze (✉)
Borys Grinchenko University in Kyiv, Kyiv, Ukraine
e-mail: n.morze@kubg.edu.ua

M. Umryk
National Pedagogical University, Kiev, Ukraine

number of hours for training on computing and coding (algorithmization and programming in national terms) has been increased within Computer Science.

On the one hand, we have strong childish interest in studying Computer Science at school; on the other hand, we have a variety of problems (e.g. technical support of schools, etc.). One of the major problems is training Computer Science teachers, namely, training related to computing and coding.

4.2 Global Ukrainian Review of the Use of Computing and Coding Competences by Teachers

As mentioned above, coding is included into state compulsory programme of Computer Science; however, in most Ukrainian schools, it is replaced by training on beginner level of MS Office programmes such as text editors and presentations. Computer Science teachers often have problems with coding themselves. It happens that even experienced teachers may not have teaching tools needed for the school curriculum.

To investigate this problem and find ways to solve it, the questionnaire on determination of the level of computing and coding competence of teachers is developed.

The basis of this survey is taken from Programmer Competency Matrix (Sijin 2014), but adapted for the Ukrainian teachers. Programmer Competency Matrix consists of five blocks of competences:

- Computer Science
- Software Engineering
- Programming
- Experience
- Knowledge

Each competence has four levels of progression: from pre-beginner (level 0) to professional (level 3). The author notes that:

> …the knowledge for each level is cumulative; being at level n implies that you also know everything from the levels lower than n. (Sijin 2014)

As for questions of the questionnaire, block of questions about gender, general pedagogical experience and experience as a programmer are placed. Questions of the questionnaire are as close to the Programmer Competency Matrix as possible.

As a result, the questionnaire consists of 5 modules with 25 competences in total. Each competence includes four levels of progression. The next level can be completed only in case of completion of previous one in matrix. So, total number of questions in questionnaire is $25 \times 4 = 100$. The Programmer Competency Matrix has been adapted for Computer Science teachers in the following way. The first and second levels are changed as part of the requirements to knowledge, skills and experience of children of the Ukrainian schools with Computer Science curriculum.

4 Formation of Computing and Coding Competences of Computer Science Teachers...

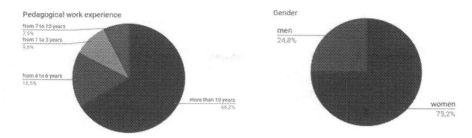

Fig. 4.1 Information on participants

The first level of the questionnaire corresponds to the standard level of the national curriculum. The second level of the questionnaire corresponds to the academic and professional level of the national curriculum. The third and fourth levels correspond to profound professional knowledge in computing and coding.

That is, the first and second levels are the basic in training of computing and coding in schools. The teacher cannot teach children coding at school without having competences at these levels in accordance with the requirements of national curriculum. The third and fourth levels for teacher are the two to which they seek.

The questionnaire is held in the first quarter of 2018, and 158 Computer Science teachers are involved. More details about the participants are shown in Fig. 4.1.

The overall result of the questionnaire with a breakdown by competency levels is presented in Fig. 4.2.

83.42% of the respondents have a level 1 (pre-beginner) of computing and coding competence. 65.86% of the respondents have a level 2 (beginner) of computing and coding competence.

That is, only 74.64% of teachers have competence at the level that meets the national curriculum on Computer Science in computing and coding. Therefore, 25.36% of teachers do not have necessary level of the knowledge to share it with their pupils.

The results of the survey are considered in more detail below.

There is a result for competence in programming languages in Table 4.1.

There is a result for competence in promotion and modelling of ongoing professional development and lifelong learning (blogs) in Table 4.2.

There is a result for competence in promotion and modelling of ongoing professional development and lifelong learning (MOOC) Table 4.3.

It follows that not everyone can be a programmer, but learning of programming at school is necessary for everyone. If only because the value of programming lies in the fact that it forms at first logical thinking (structural programming), then it helps to form abstract models that are close to life (object programming). Taking into account the development of modern technologies, knowledge of programming languages will be as needed as knowledge of foreign languages.

So, the main aim should be not just to get evaluation in the certificate but to get a set of knowledge and skills that form a competency in computing and coding of a professional beginner programmer that can motivate a significant part of pupil. Well-trained teachers are really needed for this purpose.

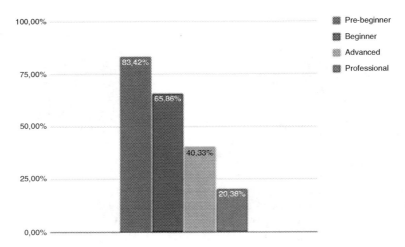

Fig. 4.2 Overall result of the questionnaire with a breakdown by the levels of computing and coding competence

4.3 The Need in Differentiation of Qualification Standards of Computing and Coding Competences of Teachers in Ukraine: Analysis of Various Standards and Curricula for Computing and Coding Competences

4.3.1 Coding in British Schools: New Computing Curriculum in England

England is the first G20 country that formally recognizes the importance of teaching children computing (Miles 2013; Swidenbank 2015). Government programme has started since September 2014, and new national curriculum was first announced at that time. The change from ICT to "computing" started, and children aged 5 and up have been learning the fundamentals of programming in schools around the country.

There were some challenges in the national British curriculum.

First, there was "skills gap" between the number of IT jobs and the people with appropriate skills to fill vacancies.

> It is predicted that just in a few years, there will be a shortage of 300,000 digitally skilled workers in London alone, with additional 900,000 ones across Europe. (Swidenbank 2015)

Lack of computer scientists was not the only one reason for changing of the national curriculum. Learning of programming skills can benefit children in other ways. Head of British Code Club Pro Maria Quevedo (Codeclub pro 2018) says:

> We're not just trying to encourage people to become developers. We're trying to encourage children to become creative.

4 Formation of Computing and Coding Competences of Computer Science Teachers... 53

Table 4.1 Result for competence in programming languages

Progression	Proficiency statements	Results of the survey
Pre-beginner (know)	I understand the purpose of the programming language and its main elements. I can give an example of modern programming languages and know how to implement the algorithm in one of the programming environments	yes 85%, no 10%, difficult to answer
Pre-beginner (use)	I have practical skills in one of the programming environments	yes 91.4%, no, difficult to answer
Beginner (know)	I have knowledge of imperative and/or object-oriented and/or declarative programming languages	yes 65%, no 12.9%, difficult to answer 22.1%
Beginner (use)	I use imperative and/or object-oriented and/or declarative programming languages in practice	yes 63.6%, no 10.7%, difficult to answer 25.7%
Advanced (know)	I have knowledge of functional programming languages	yes 41.4%, no 34.3%, difficult to answer 24.3%
Advanced (use)	I use functional programming languages in practice	yes 56.1%, no 28.1%, difficult to answer 15.8%

(continued)

Table 4.1 (continued)

Progression	Proficiency statements	Results of the survey
Professional (know)	I have knowledge of competitive programming languages (Erlang, Oz)	86.2% yes, 10.1% no, difficult to answer
	I have knowledge of logic programming languages (prolog)	72.1% yes, 17.9% no, 10% difficult to answer
Professional (use)	I use competitive programming languages (Erlang, Oz) in practice	90% yes, 7.9% no, difficult to answer
	I use logic programming languages (prolog) in practice	87.1% yes, no, difficult to answer

Namely, the main aim was not only to prepare software engineers but understanding that digital literacy can be very beneficial in a world where technologies embedded deeper and deeper into everyday lives.

Second challenge in the national British curriculum was readiness of teachers to train children coding in schools. Teachers had limited knowledge of the subject of coding. Many former ICT teachers had no experience in programming or teaching computational concepts.

To prepare pupils to the change, four distinct stages for the new computing curriculum have been designed. By the end of each key stage, pupils are expected to know, apply and understand skills and processes specified in the relevant programme of study (Fig. 4.3). The full breakdown of the changes can be found here (National curriculum in England: computing programmes of study 2013).

4 Formation of Computing and Coding Competences of Computer Science Teachers... 55

Table 4.2 Result for competence in promotion and modelling of ongoing professional development and lifelong learning (blogs)

Progression	Proficiency statements	Results of the survey
Pre-beginner	I read blogs, in particular blogs by programming teachers, constantly looking for new ones with relevant modern materials	yes 31.7%, no 61.9%, difficult to answer
Beginner	I read technical blogs, programming blogs and software development blogs and regularly listen to programming podcasts	yes 47.8%, no 42%, difficult to answer 10.1%
Advanced	I am a writer of the programming blog which contains collection of links to useful articles and tools to collect	yes, no 88.5%, difficult to answer
Professional	I am a writer for the programming blog which contains own ideas and reflections on the topic of programming and also examples of developed software	yes, no 90.6%, difficult to answer

Teachers have been preparing for the new computing curriculum in several ways.

First of all, two online guides on computing have been developed and published in the national curriculum. One of them has been designed for primary teachers (Berry 2013) and another one for secondary teachers (Kemp 2014).

At the same time, there were several training sessions for teachers with involvement of different national and private companies.

Table 4.3 Result for competence in promotion and modelling of ongoing professional development and lifelong learning (MOOC)

Progression	Proficiency statements	Results of the survey
Pre-beginner	I use MOOC or their parts for self-education	26.6% yes, 67.6% no, difficult to answer
Beginner	I have practical experience of participation in training at least in one MOOC of programming	48.9% yes, 45.3% no, difficult to answer
Advanced	I have successful experience in completion of training at least in two MOOCs of programming	79.1% yes, 15.8% no, difficult to answer
Professional	I have certificates on successful completion of trainings in MOOCs of programming	77%, 10.1%, 12.9% yes/no/difficult to answer

4.3.2 Coding and Computational Thinking in Curricula Across Europe

Many European countries are introducing coding and computational thinking as a core curriculum subject. According to the review of European Schoolnet (Computing our future. Computer programming and coding: Priorities, school curricula and initiatives across Europe 2015), the following countries have integrated coding into their curricula (Fig. 4.4).

4 Formation of Computing and Coding Competences of Computer Science Teachers...

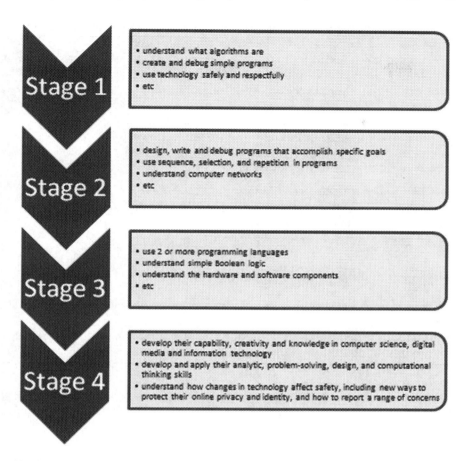

Fig. 4.3 Progression of the computing competence for pupils (in brief)

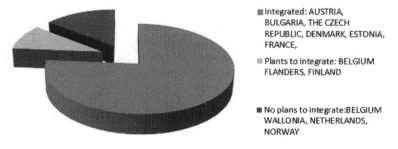

Fig. 4.4 Introducing coding into curricula. (Reproduced from (Computing our future. Computer programming and coding: Priorities, school curricula and initiatives across Europe 2015))

Countries generally have multiple reasons for integrating coding into the curricula (Computing our future. Computer programming and coding: Priorities, school curricula and initiatives across Europe 2015). First of all, the skills needed by the twenty-first century are logical thinking (15 countries) and problem-solving (14 countries). More than half of the countries, namely, 11, focus on the development of coding skills.

The European educators arise some important issues on introducing computing and coding competences in EU (Computing our future. Computer programming and coding: Priorities, school curricula and initiatives across Europe 2015, Coding and computational thinking on the curriculum 2016):

- How is coding currently integrated into curricula
- How can we further advocate for coding as a key skill for a thriving and ever-innovative digital society and economy
- How to make high-quality learning materials for coding
- How to provide training and support for teachers
- Gender aspects needed to be considered
- How to use and informal learning

Some of the complex issues on CT/coding are due to unclear terms and definitions.

To solve these and other related questions, the European Commission's science and knowledge service funds a number of programmes that could further support innovation, good practice and peer-to-peer learning of teachers in coding and computational thinking.

The example of such programmes is Taccle 3 Coding project (http://www.taccle3.eu/en/) funded by Erasmus+ that supports primary school and other teachers who want to give lessons of computing for pupils at the age of 4–14 years. The result of this project is equipping classroom teachers with the knowledge and the materials needed by developing a website of ideas and resources together with in-service training courses and other staff development events. Now resource bank, stem attitudes, resource kit, resource review, literature review and training programmes are located on portal Taccle 3 Coding.

There are a lot of useful materials in resource bank, such as Teaching Resources Blog:

- Control technologies for younger children
- Using graphic environments
- Robotics for younger children
- Controlling Arduino with Scratch

Also there are curricula from around Europe where you can find a Google Drive folder containing links to coding curricula and policy documents from around Europe.

Another example of project is about a gender issue, as (Zynczak 2016) only 17% of Google's engineers, 15% of Facebook's and 10% of Twitter's are women. In an attempt to redress the balance, there are a growing number of initiatives aimed exclusively at girls; Google's Made With Code project promotes Computer Sciences to girls.

> We started Made with Code because increasingly more aspects in our lives are powered by technology, yet women aren't represented in the roles that make technology happen. If we can inspire teen girls to see that code can help them pursue their passions, whatever they may be, then hopefully they will begin to contribute their voices to the field of technology for the benefit of us all.. (Google's Made With Code project 2018)

Many sources confirm the importance of teaching teachers programming for the more effective process of teaching children coding (Swidenbank 2015; Redecker and Punie 2017 etc.). As noted in (Coding and computational thinking on the curriculum 2016):

> Teachers need a good understanding of what CT (computational thinking) is and how to teach it. Introducing CT requires new training, possibly at large scale, as CT does not so far often feature in teachers' initial training. Support services for teachers that provide concrete advice and examples can support teachers to use coding and computational thinking in class.

To provide training for teachers, there are several ways. Note that non-formal and informal learning play a crucial role. Non-formal and informal learning opportunities can include MOOCs, peer-to-peer learning, voluntary in-school or afternoon code clubs, materials from different websites and portals like Taccle3, etc. Formal learning opportunities can include in-service training courses and other staff development events financed by government.

4.3.3 *European Framework for the Digital Competence of Educators*

According to European Commission's research, topics in 2016–2017 are structured around three main strands (the European Commission's science and knowledge service 2016):

- Twenty-First-century skills and competences
- Innovating and modernizing education and training
- Open education

It indicates that innovating and modernizing education and training are key priorities in several flagship initiatives of the Europe 2020 strategy. On the one hand, the key challenge for research and policy is to make sure that the full potential of digital technologies is used for learning and, on the other hand, to be sure that effective digital age learning is made possible through systemic and holistic change. Such change is still needed in many European countries.

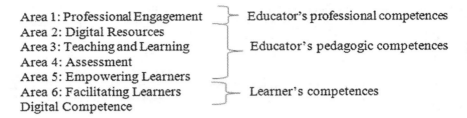

Fig. 4.5 Six DigCompEdu areas according to the European Framework

As noted in (European Framework for the Digital Competence of Educators: DigCompEdu 2017):

> ... the teaching professions face rapidly changing demands, educators require an increasingly broad and more sophisticated set of competences than before...On International and national level a number of frameworks, self-assessment tools and training programmes have been developed to describe the facets of digital competence for educators and to help them assess their competence, identify their training needs and offer targeted training.

According to the European Framework for the Digital Competence of Educators (Redecker and Punie 2017), the six DigCompEdu areas focus on different aspects of educators' professional activities (Fig. 4.5).

Therefore according to the European Framework, some aspects of programming competences for educators are in creating and modifying DR (CAMDR) competences. Skills of creating apps or games are located on the top progression of the competence (Fig. 4.6).

4.3.4 American ISTE Standards for Computer Science Educators

In 2016, former President Obama announces "Computer Science for All" initiative. Computer Science for All is the bold new initiative to empower all American students from kindergarten through high school to learn Computer Science and be equipped with the computational thinking skills they need to be creators in the digital economy, not just consumers, and to be active citizens in our technology-driven world. "Computer Science for All" initiative resulted in educators, lawmakers and Computer Science advocates spreading the gospel of coding. It also nudged more states to count Computer Science towards high school graduation requirements (Pappano 2017, Smith 2016).

The importance of IT training including computing and coding in the American educational environment speaks of that fact that IBM's chief executive, Ginny Rometty, recently wrote a letter to US President-elect Donald Trump in which she said that IT staff did not necessarily have higher education to hold high-paying posts

4 Formation of Computing and Coding Competences of Computer Science Teachers... 61

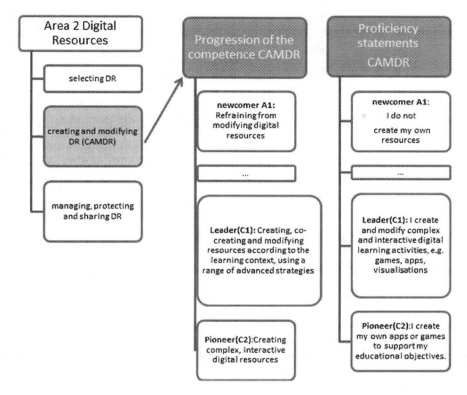

Fig. 4.6 Progression and proficiency statements of the competence CAMDR

in cybersecurity, big data, cognitive science and artificial intelligence. She asked the newly elected president to support a special 6-year programme of teaching information technology in high school.

> Let's work together to scale up this approach of vocational training, creating a national corps of skilled workers trained to take the 'new collar' IT jobs that are in demand here in America. (Rometty 2016)

Also ISTE (International Society for Technology in Education) Standards have been developed. The main idea of the education technology standards is to transform learning and teaching. ISTE is a non-profit, public-benefit corporation that is governed by an elected board of directors (ISTE 2018).

As noted in (ISTE 2018):

> The ISTE Standards work together to support educators, students and leaders with clear guidelines for the skills and knowledge necessary to move away from the factory model. These are not the typical boxes educators need to check. They provide a framework for rethinking education, adapting to a constantly changing technological landscape and preparing students to enter an increasingly global economy.

Fig. 4.7 ISTE Standards

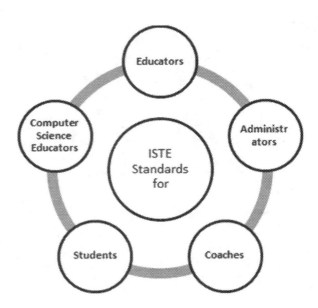

ISTE Standards are developed in five directions (Fig. 4.7).

ISTE Standards for Computer Science Educators are divided into four branches (ISTE 2018):

1. Content knowledge
2. Effective professional knowledge
3. Effective teaching and learning
4. Effective learning environment

Select those competences that are related to computing and coding competences for Computer Science educators.

(a) *On knowledge of content, we highlighted two main branches and one additional branch for computing and coding* (Table 4.4).

Two main branches strictly related with computing and coding, but additional branch has general awareness in this competence.

(b) *On effective professional knowledge, we highlighted one additional branch for computing and coding* (Table 4.5).

(c) *On effective professional knowledge and skills, we highlighted one additional branch for computing and coding* (Table 4.6).

Table 4.4 Computing and coding competences for Computer Science educators

Main branches		
Demonstrate knowledge of and proficiency in data representation and abstraction	Effectively use primitive data types	
	Demonstrate an understanding of static and dynamic data structures	
	Effectively use, manipulate and explain various external data stores: various types (text, images, sound, etc.), various locations (local, server, cloud), etc.	
	Effectively use modelling and simulation to solve real-world problems	
Effectively design, develop and test algorithms	Using a modern, high-level programming language, construct correctly functioning programmes involving simple and structured data types; compound Boolean expressions; and sequential, conditional and iterative control structures	
	Design and test algorithms and programming solutions to problems in different contexts (textual, numeric, graphic, etc.) using advanced data structures	
	Analyse algorithms by considering complexity, efficiency, aesthetics and correctness	
	Demonstrate knowledge of two or more programming paradigms	
	Effectively use two or more development environments	
	Demonstrate knowledge of varied software development models and project management strategies	
Additional branch		
Demonstrate knowledge of digital devices, systems and networks	Demonstrate an understanding of data representation at the machine level	
	Demonstrate an understanding of machine-level components and related issues of complexity	
	Demonstrate an understanding of operating systems and networking in a structured computer system	
	Demonstrate an understanding of the operation of computer networks and mobile computing devices	

4.4 Proposal for Forming Computing and Coding Competences of Computer Science Educators

Using the above analysis of various standards and curriculum for computing and coding competences offers proposal for forming computing and coding competences for Computer Science educators in Ukraine.

As a basis we take the classification American ISTE Standards for Computer Science Educators (ISTE 2018) and European Framework for the Digital Competence of Educators: DigCompEdu (European Framework for the Digital Competence of Educators: DigCompEdu 2017) (Fig. 4.8).

There are computing and coding competence areas and scope in Fig. 4.9.

Table 4.5 Computing and coding competences for Computer Science educators

Additional branch	Example	
Plan and teach Computer Science lessons/units using effective and engaging practices and methodologies	Select a variety of real-world computing problems and project-based methodologies that support active and authentic learning and provide opportunities for creative and innovative thinking and problem-solving	Select the appropriate tasks for coding
	Demonstrate the use of a variety of collaborative groupings in lesson plans/units and assessments	Use parental, command, group programming. Work on a project in a team
	Design activities that require students to effectively describe computing artefacts and communicate results using multiple forms of media	Describe and submit the technical task of the project
	Identify problematic concepts and constructs in Computer Science and appropriate strategies to address them	Know the basic general problems in coding and be able to solve them

Table 4.6 Computing and coding competences for Computer Science educators

Additional branch	Example	
Participate in, promote and model ongoing professional development and lifelong learning relative to Computer Science and Computer Science education	Identify and participate in professional Computer Science and Computer Science education societies, organizations and groups that provide professional growth opportunities and resources	Take part or organize meetings, seminars, conferences, etc. about computing and coding
	Demonstrate knowledge of evolving social and research issues relating to Computer Science and Computer Science education	Be the author of a blog on computing and coding, which contains his own thoughts as well as examples of software developed
	Identify local, state and national content and professional standards and requirements affecting the teaching of secondary Computer Science	Know and analyse national and foreign standards in Computer Science about computing and coding

The example of the table (in brief) for analysis on formation levels of computing and coding competence areas for Computer Science teachers is provided below.

Content knowledge as well as effective professional knowledge is from Fig. 4.9 (Table 4.7).

4 Formation of Computing and Coding Competences of Computer Science Teachers...

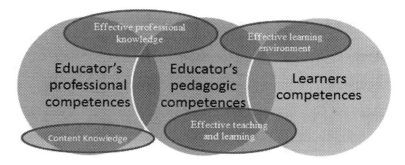

Fig. 4.8 Blend of ISTE Standards and European Framework DigCompEdu

Fig. 4.9 Computing and coding competence areas and scope

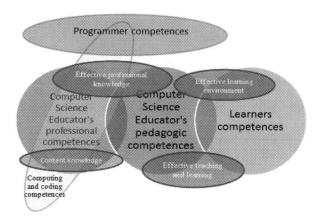

Table 4.7 Formation levels of computing and coding competences for Computer Science teachers

Formation levels of computing and coding competences for Computer Science teachers

Content knowledge

Module 1. Computer Science

Algorithms (know)

Pre-beginner	Beginner	Advanced	Professional
Know and can explain the concept of the algorithm, can describe its properties, know the basic algorithmic structures: sequence, selection, looping	Know and can explain/substantiate the affiliation of a particular algorithm to the corresponding type, the graphical representation of the basic algorithms, the correctness of the actions in the implementation of the proposed algorithm	Know and can explain the basic sorting, searching and data structure traversal and retrieval algorithms	Know and can explain the simple greedy and divide and conquer algorithms, good knowledge of graph algorithms, good knowledge of numerical computation algorithms, able to identify NP problems, etc.

(continued)

Table 4.7 (continued)

Formation levels of computing and coding competences for Computer Science teachers			
Algorithms (use)			
Able to build graphic schemes of the basic algorithms and execute the algorithm formally	Can represent algorithms in different ways; can implement the development of sequence algorithms, selection and looping algorithms; and can do their programmes implementation	Can do programme implementation of the basic sorting, searching and data structure traversal and retrieval algorithms	Able to recognize and code dynamic programming solutions, good use of graph and trees algorithms
Data structures (know)			
Know and can explain organizing of data by using one-dimensional, two-dimensional arrays	Know and can explain organizing of data in any of the following data structures: linked lists, dictionaries, queues, stacks, trees	Know and can explain organizing of data in all of the following data structures: linked lists, dictionaries queues, stacks, trees	Know and can explain at least one advanced data structures like B-trees, binomial and Fibonacci heaps, AVL/red black trees, splay trees, skip lists, etc.
Data structures (use)			
Able to recognize and code one-dimensional, two-dimensional arrays	Able to recognize and code at least one of the following data structures: linked lists, dictionaries, queues, stacks, trees	Able to recognize and code one of the following data structures: linked lists, dictionaries queues, stacks, trees	Able to recognize and code at least one of the advanced data structures like B-trees, binomial and Fibonacci heaps, AVL/red black trees, splay trees, skip lists, etc.
Systems programming (know)			
Pre-beginner	Beginner	Advanced	Professional
Know and can explain the notion of the executor of the algorithm and the system of instructions for the executor of the algorithm	Have basic understanding of compilers, linkers and interpreters	Know and can explain what assembly code is and how things work at the hardware level	Understand the entire programming stack, hardware (CPU + memory + cache + interrupts + microcode), binary code, assembly, static and dynamic linking, compilation, interpretation, JIT compilation, garbage collection, heap, stack, memory addressing, etc.

(continued)

Table 4.7 (continued)

Formation levels of computing and coding competences for Computer Science teachers			
Systems programming (use)			
Use a software environment for coding and executing algorithms	Have practical skills with compilers, linkers and interpreters, can differentiate the broadcast method with which to work	Able to read assembly code	Have practical skills with entire programming stack, hardware (CPU + memory + cache + interrupts + microcode), binary code, assembly, static and dynamic linking, compilation, interpretation, JIT compilation, garbage collection, heap, stack, memory addressing, etc.
Module 2 software engineering			
Source code version control (know)			
Pre-beginner	Beginner	Advanced	Professional
Have basic knowledge of safe storage, backup and data recovery	Know and can explain the notion of the backup software project, synchronization and emergency data recovery project	Know and can explain VSS and have basic understanding of CVS/SVN	Proficient in using CVS and SVN features
Source code version control (use)			
Have practical skills with safe storage, backup and data recovery	Have practical skills with backup software project, synchronization and emergency data recovery project	User of VSS and CVS/SVN	Can control the source code using VSS and / or CVS and SVN
Build automation (know)			
Pre-beginner	Beginner	Advanced	Professional
Have basic knowledge how to build from IDE	Know and can explain how to build the system from IDE	Know and can explain how to build the system from the command line	Can setup a script to build the basic system
Build automation (use)			
Can search for a mistake in a simple algorithm	Carry out manual testing of the developed code	Have practical skills to write automated test of code	Have practical skills to setup automated functional, load/performance and UI tests

(continued)

Table 4.7 (continued)

Formation levels of computing and coding competences for Computer Science teachers				
Module 3 programming			
More details seen in questionnaire https://goo.gl/forms/FQptJNlfQ9lvTvQK2 (Ukrainian)			
Effective professional knowledge			
Promote and model ongoing professional development and lifelong learning (books)			
Pre-beginner	Beginner	Advanced	Professional
Know, read and analyse informatics textbooks on standard level	Know, read and analyse informatics textbooks on academic, profile level	Know and read textbooks such as 21-day series, 24-hour series, dummy series, etc.	Read at least one of the following books: Steve McConnell "Code Complete" Steve Krug "Don't Make Me Think" Jon Bentley "Programming Pearls" Seif Haridi "Concepts, Techniques, and Models of Computer Programming" Donald E. Knuth "The Art of Computer Programming", etc.
Promote and model ongoing professional development and lifelong learning (blogs)			
Read blogs, in particular blogs by programming teachers, constantly looking for new ones with relevant modern materials	Read technical blogs, programming blogs and software development blogs and regularly listen to programming podcasts	Be a writer of the programming blog which contains collection of links to useful articles and tools to collect	Be a writer for the programming blog which contains own ideas and reflections on the topic of programming and also examples of developed software
Promote and model ongoing professional development and lifelong learning (MOOC)			
Use MOOC or their parts for self-education	Have practical experience of participation in training at least in one MOOC of programming	Have successful experience in completion of training at least in two MOOCs of programming	Have certificates on successful completion of trainings in MOOCs of programming

4.5 Conclusions

Coding in schools continues to be an increasing world trend. Many European countries are introducing coding and computational thinking as a core curriculum subject. Actual is the problem of formation of computing and coding competences of Computer Science teachers. As a result, we suggest new standards of computing and coding competences of Computer Science teachers in Ukraine.

Acknowledgements The research leading to these results has received, within the framework of the IRNet project, funding from the People Programme (Marie Curie Actions) of the European Union's Seventh Framework Programme (FP7/2007–2013) under REA grant agreement No: PIRSES-GA-2013-612536.

References

Balanskat, A. et al. (2015). *Computing our future Computer programming and coding Priorities, school curricula and initiatives across Europe*. http://fcl.eun.org/documents/10180/14689/Computing+our+future_final.pdf/746e36b1-e1a6-4bf1-8105-ea27c0d2bbe0. Accessed 14 May 2018.

Bogliolo, A. (2013). *CodeWeek*. http://codeweek.eu/. Accessed 14 May 2018.

Codeclub pro. (2018). https://www.codeclub.org.uk/. Accessed 14 May 2018.

Coding and computational thinking on the curriculum. (2016). https://ec.europa.eu/education/sites/education/files/2016-pla-coding-computational-thinking_en.pdf. Accessed 14 May 2018.

European Framework for the Digital Competence of Educators: DigCompEdu. https://ec.europa.eu/jrc/en/publication/eur-scientific-and-technical-research-reports/european-framework-digital-competence-educators-digcompedu. Accessed 14 May 2018.

Google's Made With Code project. www.madewithcode.com. Accessed 14 May 2018.

International Society for Technology in Education. (2018) www.iste.org. Accessed 14 May 2018.

Kemp, P. (2014). *Computing in the National Curriculum for secondary teachers*. http://www.computingatschool.org.uk/data/uploads/cas_secondary.pdf. Accessed 14 May 2018.

Learning and Skills for the Digital Era. https://ec.europa.eu/jrc/en/research-topic/learning-and-skills. Accessed 14 May 2018.

Miles, B. (2013). *Computing in the National Curriculum for primary teachers*. http://www.computingatschool.org.uk/data/uploads/CASPrimaryComputing.pdf. Accessed 14 May 2018.

Ministry of Education and Science of Ukraine. (2018). https://mon.gov.ua. Accessed 14 May 2018.

Pappano, L. (2017). *Learning to think like a computer*. https://www.nytimes.com/2017/04/04/education/edlife/teaching-students-computer-code.html. Accessed 14 May 2018.

Redecker, C., & Punie, Y. (2017). *European framework for the digital competence of educators: DigCompEdu*. http://publications.jrc.ec.europa.eu/repository/bitstream/JRC107466/pdf_digcomedu_a4_final.pdf. Accessed 14 May 2018.

Rometty, G. (2016). *IBM CEO Ginni Rometty's Letter to the U.S. President-Elect*. https://www.ibm.com/blogs/policy/ibm-ceo-ginni-romettys-letter-u-s-president-elect/. Accessed 14 May 2018.

Sijin, J. (2014). *Programmer competency matrix*. http://sijinjoseph.com/programmer-competency-matrix/. Accessed 14 May 2018.

Smith, M. (2016). *Computer science for all*. https://obamawhitehouse.archives.gov/blog/2016/01/30/computer-science-all. Accessed 14 May 2018.

Statutory guidance National curriculum in England: Computing programmes of study. (2013). https://www.gov.uk/government/publications/national-curriculum-in-england-computing-programmes-of-study/national-curriculum-in-england-computing-programmes-of-study. Accessed 14 May 2018.

Swidenbank, R. (2015). *Coding in British schools: A review of the first term*. https://www.computerworlduk.com/careers/coding-in-british-schools-review-of-first-term-3595505/. Accessed 14 May 2018.

Zynczak, H. (2016). *What closing the gender gap in tech would mean outside the industry*. https://www.fastcompany.com/3055906/what-closing-thegender-gap-in-tech-would-mean-outside-the-industry. Accessed 14 May 2018.

Chapter 5
Networking Through Scholarly Communication: Case IRNet Project

Eugenia Smyrnova-Trybulska, Nataliia Morze, and Olena Kuzminska

5.1 Introduction

The philosophy of the Internet, built on the ideas of openness and transboundary nature, has become popular in the period of globalization. The Internet is becoming a way of uniting disparate scientific and educational centers of the world.

In recent decades there has been an enormous growth of scientific collaboration across national borders. The number of internationally co-authored scientific articles has grown at an average of 14% per year. Networking is now an important means of enhancing scientific quality. The spread of generic (as Twitter, Facebook, or Google+) or specialized (as LinkedIn or Viadeo) social networks allows sharing opinions on different aspects of life every day (Colace et al. 2013).

Expanding the networking experience of teachers and, as a result, strengthening the positions of universities today are impossible under the conditions of closed systems of education and individual institutions. One of the solutions is academic mobility and the implementation of international projects and cooperation in scientific research. The strategy for supporting supranational collaboration within the European Social Fund at the level of the European Commission is manifested, e.g.,

---

E. Smyrnova-Trybulska (✉)
University of Silesia in Katowice, Katowice, Poland
e-mail: esmyrnova@us.edu.pl

N. Morze
Borys Grinchenko University in Kyiv, Kyiv, Ukraine
e-mail: n.morze@kubg.edu.ua

O. Kuzminska
Faculty of Information Technologies, National University of Life and Environmental Sciences of Ukraine, Kyiv, Ukraine
e-mail: o.kuzminska@nubip.edu.ua

by encouraging and enabling to create a network of collaboration, mutual learning, and exchange of experiences among the EU countries in the framework of the so-called learning networks. They are grassroots initiatives of the member states, which are active in some particular areas and within which the participants have the possibility of exchanging experiences, of good practices, and of joint work on the solutions to some problems. It is important to use scholarly communication tools (https://archive.org/details/OACurrRes1, last accessed 2018/01/11) to expand access to the results obtained and to organize networking among participants of international teams of researchers.

As a result of network cooperation, including online communication facilities, academic teachers, and university researchers, the scientific and IR competence of the participants in the educational process is increasing, the opportunities for academic mobility and openness are growing, and the rating of universities is increasing.

One of the most respected ratings is Webometrics (Ranking Web of Universities 2018a, b), which analyzes the presence of a given university as a research center in the Internet space. Universities give high priority to the international ranking of Webometrics because the analysis of open resources of the university in the Internet space indirectly allows us to assess the educational and research achievements of universities by comparing the same indicators (Bershadskaya et al. 2016).

The purpose of this article is to present the experience of scientific networking cooperation of researchers and mobility of six European universities (in Poland, the Czech Republic, Slovakia, Portugal, the Netherlands, Spain) and four universities from outside Europe or the EU (in Australia, Ukraine, Russia), as part of the European IRNet project (www.irnet.us.edu.pl), and to analyze the impact of such cooperation on the scientific activity and professional development of each participant scientist and, as a result, the impact on the webometrics rating of the participating universities. Identification of differences in university e-environments between selected EU and non-EU countries using knowledge mining methods was studied in Drlík et al. (2017).

One of the more important impacts was relevance of the exchange between the partner countries for ERA. In accordance with the principle of the new ERA (European Research Area) initiatives (launched in 2008), the IRNet research project aims at establishing long-lasting partnerships within EU and third countries (Fig. 5.1).

Implementation of the principle of the new ERA (European Research Area) initiatives (launched in 2008) in the context of IRNet project impact (Fig. 5.1) was realized with use of different tools, for example, via scholarly communication, in particular publications in research papers, participation in online conferences and network communities, and through the delivery of results (Smyrnova-Trybulska 2017a, b).

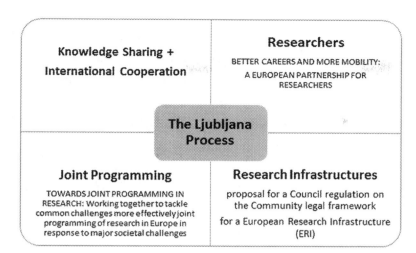

Fig. 5.1 The principle of the new ERA (European Research Area) initiatives (launched in 2008) in the context of IRNet project impact. (Source: Council Conclusions on The Launch of the "Ljubljana Process" – toward full realization of ERA)

5.2 Technical Conditioning

DESI 2018 shows that connectivity has improved but is insufficient to address fast-growing needs (European Commission – Press release. How digital is your country? Europe needs Digital Single Market to boost its digital performance. Brussels, 18 May 2018).

Ultrafast connectivity of at least 100 Mbps is available to 58% of households, and the number of subscriptions is rapidly increasing. Fifteen percent of homes use ultrafast broadband: this is twice as high as just 2 years ago and five times higher than in 2013.

Eighty percent of European homes are covered by fast broadband with at least 30 megabits per second (Mbps) (76% last year), and a third (33%) of European households have a subscription (23% increase compared to last year and 166% compared to 2013).

The number of mobile data subscriptions have increased by 57% since 2013 and reached 90 subscriptions per 100 people in the EU.

Indicators show that the demand for fast and ultrafast broadband is rapidly increasing and is expected to further increase in the future. The Commission proposed a reform of EU telecom rules to meet Europeans' growing connectivity needs and boost investments (European Commission – Press release. How digital is your country? Europe needs Digital Single Market to boost its digital performance. Brussels, 18 May 2018).

Table 5.1 Some personal activities reflected on personal webpages

Research (R)	Teaching (T)	Professional development (P)
Project reports	Workshops or seminars slides	Text or numbers
Monographies, thesis, dissertations	Textbooks	Personal info (CV)
Book chapters, papers in local journals	Websites for e-learning	Professional certification
Patent	Book reviews	Organizing events
Peer-review	Bibliographies	Certificate of registration of copyright

Source: Own research

5.3 Findings

Indicators of Webometrics and the possibilities of networking in the framework of an international project.

The initial goal of the Webometrics project (Ranking Web of Universities 2018b) was not so much to create a ranking of educational institutions but to stimulate the web publishing activity of universities. The main task of Webometrics is to motivate scientific and educational institutions to make their scientific and educational materials available to the public. When such information is made public through the Internet, it attests to a high academic level of the university. The Internet provides an exhaustive way to describe a range of events where scientific publications are just one of the components that can be found on the website (Table 5.1). In addition, providing access and promoting web publishing among teachers means that other colleagues will be aware of the results of the research, more future students can learn about the scientific and international activities of the university, companies can find suitable partners for the implementation of research projects, and organizations can easily access data for expert search. These and other reasons should be taken into account with the support of the universities of open access initiatives (Budapest Open Access Initiative 2012).

The criteria for evaluating Webometrics (Aguillo et al. 2008) change every 6 months (Fig. 5.2).

Compared to previous periods, the weight of the excellence increased by 5% (from 30% to 35%), and the presence index decreased by 5% (Ranking Web of Universities 2018a, b).

Networking of teachers from different universities within the framework of international projects will not only improve personal indicators (Table 5.1) but also the university's rating indicators; 95% is allocated to the evaluation of the scientific research work (45%) and information partnership (50%) (Fig. 5.2).

Recommendations on improving the rating indicators of universities and the use of e-portfolios of teachers were reviewed by the authors in Smyrnova-Trybulska et al. (2018a, b). Taking into account the popularity of using the networking is

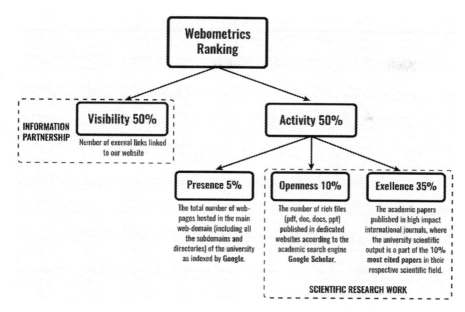

Fig. 5.2 Webometrics rankings as of January 2018: weight, characteristics, evaluation tools, support. (Source: Aguillo et al. 2008)

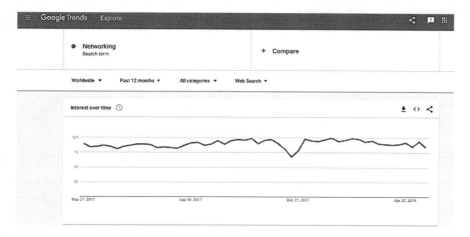

Fig. 5.3 The popularity of the networking in the worlds practice. (Source: https://trends.google.com)

confirmed by a graph obtained with Google Trends (Fig. 5.3); in this study we propose the experience of the participation of teachers from different countries in the IRNET project (www.irnet.us.edu.pl) from the standpoint of the influence of international cooperation on increasing the professional development and rating of teachers and relevant institutions (Table 5.2).

Table 5.2 Webometrics indexes of IRNet consortium universities

University	Country	Country rank	World rank	Presence rank	Impact rank	Openness rank	Excellence rank
The University of Silesia in Katowice	Poland	8	933	652	1013	1312	1159
University of Twente	The Netherlands	9	207	467	175	357	281
University of Extremadura	Spain	30	778	711	1007	723	900
Constantine the Philosopher University in Nitra	Slovak Republic	7	2574	1375	5495	3756	2395
The Lisbon Lusíada University	Portugal	33	3703	3862	6364	4712	3839
University of Ostrava	Czech Republic	15	1876	1651	3369	2003	1913
Curtin University in Perth CU	Australia	9	235	1069	227	245	276
Borys Grinchenko Kyiv University	Ukraine	92	9043	2019	72,979	9593	5777
Dniprodzerzhinsk State Technical University	Ukraine	143	12,395	13,734	15,221	6602	5777
Herzen State Pedagogical University	Russian Federation	91	4666	2052	1394	4535	5777

Source: Own research

IRNet (International Research Network) for study and development of new tools and methods for advanced pedagogical science in the field of ICT instruments, e-learning, and intercultural competences is a project financed by the European Commission under the seventh Framework Programme, within the Marie Curie Actions International Research Staff Exchange Scheme. The IRNet project aims to set up a thematic multidisciplinary joint exchange program dedicated to research and development of new tools for advanced pedagogical science in the field of ICT instruments, distance learning, and intercultural competencies in the EU and non-European countries. The program will strengthen the existing collaboration and establish new scientific contacts through mutual secondments of researchers. The main objectives of the project are the following:

1. To exchange expertise and knowledge in the field of innovative techniques of education between the EU and third countries and to suggest effective strategies of implementing new tools in the educational profession
2. To analyze and evaluate social, economic, and legal conditions, as well as methodologies and e-learning techniques being developed in the European and third countries involved

5 Networking Through Scholarly Communication: Case IRNet Project

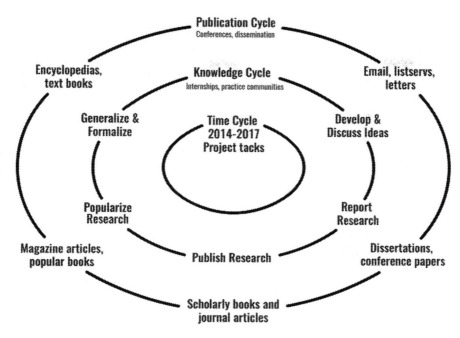

Fig. 5.4 Scholarly content and communication landscape. (Source: Adapted from http://libguides.brooklyn.cuny.edu/c.php?g=316268&p=3420483)

A network is created also by different kinds of contacts: personal contacts, scientific contacts, professional contacts, participation in joint conferences, common projects, etc. (Fig. 5.4).

Realization of network interaction of project participants. Platforms and systems were used as tools for networking scientific communication to conduct e-conferences (e.g., http://openedu.kubg.edu.ua/index.php/conf/2017#.WuQy0O-FNdg, http://www.dlcc.us.edu.pl), virtual conferences, roundtable debate, workshops, seminars in Adobe Connect (http://uex.adobeconnect.com/irnet), and discussion on the forum on IRNet website (http://www.irnet.us.edu.pl) and, additionally, on IRNet profile on Facebook (https://www.facebook.com/IRNet-1669593856645370/) as well as IRNet profile on Twitter(https://twitter.com/irnet_project, ResearchGate), except that reports were published in articles, chapters in peer-reviewed journals, books, and proceedings (e.g., IJREL (http://weinoe.us.edu.pl/nauka/seriewydawnicze/international-journal-research-e-learning), DIVAI (https://conferences.ukf.sk/index.php/divai/divai2018), ICTE (https://konference.osu.cz/icte/), etc.).

During 48 months of the project implementation, more than 220 publications were released, 23 conferences were held, more than 150 workshops and seminars were run, and more than 300 presentations and lectures were given. The main results and achievement were analyzed in detail and presented in numerous publications and reports. Presented below are some Internet sites and a review of several free social networking sites, which can be useful in the dissemination of network results and broadening of scientific cooperation.

Among some results of IRNet Project, there are:

1. *Quantitative:*

    - 204.41 months of research staff exchange have been carried out within the 4 years of the project.
    - 47 researchers have been involved in the exchange program.
    - 23 have been organized.
    - Over 150 seminars and scientific workshops.
    - 220 papers have been published by members of the network, half of publications printed in high scored journals and/or indexed in Web of Science, Scopus, and other international scientific bibliometric databases.
    - Research within seven work packages WP1–WP7 (over ten questionnaires, interviews, observations, literature analysis, statistical analysis).
    - Dissemination of results: Through the specifically designed website http://www.irnet.us.edu.pl.
    - Over 100 multimedia albums, over 10,000 photos in the gallery at www.irnet.us.edu.pl/gallery.
    - Others

2. *Qualitative:*

    - International MA program "E-learning in Cultural Diversity" was developed and accredited.
    - MOOC's "ICT tools in E-learning" (http://el.us.edu.pl/irnet) was developed and started.
    - International Journal of Research in E-learning was started (indexed in ERIH PLUS, Index Copernicus, and ten other scientific databases).
    - Model of shaping ICT competences at the micro-, meso-, macro-level was elaborated.
    - Others

The successful completion of the IRNet project provided several major outputs:

- Highest-quality competence in research in advanced pedagogical science in area of e-learning, ICT, and intercultural competences with significant influence on the development of the HEI staff and open information and educational environment from different regions/countries.
- Reinforcing ERA as internationally renowned partners of AU and initiator of cooperation projects in the next Erasmus+, cost, IVF, and H2020 with an international cooperation dimension focused on the participation of companies and development of the close cooperation with outstanding EU and AU partners.

- Synergy of the research offer with the requirements of innovative education approach and strengthening of cooperation between EU and non-EU HEIs within the framework of an open educational electronical environment, and development of SMART universities.

As a result of the activities carried out by the partners, the performed secondments, and the corresponding networking, it has been possible to present 11 project proposals to different work programs (H2020, Erasmus+, IVF, Cost).

Those which successfully received grants are summarized below:

1. Obtaining the grant no. 21720008 titled "High school teacher competence in change" (https://www.visegradfund.org/archive/results/visegrad-grants/), supported by International Visegrad Fund
2. EMOROBOTIC: Emotional Management in Primary School through Robot Programming. Government of Extremadura, Spain. 2017–2020 project number IB16090

Taking into account the different levels of project participants, special training was organized, including on networking and scientific communication (Morze et al. 2017). One of the indicators for determining the expected learning outcomes at the proposed course was considered by the Education Technology Standards for Education and Training ("ISTE," 2016), including the standards for teachers (source: [online] at http://www.iste.org/standards/standards/for-educators). The guide for implementing collaborative learning is the European Union's standards for building a higher education system and pursuing collaborative research ("Ethics for Researches. Facilitating Research Excellence in FP7," 2013, "Legal Rules of the Scientific Research under the EU Law," 2016).

An e-learning training course "Development of educational, scientific collaboration and project management with IC tools in universities" (http://e-learning.kubg.edu.ua/course/view.php?id=2879) covers the actual issues of organization of cooperation in education, assessment, and application and IC tools in scientific communication, collaboration, development of scientific projects, and research. The course was developed by the BGKU team and became one of the modules of the course; draft MOOC's "ICT tools in E-learning" were developed by a team of international experts (http://el.us.edu.pl/irnet/).

Students' training is based on mixed technology with the maximum share of distance learning (80%). When designing the course, a practical approach was used: 80% of the training material was aimed at training practical skills and competencies through the application of applied tasks and independent work on the organization of educational and scientific cooperation.

Here is an example of a task for self-executing from module 5 "Organization of scientific communication with ICT-tools."

Independent Work 8. Model of Scientific Communication.

Case: "You have decided to explore the models of scientific communication in your own experience. To do this, you plan to create a community and simulate several processes."

Progress:

1. Investigate the services for establishing scientific communication.
   - Office 365 services (https://products.office.com/uk-ua/student/office-in-education)
   - G Suite Services (https://www.google.com/intl/uk)
   - Social network: Facebook (https://www.facebook.com/)
   - Social network: ResearchGate (https://www.researchgate.net)
   - Social network: LinkedIn (https://www.linkedin.com)
2. Discuss the benefits of using one or another tool in the forum.
3. Identify and simulate several processes of scientific communication, such as setting up personal contacts, disseminating research results, and finding experts or partners to participate in projects.
4. Invite members of the group to establish communication: presentation, sending of invitations, etc. (is an integral part of the integrating collective project, in this work is not evaluated).

Carrying out independent work requires the ability to independently explore problems through searching and analyzing specialist literature from various fields of knowledge in order to be able to defend one's point of view as well as developing creativity (Table 5.3).

The fulfillment of the tasks of independent work requires from the participant a profound knowledge of the material, develops the ability to independently explore the problem through the search and analysis of special literature from various fields of knowledge, develops the ability to teach and defend their own point of view, and develops creativity.

During the project implementation, the quality of network interaction and scientific communication was monitored. The results of the publication activity of the project participants were discussed in several articles, in particular in Smyrnova-Trybulska's article (2017a, b); Smyrnova-Trybulska et al. (2017, 2018a, b).

As a result of the analysis of the network resources of the project participants, an increase in professional ties was found to increase the publication activity and effectiveness of the scientific work of teachers of different countries and the number of citations (Figs. 5.5 and 5.6).

Table 5.3 Criteria for evaluating

Criteria	Indicator	Point
Tool representation and choice argument	2 tools	2 points
Proposals for the implementation of scientific communication processes online	1 proposal	2 points
Comments on other proposals	1 comment	1 point
Total for answers and comments		5 points

Source: Own research

5 Networking Through Scholarly Communication: Case IRNet Project

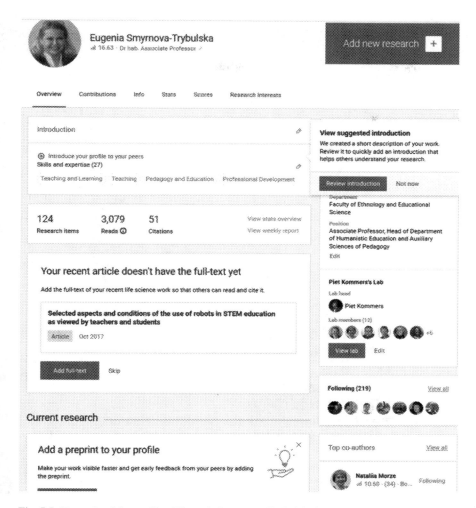

Fig. 5.5 Example of the profile of Eugenia Smyrnova-Trybulska in ResearchGate and increasing of the indicators, in particular reads (3079), citations (51). (Source: Own research)

In addition, monitoring was carried out by questioning the project participants using the questionnaire IRNet Networking research (https://docs.google.com/forms/d/1Otbu6kD0e_g-3nEbiLTIs5pSaeB3edHphw2Q2Szy_HI/viewform?edit_requested=true#responses). As a result of a survey of 17 project participants, it was found that 82.4% of respondents believe that the project network will contribute to the project development and dissemination of its results. At the same time, in the process of network interaction, 94% of respondents actively use the scientific network ResearchGate (Fig. 5.7), which is an increase of 36% compared with the beginning of the project.

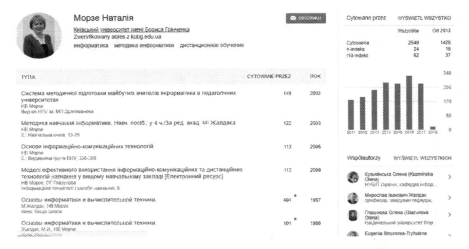

Fig. 5.6 Examples of IRNet Researchers' profiles in Google Scholar citation. Important increase of citations in 2014–2017 – time of IRNet project implementation. (Source: Own research)

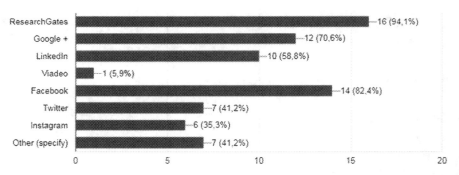

Fig. 5.7 Activity of participants in the social networks project within the framework of network interaction. (Source: Own research)

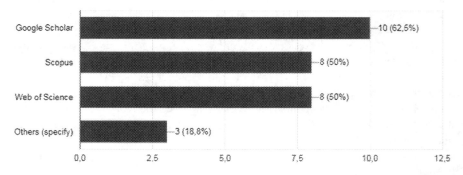

Fig. 5.8 Identification and recognition of researchers through profiles in scientometric databases. (Source: Own research)

Table 5.4 Evaluation of the influence of various forms of scientific communication on the effectiveness of joint network activities

Effectiveness of joint network activity	Internships and research trips EU	Non-EU	Conferences EU	Non-EU	Publications EU	Non-EU
Research (R)	3,35	3,62	4,36	4,4	4,74	4,82
Teaching (T)	4,15	4,46	3,7	3,56	3,64	3,56
Professional development (P)	4,24	4,35	4,12	4,68	4,56	4,7

Source: Own research

One of the indicators of the effectiveness of the participants' network activity is an increase in the indexation of publications and their citation count. Thus, according to the results of the survey on completion of the project, more than half of the project participants have profiles in science-based databases (Fig. 5.8), while 28% of the project created a profile in Scopus (created automatically if there are publications in the database) and increased h-index over 150% and a number of citations in Web of Science and Scopus over 200%.

In addition, an analysis was made of the impact of participation in conferences, internships, research trips, and joint publication activity on the effectiveness of collaborative networking activities (Table 5.4), which in turn affects professional development (P), increase of scientific productivity (R), and teaching and pedagogical efficiency (T) (Table 1) of the project participants. The degree of influence was estimated using a five-point scale: 0, none; 5, high.

Table 5.4 shows the average results of the questionnaire survey of two groups of project participants: representatives of the EU (EU) and third countries (non-EU).

Based on the results of the survey and subsequent in-depth interviews with project participants and representatives of the universities participating in the project, it can be concluded that the systemic application of forms of scientific communication is effective. In the respondents' opinion, the internships conducted within the framework of the project have the greatest impact on the effectiveness of joint network activities in the field of teaching (4,15 and 4,46 points) and professional development (4,24 and 4,35), organization and participation in conferences on development of research competence (4.4 and 4.74) and professional development (4.12 and 4.68), and preparation of joint publications to improve the quality of research (4, 74 and 4.82) and professional development (4.56 and 4.7). Solid results of the influence of each form of scientific communication on the effectiveness of joint network activities in the projects indicate the positive impact of the network on virtually all the research activities of the consortium participants.

All participants favorably rated (on average 4.2) a systematic approach in the application of forms and tools of scientific communication for the implementation of project objectives. The differences in the respondents' assessment of different groups of representatives of EU countries who estimated that the impact is somewhat lower than those of other countries, can be explained by the presence of a

Table 5.5 Results of self-efficacy of participation in the project

Indexes	EU (26)	Others (16)	Student's T distribution value (T)	Difference (Tcr-T)	Differences (p)
The increase of the publishing activity (R)	9.43 ± 0.22	9.56 ± 0.2	0.44	1.58	0.664351
Development of the new courses and their implementation at the university (T)	8.5 ± 0.24	8.92 ± 0.18	1.4	0.6	0.169419
Professional certification (P)	6.2 ± 0.24	6.73 ± 0.22	1.75	1.63	0.111603
Organization and managing of the conferences (P)	7.56 ± 0.18	8.12 ± 0.25	1.82	0.18	0.076777
Internships (P)	8.26 ± 0.24	9.2 ± 0.23	2.83	−0.83	0.007361
Projects (project activity experience) (R)	8.2 ± 0.22	9.14 ± 0.22	3.02	−1.02	0.004428
Increasing network activity, including scientific (T)	7.93 ± 0.23	8.1 ± 0.25	0.05	1.95	0.619583
Recognition (increase in citation indexes) (R)	8.62 ± 0.22	9.1 ± 0.24	1.47	0.52	0.148426

Source: Own research

greater range of opportunities (before the project): access to EU research results, participation in projects, etc.

5.4 Discussion

One of the final evaluation methods that were used as an experiment, regarding the influence of participation in the project on professional development (and as a result the increase in the university's ranking), was the self-assessment method. The questionnaire method was chosen for self-evaluation. The questions were grouped into two groups: those that are quantitatively and qualitatively measured. All the participants of the project answered the questions, and the respondents were divided into two groups: representatives of EU member countries – Poland (6 people), the Netherlands (1), Spain (5), Slovak Republic (6), Portugal (2), the Czech Republic (6) – and of third countries – Ukraine (8), the Russian Federation (5), Australia (3). These questions are divided into three categories (according to the project's tasks): professional development (P), increase of scientific productivity (R), and teaching and pedagogical efficiency (T) (Table 5.1).

On the basis of statistical data processing (Table 5.5), it can be assumed that the proposed case of using the networking through scholarly communication received a positive assessment, regardless of the country of representatives. For degrees of freedom, f = 40, the critical value of student's T distribution is Tcr = 2.021, with significance level $\alpha = 0.05$. Differences are statistically significant ($p < 0.05$) only in case of internships (P), which can be explained by different approaches in the implementation of decision to project and networking making by European and third countries.

5.5 Conclusions

On the basis of these results, we can draw the following conclusions:

1. International cooperation and participation in joint international projects promote both the development of science and contribute to an increase in the rating indicators of higher education institutions.
2. The organizations' scientific networking of researchers through scholarly communication is an effective model for the implementation of the tasks of a research international project.
3. The organization of special training in the course of the project, including on the organization of networking and scientific communication, increases the effectiveness of the project activities and the competence of individual participants.
4. Monitoring the quality of network interaction and scientific communication in the process of project implementation is a prerequisite for the creation of an active scientific network that contributes to the development of its participants and the fulfillment of project tasks.
5. On the basis of statistical data processing by project results, it can be assumed that the proposed case of using the networking through scholarly communication received a positive assessment, regardless of the country of representatives.
6. Statistically significant differences can be explained by different approaches in the implementation of the decision to undertake the project and establish networks by European and non-European countries that can be used for further research in the field of the elaborating of project proposals and the selection of the team of participants.

Acknowledgments The research leading to these results has received, within the framework of the IRNet project, funding from the People Program (Marie Curie Actions) of the European Union's Seventh Framework Program FP7/2007–2013/under REA grant agreement No: PIRSES-GA-2013-612536.

References

Aguillo, I., Ortega, J., & Fernandez, M. (2008). Webometric ranking of world universities: Introduction, methodology, and future developments. *Higher Education in Europe, 33*(2/3), 233–244. https://doi.org/10.1080/03797720802254031.

Bershadskaya, M., Voznesenskaya, Y., & Karpenko, O. (2016). Research webometrics. Ranking in the context of accessibility of higher education. *Universal Journal of Educational, 4*(7), 1506–1514. https://doi.org/10.13189/ujer.2016.040702.

Budapest Open Access Initiative. (2012). *Ten years on from the Budapest open access initiative: Setting the default to open.* [online] Available at http://www.budapestopenaccessinitiative.org/boai-10-recommendations. Accessed 16 Mar 2018.

Colace, F., De Santo, M., & Greco, L. (2013). A probabilistic approach to Tweets' Sentiment Classification Book Group Author(s): IEEE conference: *5th biannual conference of the humaine-association on Affective Computing and Intelligent Interaction (ACII).* Location: Geneva, Switzerland Date: Sep 02–05, 2013 Book Series: International Conference on Affective Computing and Intelligent Interaction, (pp. 37–42).

Competitiveness Council Conclusions of 3 June 2008 on "The Launch of the 'Ljubljana Process' – towards full realisation of ERA". http://register.consilium.europa.eu/doc/srv?l=EN&f=ST%2010231%202008%20INIT. Accessed 20 Mar 2018.

Drlík, M., Švec, P., Kapusta, J., Munk, M., Noskova, T., Pavlova, T., Yakovleva, O., Morze, N., & Smyrnova-Trybulska, E. (2017, January 1). Identification of differences in university E-environment between selected EU and non-EU countries using knowledge mining methods: Project IRNet case study. *International Journal of Web Based Communities, 13*(2): 236–261. https://doi.org/10.1504/IJWBC.2017.10004116. ISSN online: 1741-8216. ISSN print: 1477-8394.

Ethical Principles of Research in EU and International Law. (2016). Retrieved August 10, 2017, from http://www.rightsandscience.eu/project/ethical-principles-of-research-in-eu-and-international-law

European IRNet project web-site (www.irnet.us.edu.pl).

European Commission – Press release. *How digital is your country? Europe needs digital single market to boost its digital performance.* Brussels, 18 May 2018 [online] Available at http://europa.eu/rapid/press-release_IP-18-3742_en.htm. Accessed on 30 May 2018.

European Research Area (Era) Roadmap 2015–2020 https://era.gv.at/object/document/1845. Accessed 20 Mar 2018.

ISTE STANDARDS. (2016). Retrieved August 10, 2017, from http://www.iste.org/standards/standards ethics for researchers (2013). *Facilitating research excellence in FP7/European commission.* Directorate-General for Research and Innovation. Science in society/capacities FP7. Luxembourg, Publications Office of the European Union, 36 p. https://doi.org/10.2777/7491.

Morze, N., & Varchenko-Trotsenko, L. (2016). Educator's e-portfolio in the modern university. ICT in education, research and industrial applications. Integration, harmonization and knowledge transfer. In: *Proceedings from CEUR workshop* (CEUR-WS.org). Online proceedings for scientific conferences and workshops (Vol-1614, pp. 231–240). Retrieved from http://ceur-ws.org/Vol-1614/paper_68.pdf. Accessed 26 June 2016.

Morze, N., Kuzminska, O., & Liakh, T. (2017). Development of educational, scientific collaboration and project management with ic tools in universities In: E. Smyrnova-Trybulska (Ed.), *Effective development of teachers' skills in the area of ICT and E-learning* (E-learning Publishing Series, Vol. 9, pp. 347–364). Katowice-Cieszyn: Studio Noa for University of Silesia, Katowice-Cieszyn ISSN: 2451-3644 (print edition) ISSN 2451-3652 (digital edition) ISBN 978-83-60071-96-0.

Ranking Web of Universities. (2018a). *Ranking web of Universities.* January New Edition [online] Available at http://www.webometrics.info/en/node/200. Accessed 16 Mar 2018.

Ranking Web of Universities. (2018b). *Methodology.* [online] Available at http://www.webometrics.info/en/Methodology. Accessed 16 Mar 2018.

Smyrnova-Trybulska, E. (2017a). Networking is one of the effectiveness form of the international research. Some aspects. In: *Open educational e-environment of modern university* (pp. 130–139) ISSN: 2414-0325.
Smyrnova-Trybulska, E. (2017b). Mapping and visualization of scientific bibliometric domains and research network activities. In: M. Hruby (Ed.), *Distance learning, simulation and communication DLSC2017*, Brno, Czech Republic, May 31–June 2, 2017 (pp. 301–308). Brno: University of Defence. ISBN 978-80-7231-416-4.
Smyrnova-Trybulska, E., Morze, N., Kuzminska, O., & Kommers, P. (2017). Bibliometric science mapping as a popular trend: Chosen examples of visualisation of international research network results. In: P. Kommers, T. Issa, P. Isaías, & A. Hol (Eds.), *Proceedings of the International Conferences on Educational Technologies 2017 (ICEduTech 2017)* (pp. 3–10), 11–13 December 2017, Western Sydney University, Sydney, Australia. IADIS 2017. ISBN: 978-989-8533-71-5.
Smyrnova-Trybulska, E., Morze, N., & Kuzminska, O. (2018a). Academic information transparency: From teachers' E-portfolio to upgrading the rankings of universities. In M. Turčáni, Z. Balogh, M. Munk, J. Kapusta, & Ľ. Benko (Eds.), *Distance learning in applied informatics DIVAI 2018* (pp. 347–358). Nitra-Sturovo: Constantine the Philosopher University in Nitra. ISBN: ISBN 978-80-7598-059-5 ISSN 2464-7470 (print) ISSN 2464-7489 (on-line).
Smyrnova-Trybulska, E., Morze, N., & Kuzminska, O. (2018b). *Mapping and visualization of a research network: Case study.* Edukacja – Technika – Informatyka, 1. ISSN: 2080–9069 I Online ISSN: 2450-9221.

Chapter 6
Report Writing Assessment for Postgraduate Students: Lecturer's Perspective

Tomayess Issa and Theodora Issa

6.1 Introduction

Local and global organisations have been actively sourcing graduates with exceptional and specific skills, i.e. professional, interpersonal and technology skills, as these skills are essential to improve productivity and efficiency. Therefore, academics implement assessments that develop these skills such as report writing, reflective journals, wikis and teamwork assessments that will encourage specific skills to assist students in their current studies and the workforce in the future.

Report writing assessment is considered a unique technique to assess student knowledge and skills from the unit outcomes, as students prepare a document based on a topic related to the unit by following a specific template. Report writing allows students to improve their learning processes and personal and professional skills. Reports should be written concisely and clearly and be well organised. They need to identify and examine issues and events based on the current literature, and the presentation should be structured around the specific topic needs. Several studies (Benson et al. 2017; Crusan 2017; Evans 2013; Wu et al. 2013) indicate that assessments, including report writing, improve specific skills, especially critical thinking, decision-making and, most importantly, research and writing skills. This chapter aims to examine the report writing assessment design and implementation in postgraduate units to enhance students' learning processes, including skills and knowledge.

T. Issa (✉) · T. Issa
School of Management, Faculty of Business and Law, Curtin University, Perth, Australia
e-mail: Tomayess.Issa@cbs.curtin.edu.au; Theodora.Issa@curtin.edu.au

© Springer Nature Switzerland AG 2019
E. Smyrnova-Trybulska et al. (eds.), *Universities in the Networked Society*, Critical Studies of Education 10, https://doi.org/10.1007/978-3-030-05026-9_6

6.2 Report Writing Assessment

Teaching and learning in higher education needs to integrate and combine several assessments to stimulate the student learning process for the current study and workforce in the future. Generally speaking, academics work very closely with the teaching and learning department in universities to identify appropriate assessments to integrate into postgraduate units to enhance students learning, knowledge, skills and technology. These assessments are, namely, report writing, wiki contributions, reflective journals, digital presentations and teamwork-based assessments. Each assessment aims to target specific skills that assist students to become more self-confident and self-reliant in these skills in their current studies and in the future. Several studies (Caro et al. 2014; Gronlund 1998; Huot 2002; Lee 2007; Palomo-Duarte et al. 2014) indicate that assessments are essential in higher education to assist students to enhance their theoretical and practical knowledge of the unit content. Report writing assessment is a very useful tool in higher education as it helps lecturers measure students' knowledge, understanding and awareness of the unit content, as well as develop and improve the students' professional and personal skills. Report writing is intended to develop the following skills: oral presentation, researching, writing, critical thinking, decision-making and the use of the EndNote software.

The professional skills comprise reading, writing, research, information, critical thinking, decision-making, technology, digital oral presentation, drawing (i.e. concept maps) and teamwork (see Fig. 6.1). These professional skills are essential, and numerous studies (Bednarz 2014; Chu et al. 2017; Diggins 2004; Isaias and Issa 2014; Lanning et al. 2011; Pavolvich et al. 2009; Ruge and McCormack 2017;

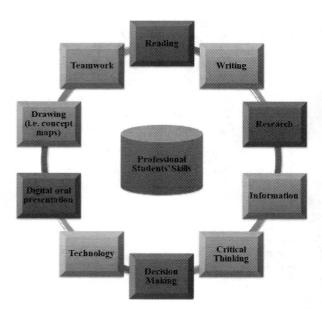

Fig. 6.1 Students' professional skills

Schlick 1992; Wallace et al. 2004; Wilen-Daugenti 2012; Worley 2008) have indicated that professional skills are essential in the business sector, as students require all the basic knowledge behind writing, reading, reflecting and very high-level thinking, and this can be achieved by practicing and interacting during class time or through technology platforms (Tucker et al. 1998).

On the other hand, personal skills encompass (see Fig. 6.2) motivation, leadership, negotiation, communication, problem-solving, time management, reflection, self-management and self-appraisal. These skills are vital for students to improve their knowledge in their studies as well as to assist them in the workforce in the future. Several studies indicate (Arlow 1991; Christie et al. 2017; Clarke 2003; Franklin 2010; Issa et al. 2012; Lin et al. 2011; Munoz-Organero et al. 2010; Pavolvich et al. 2009; Rogers 2001; Sancho-Thomas et al. 2009; Taraghi et al. 2009; Ying and Norman 2017) that universities locally and globally should endorse and shift students' mind-sets to engage with the content by thinking more critically, creatively and reflectively and reviewing and discussing the most important aspects and concepts with their colleagues, lecturers and employers. This can be achieved via the assessments, including the report writing assessments.

The report writing assessment is part of two postgraduate units offered at Curtin University; these units are Business Project Management and Green IT and Sustainability. In the Business Project Management unit, the lecturer provided a

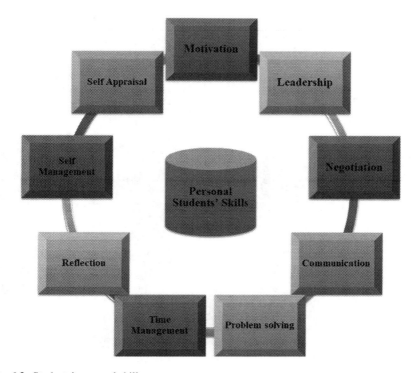

Fig. 6.2 Students' personal skills

statement related to issues such as conflict in project management, management and leaders, risks, and other topics, from an academic journal, and asked the students to evaluate this statement using a report writing template. In the Green IT and Sustainability unit, students needed to select a real-life organisation from Australia or overseas and assist them in becoming more sustainable, especially in the IT department. Firstly, students needed to identify the current IT problems or challenges in the chosen organisation's IT department. The, by using specific models and methodologies from a Green IT literature review, students developed a new IT model so the organisation could become more sustainable, with special attention to the IT departments in the organisations of their choice.

For the report writing assessment, especially in the Green IT and Sustainability unit, firstly, students presented a digital presentation (MP4) with duration of 25 min based on their IT real-life organisation. In the digital presentation, students needed to include the following sections: introduction, literature review, company details, the new sustainable strategy, recommendations and conclusion (see Fig. 6.3).

The digital presentation was marked by the facilitator providing feedback aimed at improving the report writing presentation. The report writing assessment discussed the same topic as the presentation, but students completed the report writing assessment with a different template provided by the lecturer with the following headings: executive summary, introduction, scope of the literature review, current literature review, real company details, current IT problems in the real company, models and methodologies, new sustainable model, discussion, limitations, recommendations (practical and theoretical), conclusion, reflection and references (see Fig. 6.4).

Fig. 6.3 Digital presentation template

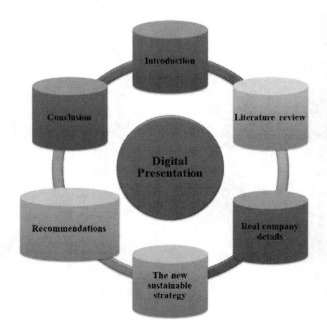

6 Report Writing Assessment for Postgraduate Students: Lecturer's Perspective

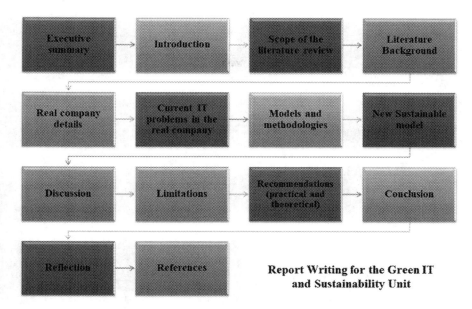

Fig. 6.4 Report writing for the Green IT and Sustainability unit

In the Business Project Management assessment, the template contains the following sections: executive summary, introduction, scope of the literature review, current literature review (based on the assessment statement and questions), discussion, recommendations, conclusion, reflection and references (see Fig. 6.5).

For the executive summary, students addressed the following areas by presenting their findings as a paragraph without citations: objectives of the report, scope of the report (narrow down the topic), information sources used (mention any limitations), findings of the research, recommendations and conclusion.

The following is needed to be included in the introduction section: introduction to the subject matter, provide the purpose and objectives of the report, state the terms of reference (what the research set out to cover), state the information sources used (mention any limitations), indicate the general make-up of the report and use decimal notation starting at the introduction, i.e. 1.0.

As the literature review section lists the key terms and the databases and journals which were used for preparing the report, this section assists the lecturer to identify how students prepared their report and which peer-reviewed journals and databases they referred to. This section also helps the students to research the correct way when report writing, especially at the postgraduate level.

The background section is based on the assessment topic. Students needed to develop headings and subheadings for this section and collect relevant and current literature to support the answer to the assessment question.

For the discussion section, students discussed the following questions in consultation with the necessary literature from journals and books: Did you answer the

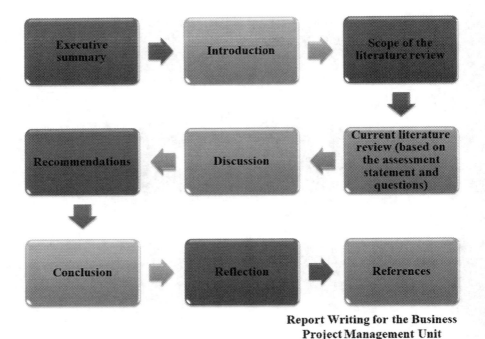

Fig. 6.5 Report writing for the Business Project Management unit

assessment question? Did you agree with the current literature regarding the question, and why or why not (please add your voice and perspective)? What are your report's limitations? And where from here i.e. the future research? In the recommendation section, the students were required to list the recommendations by cross-referencing the background section.

The conclusion section summarises the evidence and discussion provided in the body of the report. Furthermore, no new information or new references should be added at this stage.

The reflection section asked students to express their feelings about the report writing process by answering the following questions: Was this assignment as challenging as you expected, easier or more difficult, and why? What challenges did you face? How did you overcome these challenges? What have you learnt about the theories, skills (i.e. research, writing, decision-making, EndNote software, etc.) and yourself by completing the report writing assessment?

Finally, students needed to use the EndNote software for the reference section, and students should list no less than 15 academic journal references or textbooks and 8 academic journals that should be dated from 2007 to 2018 (the last 10 years).

The report writing assessment information was available from the first week of the semester, to allow the students to identify the assessment needs and to give them maximum time to locate the necessary resources for the assessment. The lecturer explained the EndNote software by providing several examples of how to use it to save references using Google Scholar and databases in the university. Furthermore, to encourage students to use the EndNote software for the report, a guest speaker from the library was invited to present a demonstration of the EndNote software. Students also needed to attend a workshop in the library for the same purpose. This technique encouraged the students to use the EndNote software in the assessment not only for the Business Project Management and Green IT and Sustainability units but also for students that started to use this software in their other units as well.

A rubric was used to mark the report writing assessment for both units. The rubric's focus was mainly on the context and purpose, content development, genre and disciplinary conventions, sources of evidence, control of syntax and mechanics and conclusion and recommendations (Fig. 6.6).

To assist the students in the report writing assessment, formative feedback was given by the lecturer to show the students their mistakes, how to better present the report writing assessment based on the assessment guidelines, and to closer meet the unit lecturer's expectations. Formative feedback is crucial, fundamental and obligatory in postgraduate units as it provides direction and guidance to students in understanding the precise and accurate nature required in report writing presentation, layout and structure. Several studies (Garrison and Ehringhaus 2007; Ghiatău et al. 2011; Hancock and Brundage 2010; Issa et al. 2014a; Ng 2014; Timmers et al. 2013; Wingate 2010) confirm that formative feedback provides a measure and substantiation of students' learning processes and identifies if students need further assistance before the final submission.

The main idea behind formative feedback is to confirm whether the students are on the right track and to allow students to learn from their faults so they can avoid these in report writing assessments not only for the Business Project Management

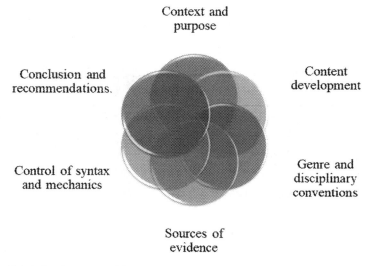

Fig. 6.6 Rubric for the report writing assessment

and Green IT and Sustainability units but also in other units in the postgraduate level. Furthermore, based on the literature (Allen and Bentley 2012; Issa et al. 2014a, b; Lynch et al. 2012; Merry and Orsmond 2008; Thomas et al. 2014), using formative feedback in report writing assessments develops more confidence, sureness and motivation among students to complete the assessment on time, to achieve the unit objectives and, importantly, to learn how to write a report for academic purposes. The lecturer may answer students' queries through face-to-face meetings, audio feedback, live feedback via wiki and email to improve and enhance student's learning and engagement. To support the formative feedback, Issa et al. (2014a) developed the foster student independent learning model (see Fig. 6.7) which helps academics and researchers to adopt the best approaches to prompt students' independent learning via feedback. Finally, the frequent feedback from the lecturers will improve and enrich students and lecturers' relationship and enhance students personal and professionals' skills.

Students managed to improve these skills by completing the report writing assessment and the majority of the students indicating that report writing is a challenging but worthwhile activity. Consequently, completing the report writing assessment changed students' mind-sets and provided them with the necessary knowledge and skills required in the workplace in the future.

Finally, students provided the following comments regarding this assessment, and from their comments, it became apparent that this assessment assisted them in two ways: unit knowledge, skills and, most importantly, professional skills from

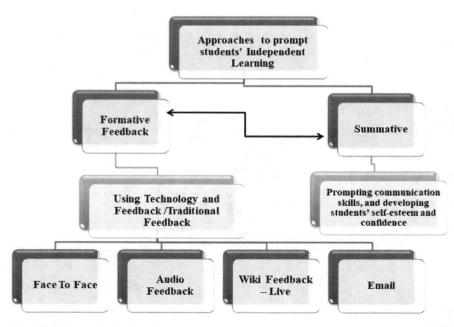

Fig. 6.7 Foster student independent learning model. (Issa et al. 2014a)

searching, researching, writing, critical thinking, decision-making and the use of the EndNote software.

The guidance provided on this report was invaluable, and I have valued the opportunity to improve my analytical, reflection and writing skills. I have been able to see the benefits of these improvements in my professional tasks, as well as the explicit benefits of a more detailed understanding of risk management processes.

I can confidently arrive at a conclusion that the benefits I derived from completing this assignment outweigh the cost. In other words, this study has been a wonderful learning experience and a valuable asset, which I would forever cherish.

I have learnt and gained rich knowledge and understanding about risks in project management and information systems. I have developed my research, writing and EndNote software skills by making an effort to contact the communication skills centre to help me proofread my report as well as contacting the librarian and arranging a time to help me and my fellow classmates to use EndNote which I believe will be really helpful and beneficial for my future studies.

I used to write down the details of my bibliography (Chicago Author-Date 16th Edition) by myself before this assignment. Professor suggested we use the EndNote to do our references. Before you start using, you might need to spend some time getting to know how to use it. After understanding how to use it, I have to say that EndNote is an easy and timesaving tool to make your references when you do your assignment.

For the last semesters, I was doing the references manually, and I lost all the marks. Now I'm comfortable using the software and it makes things easier.

At first I was facing difficulties using the software, but after a few mistakes and guidance from my professors, I became familiar with the software. The decisions that I made in various parts of the study were not an easy task. I had to analyse all the aspects of the causes and solutions. As per my self-experience in this study, I enjoyed studying the articles as the subject is very interesting and I also gathered a good knowledge on the success or failure facts of a project management process.

Thankfully through study, and in class assistance by my lecturer, I was able to learn not only how to go about the various sections of this report but also learn how to write Chicago References. In fact, one of the best things I learnt about whilst undergoing this report was the EndNote X8 referencing system for Microsoft Office Word. Before this report, I had always been sceptical of the brilliance of EndNote and as a result always wrote my references by hand instead of using EndNote or any other pieces of software. However, seeing as Chicago was a completely new system, I believed that this was the right time to learn. At first the initial learning curve for EndNote made me consistently question why I was wasting my time learning it, but by the end of the project, I found myself absolutely loving it to the extent that I never want to write references without it again.

I found the EndNote software is very useful in particular when compiling information from multiple sources. I was frustrated that I couldn't add unpublished resources easily, as I wanted to reference an assignment I had handed in last semester regarding leadership skills maturity models. I did however find that the programme would slightly glitch and I would often have to reset EndNote as it would freeze. I reinstalled the programme and contacted support; however the response was that my operating system or hardware may not be 100% compatible with the requirements.

From this assessment I've learnt what project leadership is all about and the different types of leadership styles that can be used by leaders and managers to sustain them in this twenty-first century. I have also learnt how to use the EndNote software to do referencing properly. I have also learnt that I'm able to understand project leadership and management better. Last but not least, I have learnt that through this journey, I have learnt a lot of useful skills and techniques to do a report well.

With the help of this report, I learned good presentation skills for the research paperwork using formatting styles. With the use of EndNote software, I gained knowledge of referencing the research articles and books.

The assessment has helped in learning how to reach for quality research papers and identify the most suitable article to retrieve the information from. It also helped to learn more about project management concept and the theories associated with it. More and deep knowledge on how to use EndNote was acquired on completing this assessment. Decision-making and analytical skills are something that has been practised throughout the assessment.

This assignment helped me a lot, expanding my knowledge within project management. I had the chance to get insights into the Australian, more specifically Curtin University, teaching method. Thereby I mean working with EndNote, getting continuous supervision and the type of assignment task itself. Furthermore, I gained more practice in doing research, which will help me in writing my thesis next semester. Although the assignment was more challenging than expected, I enjoyed the process itself and highly appreciate the continuous support of the professor.

The major skill I learnt throughout this journey was how to present a report in a professional manner. As mentioned, this journey was a little difficult too, but thanks to the facilitator, who was supportive throughout the journey, it became bit easier as she was very helpful by providing her guidelines and availability to everyone at every step. Overall this journey was exciting and challenging which is a life time learning experience.

This report develops analytical thinking, motivation to work sustainably, path to move from problem to solutions, brainstorming on unique topics and the list that goes on. Presentation and learning skills flourished through this critical report. This challenging work gives confidence to solve the issues systematically and strategically. Anything or any single word learnt through report is worthy and useful for future.

Overall this was one of the greatest experiences in which I have developed many skills, such as research, creativity, design, analytical thinking and being strategic and tactical. Most importantly of all, how much our environment is valuable to us and that we always need to ensure that we are doing the best and no matter what activities we are doing as individual or business members, we need to ensure to take actions that will have no negative impacts on the environment as much as we appreciate our mother nature.

6.3 Conclusion

This chapter discussed the design and implementation of report writing assessments in postgraduate units in Australia. The report writing assessment trained students to write academically, to search out appropriate databases and to enhance their personal and professional skills, especially the use of the EndNote software for referencing and citations. The report writing assessment template and marking guide was discussed to benefit researchers and academics who would like to implement this assessment in their own units. Furthermore, the researchers discussed how formative feedback is essential and vital in this assessment; as via this feedback, students learned from their mistakes and how to present the report writing assessment based on the assessment guidelines and match the unit and lecturer needs. Students indicated and confirmed that completing the report writing in their postgraduate units enhanced their personal and professional skills and helped them gain the necessary knowledge for the unit. In the future the researchers will further explore how this assessment style improves students' skills.

Acknowledgements The research leading to these results has received, within the framework of the IRNet project, funding from the People Programme (Marie Curie Actions) of the European Union's Seventh Framework Programme FP7/2007-2013/under REA grant agreement No: PIRSES-GA-2013-612536.

References

Allen, R., & Bentley, S. (2012). *Feedback mechanisms: Efficient and effective use of technology or waste of time and effort*. Paper presented at the STEM Annual Conference 2012 London.
Arlow, P. (1991). Personal characteristics in college Students' evaluations of business ethics and corporate social responsibility. *Journal of Business Ethics, 10*(1), 63–69.
Bednarz, A. (2014). *Big data skills pay top dollar: Mastering big data languages, databases and skills could be the ticket to a bigger paycheck*. Retrieved January 3, 2017, from https://www.scribd.com/document/250490075/Big-Data-Skills-Pay-Top-Dollar-Network-World
Benson, B. J, Weissenburger, J. W., & Espin, C. A. (2017). Assessing the writing performance of students in special education. In *Students who are exceptional and writing disabilities* (pp. 55–66). London: Routledge.
Caro, D. H., Sandoval-Hernandez, A., & Lüdtke, O. (2014). Cultural, social, and economic capital constructs in international assessments: An evaluation using exploratory structural equation modeling. *School Effectiveness and School Improvement, 25*(3), 433–450.
Christie, H., Cree, V. E., Mullins, E., & Tett, L. (2017). 'University opened up so many doors for me': The personal and professional development of graduates from non-traditional backgrounds. *Studies in Higher Education, 43*(11), 1–11.
Chu, S. K. W., Reynolds, R. B., Tavares, N. J., Notari, M., & Lee, C. W. Y. (2017). Twenty-first century skills education in Switzerland: An example of project-based learning using wiki in science education. In *21st century skills development through inquiry-based learning* (pp. 61–78). Singapore: Springer.
Clarke, M. (2003). *Reflection: Journals and reflective questions a strategy for professional learning*. Paper presented at the NZARE/AARE Conference Auckland, New Zealand.

Crusan, D. J. (2017). *Writing Assessment: Do we Pratice What we Preach?* Retrieved 1 June 2018, from https://corescholar.libraries.wright.edu/english/262

Diggins, M. (2004). *Teaching and learning communication skills in social work education.* Retrieved February 22, 2017, from http://www.scie.org.uk/publications/guides/guide05/

Evans, C. (2013). Making sense of assessment feedback in higher education. *Review of Educational Research, 83*(1), 70–120.

Franklin, K. (2010). Thank you for sharing: Developing students' social skills to improve peer writing conferences. *English Journal, 99*(5), 79–84.

Garrison, C., & Ehringhaus, M. (2007). *Formative and summative assessments in the classroom.* Retrieved September 14, 2012, from http://ccti.colfinder.org/sites/default/files/guyana/resources/TL/TL%20M02U03%20docs/Formative%20and%20Summative%20Assessment%20in%20the%20Classroom.pdf

Ghiatău, R., Diac, G., & Curelaru, V. (2011). Interaction between summative and formative in higher education assessment: Students' perception. *Procedia – Social and Behavioral Sciences, 11*(0), 220–224. https://doi.org/10.1016/j.sbspro.2011.01.065.

Gronlund, N. E. (1998). *Assessment of student achievement.* USA: Allyn & Bacon

Hancock, A., & Brundage, S. (2010). Formative feedback, rubrics, and assessment of professional competency through a speech-language pathology graduate program. *Journal of Allied Health, 39*(2), 110–119.

Huot, B. (2002). *Rearticulating writing assessment for teaching and learning.* USA: Utah State University Press.

Isaias, P., & Issa, T. (2014). Promoting communication skills for information systems students in Australian and Portuguese higher education: Action research study. *Education and Information Technologies, 19*(4), 841–861.

Issa, T., Issa, T., & Isaias, P. (2012). Reflective journals for the enhancement of postgraduate students learning: An Australian case study. *The International Journal of Learning, 18*, 237–252.

Issa, T., Issa, T., & Kommers, P. (2014a). Feedback and learning support that fosters students' independent learning: An Australian case study. *The International Journal of Learning, 19*, 29–39.

Issa, T., Isaias, P., & Issa, T. (2014b). Does MP3 audio feedback enhance student's learning skills? An international case study. *The International Journal of Learning, 19*, 15–28.

Lanning, S. K., Brickhouse, T. H., Gunsolley, J. C., Ranson, S. L., & Willett, R. M. (2011). Communication skills instruction: An analysis of self, peer-group, student instructors and faculty assessment. *Patient Education and Counseling, 83*, 145–151.

Lee, I. (2007). Assessment for learning: Integrating assessment, teaching, and learning in the ESL/EFL writing classroom. *Canadian Modern Language Review, 64*(1), 199–213.

Lin, H.-S., Hong, Z.-R., Wang, H.-H., & Lee, S.-T. (2011). Using reflective peer assessment to promote students' conceptual understanding through asynchronous discussions. *Educational Technology and Society, 14*(3), 178–189.

Lynch, R., McNamara, P. M., & Seery, N. (2012). Promoting deep learning in a teacher education programme through self-and peer-assessment and feedback. *European Journal of Information Systems, 35*(2), 179–197.

Merry, S., & Orsmond, P. (2008). Students' attitudes to an usage of academic feedback provided via audio files. *Bioscience Education eJournal, 11*, 1–11.

Munoz-Organero, M., Munoz-Merino, P., & Kloos, C. D. (2010). Personalized service-oriented E-learning environments. *IEEE Internet Computing, 14*(2), 62–67.

Ng, E. M. W. (2014). Using a mixed research method to evaluate the effectiveness of formative assessment in supporting student teachers' wiki authoring. *Computers & Education, 73*(0), 141–148. https://doi.org/10.1016/j.compedu.2013.12.016.

Palomo-Duarte, M., Dodero, J. M., García-Domínguez, A., Neira-Ayuso, P., Sales-Montes, N., Medina-Bulo, I., et al. (2014). Scalability of assessments of wiki-based learning experiences in higher education. *Computers in Human Behavior, 31*(0), 638–650. https://doi.org/10.1016/j.chb.2013.07.033.

Pavolvich, K., Collins, E., & Jones, G. (2009). Developing students' skills in reflective practice: Design and assessment. *Journal of Management Education, 23*(1), 37–58.

Rogers, R. (2001). Reflection in higher education: A concept analysis. *Innovative Higher Education, 26*(1), 37–57.

Ruge, G., & McCormack, C. (2017). Building and construction students' skills development for employability–reframing assessment for learning in discipline-specific contexts. *Architectural Engineering and Design Management, 13*(5), 1–19.

Sancho-Thomas, P., Fuentes-Fernandez, R., & Fernandez-Manjon, B. (2009). Learning teamwork skills in university programming courses. *Computers and Education, 53*, 517–531.

Schlick, J. (1992). Critical thinking skills. *Quality, 31*(8), 15.

Taraghi, B., Ebner, M., & Schaffert, S. (2009). *Personal learning environments for higher education: A mashup based widget concept.* Paper presented at the F. Wild, M. Kalz, M. Palmér, & D. Müler (Éd.), Mash-up personal learning environments: Proceedings of the workshop in conjunction with the 4th European conference on technology-enhanced learning (ECTEL'09).

Thomas, E., Rosewell, J., Kear, K., & Donelan, H. (2014). *Learning and peer feedback in shared online spaces.* Paper presented at The ninth international conference on networked learning, UK.

Timmers, C. F., Braber-van den Broek, J., & van den Berg, S. M. (2013). Motivational beliefs, student effort, and feedback behaviour in computer-based formative assessment. *Computers and Education, 60*(1), 25–31. https://doi.org/10.1016/j.compedu.2012.07.007.

Tucker, M., McCarthy, A., Hoxmeier, J., & Lenk, M. (1998). Community service learning increases communication skills across the business curriculum. *Business Communication Quarterly, 61*(2), 89–99.

Wallace, T., Stariha, W., & Walberg, H. (2004). *Teaching, speaking, listening and writing.* Indiana University International Academy of Education.

Wilen-Daugenti, T. (2012). Big data requires new skills. *Trade Jounral, 23*(6), 1.

Wingate, U. (2010). The impact of formative feedback on the development of academic writing. *Assessment & Evaluation in Higher Education, 35*(5), 519–533.

Worley, P. (2008). Writing skills essential in tech ed today. *Tech Directions, 68*(2), 17–19.

Wu, C., Chanda, E., & Willison, J. (2013). Implementation and outcomes of online self and peer assessment on group based honours research projects. *Assessment & Evaluation in Higher Education*, 39(1), 1–18.

Ying, T., & Norman, W. C. (2017). Personality effects on the social network structure of boundary-spanning personnel in the tourism industry. *Journal of Hospitality & Tourism Research, 41*(5), 515–538.

Chapter 7
Develop and Implement MOOCs Unit: A Pedagogical Instruction for Academics, Case Study

Eugenia Smyrnova-Trybulska, Elspeth McKay, Nataliia Morze, Olga Yakovleva, Tomayess Issa, and Theodora Issa

7.1 Introduction

In September 2013, the European Commission launched the initiative Opening Up Education to further enhance the adoption of open education in Europe (European Commission 2013). Recently the European Commission funded a number of massive open online course (MOOC) projects. One of those projects, referred to as Higher Education Online: MOOCs the European way (HOME 2014), intends to develop and strengthen an open network for European cooperation on open education and MOOCs. This is an ongoing project which was launched in 2014 and finalized in 2016 (Jansen et al. 2015).

E. Smyrnova-Trybulska (✉)
University of Silesia in Katowice, Katowice, Poland
e-mail: esmyrnova@us.edu.pl

E. McKay
RMIT University, Melbourne, Australia
e-mail: elspeth.mckay@rmit.edu.au

N. Morze
Borys Grinchenko University in Kyiv, Kyiv, Ukraine
e-mail: n.morze@kubg.edu.ua

O. Yakovleva
Herzen State Pedagogical University of Russia, St. Petersburg, Russia

T. Issa · T. Issa
School of Management, Faculty of Business and Law, Curtin University, Perth, Australia
e-mail: Tomayess.Issa@cbs.curtin.edu.au

© Springer Nature Switzerland AG 2019
E. Smyrnova-Trybulska et al. (eds.), *Universities in the Networked Society*, Critical Studies of Education 10, https://doi.org/10.1007/978-3-030-05026-9_7

7.2 What Are MOOCs? The History and Key Features of MOOCs

"The future is already here, it's just not very evenly distributed" said William Gibson (Gibson in: Clark 2013); that is certainly true of MOOCs. We have MOOC mania, but "all MOOCs are not created equal", and there's lots of species of MOOC. This is good, and we must learn from these experiments to move forward and not get bogged down in old traditionalist vs modernist arguments. MOOCs will inform and shape what we do within and without institutions. What is important is to focus on the real needs of real learners (Clark 2013).

The massive open online course (MOOC) movement is the latest "big thing" in open and distance learning (ODL). MOOCs offer both opportunities and threats that are extensively discussed in the literature, including the potential of opening up education for all at a global scale (Schuwer et al. 2015).

On the other hand, MOOCs challenge traditional pedagogy and raise important questions about the future of campus-based education. However, in discussing these opportunities and threats, the majority of the literature tends to focus on the origin of the MOOC movement in the United States (US). The specific context of Europe with its diversity of languages, cultural environments, educational policies, and regulatory frameworks differs substantially from the US context. Accordingly, the study (Schuwer et al. 2015) offers a European perspective on MOOCs in order to better understand major differences in threats and opportunities across countries and continents, including the use and reuse of MOOCs for regional or global use, via European or non-European platforms.

It is observed from available data (Open Education Europa 2014) that EU MOOC activities are mainly concentrated in Western Europe, serve a limited number of language communities and have been mainly driven by individual ambitious players from the higher education (HE) sector. Although European higher education institutions (HEIs) are aware of the importance of MOOCs as a global movement and an instrument for educational policy, many have been hesitant to adopt or engage with MOOCs. It is indicated (e.g. Yuan et al. 2014) that pedagogical issues and strategic and cost questions are among the concerns that have delayed European HEIs from entering into this movement (Jansen et al. 2015).

7.3 MOOC Types: Taxonomy Based on Pedagogy

It is important to define the taxonomy of MOOCs not from the institutional but the pedagogic perspective, by their learning functionality, not by their origins. Figure 7.1 shows a taxonomy of eight types of MOOC based on pedagogy (Clark 2013).

The history of MOOCs and their present and future have been analysed and described in the study (Gurba 2015). MOOCs and pedagogy, didactics of mass open online courses and mass open online training as a modern trend in education were

Fig. 7.1 Taxonomy based on pedagogy. (Source: Clark 2013)

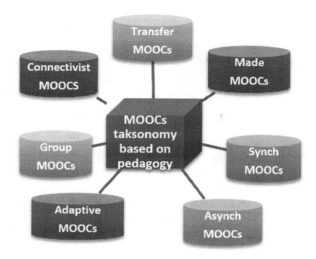

studied by researchers from different countries (Kukharenko 2013), (Lebedeva 2015). MOOCs and open education: implications for higher education were investigated by Yuan and Powell (2013). At the same time, many questions remain unanswered, including the formal aspects of MOOCs participation, types of motivation from students to participate in MOOCs, MOOCs quality and student feedback. In the paragraph below, an attempt is made to analyse some aspects of the development and implementation of MOOCs in Europe and Australia and also to present and analyse the results of a survey of students from several countries within the EU project IRNet (www.irnet.us.edu.pl) (Smyrnova-Trybulska et al. 2016).

In 2008 in the education sector, a new way of e-learning was presented, called MOOC or a mass open online course. MOOCs provide low-cost and effective teaching and learning for ordinary people around the world and locally. MOOC technology in distance learning aims to provide the visibility, knowledge and skills of students and learners on the basis of innovative, advanced methods of information and data transfer. According to Kesim and Altınpulluk (2015: 15), MOOC courses "run by elite scientists at elite universities show great interest and provide remote access to the e-environment by providing presentations, films and other training materials".

MOOCs enable students and all learners, especially in the field of distance education, to build and manage their own learning through Internet services. MOOC courses provide wide open free access for global and local students, enabling them to learn asynchronously and synchronously. This kind of teaching, unlike traditional teaching, has its functions and components, such as dynamism, accessibility, openness, the ability to cooperate and the shaping and upgrading of competences in flexible mode (Fini 2009; Martinez 2014a, b).

Integration and implementation of MOOCs in higher education can bring different challenges as well as new opportunities for students and learners such as developing and extending professional reading skills, writing, research, information processing, critical thinking, decision-making, technology, presentation in multimedia form, thought mapping, teamwork, use of languages and soft and personal skills such as motivation, leadership, competence in negotiating, communication, problem-solving, time management and self-education (Isaias and Issa 2014; Issa 2014) (Smyrnova-Trybulska et al. 2016).

The massive open online course (MOOC) movement is the latest "big thing" in open and distance learning (ODL) that threatens to transform higher education in a significant way. Put simply, MOOCs are "...courses designed for large numbers of participants, that can be accessed by anyone anywhere as long as they have an internet connection, are open to everyone without entry qualifications, and offer a full/complete course experience online for free" (OpenupEd 2015). Within this definition an important distinction needs to be made between institutionally focused xMOOCs and the connectivist origins of so-called cMOOCs. However, regardless of this distinction, the disruptive impact of MOOCs remains unclear, and we should not forget the long history of "hope, hype and disappointment" (Gouseti 2010) that characterizes many claims about the revolutionary potential of previous technological innovations in ODL (Schuwer et al. 2015).

7.4 Open Educational Resources and/vs MOOCs

In many cases, current discussions on educational reform – particularly in higher education – have moved from OER to MOOCs. Both are related to general policies of open education and reform, but there are three general differences:

1. *Use of term "open"*. The term "open" is used in connection with MOOCs to simply mean free to access and use. In reference to OER, the term means that OER has properties that allow it to be free to access but also free to reuse, revise, remix and redistribute. This redistribution of a revised resource may lead to it also being repurposed and used in a new educational setting (e.g. developed for vocational training but used in a school).
2. *Form of resource*. Unlike MOOCs, an OER is very often not an entity. It is defined by its licence and open properties, but not by its form, i.e. by being a digital course for high-scale usage. The section above states that an OER is a non-specific educational resource and can be many things, including a full course. MOOCs are designed as full courses (i.e. with full learning environments), meaning that they combine content with discussion forums and assessment tools.
3. *Audience*. The question of audience is related to the orientation towards the teacher or learner. OER are frequently focused on teachers who will use the adaptability of the resources to create their own materials or integrate the OER into their own learning environment. This is not the case with a MOOC, which is a ready-to-go course aimed at learners. For this reason, MOOCs are frequently considered a disruptive technology, whereas OER are more frequently seen as a way to enhance and augment existing learning environments. OER can be a cata-

lyst for innovation within the current education system and a means to unlock latent potential. The Hewlett Foundation says that the lockbox on education can be broken through the use of OER (The William and Flora Hewlett Foundation, 2013 cited in Orr et al. (2015)).

7.4.1 cMoocs and xMooc: Analysis of Current Research – National and International Experience

MOOCs have two different educational areas: connectivist MOOCs (cMOOC), based on connectivist technology and more focused on teachers and scientists, and MOOCs based on the content (xMOOC) and based on behavioural approach.

cMOOCs devote more attention to the organization of joint training and allow for going beyond the traditional audience. This approach includes J. Siemens, C. Down, John Groom, etc. In Ukraine, this trend has evolved from efforts of researchers B. Kukharenko and K. Bugaichuk.

The connectivist principles include:

- A variety of approaches.
- Presentation of learning as a process of forming networks and decision-making.
- Teaching and learning takes place all the time – it is always a process, not a state.
- Key skill today – the ability to see and understand relationships between meanings of fields of knowledge, concepts and ideas.
- Knowledge can exist outside the human in a network.
- Technologies help us in training.

The xMOOC educational model is essentially an extension of pedagogical models used in higher education and involves the use of video presentations, questionnaires, tests, etc. A typical example of this trend is a MOOC project called Coursera (https://www.coursera.org) and Udacity (https://www.udacity.com). They provide a unique approach that allows students to find alternative "routes" in education.

The cMOOC opens space for the introduction of nontraditional forms of education based on the needs of students, allowing students to learn from each other (Yuan and Powell 2013). Online communities solve all problems by creating networks that disseminate knowledge. For example, institutions such as MIT and the University of Edinburgh use MOOCs as an experimental company that allows you to take part in the development of new models of education, experience and the support of other agencies.

Many countries are introducing MOOCs in their different institutions, foundations, societies, as well as with government support. Main MOOC projects include:

edX (https://www.edX.org/) – a non-profit MOOC project, created by MIT and Harvard University. Currently, the project includes a large number of courses, including chemistry, computer science, electronics, medicine and others.

Students who achieve significant success in the subjects can pay a small fee and receive a certificate confirming completion of the course.

Coursera (https://www.coursera.org/) – this is a commercial company. Coursera offers courses in computer science, mathematics, business, humanities, medicine and engineering. Some universities provide a Certificate of Completion for a small fee; there are also additional courses and evaluation of teachers.

Udacity (https://www.udacity.com/) – a commercial project founded by Sebastian Thrun, David Stavens and Mike Sokolsky, offering courses in computer science, mathematics, science and business programming. After completing the course, students receive a Certificate of Completion.

Udemy (https://www.udemy.com/) – a project launched in 2010. Udemy offers more than 5000 courses, 1500 of which are not free.

P2Pu project (https://p2pu.org/en/) was launched in 2009. Process improvement and quality improvement courses are based on feedback from students and teachers.

Khan Academy (https://www.khanacademy.org/) – an online learning platform, which was founded in 2008 by Salman Khan. The organization offers several thousand video lectures on various subjects; they add various tasks, assessment of which is carried out regularly.

While edX only offers courses from Harvard and the Massachusetts Institute of Technology, Coursera gives access to a platform that can be used by any university, and Udacity has its own schedule. Other projects of open education, such as Udemy, P2Pu and Khan Academy, have been around for a long time and provide opportunities to anyone learning outside the traditional framework of universities (Yuan and Powell 2013).

7.5 MOOCs and Open Education Timeline

7.5.1 Open Courses as a Phenomenon of a Digital Society: Categories and Definitions

Open education plays an important role in ensuring equal access to education for everyone and in overcoming difficulties arising from the ever-changing circumstances in education, including:

1. Globalization and the increasing internationalization in higher education
2. Increasing demand for access to higher education
3. The changing demographics of students and increased number of adult students
4. Wide access to modern technology and communication
5. The need to change the prices, affordability and economic models for higher education

The Model of Online University is one of the most promising projects to meet the objectives of higher education. Competition between universities, with increasing differentiated and innovative use of information and communication technologies, stimulates the emergence of various forms of open learning. In this model, students learn independently, mainly on free open courses.

Open courses – open content where the term "open" is used in the context of freedom of intellectual property and allows reuse of content.

Open learning – an open practice which is regarded as a transparent activity. The difference between openness of practice and openness of content is important. Creating content takes time, effort and resources and opens numerous discussions about intellectual property rights.

The new paradigm of open education opens up opportunities for the exchange of ideas and cooperation between institutions, teachers and students locally and worldwide and for strengthening cooperation between students and teachers. The notion of open education is related to new technologies and tools, described as a *Model of Online University* (TEL-Map 2012.): an open platform, open evaluation, open education, open schedule, open source, etc.

Open learning – teachers, experts and students, through various activities, generate ideas and share them in the learning process and communicate and collaborate in solving specific practice-oriented tasks. It provides students with the possibility of independent self-study based on personal needs and interests.

Joint assessment is conducted by teachers and other students in the learning process, i.e. students' evaluating each other or in a group of "certification", in an effort to obtain openness of clear criteria for evaluation of all activities.

The open platform supports a dynamic and interactive community of open education, creating and providing intuitive operation and a stable user interface for teachers and students. Computer software is based on the principle of an information cloud, and the use of open standards facilitates the exchange of data for different platforms and services.

Open education provides opportunities for the emergence of innovation in higher education that not only supports institutions in preserving the fundamental values of education but also changes the focus from traditional teaching to learning that is based on student-centred approach and a different role of the teacher (the translator of knowledge to facilitator).

For those studying at the university, this model is provided by the MOOC (massive open online course) – an innovative form of education (Kukharenko 2011). In these courses a large number of learners can participate and can have free access to all training materials via the Internet. The initial goal of MOOC is "open" education and provision of free access to higher education for a large number of students from different countries. Unlike traditional online university courses, MOOCs have two key features:

1. **Open access** – anyone can become a learner to attend a free online course.
2. **Scale – at present,** an infinite number of students can participate.

Smyrnova-Trybulska et al. (2015) examined massive open online courses and analysed major MOOC projects and ways of running MOOCs using Wiki technology as well as analysing a selected social and educational aspects.

7.5.2 MOOC Style and Motivations

One way to support the information process of education in the higher education system is to form an information education environment (IEE). It allows for supporting the self-development of the learner by ensuring the processes of humanization of education and increasing its creativity.

An IEE is to be built as a system, essentially combining functionally and structurally informative, educational and technological elements that allow for their effective use in teacher pedagogical practice, what is important in achieving quality assurance objectives and tasks on the basis of technology in the context of computerization of education.

A list of resources was proposed and drawn up, based on the needs and expectations of Net Generation students. It includes groups and examples of resources that can be offered to teachers for use in the learning-learning process through e-learning that takes into account the needs of Net Generation students.

7.5.3 Benefits and Challenges for MOOC

According to the e-learning model of the university, these resources are not only components of IEE technology but also content and forms of organization:

- Edutainment resources (such as short videos, educational games, streaming multimedia, virtual museums and virtual worlds), all individual settings for creating your personal learning environment, virtual gadgets and services (e.g. avatars, RSS feeds, bookmarks, blogs, personal pages).
- Resources to quickly monitor student activity (common rating, quick feedback (chat, forum, frequently asked questions), collaboration resources (Google+ group, wiki, interactive whiteboard, others).
- Resources to provide innovation (various interactive environments, simulation and modelling programs, utilities). Because technology is developing very rapidly, new learning resources (Morze et al. 2015) should be considered.

In summary, it is possible to point out that the use of IEE resources in the learning process is aimed at intensifying the learning-learning process, improving the forms and methods of organizing the educational process, which envisages the transition from mechanical learning to acquiring the ability to acquire new knowledge independently.

(a) **Pedagogy**

Whilst it is known that online pedagogy is different from classroom pedagogy, there is insufficient consideration for the importance of approaching learning as a process that can be engineered. In other words, MOOCs for development must be based on a vision of learning engineering, and a certain amount of experimentation must be accepted as part of the initial investment. The MOOC management system at the institutional or country level needs to take into account some of these factors (Patru and Balaji 2016: 36).

(b) **Quality**

At an international level, different studies and reports have identified the main topics in the agenda for MOOCs. Gil-Jaurena and Titlestad (2013) compiled issues and recommendations relating to building of foundations for MOOCs and practical suggestions for their use, primarily addressed to higher education institutions which provide open, distance and flexible education; these recommendations were structured around the following strands: equity (about MOOCs and their relationship to inclusion, social justice and social mission of open education.), diversity (about considering contextual aspects when producing/consuming MOOCs), quality (about improving MOOCs considering pedagogical- and managerial-related aspects) and innovation (regarding innovation and research related aspects) (Schuwer et al. 2015: 26).

What is needed is a framework for quality assurance. The time investment by faculty in a typical MOOC in a developing country context is almost double that for a regular, on-campus course. This requires formal recognition, along with incentives. Unlike MOOCs offered by institutions in the OECD countries, a much higher level of mentoring is expected (Patru and Balaji 2016: 36).

ICDE and UNESCO (2014) stress the following as a main political challenge in the context of Open Education: "it is not only having equal access that leads to equity, it is having equal access to success, regardless of learning difficulties, social backgrounds and other barriers" (p. 2) in order to meet the overarching education goal of the post-2015 education agenda, that is, "to ensure equitable and inclusive quality education and lifelong learning for all by 2030" (UNESCO 2015, p. 5). The different categories identified in the literature complement the categorization we propose here (micro/macro level). At European level, those same concerns about equity, diversity, quality and innovation are reflected.). (Schuwer et al. 2015: 27)

(c) **Assessments and Credit**

Krause and Lowe (2014) present a useful synthesis of the claims made about the promise and perils of MOOCs. On the one hand, they show that MOOCs have the potential to challenge the closed and privileged nature of academic knowledge in traditional universities. That said, in many respects this feature of openness is a profound second order outcome of the Internet rather than a result of MOOCs per se. Nevertheless, the growth of the MOOC has potential to address the problem of meeting increasing demand for higher education, particularly in developing countries where it is almost impossible to build sufficiently traditional institutions to cope with the number of prospective students. In this regard, Daniel (2012) believes the new openness movement is a real game changer, as it has potential to widen access to lifelong learning, address key gaps in skill development and ultimately enhance the quality of life for millions. There is even some hope in Europe that MOOCs may be able to play an important role in closing the growing inequality gap and in reducing youth unemployment. In this regard, the European Credit Transfer and Accumulation System (ECTS) can probably play a role in bridging non-formal and formal learning. ECTS (2009) describes the ECTS as:

> a tool that helps to design, describe, and deliver programmes and award higher education qualifications. The use of ECTS, in conjunction with outcomes-based qualifications frameworks, makes programmes and qualifications more transparent and facilitates the recognition of qualifications. ECTS can be applied to all types of programmes, whatever their mode of delivery (school-based, work-based), the learners' status (full-time, part-time) and to all kinds of learning (formal, non-formal and informal). (p. 7) (Schuwer et al. 2015)

(d) **Sustainability**

Currently, the main questions linked to MOOCs range from the sustainability of their business model to their ability to generate meaningful credentials for career-oriented or lifelong learners. (Patru, Balaji, 2016: 67). Sustainability and costs of MOOCs were analysed and described in more detail by Nkuyubwatsi (2014), and Truyen (2014). The costs of MOOCs production and uncertainty about sustainability in lifecycle planning are also mentioned as threats. Examples of inequality in access are mentioned: persistence in MOOCs only achievable for privileged learners (those who have previously attained higher education qualifications); publishing MOOCs is only achievable for large, well established institutions; and massiveness may disincentivize MOOCs for smaller language groups. (Schuwer et al. 2015: 30).

Other theoretical, methodological, practical aspects of development, implementation and evaluation of MOOC were studied and described in Belanger and Thornton (2013), Downes (2010), European Commission/EACEA/Eurydice (2015), Gaebel et al. (2014), Guthrie et al. (2013), Inamorato dos Santos et al. (2016), Larry (2012), Mackness et al. (2010), Mcauley et al. (2010), Smyrnova–Trybulska et al. (2017), Stephen (2008), Wickramasinghe et al. (2015).

7.6 MOOC Implementation

Objective of the Research
The main objective of the research was:

- To define and test a **computer-oriented methodological and theoretical scientific system** for developing competences in the area of e-Learning and ICT for future and in-service teachers
- And the others:
- To develop, theoretically justify and experimentally verify the **basic concept** of shaping the location of ICT teachers competences in the use of information and communication technologies and remote forms of teaching in their professional activities

- To develop, theoretically justify and experimentally verify the **basic components of a computer-oriented system** of methodological preparation of contemporary specialists, in particularly future and active teachers to use ICT and distance forms of teaching in the educational process and intercultural competences
- To develop the **content, forms, methods and technologies**
- To **define and test a computer-oriented methodological and theoretical scientific system** for competences developing, which includes:
  1. **Psychological** and **pedagogical** aspects
  2. Organizational and methodical security **curriculum**
  3. Implementation of the social contract in such educational requirements for training future and in-service teachers
  4. Protection of the learning process of computerization measures, **information, methodological and technical support** of the school and the cognitive activity of in-service and future teachers and other specialists with extensive use of distance forms of learning, based on Internet technologies
  5. **Adequate information on competences components including e-learning and intercultural competences**

Aims of the Practical Implementation

- Development, verified in empirical **research, of an e-learning course MOOC "ICT tools for e-learning"**, improving efficiency of the educational process-oriented development of ICT and e-learning competencies and other components of the system such as content, means, methods, forms of teaching and so on
- Development of the curriculum of the MA course **"E-learning in Cultural Diversity"**, the international specialization and start within the framework of Erasmus Mundus programme

The **ADDIE model** is a framework that lists generic processes that instructional designers and training developers use (Fig. 7.2).

It represents a descriptive guideline for building effective training and performance support tools in five phases:

- Analysis
- Design
- Development
- Implementation
- Evaluation

The Concept of the Learning System is based on the ADDIE model and on the following pedagogical theories: behaviourism, constructivism, connectivism, constructionism, programming teaching and others.

Methods

- General environment of theories and methodologies of online teaching and learning
- Self-learning approaches and techniques

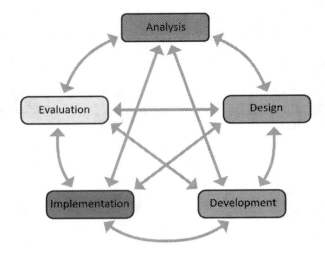

Fig. 7.2 ADDIE model. (Source: Smyrnova–Trybulska (2018: 278) based on McGriff 2000; Heba et al. 2014a, b)

- Learning styles and teaching process
- Objectives and teaching taxonomies
- Teaching and learning methods *(method of the project, Wiki, WebQuest, programming learning and teaching, discussion on the forum in the course, use of the social media)*
- Teaching and learning models
- Methodology and techniques of e-learning
- Methodology of producing e-contents
- Evaluating of the teachers' skills necessary to work in ICT environment

Organizational Forms

- Online learning
- E-learning
- MOOCs
- Blended learning
- Distance learning
- Face-to-face (no more than 50%) (MA courses international (or native))

Additionally

- Teaching models and forms
- Pedagogic management of the project
- Planning and coordination of courses
- Personal and institutional ICT plan
- Others

Means

- **Electronic:** ICT applications, educational computer programs, multimedia, didactic video, Internet resources, web services (YouTube, Wikipedia, Wiki portals, social media, etc.), component (activity) LCMS systems (Moodle) and others

Fig. 7.3 Bloom's taxonomy. (Source: Anderson and Krathwohl (eds.) 2001)

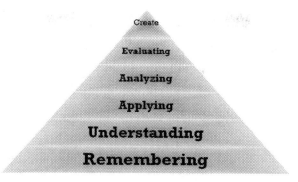

- **Partly traditional:** books, textbooks, exercise books, printed teaching materials, journals, conference proceedings, monographs and others

Technologies

- LMS system Moodle and other LMS
- ICT tools used in MOOC
- Web 2.0 and web 3.0
- Others

The Learning System Concept is based on revised of Bloom's taxonomy (Fig. 7.3).

Tables 7.1 and 7.2 contain examples of kinds of knowledge (for modules 1–10).

Contents, Aims and Structure of the MOOC "ICT Tools for E-learning" (Fig. 7.3)

The structure of the course includes:

Introduction

1. **E-learning in higher education**
   - E-learning in higher education. Comparison of traditional and innovative methods and technologies
   - Twenty-first century skills and e-learning
   - System of ICT tools for developing twenty-first century skills and implementing e-learning in modern universities and institutes of teacher training

2. **ICT tools for presentation of content and tools for making didactic video**
   - Preview of analysing tools for presentation of content
   - Comparison and evaluation of tools for presentation of content
   - Developing practical skills of using tools for presentation of content in education
   - Preview of analysing tools for making didactic videos
   - Comparison and evaluation of tools for making didactic videos
   - Developing practical skills with use of tools for making didactic videos

Table 7.1 Table of knowledge (for modules 1–10)

	The cognitive domain (knowledge-based)
Remembering	Recall facts and basic concept (define, duplicate, list, memorize, repeat, state)
Understanding	Explain ideas and concepts (classify, describe, discuss, explain, identify, locate, recognize, report, select, translate)
Applying	Use information in a new situation, solve, demonstrate, interview, complete, model, construct, report, dramatize, sketch, exhibit, make, prepare "How would you explain…?" "Can you write in your own words…?" "Clarify why…"
Analysing	Classify, interpret, differentiate, compare, organize, examine, investigate, inquire "Why do you think…?" "What conclusions can you draw..?" "What ideas justify…?"
Evaluating	Imagine, invent, develop, judge, formulate, hypothesize, predict "What can happen if..? Can you predict an outcome? Can you invent?"
Creating	Design, produce, critique, debate, assess, consider "What is your opinion of...? How can you determine..?"

Table 7.2 Table of knowledge (for module 1–10)

Remembering: can the student recall or remember the information?	Define, duplicate, list, memorize, recall, repeat, reproduce state
	Define the learning management system
	Present the list of well-known LMS system
Understanding: can the student explain ideas or concepts?	Classify, describe, discuss, explain, identify, locate, recognize, report, select, translate, paraphrase
	Classifying the LMS systems
	Identify the activities of learning management system
Applying: can the student use the information in a new way?	Choose, demonstrate, dramatize, employ, illustrate, interpret, operate, schedule, sketch, solve, use, write
	Choose the most popular and multifunctional LMS system
	Illustrate the activities, supported by LMS Moodle
Analysing: can the student distinguish between the different parts?	Appraise, compare, contrast, criticize, differentiate, discriminate, distinguish, examine, experiment, question, test
	To compare the LMS systems according some criteria's.
	Differentiate the resources and activities supported different educational activities.
Evaluating: Can the student justify a stand or decision?	Appraise, argue, defend, judge, select, support, value, evaluate
	Defend one's own position concerning more adequate LMS system
	Evaluate and assessment of DL course according some criteria's
Creating	Design, produce, critique, debate, assess, consider "What is your opinion of...? How can you determine..?"

3. **Tools for adaptive learning: learning styles**
   - Cognitive domain
   - Psychomotor domain
   - Affective domain

4. **Tools for mind maps and infographics knowledge**
   - Preview of analysing tools for mind maps and infographics knowledge
   - Comparison and evaluation of tools for mind maps and infographics knowledge
   - Developing practical skills with use of tools for mind maps and infographics knowledge

5. **Gamification in education**

   Module objectives:
   - Learn what game elements are used in gamification of learning process
   - Learn about types of gamification
   - Learn about motivation and techniques for improving knowledge
   - Learn about different types of games

6. **Tools for communication and collaboration**

   The topic appeals to:
   - University faculty and management, teachers, professionals and MSc students who want to use ICT tools for collaboration in education online and in blended learning, privately or as part of an educational institution or company
   - General public, keen on becoming familiarized with blended learning and to implement it in their educational institution

7. **Tools for formative assessment and control**
   - Preview of analysis of ICT tools for formative assessment and control
   - Comparison and evaluation of ICT tools for formative assessment and control
   - Developing practical skills with the use of ICT tools for formative assessment and control

8. **Digital storytelling**
   - Preview of analysing tools for storytelling
   - Comparison and evaluation of tools for storytelling
   - Developing practical skills using storytelling tools
   - Previous tasks for testing in real scenarios

9. **ICT tools for developing intercultural competences in e-learning**
    - Preview of Analysing ICT tools for developing intercultural competences in e-learning
    - Comparison and evaluation of ICT tools for developing intercultural competences in e-learning
    - Developing practical skills with the use ICT tools for developing intercultural competences in e-learning

10. **Social presence and online tutoring**
    - To define online tutoring and its methodology
    - To outline clusters of ICT tools applied for the purposes of online tutoring
    - To define the role and functions of social media in the context of online tutoring
    - To provide recommendations on enhancing interactivity and social presence in online tutoring. To outline competences required for online tutors

To discuss practices of experts in teaching students with special needs and ways of facilitating their teaching with ICT tools (Fig. 7.4).

Methodology of MOOCs Design (Fig. 7.5)
As stressed by Spanish researchers: "The development of a MOOC involves the implementation of a complex process of planning, design and development. This process requires the participation of different professionals and work areas. The efficiency of the production system needs to establish specific methodologies. These should address the specific characteristics of the context of development, and they must combine strategies and techniques from different areas: instructional design, audiovisual production and multimedia development" (Barrio et al. 2017: p. 183). In their own study, Olazabalaga et al. (2016) analysed the trends and methodologies

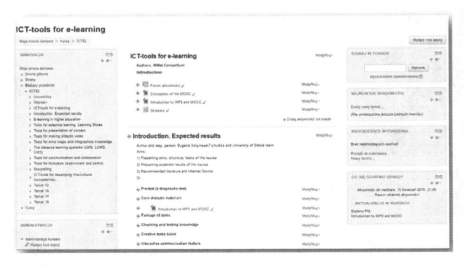

Fig. 7.4 MOOC "ICT tools for e-learning". (http://el.us.edu.pl/irnet)

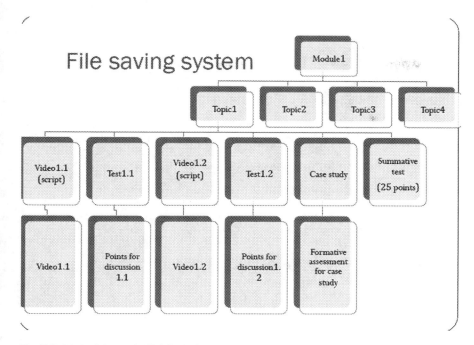

Fig. 7.5 Methodology of MOOCs design

in area research on MOOCs. Gurba (2015) described the MOOC history and future. In Yousef et al. (2014), an empirical examination is presented of criteria to assure design quality of MOOCs; 29 criteria were identified to measure the instructional design and assessment categories which represented the pedagogical dimension. Daradoumis et al. (2013) focused on a review of massive e-learning (MOOC) design, delivery and assessment.

Figure 7.5 shows the structure of one of the modules of MOOC; Table 7.3 compares the structure of DLC and MOOC.

Limitations and Future Research

A survey was conducted in several IRNet project partner universities: University of Silesia (US), Poland; Borys Grinchenko Kyiv University (BGKU), Kiev; Herzen State Pedagogical University of Russia (HSPU), Saint Petersburg, Russia; and Curtin University (CU), Perth, Australia. Presented below are the survey results with participation of 99 respondents. The questionnaire was developed in Google Drive (Google Form) and was anonymous, and students of different specializations were invited to complete it. The University of Silesia conducted the survey at the Faculty of Ethnology and Sciences of Education among students of the humanistic specialization: Integrated Primary Education and Kindergarten Education, Kindergarten Education with Child's Development Early Support, Social-Cultural Animation with Cultural Tourism and Integrated Primary Education and Pedagogical Therapy; in total 99 students took part in the survey.

Table 7.3 Comparing the structure of DLC and MOOC

Detailed structure of an Internet-based distance course	MOOC: Module study scheme

Introduction
 Course description: Goals, objectives, registration procedures, course structure, skills and knowledge (both in terms of IT and course subject matter) required prior to taking the course and upon its completion, information on documents, assignments required to obtain credit for the course (text or html documents) Reading list: core reading, additional reading, Internet resources (a listing of recommended core and additional sources with which participants need to familiarize themselves during the course – a text, PDF or html document)
 Glossary of terms containing basic concepts and key terms related to the course topics (types of dictionary: encyclopaedias, ordinary Glossaries, FAQ's, etc.).
 Forum, a course feature facilitating discussion on a given course (News Forum, Discussion Forum).
 Participant registration survey designed to collect information on the profile of potential students, contains questions relating to various issues (Survey, Questionnaire).
 Thematic Modules N (1 < N < 10)
 Pretest (a diagnostic test) (a package of quizzes (tests) designed to gauge participant knowledge of the course material)
 Core didactic materials for a given course subject area (Lessons (didactic materials and self-testing quiz), Glossaries, Encyclopaedias, links, files (text files, PDF, audio files, video files, multimedia presentations, other.
 Package of tasks designed to help participants assimilate material, to help the instructor check student understanding of the material, to consolidate and apply the knowledge.
 Checking students' knowledge (Lessons, Glossaries, Encyclopaedias, reference links to Internet resources, files stored in folders (text files, PDF, audio files, video files, multimedia presentations, other material)
 Creative tasks block designed to help the student to work independently to assimilate knowledge, skills and to develop ways to solve specific problems, to complete individual projects; practical tasks (individual and group ones) (Assignments (various types: Advanced uploading of files, Online text, Upload a single file, Offline activity), Journals, Workshops, Forums, audio recorder, Wiki, etc.)
 Interactive communication feature, enabling students to communicate with one another and with instructors synchronously (Chat, instant messaging software (Skype, NetMeeting, Gadu-Gadu, Yahoo Messenger, ICQ, etc.)) and asynchronously (Forum, E-mail, Internal Messaging System, etc.)
 Additional reference material for a given subject area (Lessons, Glossaries, encyclopaedias, reference links to Internet resources, files stored in folders (text files, PDF, audio files, video files, multimedia presentations, other material)
 Checking students' knowledge (Test quiz) (Quiz, Hot Potatoes Quiz)
 Conclusion module (Conclusion of the course)
 Examination designed to test (Quiz).
 Final evaluation survey (Survey, Questionnaire).
 Self-reflective survey (Survey, Questionnaire) (Smyrnova-Trybulska 2009)
	Module study scheme
	   Video, Points for discussion + Individual tasks (Interactive tasks) + Self-assessment test – no points
	   video Points for discussion+ Individual tasks (Interactive tasks) + Self-assessment test – no points
	   Presentation on the topic
	   Lecture notes
	   Selected bibliography
	   Additional bibliography
	   Graded test
	 Topic 1
	   Video points for discussion + Individual tasks (Interactive tasks) + Self-assessment test – no points
	   video Points for discussion+ Individual tasks (Interactive tasks) + Self-assessment test – no points
	   Presentation on the topic
	   Lecture notes
	   Selected bibliography
	   Additional bibliography
	   Graded test
	 Topic 2
	 ……
	 Summative test

7 Develop and Implement MOOCs Unit: A Pedagogical Instruction for Academics...   121

The purpose of this section is to describe the empirical results derived from the data set of the three independent research studies: the MOOC platform evaluation, involving 99 participants; the HPSU questionnaire, involving 32 participants; and the survey questionnaire, involving 99 participants. The 99 participants for Study 1 and Study 3 were the same people.

Research Instruments

Test instruments were prepared by researchers from the IRNet project consortium (www.irnet.us.edu.pl), to investigate the development of MOOC platforms and to test the effectiveness of such computer-oriented methodological and theoretical scientific e-learning systems. The intention was to prepare a range of questionnaire items to interrogate people's attitudes, knowledge and MOOC experiences, to evaluate multiple levels of knowledge. This work was in accordance with research (Izard 2006) that would provide a rectangular distribution of rates-of-agreement over an extended number of questions relating to knowledge of current e-learning delivery platforms. These questions took the form of three separate instruments where respondents were asked to provide ranking responses to each question.

The responses were analysed using the QUEST Interactive Test Analysis System (Adams and Khoo 1996; Wu and Adams 2007). Central to QUEST is a measurement model developed in 1960 by the Danish statistician George Rasch (1960). The initial analysis of the data with QUEST used an iterative procedure to describe the unidimensional scale with equal intervals along the vertical axis, to represent individual performance (case achievement) and questionnaire item difficulty on the same scale (McKay 2007). The estimation procedure investigated the probability of an individual with a particular level of achievement making particular responses to a range of questionnaire items. The diagram showing the pattern of peoples' responses and questionnaire items is known as a variable map (see Figs. 7.6 and 7.7). There were no questionnaire items that were in common across the three data sets, which means that there was no possibility of anchoring the responses across three independent data sets, to provide a linked evaluation analysis. Instead these three data sets will be reported here as independent evaluations. In study 1 the estimate could only compute responses from 21 participants, due to the 78 participant answers that were considered as "perfect score" and therefore were not able to be included in the estimate.

Fig. 7.6 QUEST variable maps

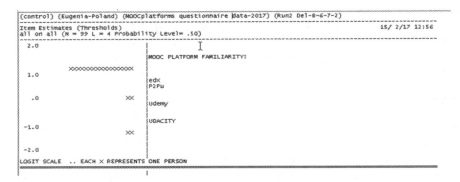

Fig. 7.7 QUEST variable map – MOOC platforms US questionnaire result

Data Analysis

The questionnaire outcomes were evaluated in terms of the QUEST instigated Rasch analysis (Bond and Fox 2015) generating a set of hypotheses regarding the knowledge and experience of the participants with regard to MOOC deployment of their learning resources. QUEST allows for improved analyses of an individual's answers relative to other participants (McKay 2000) and relative to the questionnaire item agreement levels. See an example of this in Figs. 7.6 and 7.7 where each participant or "case" is depicted by an "x" and questionnaire items are shown on the right side of the map. The Rasch item response theory (IRT) estimates the probability of an individual making a certain response to a questionnaire item.

Findings Exhibit 1
Which MOOC platforms are you familiar with?

1.	edX
2.	Coursera
3.	Udacity
4.	Udemy
5.	P2Pu
6.	Khan Academy
7.	Prometheus
8.	Am not familiar with MOOC platforms
9.	Others

In this study, there were 99 respondents all from the University of Silesia. Respondents were invited to participate through DLC. The questionnaire was delivered online in Google Drive.

The QUEST software package provides item fit statistics. And so, the mean square fit statistics provide a useful way of judging the compatibility of the Rasch model and the data. Following examination of the "fit" of the items (see Fig. 7.8), item 7 to the right side of the dotted line showed more variation from the Rasch

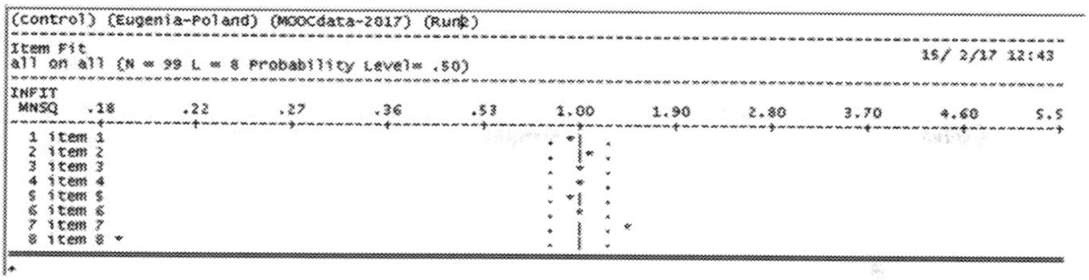

7 Develop and Implement MOOCs Unit: A Pedagogical Instruction for Academics… 123

```
(control) (Eugenia-Poland) (MOOCdata-2017) (Run1)
Item Fit
all on all (N = 99 L = 8 Probability Level= .50)                                   15/ 2/17 12:43
INFIT
MNSQ    .18       .22      .27      .36      .53    1.00    1.90    2.80    3.70    4.60    5.5
         +---------+--------+--------+--------+-------+-------+-------+-------+-------+-------+
  1 item 1                                            . *|
  2 item 2                                            .  |*  .
  3 item 3                                            .  |   .
  4 item 4                                            .  ▼   .
  5 item 5                                            . *|   .
  6 item 6                                            .  |   .
  7 item 7                                            .  |  .*
  8 item 8 ▼                                          .  |   .
```

Fig. 7.8 Initial QUEST item fit map

```
(control) (Eugenia-Poland) (MOOCdata-2017) (Run2 Del-8-6-7-2)
Item Fit
all on all (N = 99 L = 4 Probability Level= .50)                                   15/ 2/17 12:56
INFIT
MNSQ    .50       .56      .63      .71      .83    1.00    1.20    1.40    1.60    1.80    2.0
         +---------+--------+--------+--------+-------+-------+-------+-------+-------+-------+
  1 item 1                                            .  |   .
  3 item 3                                            .  |*  .
  4 item 4                                            . *|   .
  5 item 5                                            . *|   .
```

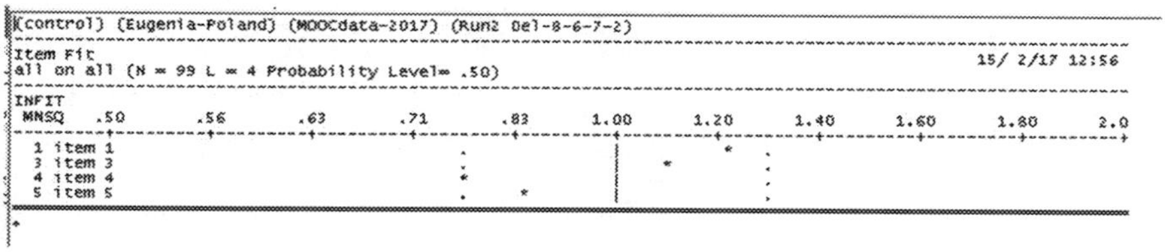

Fig. 7.9 Initial QUEST item fit map

model than was expected and as such was the first item to be removed from the QUEST estimate as it was considered as an under fit of the model, while item 8 to the left side of the dotted line indicated less variation than expected and, as such, was also removed from the analysis, leaving the following reliable evidence for conveying a good Rasch fit for the items 1, 2, 3, 4, 5 and 6 (Fig. 7.8).

Figure 7.8 shows evidence that the behaviour of the questionnaire-items were a good fit for the remaining items: −1; −3; −4; and −5: that the consistent behaviour of these items reveals their popularity compared with the other products: Khan Academy and the Prometheus, were unknown to the participants (Fig. 7.9).

Item 9 was removed from the QUEST estimate as there were no responses.

Figure 7.10 shows there were two respondents more likely to have knowledge of Udacity and another two people who were familiar with Udemy, while the rest of the respondents (91) knew about edX, P2Pu, Edemy and Udacity. There were no responses that recognized Khan Academy and Prometheus.

Findings Exhibit 2

In this study, there were 32 participants all from the HSPU. Respondents were invited to participate through online version of the questionnaire, delivered via Google Forms tool (Fig. 7.11).

From an examination of Fig. 7.12 the behaviour of the questionnaire items relative to each other and relative to the participants answering, it can be seen that there were five participants who did not agree about questions 1 to 8, while the majority (26 participants) had undergone a MOOC and had opinions on the type of course that was better for teacher training and to use for extending basic knowledge. Be that

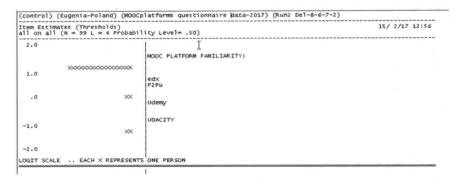

Fig. 7.10 QUEST variable map – MOOC platforms US questionnaire result

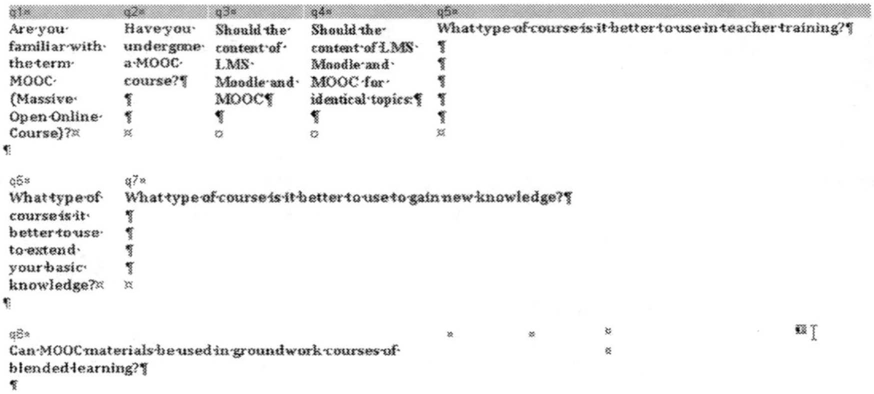

Fig. 7.11 QUEST variable map – MOOC platforms US questionnaire result (continue)

as it may, there were only 8 of those 26 participants who demonstrated the probability to be more likely to have opinions on familiarity with MOOC delivery, whether a MOOC could be used in groundwork for blended learning courseware and which type of delivery is better to elicit new knowledge.

To this end, the reliability of these questionnaire items can be witnessed in Fig. 7.13 as it represents the final fit map, once questionnaire items 3 and 4 were removed from the data analysis due to them lying on the left side of the dotted Rasch model threshold lines (between 0.63 and 0.73), leaving the behaviour of the remaining questionnaire items to be considered as reliable items. Examining the structure of these two questions may reveal that participants may have had difficulty understanding the question.

7 Develop and Implement MOOCs Unit: A Pedagogical Instruction for Academics...

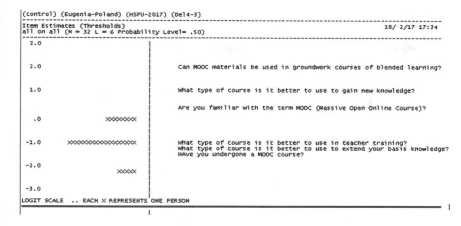

Fig. 7.12 QUEST variable map – HSPU questionnaire result

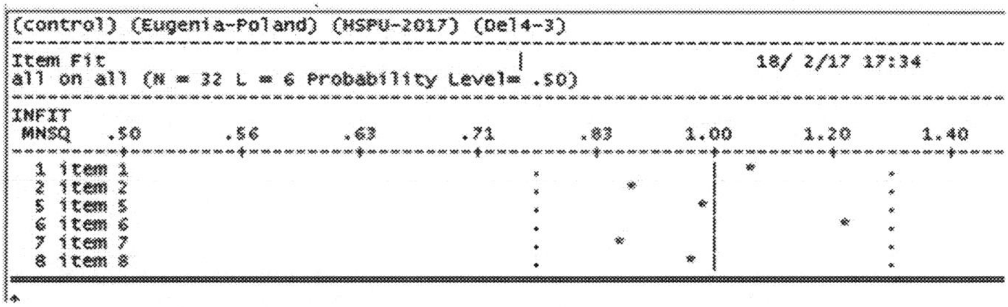

Fig. 7.13 QUEST HSPU fit map

Findings Exhibit 3

(i) **Are you familiar with the term MOOC (massive open online course)?**

   Yes – **1**
   No – **2**

(ii) **Have you undergone a MOOC course?**

   Yes – 1
   No – 2

(iii) **Should the content of LMS Moodle and MOOC**

   Be different – 1
   Be the same – 2
   Be partially the same – 3

(iv) **Should the content of LMS Moodle and MOOC for identical topics:**

Be different – 1
Be the same – 2
Be partially the same – 3

(v) **What type of course is it better to use in teacher training?**

MOOC – 1
LMS Moodle – 2
Both types – 3

(vi) **What type of course is it better to use to extend your basic knowledge?**

MOOC – 1
LMS Moodle – 2
Both types – 3

(vii) **What type of course is it better to use to gain new knowledge?**

MOOC – 1
LMS Moodle – 2
Both types – 3

(viii) **Can MOOC materials be used in groundwork courses of blended learning?**

Yes – 1
No – 2

In this study, there were 99 participants. Figure 7.13 provides a graphical comparison of how the behaviour of each questionnaire item, relative to each question and relative to the participants' answering style, confirms the following: there were eight participants who were unable to provide reliable answers to any of the questions. Yet of these eight participants, there were five who would be more able to provide opinions on the content of LMS Moodle and MOOC for identical topics and which type of course was better to use in teacher training.

There was only one participant who reports they had not undergone a MOOC or an LMS course. While there were seven participants who answered such to reveal they felt that an LMS Moodle was better to use to extend basic knowledge. Eleven participants were identified as thinking that the content of LMS/Moodle should be the same. While six others had answered all questions thus far (on the logit scale shown in Fig. 7.8),), they were not as likely to agree with the rest of the questionnaire items (questions −3,−4, −5, −6, −7 and −8). And so, the second largest group of 17 participants agreed on the partial sameness of the LMS/Moodle content (questions −3, −6 and −7); while at the same time would be less probability for them to reach an opinion on questions −4 and −5), relating to content of LMS/Moodle to be partially the same and whether both types were better for teacher training. Yet there were 10 participants who were identified as showing that they thought this was possible.

7 Develop and Implement MOOCs Unit: A Pedagogical Instruction for Academics…   127

```
(control) (Eugenia-Poland) (Survey QuestionnaireData-2017) (Run-1)
Item estimates (Thresholds)
all on all (N = 99 L = 8 Probability Level= .50)                    15/ 2/17 13:50

  3.0
                 XXXXXXX
  2.0
                 XXXXXXX
  1.0         XXXXXXXXXXXXXXX
           XXXXXXXXXXXXX       Identical topic content of LMS Moodle&MOOC should be partially be the same .. Better to use both types of courses in teacher training.
                    XXXXX      Content of LMS Moodle&MOOC should be partially be the same. .. Both types are better to use to extend basic knowledge & to gain new knowledge.
   .0                          Unfamiliarity with the term MOOC (Massive open online course).
           XXXXXXXXXX           Content of LMS&MOOC should be the same.
                XXXXXX         LMS Moodle is better to use to extend basic knowledge.
 -1.0                X         Have not undergone a MOOC or an LMS course.
                XXXXX          LMS and MOOC content for identical topics should be the same, and are better to use in teacher training.
 -2.0
                    XX
 -3.0
LOGIT SCALE  .. EACH X REPRESENTS ONE PERSON
```

Fig. 7.14 QUEST variable map – survey instrument result

```
(control) (Eugenia-Poland) (QuestionnaireData-2017) (Run-1)
Item Fit
all on all (N = 99 L = 8 Probability Level= .50)              15/ 2/17 13:50
INFIT
MNSQ    .50      .56      .63      .71      .83     1.00     1.20     1.40
      --------+--------+--------+--------+--------+--------+--------+----
1 item 1                                  x             *          .
2 item 2                                                  **       .
3 item 3                                          *                .
4 item 4                                     *                     .
5 item 5                                      *                    .
6 item 6                                             *             .
7 item 7                           x                               .
8 item 8                                                        *. 
```

Fig. 7.15 QUEST fit map – survey instrument result

Finally, at the upper-participants level on this variable map, there are a total of 34 participants who demonstrated they agreed with the questioning of all the given items, while 16 participants were unchallenged by this questionnaire, as their responses revealed they were in agreement with the complete questionnaire. The last mentioned questionnaire item brought forward the negative response to whether MOOC materials could be used in groundwork courses of blended learning (Fig. 7.14).

The data represented in Fig. 7.15 presents the evidence that this study was able to present the best Rasch model fit map where all questionnaire items were showing validity and reliability of the instrumentation (the behaviour) of the items relative to each item while at the same time relative to the participants' answers.

7.7 Implications for Higher Education Including Policy

Widening participation in HE is a major component of the government education policy – to increase not only the numbers of young people entering HE but also the proportion from under-represented groups (e.g. those from lower-income families, people with disabilities and some ethnic minorities) (https://en.wikipedia.org/wiki/Widening_ participation).

In their own publication, Patru and Balaji (2016) stressed the promoting a culture of quality in higher education. Quality lies at the heart of higher education policies in all countries around the world. However, the demand for higher education is increasing well beyond the capacity of traditional institutions. Thanks to technology, teaching and learning are now less constrained by time and place. Online learning holds the potential of delivering quality education to anyone, anywhere. Many of the online self-paced courses offered outside of traditional higher education are of high quality, enabling learners' access to new knowledge, new skills and new professional opportunities. In a world of growing virtual mobility, and in an effort to address a more diverse range of learning options for working adults, more and more open and distance teaching universities have expressed their intention to promote the large-scale delivery of certified short learning programmes (SLP) and to incorporate MOOCs into these courses as flexible building blocks. Governments should develop or strengthen quality assurance frameworks for the recognition, validation and accreditation of flexible learning pathways as part of their broad development agenda (Patru and Balaji Eds., 2016: 13).

7.8 Discussion

Education 2030: A new vision for education. Education 2030 must be seen within the broader context of development today. MOOCs can contribute to SDG 4: Ensure inclusive and equitable quality education and promote lifelong learning opportunities for all. The Education 2030 Framework for Action, adopted at Incheon (Republic of Korea) in May 2015, recognizes lifelong learning for all as one of the underpinning principles of this new vision, stating that "all age groups, including adults, should have opportunities to learn and continue learning". It also calls on countries to "develop policies and programmes for the provision of quality distance learning in tertiary education, with appropriate financing and use of technology, including the Internet, massive open online courses (MOOCs) and other modalities that meet accepted quality standards to improve access." MOOCs could be successfully designed and adapted to support the expansion of access to post-secondary education for all categories of learners and to maintain their motivation. They could also play a significant role in providing learning opportunities for those in fragile/emergency situations. (Patru and Balaji 2016).

7.9 Conclusion

The purpose of this study was to identify specific criteria for developing and implementing a MOOC unit. The authors described a pedagogical instruction for academics via case study – elaborating a MOOC prototype version "ICT tools in e-learning". In addition a questionnaire was developed with the purpose of interrogating student's attitudes, knowledge and MOOC experiences, together with revealing their notion of MOOC delivery, whether a MOOC could be used in groundwork for blended learning courseware and which type of delivery is better to elicit new knowledge to evaluate multiple levels of knowledge. The results show that although MOOCs appear to be one of actively and deeply studied directions in pedagogical science and practice, learners still are not completely sure of MOOCs actual advantages and do not always have sufficient experience of undergoing a MOOC. That is why the developed MOOC prototype version can be very useful in the practice of familiarizing students with the MOOCs phenomenon.

Acknowledgement The research leading to these results has received, within the framework of the IRNet project, funding from the People Programme (Marie Skłodowska-Curie Actions) of the European Union's Seventh Framework Programme FP7/2007-2013/under REA grant agreement No: PIRSES-GA-2013-612536 and statutory research.

References

Adams, R. J., & Khoo, S.-T. (1996). *QUEST: The interactive test analysis system.* Melbourne: Australian Council for Educational Research.
Anderson, L. W., & Krathwohl, D. R. (Eds.). (2001). *A taxonomy for learning, teaching, and assessing: A revision of Bloom's taxonomy of educational objectives.* New York: Longman.
Barrio, M. G., Fernandez, M. R., & Garcia, S. A. (2017). Production methodology for the development of audiovisual and multimedia content for MOOC. *RIED-Revista Iberoamericana de Educacion a Distancia, 20*(1), 183–203.
Belanger, V., & Thornton, J. (2013). *Bioelectricity: A quantitative approach – Duke University's first MOOC* [Online]. Available at: http://hdl.handle.net/10161/6216. Accessed 26 November 2014
Bond, T. G., & Fox, C. M. (2015). *Applying the Rasch model: Fundamental measurement in the human services* (3rd ed.). New York/London: Routledge/Taylor & Francis.
Clark, D. (2013). *MOOCs: Taxonomy of 8 types of MOOC.* Donald Clark Paln B, Tuesday, April 16, 2013, [online] at http://donaldclarkplanb.blogspot.co.uk/2013/04/moocs-taxonomy-of-8-types-of-mooc.html. Accessed 20 Mar 2016.
Coursera [Online]. Available at: www.coursera.org. Accessed 26 November 2014
Daniel, J. (2012). Making sense of MOOCs: Musings in a maze of myth, paradox and possibility. *Journal of Interactive Media in Education, 18*(3). https://doi.org/10.5334/2012-18.
Daradoumis, T., Bassi, R., Xhafa, F., & Caballe, S. (2013). *A review on massive E-learning (MOOC) design, delivery and assessment.* IEEE, Compiegne, France, 28–30 Oct 2013, ISBN:978-0-7695-5094-7.
Downes, S.. (2010). *Fairness and equity in education.* Huff Post Education, August 20, 2014, [online] at http://www.huffingtonpost.com/stephen-downes/democratizing-education_b_794925.html. Accessed 20 Mar 2016.
ECTS. (2009). *ECTS users' guide.* Luxembourg: European Communities.
European Commission. (2013). Communication from the Commission to the European Parliament, the Council, the European Economic and Social Committee and the Committee of the Regions. Opening up Education: Innovative teaching and learning for all through new Technologies and Open Educational Resources. COM(2013) 654 final In European Commission/EACEA/Eurydice, 2015.
European Commission/EACEA/Eurydice. (2015). *The European higher education area in 2015: Bologna process implementation report.* Luxembourg: Publications Office of the European Union http://eacea.ec.europa.eu/education/eurydice/documents/thematic_reports/182EN.pdf

Fini, A. (2009). The technological dimension of a massive open online course: The case of the CCK08 course tools. *The International Review of Research in Open and Distributed Learning, 10*(5).
Gaebel, M., et al. (2014). *E-learning in European higher education institutions: Results of a mapping survey conducted in October–December 2013*. Brussels: EUA.
Gil-Jaurena, I., & Titlestad, G. (2013). *ICDE: "Mind to MOOCs"– draft issues and recommendations*. Retrieved from http://www.icde.org/filestore/News/2013_July-Dec/SCOP_2013/ICDEMindtoMOOCsdraftissuesandrecommendationsver1-120131125.pdf
Gouseti, A. (2010). Web 2.0 and education: Not just another case of hype, hope and disappointment? *Learning Media and Technology, 35*(3), 351–356. https://doi.org/10.1080/17439884.20 10.509353.
Gurba, K. (2015). *MOOC Historia i przyszłość*, Kraków 2015 137 s. ISBN:978-83-7438-470-4.
Guthrie, J., Burritt, R., & Evans, E. (2013). Challenges for accounting and business education: Blending online and traditional universities in a MOOC environment. The virtual university: Impact on Australian accounting and business education (pp. 9–22). Http://Www.Ekspercibolonscy.Org.Pl/Sites/Ekspercibolonscy.Org.Pl/Files/Ii_Tsw_Dp_Weryfikacja_3_4_1.Pdf
Heba, A., Kapounová, J., & Smyrnova-Trybulska E. (2014a). Mathematics and eLearning or how to work with students before exam. In: *Information and communication technologies in education overview in Visegrad countries*, Ostrava, 2014, s. 92–102. ISBN:978-80-7464-701-7.
Heba, A., Kapounová, J., & Smyrnova-Trybulska, E. (2014b). Theoretical conception and some practical results of the development of mathematical competences with use of e-learning. *International Journal of Continuing Engineering Education and Life-long Learning, 24*(3/4), 252–268. ISSN online 1741-5055, ISSN print 1560-4624.
HOME. (2014). *Higher Education Online: MOOCs*. https://home.eadtu.eu/results
ICDE & UNESCO. (2014, November 20th). *Policy forum. ensure equitable quality education and lifelong learning for all by 2030: The contribution of open, online and flexible higher education to the post-2015 global education agenda*. Bali, Indonesia. Retrieved from http://icde.org/en/context/unesco/icde_-_unesco_policy_forum/
Inamorato dos Santos, A., Punie, Y., & Castaño-Muñoz, J. (2016). *Opening up education: A support framework for higher education institutions*. JRC Science for Policy Report, EUR 27938 EN.
Isaias, P., & Issa, T. (2014). Promoting communication skills for information systems students in Australian and Portuguese higher education: Action research study. *Education and Information Technologies, 19*(4), 841–861.
Issa, T. (2014). Learning, communication and interaction via Wiki: An Australian perspective. In H. Kaur & X. Tao (Eds.), *ICTs and the millennium development goals* (pp. 1–17). Berlin: Springer.
Izard, J. F. (2006). *Quality assurance: Asking the right questions*. 32nd Annual Conference of the International Association Assessment, May 21–26. Singapore.
Jansen, D., Schuwer, R., Teixeira, A., & Aydin, C. H. (2015). Comparing MOOC adoption strategies in Europe: Results from the HOME project survey. *International Review of Research in Open and Distributed Learning, 16*(6), 116–136.
Kesim, M., & Altınpulluk, H. (2015). A theoretical analysis of MOOCs types from a perspective of learning theories. *Procedia-Social and Behavioral Sciences, 186*, 15–19.
Krause, S., & Lowe, C. (2014). *Invasion of the MOOCs: The promise and perils of massive open online courses*. San Francisco: Parlor Press.
Kukharenko, V. N. (2011). Innovation in E-learning: A massive open online course/V. N. Kuharenko//Higher education in Russia. – 2011. – No 10. – pp. 93–99. ISSN 0869-3617.
Kukharenko, V. (2013) *Didactic of massive open online courses MOOC Omsk, 2013* [on-line] at http://www.slideshare.net/kvntkf/mooc-omsk/. Accessed 28 Aug 2014.
Larry, C. (2012). *MOOCs and pedagogy: Teacher-centered, student-centered, and hybrids (Part 1)* [Online]. Available at: http://larrycuban.wordpress.com/2013/02/13/moocs-and-pedagogy-part-2/. Accessed 26 November 2014

Lebedeva, M. (2015). Mass open on-line training courses as a trend in education progress. *Man and Education, 1*(42), 105–109. in Russian.

Mackness, J., Sui, M., & Roy, W.. (2010). *The ideals and reality of participating in a MOOC* (2010): 266–275 [Online]. Available at: http://www.lancaster.ac.uk/fss/organisations/netlc/past/nlc2010/abstracts/Mackness.html. ISBN:978-1-86220-225-2. Accessed 26 November 2014

Many more academic courses to be freely available online' The Hankyoreh [Online]. Available at http://english.hani.co.kr/arti/english_edition/e_national/676825.html . Accessed 26 November 2014

Martinez, I. (2014a). *The effects of nudges on students' effort and performance: Lessons from a MOOC* (Working Paper). http://curry.virginia.edu/uploads/resourceLibrary/19_Martinez_Lessons_from_a_MOOC.pdf. Accessed 10 Aug 2016.

Martinez, S. (2014b). *OCW (Open Course Ware) and MOOC (Open Course Where?).* Proceedings of Open Course Ware Consortium Global 2014. http://conference.oeconsortium.org/2014/wp-content/uploads/2014/02/Paper_16.pdf. Accessed 10 Aug 2016.

Mcauley, A. et al. (2010). The MOOC model for digital practice. 33 [Online]. Available at: http://www.elearnspace.org/Articles/MOOC_Final.pdf. Accessed 26 November 2014

McGriff, S. J. (2000). *Instructional system design (ISD): Using the ADDIE model.* Retrieved January 17, 2005, from http://www.personal.psu.edu/faculty/s/j/sjm256/portfolio/kbase/IDD/ADDIE.pdf

McKay, E. (2000). Measurement of cognitive performance in computer programming concept acquisition: Interactive effects of visual metaphors and the cognitive style construct. *Journal of Applied Measurement, 1*, 257–286.

McKay, E. (2007). Planning effective HCI to enhance accessibility, ISSN 1615-5289. *Universal Access in the Information Society, 6*, 77–85.

Morze, N., Smyrnova-Trybulska, E., & Umryk, M. (2015). Designing an e-university environment based on the needs of net-generation students. *International Journal of Continuing Engineering Education and Life-Long Learning, 25*(4), 466–486.

Nkuyubwatsi, B. (2014). Fostering collaborative investment in Massive Open Online Courses (MOOCs). In D. Jansen & A. Teixeira (Eds.), *Position papers for European cooperation on MOOCs* (pp. 44–57). Heerlen: EADTU. Retrieved from http://home.eadtu.eu/images/Position_papers_for_European_cooperation_on_MOOCs.pdf.

Olazabalaga, I. M, Garrido, C. C., & Ruiz, U. G. (2016). Research on MOOCs: Trends and methodologies, PORTA LINGUARUM (pp. 87–98), Special Issue.

Open Education Europa. (2014). *Report on web skills survey* [online]. http://www.openeducationeuropa.eu/sites/default/files/news/MOOCs-for-web-skills-survey-report.pdf. Accessed 21 Sept 2014.

OpenupEd. (2015). *Definition massive open online courses.* Heerlen: EADTU. Retrieved from http://www.openuped.eu/images/docs/Definition_Massive_Open_Online_Courses.pdf.

Orr, D., Rimini, M., & Van Damme, D. (2015). Open educational resources: A catalyst for innovation. In *Educational research and innovation.* Paris: OECD Publishing.

Pappano, L. The Year of the MOOC. *The New York Times* 2.12 (2012): 2012 [Online]. Available at: http://www.nytimes.com/2012/11/04/education/edlife/massive-open-online-courses-are-multiplying-at-a-rapid-pace.html?pagewanted=all&_r=0. ISSN 0362-4331. Accessed 04 November 2012

Patru, M., & Balaji, V. Eds. (2016). *Making sense of MOOCs a guide for policy-makers in developing countries* UNESCO and commonwealth of learning, 2016 ISBN:978-92-3-100157-4.

Poland MOOC platform [Online]. Available at: http://fmn.org.pl/polska-platforma-mooc/, https://www.youtube.com/watch?v=LqkQDnaoY7M. Accessed 28 February 2015

Porto Declaration on European MOOCs [Online]. Available at: http://home.eadtu.eu/images/News/Porto_Declaration_on_European_MOOCs_Final.pdf. Accessed 28 February 2015

Prometheus : [Online]. Available at: http://prometheus.org.ua. Accessed 26 November 2014

Rasch, G. (1960). *Probabilistic models for some intelligence and attainment tests.* Copenhagen: Nielsen & Lydiche.

Schuwer, R., Gil-Jaurena, I., Aydin, C. H., Costello, E., Dalsgaard, C., Brown, M., Jansen, D., & Teixeira, A. (2015). Opportunitiesand Threatsof the MOOC movement for higher education: The European perspective. *International Review of Research in Open and Distributed Learning, 16*(6).

Smyrnova-Trybulska, E. (2009). On principles of the design and assessment of distance courses [in:] distance learning, simulation and communication, 2009, proceedings, editor: Miroslav Hruby, Brno, Czech Republic, May 6, 2009, s.159–165. ISBN:978-80-7231-638-0.

Smyrnova–Trybulska, E. (2018). Technologie informacyjno-komunikacyjne i e-learning we współczesnej edukacji [Information and Communication Technologies and E-learning in Contemporary Education]. Katowice: Wydawnictwo Uniwersytetu Śląskiego. 572 s. ISSN 0208-6336 ISBN:978-83-226-3070-9 (wersja drukowana) ISBN:978-83-226-3071-6 (wersja elektroniczna).

Smyrnova-Trybulska, E., Morze, N., Varchenko-Tritzenko. (2015). MOOCs –selected social and educational aspects. In M. Hruby (Ed.), *Proceedings of the distance learning, simulation and communication*, 2015. Brno, Czech Republic, May 19–21, 2015, s.159–165.

Smyrnova-Trybulska, E., Ogrodzka-Mazur, E., Szafrańska-Gajdzica, A., Morze, N., Makhachashvili, R., Noskova, T., Pavlova, T., Yakovleva, O., Issa, T., & Issa, T. (2016). MOOCS – theoretical and practical aspects: Comparison of selected research results: Poland, Russia, Ukraine, and Australia. In P. Kommers, T. Issa, T. Issa, E. McKay, & P. Isaías (Eds.), *Proceedings of the international conferences on internet technologies & society (ITS 2016) educational technologies 2016 (ICEduTech 2016) and sustainability, technology and education 2016 (STE 2016)* Melbourne, Australia 6 – 8 December, 2016. IADIS 2016, s. 107–114.

Smyrnova–Trybulska, E., Morze, N., Yakovleva, O., Issa, T., & Issa, T. (2017). Some methodological aspects of MOOCs developing. In E. Smyrnova-Trybulska (Ed.), *Effective development of teachers' skills in the area of ICT*. Vol. 9 (2017) Katowice-Cieszyn: Studio Noa for University of Silesia, Katowice-Cieszyn ISSN: 2451-3644 (print edition) ISSN 2451-3652 (digital edition) ISBN:978-83-60071-96-0, pp. 139–158.

Stephen, D. (2008). CCK08 – The Distributed Course. The MOOC Guide. Retrieved September 11 2013 [online] at https://sites.google.com/site/themoocguide/3-cck08%2D%2D-the-distributed-course. Accessed 26 Mar 2016.

TEL-Map. (2012). *TEL-Map UK HE Scenarios* [Online]. Available at: http://www.learningfrontiers.eu/?q=content/context-scenarios-task-7-2. Accessed 26 November 2014

Truyen, F. (2014). MOOCs from a university resource management perspective. In D. Jansen & A. Teixeira (Eds.), *Position papers for European cooperation on MOOCs* (pp. 11–18). Heerlen: EADTU. Retrieved from http://home.eadtu.eu/images/Position_papers_for_European_cooperation_on_MOOCs.pdf.

Udacity [Online]. Available at: www.udacity.com. Accessed 26 November 2014

UNESCO. (2015). *Position Paper on Education Post-2015*. Retrieved from http://en.unesco.org/post2015/sites/post2015/files/UNESCO Position Paper ED 2015.pdf

Wickramasinghe, S., Kumara, W. G. C. W., & Jayasekara, J. M. N. D. B. 2015. "ICT education for non-ICT professionals through e-learning", Ubi-Media Computing (UMEDIA) 2015 8th International Conference on, pp. 212–217.

Wu, M., & Adams, R. (2007). *Applying the Rasch model to psycho-social measurement: A practical approach.*

Yousef, A. M. F. et al. (2014). What drives a successful MOOC? An empirical examination of criteria to assure design quality of MOOCs. In: Advanced Learning Technologies (ICALT), 2014 IEEE 14th International Conference on. IEEE, 2014. pp. 44–48.

Yuan, L., & Powell, S. (2013). *MOOCs and open education: Implications for higher education* [Online]. Available at: https://www.researchgate.net/publication/265297666_MOOCs_and_Open_Education_Implications_for_Higher_Education.

Chapter 8
Synchronous Virtual Classrooms in Problem-Based Learning to Mentor and Monitor Students in Higher Education

Juan Arías Masa, Rafael Martín Espada, Prudencia Gutiérrez-Esteban, Gemma Delicado Puerto, Sixto Cubo Delgado, Laura Alonso-Díaz, and Rocío Yuste Tosina

8.1 Introduction

Problem-based learning is characterized by posing a challenging state to solve that "forces a student to generate solutions and that is used by the teacher to reach theoretical aspects inductively, which have not been explained before and whose proposal is made in the exposition of it (…). In PBL, the problem is given to the students, they have to look for information and return to the problem in order to determine its possible solution (…). In PBL, the essential thing is not knowledge acquisition itself but a personal development of people in training" (Leal y León 2017, p. 42).

ABP is certainly not a novel methodology according to (Branda 2001) p. 80, *prof. Alejandro Pulpeiro citó a Arquímedes, y yo desearía citar a Amos Comenius quien, en el siglo XVII en sus clases iniciales de lenguaje, les daba a los estudiantes un dibujo mostrando una situación, y les decía: "Mañana traigan lo que ven por escrito en alemán, checo y latín." Pero, —decían los estudiantes—"no sabemos ninguna gramática". La repuesta de Comenius era: "Ese es problema de ustedes, tienen que ir a buscarla y aplicarla."*.[1] Thus, PBL is nothing original; what was innovative in 1969 was the use of a scenario or a problem as the starting point to

---

[1] *P. Alejandro Pulpeiro quoted Archimedes, and I would like to quote Amos Comenius who, in the seventeenth century, in his initial language classes, gave the students a drawing showing a scenario, and told them: "Tomorrow bring what you see by writing in German, Czech and Latin." "But," the students said, "We do not know any grammar." Comenius's response was: "That's your problem, it is just up to you to find it and apply it."*

J. Arías Masa (✉) · R. Martín Espada · P. Gutiérrez-Esteban · G. Delicado Puerto ·
S. Cubo Delgado · L. Alonso-Díaz · R. Yuste Tosina
University of Extremadura, Badajoz, Spain
e-mail: jarias@unex.es; pruden@unex.es; gdelpue@unex.es; sixto@unex.es; laulonso@unex.es; rocioyuste@unex.es

learn medicine at the McMaster school, which was certainly a notable success (Graaff and Kolmos 2009).

Hence, Luengo Caballero (2014) identifies the following features of problem-based learning:

1. It is a methodology mainly focused on students. Learning focuses its attention on acquiring prominence in class.
2. The problem is by itself the focus of instruction and an encouragement to learn. In this way, problems must be selected to achieve a conceptual, procedural, and attitudinal learning. The ideal style of the proposed problem in the PBL methodology must be real or realistic.
3. It is carried out through a cooperative (or collaborative) context, preferentially within small groups. Likewise, students play a key role in knowledge acquisition. It also catches students' commitment to solve the problem.
4. The role of the teacher shifts to being a facilitator of knowledge acquisition and becoming a guide of learning processes. This leads us to think that students acquire a leading role throughout the whole process of methodology development, while teachers play a secondary role (although he/she does not lose its importance and relevance).
5. Regarding developed skills, problem-solving and decision-making gain greater relevance. Also, PBL methodology fosters self-directed learning (necessary for the acquisition of new information in the teaching-learning process).
6. PBL is a working model suitable for different knowledge areas.

According to Mckeachie and Svinicki (2006), PBL is currently one of the most important deployment areas in higher education, along with active learning, collaborative learning, and technology. In addition, it is likely that learned and generated knowledge from problem-solving in realistic contexts will aid to support the cognitive theory, in case such knowledge would be required afterward. Therefore, PBL is not the result of combining ordinary knowledge contents with complementary problems, but rather problems are the essential part of the course itself (Biggs 2011). Meaning the objective pursued is not to solve specific problems, but rather the resolution process represents the very act of learning and, consequently, the acquisition of skills related not only with contents but also with the organizational skills. That is, those mainly related to the acquisition of professional skills, which should be the ultimate goal of higher education students.

Particularly (Leal y León 2017), this method develops a series of skills such as critical thinking, analysis, synthesis and evaluation, learning of theoretical concepts, or the application of some others previously gained.

Some of the benefits of PBL can be found in (Cawley 1989) who indicates that with this methodology students can cultivate skills to assimilate concepts while improving their critical and analytical skills and, of course, the ability to search for solutions. However, within the traditional methodologies, which were fundamentally focused on the expository method, diagnostic and problem-solving skills have not been adequately considered even though they are so important in engineering.

Under this model, a student does not remain reflecting on the usefulness of what he learned but rather takes an active, relevant, and committed role with the resolution of real-life problems (Nasr and Ramadan 2005). This pedagogical strategy (Echavarria 2010), although widely accepted in the medical education field, still finds some important barriers when being introduced in engineering syllabi (Yusof et al. 2004). This is not exactly the case of the University of Extremadura, where PBL methodology has been successfully applied to Engineering Teaching and is widely accepted, since the Service for Orientation and Teacher Training (SOFD) offers important support and training to implement it. In fact, some members of this research team have continuously applied PBL methodology since the 2012–2013 academic year, as can be seen in (Carmona-Murillo et al. 2013), as well as in the analysis of syllabi of a number of courses within the degree mentioned above.

However, in Spain and in the field of engineering, the father of this kind of advance was Valero, working for the Polytechnic School of Castelldefels (EPSC), at the Polytechnic University of Catalonia (Valero-García 2005 and Alcober et al. 2003). In this field, it is possible to identify some particular features of PBL, such as the ability to stress autonomous learning processes (Posada Álvarez 2004) and collaborative learning (Carrió Pastor 2007), making it possible to meet established competencies that university students must achieve. It also highlights the ability to foster meaningful learning linked to developing practical activities that take place surrounded by PBL methodology (Gil et al. 2010). Numerous other skills are promoted in different PBL development phases (Davies et al. 2011).

It is also important to remind the described experience in (Arias and Martin-Espada 2015) where PBL methodology was used combined with synchronous virtual classrooms (SVC). Indeed, the combination of PBL with technological platforms for online education in a synchronous way has been applied in some fields previously, being the term renamed as ePBL (King et al. 2010). So it was renowned that positive effects of the PBL methodology in a virtual environment improved learning outcomes (Baturay and Bay 2010).

In addition, students who were part of this project during the first 4 months of the 2014–2015 academic year had enough experience in this PBL methodology and are familiar with the processes involved. That was due to the fact that they collected some other PBL experiences in advance, such as in the courses taught in prior semesters Advanced Communications (Carmona-Murillo et al. 2013) or Computer Networks (Arias Masa et al. 2013). In fact, there are several similar papers and research projects developed in the same university college, which can be found in Arias Masa et al. (2013) and Gonzalez Macias et al. (2014).

On the other hand, SVC are described by Alonso Díaz et al. (2014), who tested diverse experiences, in higher education as described in this chapter, but articulated with different tools and platforms. And they pointed out that the most significant fact is not the tool itself but the methodology to develop it, so finally they proposed three basic actions to be considered, namely:

- Teaching planning
- Teacher management
- Technical management of tools

Getting a little further with SVC, in (Arias Masa and Bonilla Gutierrez 2011), an innovative definition can be found which states that "it is a teaching and learning space through which computers, together with communication networks, make it possible to take place a real class without a physical presence in the same space shared by teachers and students." Based on it, SVC was used as the elementary tool to solve online communication problems, as students participating in the experience were located in different contexts. Among all potential and available SVC tools in the university scope, basically two of them were selected and used in this study, Adobe Connect and Google Hangout, since both meet basic operating requirements according to (Arias Masa and Bonilla Gutierrez 2011) and which are shown below:

- Audio communication tools
- Direct instant messaging
- User profiles configuration which can coexist in the virtual room
- Presence control
- Interactive whiteboard
- Monitoring and evaluation tools
- Shared and remote desktop

8.2 Context of the Teaching Experience

It was carried out during the academic year 2014–2015 in an Information Security course, which is jointly taught in the Degree in Telecommunications Engineering (GIT) and in the Degree in Computer Engineering in Information Technologies (GIITI) at the college located in the town of Mérida, a campus belonging of the University of Extremadura (Spain).

Information Security is a course taught throughout the third year for GIITI and the fourth year for GIT students. It is planned in lectures, which take 75% of the time, and lab sessions the remaining. Problem-based learning (PBL) hereafter was chosen to be implemented in theoretical classes.

The main goal of this study is to assess methodological strategies when synchronous virtual classrooms (SVC) are used as a collaborative work tool in a PBL environment, aimed to develop teaching-learning activities for engineering students in higher education.

The course under study is divided into ten sections, which are summarized in Table 8.1. Specifically for this project, section number two "Legal Aspects of Computer Security" to learn to use PBL has been addressed. It was proposed at the beginning of the course, making use of time dedicated to those activities that must be carried out within ECTS (European Credit Transfer System). These ECTS tutorials extend the concept of the traditional ones offered in Spanish universities, prior to the introduction of the degrees under the new European Higher Education Area. In particular, new ECTS tutorials combine some objectives such as monitoring, orientation, reflection, and social construction of knowledge in a dynamic, planned,

Table 8.1 Topics summary of the information security course

Module I. Security principles/introduction	
Topic 1	Introduction to information security
Topic 2	Legal aspects of information security
Module II. Cryptography	
Topic 3	Introduction to cryptography
Topic 4	Cryptography private-key
Topic 5	Cryptography public-key
Topic 6	Summarizing functions
Module III. Network security: Internet	
Topic 7	Perimeter security
Topic 8	Other security tools
Topic 9	Services in secure networks
Topic 10	Security protocols
Module III. Network security: Internet	
Lab activity I	Introduction to the programming environment in practices
Lab activity II	Uses and analysis of some security tools
Lab III	DES and S-DES (DES simplified) algorithms
Lab activity IV	PGP Tool

and structured action (Giráldez et al. 2012), which perfectly fits into the intentions of our experience.

As described in (Arias and Martin-Espada 2015), in this research project, four phases have been designed:

- Phase I. Problem presentation
- Phase II. Research
- Phase III. Project execution
- Phase IV. Solution presentation and evaluation

These four phases represent a synthesis of the seven steps that (Must et al. 2007) have proven effective for future engineers training:

- Step 1. Clarify terms and concepts that are not very clear
- Step 2. Define the problem
- Step 3. Analyze the problem (Brainstorming)
- Step 4. List the analysis and possible solutions
- Step 5. Formulate learning objectives
- Step 6. Private research toward learning objectives
- Step 7. Synthesize and present new information

Correspondence between the previous steps and the four phases shown above: steps 1 and 2 are carried out together in phase I, while steps 3, 4, 5, and 6 are carried out in phases II and III, and, finally, step 7 is included in phase IV "Solution Presentation and Evaluation." In any case, the seven steps are formulated in terms of the activities that students need to perform, while phases described in (Arias and Martin 2015) are based on the stages that the learning management process must follow with PBL methodology and the way this approach itself should be managed, both from the point of view of the students and the teaching team.

8.3 Procedure: Project Development

This Information Security course goes from the beginning of September to the end of December. Concerning this PBL experience, the teaching team decided to implement it from the very beginning. In the final weeks of the semester, students should focus on a great load of works for different courses, and probably they are overwhelmed; however, the first weeks can be useful for students to keep pace with the recommended study schedule.

Thus, the total available time is limited to about 9 weeks out of 15. The project schedule was designed to arrange face-to-face seminars through the SVC tool every 15 days, meaning that the tasks should be monitored every alternate week. As a result, a total of five virtual meetings were held, coinciding with odd weeks within the course. The purpose of the first meeting was to develop the abovementioned phase "Definition of the problem" and the last one, the group solution presentation and evaluation. The goals of the intermediate meetings were to supervise tasks and help each group as needed to progress and develop the intermediate phases of research and effective execution of the project.

In relation to the number of students in each group, according to Abrandt Dahlgren and Dahlgren (2002), they suggest that the optimal number should be between six and ten members. In this case, given that there have already been multiple PBL experiences with smaller groups at the University College of Mérida, producing highly positive results, as can be seen (Gonzalez Macias et al. 2014 and Gonzalez Macias et al. 2014), the number of members per group is set to a minimum of five. In Fig. 8.1, it can be observed a sample session in the SVC tool Adobe Connect AVS.

Concerning the procedure for implementing the project, similar to that used in Arias and Martin (2015), it can be highlighted that, in this case, the starting point was the topic to be addressed, namely, "Legal Aspects of Computer Security." However, in this experience, each group was randomly assigned a different subtopic within a broad range of topics, as shown in Table 8.2, in order to focus the particular problem on its application to real-life situations on the basis of their university student context.

At the same time, it is important to point out that the selection of problems is an essential part of the PBL pedagogical strategy, as it motivates and challenges students with genuine complications. Indeed, creating an appropriate problem for a PBL project is, therefore, a critical issue that helps determine whether a student's work will be successful or not (Vizcarro and Juárez 2008). In this case, the topic named Information Security enjoys great popularity as a worldwide concept among

8 Synchronous Virtual Classrooms in Problem-Based Learning to Mentor... 139

Fig. 8.1 Sample session in the SVC tool Adobe Connect

Table 8.2 Subtopics to be assigned to each group

Number	Title
1	Data protection
2	Copyright
3	Electronic access to public administrations
4	Telecommunications and data recording
5	Electronic signature
6	e-Commerce
7	Critical infrastructures protection
8	Criminal code and reform

students and European citizens overall (European Commission and DG-COMM 2017). However, such topic syllabus includes very specific contents, such as some encryption algorithms and additional essential characteristics related to complex technical contents. In order to avoid a negative atmosphere among students, in terms of the usefulness of the content, the problem raised in the PBL project was chosen to develop the legal aspects of information security from the students' context. Furthermore, students had to think about what was intended to be protected, to ana-

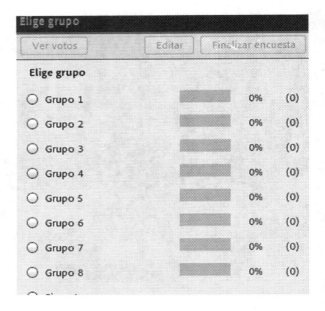

Fig. 8.2 Students' distribution method in groups using the survey tool of SVC Adobe Connect

lyze why legislation is therefore needed and finally its importance in this area for preserving privacy in the digital age. It was explained in this way, and students assumed the project basic principles. Thus, the teaching team intended to connect the topic itself and the contents of the Information Security course with social life aspects that can be affected and then are protected by the law to a greater or lesser extent.

As a result, eight topics were distributed among the eight groups for PBL projects. They were designed in the first ECTS session via SVC tool. It should be noted, at this point, that each group was randomly created using the Adobe Connect survey tool, as can be seen in Fig. 8.2. This fact is central since it is possible to avoid the creation of groups of friends, a fact that makes the essence of PBL project distorted. The essence of PBL is the ability to function in a group from an integrative perspective. Thus, a simple subdivision of tasks and then the subsequent development of each part individually are avoided.

Although in this introduction document we indicated that the optimal size of the groups for PBL project was five members, in this experience it has been necessary to arrange for a total of 37 students registered in the course. Therefore, there was an option to form 5 groups with 5 members and 2 additional groups of 6 students (5x5 = 25, plus 2x6 = 12, of a total of 37 students) or a second option that consisted of carrying out 6 groups of 5 members and 2 small groups of 4 students, which is the one adopted by our project. The main goal was having eight groups that needed to complete each eight subtopics that would cover the main theme, namely, legal aspects of information security.

In this way, face-to-face seminars in phases II and III were carried out alternatively in the SVC tools Adobe Connect and Google Hangout, the latter being the one that the students used for their internal group sessions, since they were more accessible for them because they were free of charge and did not require any license from the university to be used, as in the first option. The final presentation of works was carried out exclusively in SVC Adobe Connect tool, since Google Hangout does not fit for the purpose because students cannot access simultaneously to the virtual room.

8.3.1 Phase I: Problem Presentation

Following the procedure described in Arias and Martin (2015), this phase is carried out in the SVC tool during an online face-to-face session. On this occasion, Adobe Connect was used as SVC tool. However, in order to contact with all the students and schedule seminar times and ways of communication and documentation, a Moodle virtual classroom inside the LMS Virtual Campus of the University of Extremadura (AVUEX) was utilized. It is fully available for students and teachers enrolled in the course, and they are very familiar with it.

This phase, "Presentation of problem," was already carried out in the SVC tool previously selected. The first action that students had to accomplish, once they entered the virtual classroom, was to perform the basic audio configuration test, though some students do not consider it imperative. It can be said that it is essential for a positive seminar development, individual identification within the virtual room. Once the previous steps have been completed, the following stages can take place.

8.3.1.1 Stage 1: PBL Group Choice

As detailed above, students were randomly allocated to PBL groups, as shown in Fig. 8.2. It can be considered that students were very satisfied with this arrangement (Arias and Martin 2015), and it can be seen in Fig. 8.3. In this figure, it can be perceived how 75% of the students strongly agree, that added the 20% who agree, show a 95% of students positive with this kind of selection, which is a certainly high percentage (Fig. 8.3).

In this stage, besides the distribution of students in PBL groups, the assignment to each group of the subtopic to work on also takes place. Given that students were randomly assigned to groups (see Fig. 8.2), this next step, the assignment of topics to the different groups, is to be done in an arbitrary way as well, selecting them from those ones included in the list shown in Table 8.2. The results of such action are shown in Table 8.3, where students' names were replaced by their initials. Figures 8.5 and 8.6 show the question asked to the students inquiring about this system of distributing workload among the PBL groups and their satisfaction with it. Something to take into account is that a 12% of the total of students does not consider this method suitable.

Fig. 8.3 Level of students' satisfaction with group choice

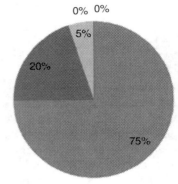

Fig. 8.4 Question for students' opinion on topics assignment

Table 8.3 Final assignment of topics to working groups

Number	Title	Student acronym
1	Data protection	ACG, CGH, JAVB, MGM, AMCD
2	Copyright	IGR, PMN, SGC, GSB, NVG
3	Electronic access to public administrations	JLCG, JFGM, FRL, DBN, SLR
4	Telecommunications and data recording	SEB, MHM, JML, MBG, SCG
5	Electronic signature	DFM, MRR, PMMA, DRM, MESM
6	e-Commerce	VMCS, GCC, GBU, JAM, EJLV
7	Critical infrastructures protection	JAFP, SMC,JFG, DGH
8	Criminal code and reform	DGC, JPGS, DWBR, SGM

8 Synchronous Virtual Classrooms in Problem-Based Learning to Mentor... 143

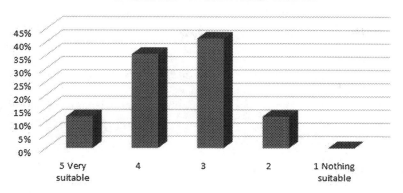

Fig. 8.5 Students' opinion

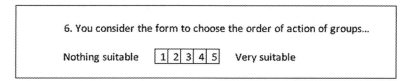

Fig. 8.6 Students' opinion question about the way of selecting order of presentations

8.3.1.2 Stage 2: Preparation of the Team Notebook

The team notebook can be an essential tool for the effective management of collaborative work, since according to Domínguez Fernández et al. (2011) it is a tool to consolidate the group and schedule the tasks and their fair distribution among the different team roles. The template proposed for this experience was adopted by all groups and is based on the one proposed by Arias and Martin (2015), where the following roles are established:

- Coordinator (fixed)
- Seminar secretary (fixed)
- Task scheduler and manager in the group (rotating)
- Technical documentation writer (rotating)

As there are four roles and five members in each group, two rotating roles were established in the groups of five students that alternated among three members, apart from the coordinator and the secretary; obviously, in the two groups of four members, each role was assigned to students individually and permanently.

On the other hand, the following guidelines were proposed:

- Do not miss the scheduled group seminars unless it is due to exceptional circumstances.
- Assume responsibility for the work process of your group, both individually and collectively.
- Have the willingness to help your colleagues if they have not finished a task.
- Punctuality when attending group seminars.
- If any student breaks one of these rules for three times, he will be penalized with additional tasks.

8.3.1.3 Stage 3: Initial Agenda

There were two types of seminars: on the one hand, group seminars and, on the other hand, general seminars. It was proposed that all of them were carried out through the SVC tool, so it was necessary to properly manage the group agendas to share the same SVC platform.

As explained above, the SVC tool was a specific Adobe Connect virtual room under the University of Extremadura license agreement. Although there are many alternatives to manage a common classroom, in this particular case, for example, Google Calendar web app was used, where only group secretaries had access to edit. Thus, there were no conflicts due to the fact that simultaneous access was possible.

8.3.1.4 Output from Phase I

The output of this phase was included in the team notebook, and, basically, the following elements were incorporated:

- Group members
- Responsibility description of each member
- Internal group guidelines
- Scheduled seminars

8.3.2 Phase II: Research

This phase was carried out by the students in their own seminars with teaching team involvement, acting as tutors for the activity; however, they voluntarily managed time and mainly the contents to be treated. Of course, relevant annotations were made in the team notebook as a summary or minute, containing all the aspects dealt with and agreed upon. It must be clear that each group worked independently on their own research topic.

This phase does not propose any deliverable for the teaching team. In fact, in the experiences, there is a constant return to this phase from the following "Development of the project," because according to the opinion of the students, there are several concepts that had to be "polished" or reconsidered once they were addressed again in this phase.

In any case, the team notebook, although it is not defined as a deliverable in this phase of the project, it is just an element that must be completed by the students on a continuous basis throughout the project.

8.3.3 Phase III: Project Implementation

During the project implementation, as described by Arias and Martin (2015), the most outstanding milestones in order to detect possible deviations and anomalies by the teaching team are:

- Group member cohesion
- Monitor project progress in terms of tasks accomplished
- Team notebook review

The following documents must be available as deliverables:

1. Definitive team notebook. It must be a complete team notebook, where all the important information from all seminars must be recorded.
2. Document describing the work developed with a classic format of cover, index, summary, contents, personal assessment and bibliography.
3. Document for projects presentation and defense. Usually, it is a "PowerPoint" or "Prezzi" file with slides or images to be used during the discussion section.

8.3.4 Phase IV: Solution Exposition

This phase was carried out following the guidelines described by Arias and Martin (2015), where it was summarized that:

- All papers must be published prior to the final public presentation. To do that, a task element was defined in the course virtual classroom of the Virtual Campus to which we referred earlier. The student who held the role of team secretary was in charge of uploading that task to the platform. The specific objective of this task was to allow the teaching team to review the work carried out by the students before the exposition and, at the same time, to avoid any changes that could be implemented in real time according to what could be observed in previous expositions following the order of presentations. It must be taken into account that, in this case, having eight groups means that not entirely 100% of presentations could be performed in the same day due to lack of time.

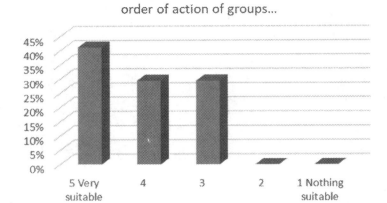

Fig. 8.7 Extracted results from question about selection procedure of presentations order

- The order for presentations of group projects was randomly selected, and its results can be seen in Fig. 8.7. It was widely accepted by the vast majority of students. A figure close to 70% of students was satisfied with the outlined procedure (Fig. 8.7).
- In addition to assessing the criteria to select the order of group presentations, it was similarly evaluated on the random method to order individual student presentations. Such individual participations are part of the group presentation, and this way of ordering is done with the intention that every student of a group can master all the aspects on a topic on which the group has been working and not only that part in which they have been mostly involved according to the task distribution.
- The final results are shown in Fig. 8.9, and it can be seen that 18% of total number of students disagree with this approach. As mentioned at the beginning of the document, students belonged to two different degrees, and while those of the Telecommunications Engineering degree (GIT) had actively participated in these methodologies in previous courses, Computer Engineering students (GIITI) faced this working method for the first time. Thus, it is conceivable that within this percentage of students who consider it inappropriate, a significant part of them should belong to GIITI. This last sentence is purely speculative when it comes to justifying this discrepancy, because at the time of preparing this document there is no evidence of such fact. However, after analyzing the students' answers to open questions in the survey and some oral opinions collected by the teaching team, they concluded that there is a lack of student awareness of the great usefulness of this system, designed for the global and interdisciplinary acquisition of knowledge and, ultimately, the development of professional skills (Figs. 8.8 and 8.9).

8 Synchronous Virtual Classrooms in Problem-Based Learning to Mentor... 147

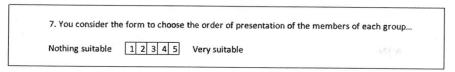

Fig. 8.8 Student opinion question about the order of individual students' presentations

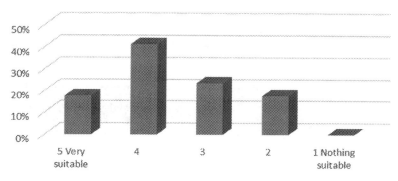

Fig. 8.9 Results of collecting student opinion about the order of individual students' presentations

- Finally, presentations were peer reviewed. For this co-evaluation, the online questionnaire shown in Fig. 8.10 was used. Results of co-evaluation are presented in the Results section.

The co-evaluation questionnaire shown in Fig. 8.10 was validated by experts and scholars in previous courses. It has been used in a great number of experiences of evaluation as in (Traver and Arias 2016) and (Traver Becerra et al. 2015).

8.4 Project Assessment

For project evaluation of this PBL experience combined with a SVC tool in the course of Information Security, the following elements were used:

1. Online questionnaire for students to ask them their opinion about the work developed. This questionnaire was validated by experts in the course within a teaching innovation project described in (Carmona-Murillo et al. 2013). Some of the study results were shown in previous tables and figures.
2. Co-evaluation is based on the same process developed and described in (Traver Becerra et al. 2015). It is designed through an online questionnaire and whose results can be found in the Results section.

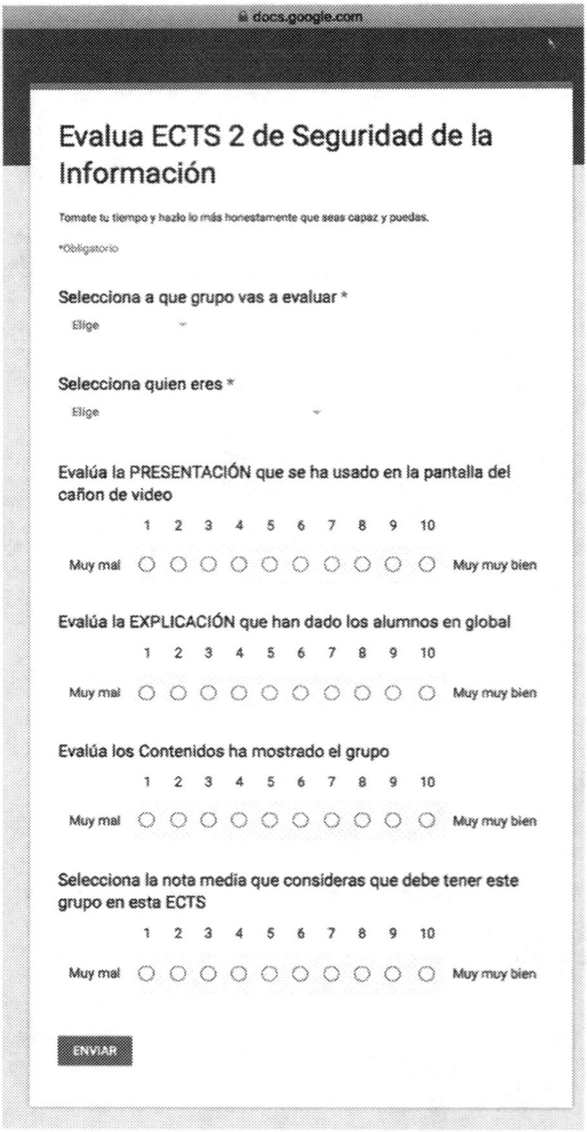

Fig. 8.10 Co-evaluation questionnaire

3. Review of all documentation submitted by students to the teaching team. For that, they should be using an appropriate evaluation rubric. In this case, it was followed what is specified in (Arias Masa and Arevalo Rosado 2014) where the evaluation rubric for assessing students' tasks in the Telematics Engineering Degree is collected.

Fig. 8.11 Students' preference between SVC versus face-to-face formats

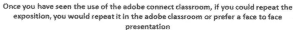
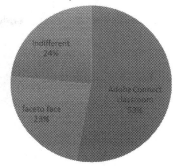

Fig. 8.12 Usefulness of the SVC tool usage for their professional training process

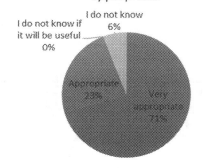

In this project, it was employed the named "level test" in a different way as followed in (Arias and Martin 2015) since each PBL group had worked with a different topic. The original test was designed to compare the quality level of different presentations about a similar theme.

Concerning all items included in the questionnaire (Carmona-Murillo et al. 2013), those ones related to the comparison between SVC and the face-to-face works must be highlighted. Results can be seen in Fig. 8.11. In that, it can be seen that if the number of students positive about virtual classrooms is added to the percentage of those who show indifference to them, the resulting figure constitutes the majority of the students.

In addition to the previous item, in Fig. 8.12, it can be observed how a 93 per cent of students consider that using a SVC tool is very suitable for their professional training. Consequently, they believe that it is a very useful method for acquiring some transversal and professional competencies necessary in their groundwork process.

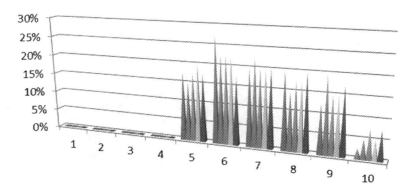

Fig. 8.13 Content co-evaluation. Results shown for each group

Concerning the result of the co-evaluation, it can be summarized as shown in the following figures, where the most outstanding information is depicted. Data entries from students are individually analyzed and gathered to obtain each PBL group assessment.

Figure 8.13 shows co-evaluation made by their peers. Students assessed the PBL group presentation related to the contents shown; consequently, each group was evaluated by the rest of the students who did not belong to them. Each color of the graph represents one different PBL group. On the abscissa axis, the scale of assessment is adjusted from 1 to 10, where each student could mark for the content evaluation according to the expositions of each group. The ordinate axis presents the percentage values of students who give that assessment mark, that is to say, the relative frequency. In the picture, it can be seen how all the assessment given values are above five, which means a passing grade. Most marks are in the range from 6 to 8, and very few students give the maximum value.

Figure 8.14 shows the average rating of the co-evaluation. In such figure it can be seen how there is a large majority of values around eight. Most students' given values are joined in nine. This leads us to conclude that final presentations were perceived to be made with a high level of quality.

Regarding the students' opinions about a SVC tool used in this project, Adobe Connect, they were collected through an open question "write at least three advantages of using the Adobe Connect Virtual Classroom." Results can be summed up in the following themes:

- One hundred percent of students highlight the flexibility of these platforms, regarding schedules and location. They are several answers such as "it allows to connect to all the students from any place" by user 2 or "comfort of being able to do it in your house" by student 6.
- Almost 50% of students highlight the effective learning of a useful tool for the labor market, with answers such as "perform teleworking in future companies" (user 10) and "it serves us as a training for possible online actions in the future," contributed by user 2.

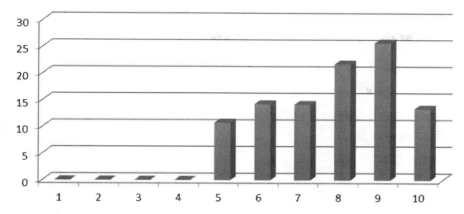

Fig. 8.14 Co-evaluation results of each PBL group presentations

- It also stands out with 30% of the respondents (it must be remembered that they freely give an opinion in an open question) they value as a very positive aspect the lesser pressure they have when they make presentations. Responses of this nature are "since it is not face-to-face, I consider that we are less stressed at the time of presenting in front of the rest of the students" by user 16 or "being at home, you are less stressed and can speak more properly" of user 9.

Regarding the negative aspects, there is a large majority of students who refer to technical problems (60%), providing with comments such as "audio problems, which are a bit annoying, although they do not have to do with the platform" or "the quality of the videoconferencing depends on the Internet connection." It is worth highlighting some singular opinions, although they are not in the majority. They should be taken into account because they provide a diverse interpretation of the most immediate issue, the technical problems of this variety of tools. It can be seen different comments that reflect on signs of concentration problems (user 15: "the student, when he/she remains silent, easily lost concentration") or express feelings as the coldness of presentations (user 13: "presentations are duller because they lack body language as in face-to-face format; in this way it costs much more to hold colleagues' attention"). These students' opinions present an interesting aspect of SVC tools that should be considered by the teaching team when resuming these types of experiences.

Finally, some other advantages are found in the SVC uses combined with the PBL methodology and must be outlined below:

- With the SVC tool, it has been possible to get rid of the passive attitude that some member of the PBL group could have had in the physical face-to-face seminar. This is so because, given that inside a group each one has their assigned role, they have to take charge of carrying it out.
- With the SVC tool, members of each working group have flown the information gathered in the individual research and allowed it to be shared in real time.

- The organization and management of each group seminar, both individually and generally speaking, have been highly favorable through the use of SVC.
- From all the features that a SVC tool has, most students have chosen the shared desktop ability as an essential tool for sharing information.
- In short, as a tool for collaborative work itself, a SVC tool is a high-quality one.

8.5 Conclusions

The described experience presents an effective combination of a pedagogical strategy, such as problem-based learning (PBL), together with a technological innovation named synchronous virtual classrooms (SVC). It was created to develop a hybrid model of teaching, as it can complement the face-to-face classes based on the transfer of contents, in specific courses of our engineering degree.

Based on the results presented in this paper, it can be said that the experience has been highly satisfactory for both the students and the teaching team. On the one hand, it has been successful for students, because it addresses one of the most complex topics of the course: the acquisition of specific skills that are explicit in the statement of the problem. Besides, in addition to these precise competencies, a series of transversal abilities which must be acquired by the students throughout the degree in all of their courses have also been worked on. In fact, after adopting European Higher Education Area (EHEA), it is essential to achieve an interdisciplinary nature that confers a holistic vision of university education.

Indeed, the synchronous virtual classrooms (SVC), despite of creating a more rigid environment than the face-to-face formats, do not generate rejection among students. On the contrary, in general, some of the analyzed characteristics are positively perceived and, in addition, they allow teaching teams to incorporate appropriate formalities to develop optimal skills for the resolution of real-life problems, such as collaborative work.

Moreover, access and location possibilities for students when working with SVC tools allow PBL strategies to provide suitable conditions for its development and arrange it to short formats such as ECTS tutorials. These compulsory parts of the syllabus, if done in a face-to-face format, would have forced the possibilities of development. And, finally, if their application is provided with conditions that ensure the effective work of all the members of a group, such as the randomness of selection or the order of presentation, the results show an optimal efficiency of the third effort, time, and learning.

Therefore, based on the experience presented in problem-based learning on SVC tools, it can be stated that currently they are a precise valid tool for hybrid, face-to-face, and distance teaching. All in all, it has been shown that students rated the experience as very positive, mainly when evaluating the collaborative work by using these tools. This leads us to recommend the use of problem-based learning methods on SVC platforms for those projects to be developed within a course, such as for the problem design, as the group management and the final presentations of results.

Acknowledgments The research leading to these results has received, within the framework of the IRNET project funding from the People Programme (Marie Curie Actions) of the European Union's Seventh Framework Programme FP7/2007–2013/under REA grant agreement.

References

Abrandt Dahlgren, M., & Dahlgren, L.-O. (2002). Portraits of ABP: Students' experiences of the characteristics of problem-based learning in physiotherapy, computer engineering and psychology. *Instructional Science, 30*(2), 111–127.

Alcober, J., Ruiz, S., & Valero, M. (2003). Evaluación de la implantación del aprendizaje basado en proyectos en la EPSC (2001–2003). In *XI Congreso universitario de innovación educativa en enseñanzas técnicas*. Vilanova i la Geltrú: Escola Universitària Politècnica de Vilanova i la Geltrú.

Alonso Díaz, L., Gutiérrez Esteban, P., Yuste Tosina, R., Arias Masa, J., Cubo Delgado, S., & Diogo Dos Reis, A. (2014). Usos de aulas virtuales síncronas en educación superior. *Pixel-Bit. Revista de Medios y Educación, 45*, 203–215.

Arias, J., & Martin, R. (2015). *Problem-based e-learnign (ABP) using synchronous virtual teaching*. New York: Nova Science Publishers, Inc.

Arias Masa, J., & Arevalo Rosado, L. (2014). Rubrica de contenido de tareas para el Grado de Ingeniería Telemática. *XXII Jornadas Universitarias de Tecnología Educativa*. Toledo.

Arias Masa, J., & Bonilla Gutierrez, M. (2011). Requisitos mínimos para aulas virtuales síncronas. *XIX Jornadas Universitarias de Tecnologla Educativa*. Sevilla: RUTE.

Arias Masa, J., Valenzuela-Valdés, J. F., Carmona Murillo, J., González-Macías, J. C., Martín Tardio, M. A., & Pardo-Fernández, P. J. (2013). Diseño de Gestión de Errores en paquetes IPv4 Project-based learning for Error Handling in IPv4 Packets. *Sistemas e Tecnologias de Informação, 45*.

Baturay, M. H., & Bay, O. F. (2010). The effects of problem-based learning on the classroom community perceptions and achievement of web-based education students. *Computers & Education, 55*, 43. https://doi.org/10.1016/j.compedu.2009.12.001.

Biggs, J. B. (2011). *Teaching for quality learning at university: What the student does*. Maidenhead: McGraw-Hill Education.

Branda, L. (2001). Aprendizaje basado en problemas, centrado en el estudiante, orientado a la comunidad. *Aportes Para Un Cambio Curricular En Argentina*, 79–101.

Carmona-Murillo, J., González-Macías, J. C., Martín-Tardío, M. A., Pardo-Fernández, P. J., Arias-Masa, J., & Valenzuela-Valdés, J. F. (2013). Problem-based learning for skills development in advanced communications. In: *Information systems and technologies (CISTI), 2013 8th Iberian conference on* (pp. 1–7). IEEE.

Carrió Pastor, M. L. (2007). Ventajas del uso de la tecnología en el aprendizaje colaborativo. *Revista Iberoamericana de Educación, 41*(4), 5.

Cawley, P. (1989). The introduction of a problem-based option into a conventional engineering degree course. *Studies in Higher Education, 14*(1), 83–95.

Davies, J., Graaff, E. De, & Eds, A. K. (2011). *ABP across the diciplines: Research into best practice*. ABP 2011.

Domínguez Fernández, G., Prieto García, J. R., & Álvarez Bonilla, F. J. (2011). El cuaderno de equipo. Eje de la metodología de aprendizaje cooperativo en una asignatura del máster de Educación. *REDU. Revista de Docencia Universitaria*.

Echavarria, M. V. (2010). Problem-based learning application in engineering. *Revista EIA*.

European Commission, & DG-COMM. (2017). *Special Eurobarometer 464a. Europeans' attitudes towards cyber security*. Brussels. Retrieved from http://ec.europa.eu/commfrontoffice/publicopinion/index.cfm/Survey/getSurveyDetail/instruments/SPECIAL/surveyKy/2171

Gil, J., Pérez, A. L., Suero, M. I., Solano, F., & Pardo, P. J. (2010). Evaluation of the effectiveness of a method of active learning based on Reigeluth and Stein's Elaboration Theory. *International Journal of Engineering Education, 26*(3), 628–641.

Giráldez, R., Troncoso, A., & Aguilar-Ruiz, J. S. (2012). *Diseño Y Aplicación De Una Acción Tutorial Para Asignaturas De Programación En La Escuela Politécnica Superior*. Seville: Revista Universidad Pablo de Olavide Sevilla Innova.

Gonzalez Macias, J. C., Martín-Tardío, M. A., Pardo-Fernández, P. J., Valenzuela-Valdés, J. F., Arias Masa, J., & Carmona Murillo, J. (2014). Proyecto de innovación docente en normalización y proyectos de telecomunicación. In Educación Editora (Ed.), *Experiencias e innovación docente en el contexto actual de la docencia universitaria* (pp. 361–366). Barbadás/Ourense: Educación editora Vigo.

Graaff, E., & Kolmos, A. (2009). *History of problem-based and project-based learning*. University Science and Mathematics Education in Transition. https://doi.org/10.1007/978-0-387-09829-6

King, S., Greidanus, E., Carbonaro, M., Drummond, J., Boechler, P., & Kahlke, R. (2010). Synchronous problem-based e-Learning (eABP) in Interprofessional health science education. *Journal of Interactive Online Learning*.

Leal, M. M., y León, M. R. (2017). La innovación y mejora docente a través del aprendizaje por problemas y la tutorización. In: *El aprendizaje basado en problemas como experiencia de innovación y mejora docente universitarias* (pp. 35–54). Madrid: Editorial sintesis, S.A.

Luengo Caballero, S. (2014). *El aprendizaje basado en problemas en la educación primaria: implementación en el aula*. Bachelor Degree Final Essay. Universidad de Extremadura.

McKeachie, W. J., & Svinicki, M. (2006). *McKeachie's teaching tips: Strategies, research, and theory for college and university teachers* (12th ed.). Boston: Houghton-Mifflin.

Moust, J. H. C., Bouhuijs, P. A. J., & Schmidt, H. G. (2007). *El aprendizaje basado en problemas: guía del estudiante* (Vol. 1). Cuenca: Univ de Castilla La Mancha.

Nasr, K. J., & Ramadan, B. (2005). Implementation of problem-based learning into engineering thermodynamics. In *ASEE Annual Conference and Exposition, Conference Proceedings*.

Posada Álvarez, R. (2004). Formación superior basada en competencias, interdisciplinariedad y trabajo autónomo del estudiante. *Revista Iberoamericana de Educación, 35*(1), 1–33.

Traver, M., & Arias, J. (2016). Mejora de las competencias transversales mediante Co-evaluación en Ingeniería Telemática. *CIAIQ2016*, 1.

Traver Becerra, M., Hidalgo Izquierdo, V., & Arias Masa, J. (2015). Co-evaluación de las "ECTS" en Ingeniería Telemática. *XXIII Jornadas Universitarias de Tecnología Educativa JUTE 2015*, 196.

Valero-García, M. (2005). Las dificultades que tienes cuando haces ABP. In: *La Educación Superior Hacia La Convergencia Europea: Modelos Basados En El Aprendizaje (Capítulo 8)*. Universidad de Mondragón.

Vizcarro, C., & Juárez, E. (2008). ¿Qué es y cómo funciona el aprendizaje basado en problemas? In: *La metodología del Aprendizaje Basado en Problemas*.

Yusof, K. M., Aziz, A. A., Kamarudding, M., Hamid, A., Ariffin, M., Hassan, A., Hassim, M. H., Hassan, S. A. H. S., & Nma, A. (2004). Problem based learning in engineering education: A viable alternative for shaping graduates for the 21st century ? In: *Conference on engineering education*.

Chapter 9
Multilevel Study of the Higher Education Challenges Caused by the Migration Crisis in Turkey

Iryna Sekret and Darco Jansen

9.1 Introduction

According to the European Commission evaluations, in 2014 over 2.3 million third-country nationals attained resident permits in the EU, and approximately 1.3 million asylum applications were recorded in 2015. Taking the education and qualifications into concern, it states that non-EU migrants residing in the EU have a lower than average level of skills and qualifications; at the same time, two thirds of highly educated third-country migrants are employed in low- or medium-skilled occupations or simply fail to find any job (EU boosts 2017 commitment to education for children in emergencies, 2016).

This study focusses on the situation in Turkey which has become the largest refugee population country in the world according to the official estimations of the European Commission (Turkey: Refugee crisis, 2016). About 3 million refugees registered in Turkey include Syrians, Iraqis, Afghan, Iranian, Somalian and other nationalities.

The special focus is on the current situation in higher educational establishments and the refugees' impact on the teaching and learning processes. With this purpose the instructors from universities located in different parts of Turkey were invited to respond to a specially designed questionnaire for obtaining their insights on the problems and specifics of teaching refugees.

I. Sekret (✉)
School of Foreign Languages, Abant Izzet Baysal University, Bolu, Turkey
e-mail: iryna.sekret@ibu.edu.tr

D. Jansen
EADTU, Maastricht, The Netherlands
e-mail: darco.jansen@eadtu.eu

9.2 Methods

The research was conducted with a combination of the qualitative and quantitative methods which include:

1. Literature review and documentation analysis with a purpose to research on the current challenges caused by the migration crisis in Turkey, scrutinising governmental policies aimed to facilitate educational adaptation and assimilation of refugees in the country.
2. A questionnaire designed to get responses from experts, instructors and administrative personnel from the educational institutions in Turkey to reveal and analyse the internal policies and practices of dealing with refugees. The tool was developed to elicit information on the problems experienced by the education stakeholders and instructors' approaches when dealing with the cultural diversity in the classroom, specifics of the migrants' learning and behaviours, the teachers' observations and solutions resulted from their teaching practices.
3. Observations while communicating with refugees, experts and agencies dealing with the problems of refugees and their adaptation in Turkey, teaching practices and self-observations when teaching classes containing the Syrian refugees.

9.3 Literature Review

9.3.1 Methodological Background

According to the European Commission evaluations, in 2014 over 2.3 million third-country nationals attained resident permits in the EU, and approximately 1.3 million asylum applications were recorded in 2015. Taking the education and qualifications into concern, it states that non-EU migrants residing in the EU have a lower than average level of skills and qualifications; at the same time, two thirds of highly educated third-country migrants are employed in low- or medium-skilled occupations or simply fail to find any job (EU boosts 2017 commitment to education for children in emergencies, 2016).

Bearing this situation in mind, the European Commission stresses the necessity of actions which are aimed to improve skill levels and qualifications among the migrants and the use of their existing skills and qualifications to support effective integration into the labour market.

In Brussels, 7 December 2016, the European Commission presented a new initiative for Europe's youth "Investing in Europe's Youth" which covers four key areas of critical importance: employment, mobility, solidarity and participation and education and training (Investing in Europe's Youth, 2016).

Discussing the youth's employment, it states that although youth unemployment is steadily dropping, it still remains too high. In this context learning and studying in another country is viewed as a great added value for young people to develop their skills, improve their career chances and enhance European citizenship. Learning abroad is believed to provide experience in cross-cultural communication and developing specialist skills. Experience gained abroad is a major advantage for young people when applying for a job, due to the fact that employers appreciate such additional assets as the capacity to show initiative, adaptability in different cultural environments and linguistic skills. Vocational education and training systems, in particular apprenticeships, are regarded as a tried-and-tested way to equip young people with relevant skills and facilitate their transition from school to the labour market; but it is important to note if there are sufficient apprenticeship places available and they are of a good quality.

In the context of the development of the European community, solidarity is stressed to be a shared value. To meet the need, young Europeans should have more and easily accessible opportunities to express their solidarity while gaining certified experience and skills that can open new opportunities for their employment, learning and socialisation.

Continuing with the education, the European Commission stresses that the quality and accessibility of education are of critical importance in order to sustain Europe's social cohesion, growth and competitiveness. However, as evidence shows, there is still a high share of young people who do not acquire knowledge, skills or competences required for the needs of the modern labour market, be it basic skills (literacy, mathematics) or key competencies (such as digital skills or an entrepreneurial mindset). It is required that education systems should be tuned to equipping young people from all backgrounds with the knowledge and skills they need in life.

The New Skills Agenda for Europe already announced specific measures to develop required skills of Europeans, with a particular focus on adult learning, vocational education and training and higher education. With the "Investing in Europe's Youth" initiative, the Commission is placing a particular emphasis on school and higher education. To enhance equipping Europeans with the digital skills required for their careers, the Commission launched on 1 December 2016 the Digital Skills and Jobs Coalition, together with member states, companies, social partners, NGOs and education providers (A New Skills Agenda for Europe: Skills and Integration of Migrants 2016).

9.3.2 *MOOCs as an Alternative Means of Education to Provide Access for Learning to Migrants*

UNESCO and the Commonwealth of Learning (COL) joined their efforts to develop a guide to massive open online courses (MOOCs), where open and online education is seen as an innovation driver for improving education and as a basis for transforming secondary and higher education systems. In this respect, MOOCs are viewed to be excellent for promoting lifelong learning (Sekret and Doş 2018).

Among benefits of MOOCs which may serve for the learning needs of migrants and refugees are the following (Making Sense of MOOCs: A Guide for Policy-Makers in Developing Countries 2016):

1. Courses are offered free of charge to any number of people, anywhere and anytime; therefore, MOOCs enable access to higher education and beyond for people who cannot afford a formal education and are disadvantaged.
2. MOOCs can reduce the disconnect between the skills and aptitudes of the majority of university graduates and the needs of the industry sector in many countries. This disconnect is triggering huge unemployment among youths and adults, particularly women.
3. MOOCs can be useful in providing job-oriented training and skills development.
4. MOOCs emerged from the open education movement. As such, they enable free access to high-quality content and resources, which might be too costly for higher education institutions in developing countries to produce.

Due to the present evidence, the provision of MOOCs in Europe and other continents tends to grow. Together with that the implementation of MOOCs may be hindered because of diverse languages, cultures, settings, pedagogies and technologies (Jansen and Goes-Daniels 2016).

Considering MOOCs for the learning needs of refugees, the currently existent practice should be mentioned. Among them:

- Kiron online university for refugees (Germany). Kiron is a crowdfunding project, conceived to give refugees access to higher education. Programmes are a combination of 2 years of online studies and 1 year of classroom studies at a partner university. The programme is provided in English, German and Arabic (http://www.dw.com/en/kiron-education-for-refugees/a-19311256).
- The University of Louvain (Belgium). The University of Louvain together with the Croix-Rouge de Belgique offers asylum seekers to (re)connect with the university education via its MOOC programme, a set of online courses open to everyone (https://www.uclouvain.be/en-mooc-refugees.html).
- Coursera for Refugees. The US Department of State and massive open online course provider Coursera are partnering to launch Coursera for Refugees, a programme that offers career training to displaced people around the world. The programme focusses on non-profits that help refugees, which will be able to apply for fee waivers to access the Coursera course catalog. The organisations will then be able to offer free access to MOOCs to the refugees they serve. Coursera is the latest MOOC provider to offer educational services to refugees. Earlier this year, edX partnered with Kiron, a free education provider for refugees, to offer college credit to Syrian migrants (https://www.insidehighered.com/quicktakes/2016/06/20/launch-moocs-refugees-program).
- Edraak – MOOC platform. Edraak is a massive open online course (MOOC) platform that is an initiative of the Queen Rania Foundation (QRF). Through its partnership with edX, the platform gives Arab learners access in Arabic to

courses taught and developed at top-tier institutions like HarvardX, MITX and UC BerkelyX. All courses are delivered at no cost to the learner. QRF envisions the use of the platform to showcase Arab role models by broadcasting short online courses by practitioners and professionals from a variety of fields spanning the arts and sciences (https://www.edraak.org/en/courses/).

Analysis of the practical implementation of MOOCs in the refugee camps is reported to demonstrate the following specifics:

- Female participation is rather low due to the household responsibilities or insufficient digital skills;
- More than 90% of MOOC participants are male;
- Computer illiteracy may hinder the participation; at the same time, it may trigger learning curiosity of the students regardless of their age and prior learning experience;
- Navigating MOOC platform may be a challenge for new learners; they may need support from facilitators located in their areas;
- Insufficient number of equipment may cause troubles for consistency of session attendance and fulfilling learning assignments;
- Low levels of interactivity in MOOC design may become frustrating; therefore, the presence of the learning facilities in camp may be helpful;
- Offline meetings are essential to facilitate understanding via face-to-face discussions and clarifications;
- Preferences in online learning are given to those courses which develop knowledge and skills transferable to the needs of the local community.

9.4 Current Situation in Turkey: Education Policies, Schooling for Refugees and MOOCs

9.4.1 Education Policies in Turkey

Turkey is reported to become the largest refugee population country in the world according to the official estimations of the European Commission. About 3 million refugees registered in Turkey include Syrians, Iraqis, Afghan, Iranian, Somalian and other nationalities.

In January 2017, the Government of Turkey estimated that it spent over €11.4 billion to provide assistance for refugees since the beginning of the Syria crisis.

Out of the close to 2.8 million registered Syrian refugees in the country, some 260, 000 people are hosted in 26 camps run by the Disaster and Emergency Management Presidency of Turkey (AFAD), where refugees have access to shelter, health, education food and social activities.

Despite these efforts, 90% of the Syrian refugees (over 2.5 million persons), as well as many refugees from other nationalities, live outside the camps under the challenging circumstances with depleted resources. Education in emergencies remains one of the most underfunded areas.

Considering education for the Syrian refugees in Turkey, a need to establish schools for learners of all ages was one of the earliest to be recognised (Nielsen and Grey 2013).

On the way of establishing educational institutions and providing education to the Syrian students, a number of problems were indicated (Nielsen and Grey 2013).

1. The curricula of the camp schools though being administrated by the Turks are not recognised or sanctioned by the Turkish education authorities; therefore, the licensed Turkish teachers cannot be assigned to those establishments.
2. The camp education relies heavily on volunteers from refugees and may often be inconsistent in time and curriculum.
3. The language remains a barrier for the Turkish teachers to educate the Syrian students who speak Arabic and together with the lack of the Turkish language may have little motivation to learn it due to the uncertainty if they will stay in the country or will have to leave it. Knowing Turkish and obtaining the Turkish education do not guarantee opportunities for further education and advanced career in Turkey.
4. In case the camp school follows the curriculum of the Turkish school, the students from the camp schools cannot readily transfer their credits to the correspondent levels at the Turkish official schools. Simultaneously, the Turkish language and education will not be easily transferred to Syria.
5. Teenage students in the camps generally do not have access to the secondary schooling that would help them enter universities in Turkey or, for a variety of reasons, in Syria. One source of tension between the Syrian parents and the Turkish authorities was the Syrian demand for special classes for advanced students whose preparations for the university entrance exams were interrupted by the war.
6. Another tension is caused by the Syrian parents' reluctancy to send their children to the mixed gender classes, or insisting on their teenage daughters to wear headscarves in school which is not accepted by the official Turkish education policy.
7. Among the Turk population, together with the overall sympathy towards the people from the neighbouring Muslim countries, the tension starts growing like to the guests who are overstaying the hospitality – the Turks blame the refugees for the inflation and rise of prices, too many benefits granted by the Turkish government, cultural inconsistency, differences in lifestyles, attitudes towards work and learning, epidemic situations, etc.

Due to the limitations of the camp schools, the Syrian special schools following the Syrian curriculum were being opened outside of the camps with fundings from the local administration and charity organisations. Examples of such endeavours are frequent in the south-east of Turkey, affected by the Syrian migration the most (Gaziantep, Mersin, Hatay, etc.) (Alemdar 2016).

Together with establishing the full circle education schools for the Syrians, there were attempts to open institutions of the higher education which had to undertake processes of licensing and accreditation to function at the legal basis. In many cases such attempts failed due to the lack of funding and restrictions in the educational policies of Turkey.

On 25 October 2016 in Ankara during the conference "Refugee Children Access to Education" which brought together representatives of UNICEF, governing bodies, educators and teachers, a huge range of currently burning problems were highlighted by the speakers. They included:

- Overcrowded classes with the number of learners getting to 50 and more;
- Lack of the transportation means to deliver the students from camps to schools or from other places of their residence places;
- Lack of textbooks and learning materials appropriate for the refugees, concerning their educational, cultural and language background;
- Bullying at schools from the side of the Turk students;
- Lack of social programmes and solutions facilitating the refugees' adaptation at schools;
- Teachers are not prepared to deal with the psychological problems experienced by the refugees during their learning and interaction with their peers;
- Due to the adaptational problems, bullying, language barrier and learning difficulties, the learning motivation of refugees decreases, and the rate of dropout is getting higher;
- The refugee children have to combine learning with work and, in a number of cases, to leave school for the sake of earning for life due to the fact that their parents cannot get employed because of the lack of language, required qualifications, education, etc.;
- Classrooms contain learners of different ages; this fact complicates the learning process; the Syrian teenagers and adults feel uncomfortable to share the same classrooms with the learners who are much younger (Demirbuken 2016; Education for Refugee Children in Turkey 2016).

Among the suggestions uttered at the conference to tackle with the highlighted problems were the following actions: (1) to search for alternative methods of teaching which include online learning, MOOCs (massive open online courses) considering international teaching experience in Europe and the USA; (2) to train teachers to apply specific methods of instruction based on the principles of individualisation, student-centred learning, cultural awareness and technology-enhanced teaching; (3) to establish consortiums between international organisations, researchers, educators, governing bodies and teachers to identify the problems, develop effective solutions and monitor their effects on the factual situation of the refugee education; and (4) to initiate projects on developing teaching materials to meet special learning needs of refugees (Jansen and Sekret 2016).

Analysis of the educational policies concerning enrolment of refugees to the universities of Turkey allowed to define that the Turkish universities accept international students in four ways: (1) with scholarships (Presidency of Turks Abroad and

Related Communities), (2) undergraduate transfer, (3) special students and (4) international students with the applications according to the university requirements.

The Syrian refugee students can be accepted following the mentioned conditions:

1. Students from Syria and Egypt can come and study in universities of Turkey within the undergraduate transfer after 2013 according to the regulation issued by the Council of Higher Education (YÖK 2016).
2. Special student programme refers to those who want to study at another university on temporal terms. The Turkish government offers an opportunity for refugee students to start education within special student programmes if they don't have official documents for the undergraduate transfer.
3. International student programme is the programme where all international students can apply. In Turkey for the 2016–2017 academic year, most of the refugee students were enrolled to higher institutions on terms of the undergraduate transfer system.

Based on the regulation issued in September 2013 (Resmigazete 2013), the Council of Higher Education made a meeting on 9 October 2013 and stated the following regulations (YÖK 2016):

- Before the 2013–2014 academic year, students from Egypt and Syria (the Syrian, Egyptian and Turkish nations only) who were studying for associate, undergraduate and graduate degrees (except Medicine and Dentistry) can be transferred to the Turkish higher institutions.
- If students have official papers, they can continue their first, second, third or fourth year courses in the higher institutions of Turkey.
- The department quota for refugees must not exceed the 10% of the total quota of the application year.
- The students who don't have official papers can apply only to Gaziantep University, Kilis 7 Aralık University, Osmaniye Korkutata University, Urfa Harran University, Hatay Mustafa Kemal University, Adana Çukurova University and Mersin University.

Considering conditions of online learning and MOOC offerings in Turkey, according to the recent data, the MOOC movement is still in its infancy stage. There are only a few universities and a couple for-profit initiatives that provide online courses and develop MOOCs for broad masses of learners. It states, however, that demand for MOOCs is growing faster than the supply side, especially in the corporate settings, where the training departments motivate their employees to take Coursera and EdX courses. Besides, Khan Academy is offering courses in Turkey in Turkish, and not only corporations but also educational institutions and single users show great interest in these courses.

9.4.2 The Potential of MOOCs for Enhancing the Refugee Higher Education in Turkey

Recent studies on the status of MOOCs in higher institutions of Turkey reveal that a big number of the Turkish institutions participants are not really aware of MOOCs. Those universities that offer MOOCs do this mainly for the sake of the international and national visibility.

The situation is caused by the following factors (Aydin 2016):

1. Language barriers – a big majority of MOOCs are supplied in English, though quite a big number of the Turkish citizens don't have sufficient English language proficiency.
2. Recognition of the prior learning in MOOCs – it is defined as problematic in the country due to the lack of the corresponding standards and regulations. As a result, the institutions hesitate to recognise the prior learning in MOOCs, even if the certificates are issued by the universities and especially by the private institutions, though they do not have enough reputation and may be not accepted by employers or other institutions.
3. Reputation of open and distance education is another disputable question. Due to the unsuccessful past and current implementations, distance learning is not considered as valuable as the face-to-face traditional education. The Higher Education Council (HEC), a government agency controlling and taking all the decisions about higher education in Turkey, encourages all the public universities to offer distance education. However, the main reason behind this encouragement is related to the income provided by the open and distance learning, which is considered as a good business rather than a substantial form of the instruction delivery.
4. Legislations – although the government (via HEC) encourages the universities to offer open and distance learning, insufficient and problematic legislations make the development of the online learning implementations rather obscure and complicated.
5. Knowhow – although the country has a long history in open and distance learning, a big majority of universities do not have enough proficiency in online learning.
6. Infrastructure – some professors, experts or institutions are willing to offer MOOCs, but they do not have access to the required technological infrastructure.

9.4.3 Case Study: Analysis of the Refugee Situation in Higher Institutions in Turkey

In order to shed the light on the current situation concerning refugees in higher institutions in Turkey and with a purpose of discussing possible solutions and perspectives through the lenses of the global European policies, we invited experts and instructors to share their experiences and visions on the problem via a specially designed questionnaire.

The tool was developed to answer the following research questions:

1. What is the involvement of refugees in higher institutions in Turkey?
2. What kind of problems are caused by the refugee enrollment to the university programmes?
3. How does the refugees' presence affect teaching and learning processes?
4. What is the potential of MOOCs as an alternative means of providing education to refugees from the point of views of educators?

The questionnaire consisted of 24 questions purposed to obtain data on the status of the participant and their institutions; the refugee situation in the institutions; their effects on the administrative, teaching and learning processes; technological supply and teaching materials used in the class; attitudes and policies towards MOOCs; and visions on the MOOC implementation for the refugees' learning needs.

The experts from 11 (eleven) institutions of Turkey responded to the inquiry.

As the institutions whose representatives responded to the questionnaire are situated in different parts of Turkey (the south-east, the Central Anatolia Region, the Black Sea Region, the western part of Turkey), it provides an idea of the overall situation in the higher education in the country.

Simultaneously it should be noted that the data and conclusions may be affected by the following limitations:

- The respondents in this study work mostly at the humanitarian departments, while other departments, i.e. technician, medical, etc., may provide different responses.
- The participants are educators with different academic levels whose responsibilities may have little to do with the overall policies of the institutions.
- The questionnaire was designed and administrated to the instructors, the questioning of the refugee students was not included in the current study but definitely would provide solid basis for further speculations on the problem.
- If to conduct the study separately in different regions of Turkey, it may provide more accurate results as the socio-ethnical composition of the refugees in different regions of the country differs together with the time of the refugees entering the area.

Statistically the data was derived from the instructors with different academic levels from three private, five public and three mixed financed institutions. Eight universities provide education mainly on campus; three are mixed, providing blended learning in campus and online.

All the participants are from the middle-sized universities mainly between 15.000 and 50.000 students.

Six institutions report on a little number of the refugee students (the central and Black Sea regions of Turkey); four universities responded about having up to 10% of refugees; and one establishment stated to educate up to 30–50% of the refugee students (the south-east of Turkey). The origin of the refugee students is noted to be mostly from Syria, and the second country by the number of the refugee students mentioned by the respondents is Iraq, studying mostly in the central part of the country.

The refugees' socio-economic status is mentioned to be rather low, only 2 of the 11 participants which work at the private universities declared that their students have more than average economic opportunities.

To deal with the refugee students and their adaptation, the universities are not reported to explore any external staff and use their own resources.

To proceed with the data analysis and their discussion, we will follow the research questions laid out above.

1. The refugee students' involvement in the higher education in Turkey

Eight of the eleven participants from different universities stated they have the refugee students. That means that the refugee students have opportunities to study at the higher institutions of Turkey, which are protected by the regularities issued by the Council of Higher Education. Gaziantep University is a state university which is reported to provide learning programmes with the Arabic language as a medium of instruction. The university also offers the Turkish and English programmes applicable for the Syrian refugee students. Seven universities are situated close to the Syrian border and also offer special student programmes where the refugee students can apply without official papers.

Many state universities of Turkey provide the Turkish language course to get certification (TOMER) as a prerequisite for the refugees to apply to the university departments as international students. All these regulations provide sound opportunities for the refugee students to get access to the higher education in Turkey.

2. The problems the refugee students experience in the higher institutions and their effect on the learning and teaching processes

The Syrian and Turkish educational systems are completely different in terms of their aims, educational programmes, administration, assessment and evaluation. These differences cause problems at the levels of formalities, educational programmes and compatibility of programmes. Another problem is the language as a barrier to follow the classes at the level of the academic Turkish language. Three of the respondents noted that they had no problems with adapting the refugees to their courses. Three of them declared that they give individual assignments to the refugee students to catch up with their peers if needed. Two participants responded that they give additional consultations to the refugees, while the other two instructors

Table 9.1 Teaching materials applied in teaching practices

Textbooks	8
Teacher-sharing resource websites	6
Open online resources	6
News sources	3
Political organisations or parties	2
International organisations	2
Governmental bodies	2

Table 9.2 Teaching technologies in use

Desktop computers	10
Large screen digital display	7
Audio-visual recording or editing equipment	7
Tablets or smart phones	5
Physical manipulatives (blocks/other objects)	3

Table 9.3 Online websites and applications implemented by the university instructors in teaching

Youtube	Google apps	Quizlet	Blogger
Moodle	Edmodo	BBC Learning	StoryJumper
Facebook	Turnitin	Camtasia	Onlineenglish
Wikipedia	Kahoot	Snagit	Audioboom

indicated that their teaching style remained the same. It is the evidence that despite the differences in educational programmes and other difficulties, the refugee students may continue their education in higher institutions though some extra consultations and individual assignments are beneficial for their support. Together with that, it should be noted that discrepancies in the educational levels and degrees, differences in the educational policies, resistence of the teaching and administrative stuff to the refugees, cultural, behavioural and communicational misinterpretations may hinder the refugee education in the higher institutions.

The respondents were questioned about the teaching materials they use for their teaching. It was indicated that textbooks remain to be the main sources, added with the teacher materials from the websites and open online resources (Table 9.1).

Table 9.2 shows the technologies which are used by the instructors in their teaching.

As it is obvious from Table 9.2, the instructors report about implementing different kinds of technological equipment in their teaching processes. Mostly they mention desktop computers, large screen digital displays and audio-visual recording or editing equipments, tablets and smart phones.

The respondents notify that they use different kinds of online websites and applications. Youtube, Moodle and Facebook are reported to be applied the most. They also refer to such educational websites as Edmodo, Moodle and Onlineenglish (Table 9.3).

Table 9.4 The instructors' experience with MOOCs

Yes, I am participating in the development of MOOCs	3
Yes, I have been following some MOOCs	2
I know what MOOC is and believe that MOOC can substitute traditional classroom environment	2
I heard about MOOC, but I can't say I fully understand what it is	2
I have no idea what MOOC is	1
I know what it is, but I don't have personal experience	–
I know what MOOC is and believe that it is a substantial support for the main educational programme	–

Table 9.5 Do you think refugees won't be able to follow MOOCs within the programme of your institution?

	Agree	Neutral	Disagree
The scarcity of Internet connection		1. xxxx	2. xxxx
Absence of required skills to follow online course	3. xxx	4. x	5. xxxx
Lack of motivation for learning	6. xxxx	7. xx	8. xx
They don't need such complications	9. xx	10. xxxx	11. xx
They are not interested in upgrading their education	12. x	13. x	14. xxxxxx
The content of MOOCs can be difficult for the refugees to understand and learn	15. xxxx	16. xxx	17. x
The differences of the refugees' culture and the culture of the MOOCs providers	18. xxxxx	19. xx	20. x

All together the data indicate that the instructors use open online resources for their teaching, and the technical equipment which is available in their classes can be effectively used for online learning in a broader sense, i.e. joining the MOOCs and integrating online courses into the teaching practice.

To the question if some additional courses for the refugee students can be beneficial to enhance their knowledge, all the respondents agreed on the importance of such endeavours and accepted the value of online learning for the refugee students.

The participants were also asked if they had any experience with MOOCs. It was found out that only one participant didn't know anything about MOOCs. All the other participants have knowledge about MOOCs, but it is interesting to note that none of them have sufficient experience with such a form of learning. Two of the respondents reported to have been following some MOOC courses (Table 9.4).

The respondents were also asked about their views on MOOCs, and all of them agree that MOOCs can be a sustainable method for offering courses and a solution to provide access to the higher education for the refugees. The respondents also stated that MOOCs can be more beneficial for the refugees than traditional classes.

Table 9.6 If to implement MOOCs into the programme of the refugees' education, which courses would be of primary need?

	Agree	Neutral	Disagree
The English language	21. xxxxx	22. xx	23. x
The language of the country of their settlement	24. xxxxxxx	25. x	26. x
Social sciences	27. xxxxxxx	28. x	
Fundamental sciences (math, physics, etc.)	29. xxxx	30. xxxxx	
Vocational courses	31. xxxx	32. xx	33. xx
Cultural studies	34. xxxxxx	35. xx	
Tutoring on applied skills (e.g. crafting)	36. xxxxxxx		37. x

To the question if their institutions would open a MOOC course, and if the refugees would follow such a course, the respondents stated that motivation for MOOC course may be the biggest problem. The second indicated problem is viewed to be the content as being difficult for the refugee students to understand, and the diversity of cultural issues can also cause a problem in following the course (Table 9.5).

Another concern of the research was to find out if any MOOCs can be provided, which courses from the respondents' point of view would be beneficial for the refugee students to follow. The data indicate the importance of the language, vocational training, social and cultural studies as the most important (Table 9.6).

9.5 Conclusions

Based on the study conducted, the following conclusions can be laid out.

1. The Government of Turkey and Council of Higher Education have been taking measures to facilitate the refugee student's enrollment to the institutions of higher education by issuing special regulations which consider different situations and complicated cases concerning applications and documentations. Simultaneously, the Turkish language as a main means of instruction and lowered economical status of the refugees hinder their enrollment and further learning in universities. The Arabic-medium education programmes, initiated in some institutions in the south-east of Turkey, are another measure to make education more accessible for the refugees from the Arab countries.
2. Despite all efforts from the governmental bodies, charity organisations and local authorities, the overall situation with education for the refugee seeks desperately for solutions due to the huge number of newcomers to the country; lack of teaching materials; technical, administrative and human resources to cope with the problems caused by the language barrier; lack of possibilities for the official employment; growing psychological tense in the society; sociocultural discrepancies.
3. The distribution of the refugee students in the higher education of Turkey, their origins and sociocultural backgrounds differ depending on the geographical

location of the institution. The universities in the south-east of Turkey declare a higher percentage of the Syrian refugees, while the institutions in the central part of Turkey contain more refugees from Iraq.
4. The refugee students may continue their education in the higher institutions though some extra consultations and individual assignments are beneficial for their support. Together with that it should be noted that discrepancies in the educational levels and degrees, differences in the educational policies, teaching stuff and administrative stuff resistance to the refugees, cultural, behavioural and communicational differences may hinder the refugee education in the higher institutions.
5. The findings of this study showed that university instructors are applying open online resources in their teaching; they use social media resources, websites and teaching materials. Though knowing about the MOOCs, the educators have scarce experience of dealing with such form of delivering instruction, as a result it may hinder the implementation of MOOCs into practice. The overall attitudes towards online learning are proved to be positive, MOOCs are regarded as beneficial for the specific learning needs of the refugee students.
6. Therefore, taking into consideration the current problems of the traditional face-to-face schooling for refugees, i.e. overcrowded classes, lack of learning materials, cultural discrepancies, etc., online learning can be positively recommended as an alternative means of providing access to the education for the refugees.

However, discussing the potential of MOOCs as an alternative means of the education for the refugees, the following measures should be undertaken:

- To raise the reputation and assure the quality of online courses, it is advisable to establish partnership among reputable institutions from Turkey and abroad to join the efforts and develop qualitative content to meet the learning needs of the refugees and other groups of migrants;
- To eliminate the language barrier to the qualitative education, the courses should be provided in multiple languages, together with the online language courses designed to meet the needs of the English learners and those who would like to learn Turkish for professional and academic purposes;
- To enhance the development and implementation of MOOCs, it is essential to raise awareness among the stakeholders about benefits of MOOCs especially in cases of problematic access to the formal education caused by financial, socio-cultural, geographical, etc. conditions.

Acknowledgements The study was conducted with the application of the methodology of the Erasmus+ Project MOONLITE "Massive Open Online courses eNhancing Linguistic and Transversal skills for social inclusion and Employability" under the Key Action "Cooperation for innovation and the exchange of good practices".

References

A New Skills Agenda for Europe. (2016). Working together to strengthen human capital, employability and competitiveness. Available at https://ec.europa.eu/transparency/regdoc/rep/1/2016/EN/1-2016-381-EN-F1-1.PDF. Accessed 19 Feb 2019.

Alemdar, M. (2016). Türkiye Eğitim Program. Report of Concern Worldwide Consulting Group at the conference "Refugee Children Access to Education", 25 October, 2016, Ankara, Turkey.

Aydin, H. (2016). *Current status of the MOOC movement in the world and reaction of the Turkish higher education institutions*. EADTU- Anadolu. Retrieved from http://home.eadtu.eu/news/112-country-reports-on-uptake-of-moocs-by-heis. Accessed 15 Apr 2017.

Demirbuken, H. (2016). Mülteci Çocukların Eğitime Erişim Eşitliği Araştırması. Report of UDA Consulting Group at the conference "Refugee Children Access to Education", 25 October, 2016, Ankara, Turkey. http://www.udaconsulting.com. Accessed 30 Oct 2017.

Education for Refugee Children in Turkey. (2016). Report of UNICEF at the conference "Refugee Children Access to Education", 25 October, 2016, Ankara, Turkey.

Education for the Syrian Children. Report of International Blue Crescent Relief and Development Foundation at the conference "Refugee Children Access to Education", 25 October, 2016, Ankara, Turkey.

Empowering Syrians in Turkey. Report of GFA Consulting Group at the conference "Refugee Children Access to Education", 25 October, 2016, Ankara, Turkey.

EU boosts 2017 commitment to education for children in emergencies. European Commission – Press release. Retrieved from http://europa.eu/rapid/press-release_IP-16-4090_en.htm. Accessed 16 Apr 2017.

Investing in Europe's Youth: Questions and Answers. Press release. Retrieved from http://europa.eu/rapid/press-release_MEMO-16-4166_en.htm. Accessed 10 Oct 2017.

Jansen, D., & Goes-Daniels, M. (2016). *Comparing Institutional MOOC strategies: Status report based on a mapping survey conducted in October–December 2015*. EADTU, August 2016. ISBN:978-90-79730-23-0.

Jansen, D., & Sekret, I. (2016). *MOOC as TOOL to provide access to education for refugees*. Presentation at the conference "Refugee Children Access to Education", 25 October, 2016, Ankara, Turkey.

Making Sense of MOOCs: A Guide for Policy-Makers in Developing Countries. (2016). Ed. by Patru M. & Balaji, V. Published by the United Nations Educational, Scientific and Cultural Organization (UNESCO), 2016. Available at http://www.unesco.org/open-access/terms-use-ccbysa-en. Accessed 10 Oct 2017.

Nielsen, S. I., & Grey, M. A. (2013). Schooling in a crisis: The case of Syrian refugees in Turkey. Retrieved from: http://odihpn.org/magazine/schooling-in-a-crisis-the-case-of-syrian-refugees-in-turkey/. Accessed 15 Apr 2017.

Resmigazete (2013). http://www.resmigazete.gov.tr/eskiler/2013/09/20130921.htm. Accessed 20 Apr 2017.

Sekret, I., & Doş, B. (2018). MOOCS as an alternative tool for providing access to education for refugees: A pilot study in turkey. In M. Hruvy (Ed.), *Distance learning, simulation and communication proceedings* (Selected papers) (pp. 171–172). University of Defence, Brno, 2017, ISBN:978-80-7231-415-7.

Turkey: Refugee crisis. European Commission: Humanitarian Aid and Civil Protection. Retrieved from http://ec.europa.eu/echo/files/aid/countries/factsheets/turkey_syrian_crisis_en.pdf. Accessed 10 Apr 2017.

YÖK. (2014). www.yok.gov.tr/web/guest/ek_madde_2. Accessed 10 Apr 2017.

YÖK. (2016). www.yok.gov.tr/web/guest/yurt-disindan-kabul-edilecek-ogrenci-kontenjanlari. Accessed 15 Apr 2017.

Chapter 10
From Face-to-Face Teaching to Online Tutoring: Challenges, Solutions and Perspectives

Iryna Sekret, Soner Durmus, Melih Derya Gurer, and Orhan Curaoglu

10.1 Introduction

In the information era and rapid development of ICT tools, online education has become an important invention providing a wide range of possibilities for lifelong learning. Developments in telecommunication and computer technologies made designing online courses and establishing networked cultures much more affordable and manageable for educators at all levels of learning.

Together with the technological and educational advancements, and due to the growing competition among educational establishments, universities are urged to provide a larger variety of forms and methods of learning to meet the needs of technologically enhanced society (Sekret 2012a, b; Sekret and Kommers 2014). In this respect academicians and instructors are required to revise their professional competences in order to adjust their teaching practices to the conditions of ICT-enhanced learning environments.

One of the worldwide growing tendencies in education nowadays is the implementation of online learning in the contexts of the university formal education. This process is accompanied with many problems and difficulties, and one of them is switching the university instructors from the mode of face-to-face teaching to ICT-mediated learning environment.

As it often happens, the university instructors who are already experienced in face-to-face teaching, become expected to switch to the mode of online tutoring and adjust their teaching strategies to the conditions of ICT-mediated learning environment. During this process they experience a huge variety of problems which affects

---

I. Sekret (✉)
School of Foreign Languages, Abant Izzet Baysal University, Bolu, Turkey
e-mail: iryna.sekret@ibu.edu.tr

S. Durmus · M. D. Gurer · O. Curaoglu
Faculty of Education, Abant Izzet Baysal University, Bolu, Turkey

their performance, motivation to be involved in such kind of activities and, consequently, the quality of online tutoring as a whole and students' learning outcomes.

Such problem was mentioned by Vlachopoulos (2008), when many instructors who are new to online teaching, without relevant background or experience of online pedagogy, are asked to contribute to the development and delivery of online courses. In this situation one cannot but agree with Sheena O'Hare (2011) stating that "There is a real danger that these members of staff are being asked to run before they can walk without a clear picture of what the role looks like and whether it is very different from what they have previously experienced". As Tomei (2006) states, "online teachers have to be different from and more demanding than on-site teachers" which is conditioned by the specifics ICT-mediated learning environment (Tomei 2006).

Referring to such problems, the current study aims to analyse experience of the instructors after their first year of teaching online in order to identify the problems and challenges they are facing and to outline a complex of solutions to enhance their performance and a quality of teaching online.

10.2 Methodology of Online Tutoring

Nowadays a big amount of research and studies focus on the problems of online learning. The scope of the questions under concern ranges from the pure theoretical, defining pedagogy and methodology of online learning, to those describing online practices and case studies.

Due to a variety of pedagogies and approaches applied, the concept of online learning turns to be a broad one including different forms of ICT-mediated learning. While most researchers define this concept as the access to learning experiences via the use of some technology (Carliner 2004; Gümüş and Okur 2010; Regan et al. 2012) and as wholly online learning (Oblinger and Oblinger 2005), others consider it as a new form of distance learning (Benson 2002). Khan (2005, p. 3) defined online learning as "an innovative approach for delivering a well-designed, learner-centered, interactive, and facilitated learning environment to anyone, any place, any time by utilizing the attributes and resources of various digital technologies along with other forms of learning materials suited for open, flexible, and distributed learning environments".

In the literature, online tutoring is often referred to as a process of teaching in an online, web-based or virtual environment in which teachers and learners are separated by time and place (Denad 2003; Flowers 2007).

According to the definition brought by Cornelius and Higgison (2001), tutoring or moderating includes "those aspects of a teacher's work which involve managing and 'animating' interactions with and among learners, especially with respect to their participation in networked learning activities".

As Vlsachopoulos (2008) and Sheena O'Hare (2011) notified, the role of online educator is defined in a wide range of roles including tutor, teacher, facilitator, promoter, manager, discussion leader, negotiator and E-moderator. Despite the term given, the role and functions of the online tutor are complex and require specific skills and competences (Sheena O'Hare 2011).

In the model described by Arrizabalaga et al. (2010), online tutors are defined as tutors-authors and content experts experienced in on-site teaching. The scope of their duties include planning tutoring activities to assure their presence at each one of them, guiding discussions on the topic and answering questions related to contents, evaluating answers, detecting students' progress and communicating with students through messages on the forum or via email (Arrizabalaga et al. 2010).

Online tutor has to operate the whole process of learning online. This task should be done systematically and based on the principles of online pedagogy. Methodology of online tutoring should consider context, subject and types of learning activities conducted by the online tutor. In order to do these activities, online tutor is required to possess specific skills and competences. According to Khan (2001) and Marcelo et al. (2002), any tutor, counsellor or mentor has to own a suit of skills and competences that will be extremely relevant for doing their job in the online environment.

Seoane et al. (2007) and Guichon (2009) defined some specific issues of e-learning in lifelong learning contexts. Being related to the scope of activities performed by online tutors, they include competences in the subject matter; technological skills; methodological, didactical and psycho-pedagogical skills; communication skills; social skills and leadership; evaluation; and quality skills.

It is stressed that the tutor should improve a leadership position by promoting collaborative working atmosphere inside a learning community (Sekret 2016), which is possible to be in achieved through the introduction of the collaborative learning model.

To add to the aspects mentioned above, it is important to consider conducting knowledge assessment and evaluation online. Due to a variety of assessment techniques and lack of face-to-face interaction, great attention should be given to the successful design and implementation of the student assessment in the online courses (Yukselturk and Curaoglu, 2010).

The technological aspect of online tutoring is important issue to consider. Thus, Hawkridge and Wheeler (2010) notify that blogs, wikis and podcasts provide essential supplement to the established systems in online tutoring such as email, virtual learning environments (VLEs, such as Blackboard) and computer conferencing. Together with that they discuss possibilities of Second Life to meet students' needs for tutoring and specifics of interacting in such online environments (Hawkridge and Wheeler, 2010).

The problems of enhancing interactivity of online tutoring by implementing social media are raised in the recent studies by Salmon et al. (2015), Williams and Sekret (2018). According to the authors' findings, although some participants of structured online learning benefit from social media by crediting it with networking and knowledge-sharing opportunities, others object or refuse to engage with social media, perceiving it as a waste of their time (Salmon et al. 2015).

Gray et al. (2010) argue that university-utilised learning management systems (LMSs) and social media platforms both enable file sharing, collaboration and discussion although social media platforms tend to be more popular with students for peer-to-peer interactions (Davies et al. 2010; Veletsianos and Navarrete 2012; Sekret 2012a, b; Sekret and Williams 2013) due to their familiarity and flexibility (Salmon et al. 2015).

Considering results of the literature review and analysis of the case studies focusing on the specifics of online tutoring, we assume that online tutoring is characterised by the following features (Sekret 2016):

1. Methodology of online tutoring is based on the principles of constructivist and social-constructivist pedagogies.
2. Main components of online tutoring include (a) adopting a specific pedagogy or an educational method, which conditions ways and strategies of the learning content delivery and provides social support for the learning group, (b) organisation and coordination of supplying services of online tutoring, (c) a coherent system of ICT tools with the manageable interface and (d) technical support for the online tutoring system to function smoothly and to be adjusted to the learning purposes.
3. Forms of providing online tutoring depend on the learning needs, content of learning, the scope of the topics under discussion, number and character of its participants. Therefore, we can distinguish (a) many-to-one online tutoring, (b) peer online tutoring, (c) one-to-one tutoring, (d) tutoring provided by the automated tutoring systems, (e) online tutoring as e-moderation for facilitating the mainstream learning, etc.
4. Online tutoring can be conducted in synchronous and asynchronous modes, or combining both modes of communication and interaction.
5. Alongside with delivering the learning content, effective online touring entails scaffolding, weaving, facilitating discussions and providing feedback. Due to the specifics of the ICT-mediated learning environment and absence of possibilities for face-to-face interactions, the mentioned teaching processes, which are extremely essential for learning and being realised naturally in a traditional classroom, remain to be a problematic area for the online tutoring class. They require to be transformed and adapted to the conditions of online tutoring via appropriate ICT tools and communication strategies.
6. Online tutoring is conducted in most cases via virtual learning environments (VLE) or LMS involving also other ICT tools and social media for developing learning content (presentations, video, podcasts, etc.) and facilitating communication in the learning group (Smyrnova-Trybulska et al. 2017; Williams and Sekret 2018).

10.3 The Study

10.3.1 Aims, Methods and Procedures

The study was aimed to analyse 1 year experience of implementing online tutoring in the framework of the formal university education in Turkey. The research is a qualitative study based on the free interview of the focus group of the online tutors and ICT experts.

Due to the fact that it was the first experience of online tutoring for most of the university instructors, there was a concern about the ways how they were adjusting their face-to-face teaching styles and techniques to the conditions of online tutoring.

The question under discussion was: "What problems did you experience when teaching online?"

The managerial stuff of the online learning centre were asked to comment on their experience of arranging technical issues of online courses and problems they had to settle together with the instructors. Also they shared their observations on the overall tendencies and dynamics on the part of the online tutors and students. The instructors shared their own experiences of teaching online courses, the problems they had to face, specifics of the students' behaviours and strategies of learning and communication.

10.3.2 Focus Group

The focus group consisted of ICT experts responsible for managing the system of online tutoring and ICT supply, and the university instructors and academicians experienced in on-site teaching. The overall number of the participants in the focus group was 28 persons, with males in the age of 35–50 years old.

10.3.3 Specifics of the Online Tutoring System

In order to shed the light on the specifics of the online tutoring system of the institution under consideration, it is essential to provide some details of its functioning.

The system of the online learning applications was initially established in August 2014. In order to support online education environment, an LMS was hired from a private company in Turkey. This institution is one of the leading companies on online education in Turkey and creates LMSs and online course contents for private and governmental organisations.

After analysis and evaluation of both open-source and commercial LMSs with a team consisting of the experts from the instructional technology department at the university and considering the university conditions such as budget, the number of students, teachers and information technology experts at the university, an agreement was made with the company, and LMS was hired to enrol up to 10,000 students. The LMS was installed in a cloud computing environment and serviced by the company. The web conferencing tool was also purchased, and installed into two server computers at the computing service of the university. It was integrated with the LMS and could be used by 2000 persons at the same time. The company ensured to respond to a failure in the LMS and the integration of LMS with the web conferencing tool.

The LMS is composed of several modules in order to help the application of learning and instruction in online learning environment. The modules of the LMS are course content, quiz, assignment, file sharing, web conferencing, user tracking, announcement, messaging and discussion. In addition, the roles of users in the LMS are system manager, teacher, assistant teacher, department head and student.

10.4 Results and Discussion

The findings from the discussions and interviews were analysed, and the identified problems were clustered in four categories: (a) technical, (b) managerial, (c) instructional and (d) psychological (Table 10.1). The identified points were admitted and agreed upon by all the participants of the focus group.

Analysis of the instructors' and ICT experts' feedbacks allowed to outline a complex of solutions for enhancing quality of online tutoring at the university level. Among them are:

1. Providing intensive pre-training programme on the specifics of online tutoring, differences between the face-to-face setting and ICT-mediated environment on strategies of teaching, communication and interaction. It should be done in an active, collaborative and project-based mode to develop necessary skills and competences within a short period of time.
2. Organising workshops and trainings on ICT usage for different purposes of online tutoring.
3. Providing orientation for the students before the online course. It should focus on regulations and requirements, codes of behaviour, communication and interaction with the instructor and peers during online sessions and in the asynchronies mode of communication.
4. Establishing teams of the content developers, designers, evaluators, software developers, etc. to perform collaboratively at the design, delivery and evaluation of the online courses.
5. Realising continuous collecting data on the feedbacks from instructors and students on the online courses, learning contents and strategies, specifics of ICT tools functioning, teaching practices and their effects on the learning outcomes.

Table 10.1 Problems of switching from face-to-face learning to online tutoring: analysis of the online tutors' reflections

Technical	Managerial	Instructional	Psychological
Internet connection	Ethical regulations (time, conditions, ways of communication and interaction, behaviour within online course)	Organising interactivity among the students during online session	Students' motivation to take online course – preference to face-to-face learning
Downloading/uploading materials	Students' attendance issues (free/obligatory)	Providing lectures and assuring active learning	Instructors' motivation to deliver online courses –preference to face-to-face teaching
Changing status of the participants, adjusting, switching on/off – time consuming and distracting from the content	Instructors' work overload (developing content, managing the course, checking assignments, quizzes, providing feedback to students, managing the class if it is oversized)	Assuring attendance and active participation of the learners in online session	Diversity of students; different groups require different approaches (educational levels, cultural background, ages, social status, etc.)
Compatibility of LMS with other ICT tools (social media, free/non-free)	Lack of pre-training for the online instructors	Providing timely and effective evaluation (formative/summative)	Affective issues (attitudes towards online learning, teaches/students' anxiety, preoccupations, etc.)
Lack of reliable connection between different parts of the campus and regional areas of the students' location	Lack of pre-instruction of the students on the code of behaviour and strategies of learning within online course	Regulations on the content and ways of its delivery	Psychomotor abilities to joint and follow the course (students with learning disabilities)
Insufficient technical supply (studio for video recording lectures for asynchronous mode of delivery, licenced software)	Need for knot-knit teams to be established (content developers, designers, evaluators, software developers, etc.)	Necessity to develop own learning content because the purchased one does not meet the requirements and needs of the institution	Possibilities to consider students' learning styles
Compatibility of the university's technical abilities and students' technical capabilities/possibilities to joint and follow		How to develop content (tools, methods, forms of representation)	
		Course and teaching/learning quality assurance (consistency of the content, assignments, ways of evaluation)	

6. Reflecting and reacting effectively on the problems which appear during the course delivery and afterwards to enhance the quality of online tutoring and learning outcomes.

Based on the findings and their analysis, we developed an outline of skills and competences required for an online tutor to perform effectively. They are as follows:

Pedagogy and methodology of online tutoring:

- Know pedagogies and methodologies of online tutoring.
- Be aware of differences of face-to-face and online teaching.
- Be familiar with practices and trends of online tutoring, etc.

Online instruction:

- Be competent and professional in the area of the subject taught.
- Possess a repertoire of techniques of online tutoring within the following teaching activities: (a) delivering the learning content online, (b) establishing connections with the learners and among them, (c) facilitating communication and discussions during the online delivery of learning, (d) getting and providing meaningful feedback, (e) monitoring the knowledge progress and (f) knowledge assessment and evaluation.
- Be knowledgeable and skilful as for providing a variety of e-activities (online learning activities) appropriate for the learning content, needs and purposes of online tutoring.
- Know techniques of online scaffolding in a view of limitations of ICT-mediated learning environment.
- Be able to weave different resources and data in the streamline of the learning.
- Be flexible as for the learning content, learners needs and ways of communication and interaction with the students.
- Be open for new experience and competences in the professional area and in the area of online tutoring, etc.

Managing ICT tools:

- Be competent of ICT tools required for purposes of online learning.
- Able to manage the main ICT tool aimed to provide online tutoring environment.
- Know and be able to apply alternative ICT tools for different purposes of online tutoring.
- Be able to evaluate effectiveness of other ICT tools and to implement them for the needs of online learners.
- Be sensible on the balance of ICT tools in order to facilitate learning and communication and not to overburden the learners and the course.
- Know how to replace ICT tool with the other means or a way of teaching in a case of technical problems or faults of ICT tool functioning, etc.

To sum up the results obtained from the literature review and the findings from the case study, it is essential to state that effective online tutoring should be based on the following principles.

Independent Learning and Students' Autonomy Online tutoring is called to foster students' independent learning. In this context, developing a student's autonomy is a principal phenomenon of online tutoring, which stands for specific learning conditions of online tutoring and aims of independent learning. In the situation of online tutoring, a learner's autonomy can be interpreted as a learner's ability to define their own learning goals and needs, being responsible for their learning in a sense of being able to regulate their determination to study, to continue learning and achieve the learning goals.

Collective Knowledge Construction Together with the development of a learner's autonomy, online tutoring presupposes collective knowledge construction. The lecturer is no longer the only source of knowledge and information, but on the contrary, learners develop the knowledge and ideas through their interaction with different sources. For this purpose, a tutor's ability to weave different data and views into one stream of knowledge is of prime importance in order to facilitate learners' deeper understanding of the learning content and to develop their critical thinking when dealing with various information resources.

Transformative Learning As far as the learning is no longer restricted with the traditional limits as for the content, ways of communication and sources of knowledge, it acquires new features of being transformative and flexible. It is essential for online tutors to demonstrate their students' meaningful and logical connections between bulks of knowledge, experiences, information and data, in order to make knowledge and skills obtained in a course of learning transformative and easily adjustable to the needs and situations of the learner's everyday life and professional tasks.

Establishing Communities of Practice Online tutoring assumes collective knowledge construction, which occurs in specially established communities of practice. Such communities include learners enrolled in the course, their instructors and outside experts. They may involve broader circles of individuals and groups who are interested in the subject or having expertise in the subject area. The main aim is to provide socialisation for the learners, to organise discussions and to communicate on the issues of the course. Such practices contribute to the students' deeper understanding of the course and its content, making learning transformative and flexible, sharing experiences and broadening professional and cultural visions.

Dialogical Learning Collective knowledge construction and practising within the learning communities occur via dialogical interaction. It entails equality in exchanging of information, sharing views, experiences and responsibilities, switching the roles from the learner to the tutor (as, e.g. in peer online tutoring). As a result, learning tends to turn from the one way knowledge delivery to the spatial mode, acquiring dialogical features.

Self-Reflection In the context of online tutoring, self-reflection acquires special significance as it is a main moving factor for learners to realise their learning and determine their learning aims, needs and, therefore, learning content. Self-reflection is also important for the online tutor in order to sense the streamline of the course, to introduce changes when it is required and to tune the content and teaching strategies to the needs of the learners. Self-reflection is a main regulating tool for the success and efficiency of the online tutoring as a whole.

10.5 Conclusion

The aim of the paper was to reveal issues related to online tutoring at the university-level courses. The focus group was formed to discuss problems they experienced while teaching online. The findings from the discussions and interviews were categorised into four clusters of problems: (a) technical, (b) managerial, (c) educational and (d) psychological.

The technical issues include problems with Internet connection, downloading or uploading learning materials, changing status of the participants, compatibility of LMS with other ICT tools, compatibility of the university's technical abilities and students' technical capabilities/possibilities to joint and follow the course, lack of sufficient technical support.

The managerial issues refer to the problems of ethical regulations, students' attendance and participation, instructors' work overload, lack of pre-training of the online instructors and students, establishing teams for the content elaboration, designing, implemention and evaluating an online course.

The instructional problems entail organising interactivity among the students, conducting online lectures and assuring active learning, facilitating students' active participation during online sessions, providing fair and timely evaluation and developing the content and defining strategies of its delivery.

The psychological issues deal with students' and instructors' motivation, diversity of students' learning styles and psychomotor abilities, affective issues such as anxiety, attitudes, etc.

Based on the findings from the focus group discussion, a complex of solutions was provided to the online instructors in order to enhance their competences and to deal with the problems identified. They included (1) intensive pre-training programme on the specifics of online tutoring; (2) organising workshops and trainings on ICT tools usage for different purposes of online tutoring; (3) providing pre-course orientation for the students focusing on regulations and requirements; (4) establishing teams of the content developers, designers, evaluators, software developers, etc.; (5) collecting data on a constant base concerning the feedbacks from instructors and students; and (6) reflecting on the problems in order to enhance the quality of online tutoring and learning outcomes.

Analysis of the data and implementation of the solutions mentioned above brought to the outline of skills and competences required for effective and efficient online tutoring. They are categorised into three areas: (1) pedagogy and methodology of online tutoring, (2) online instruction and (3) managing ICT tools.

Therefore, the effective online tutoring can be defined as the mode of learning which is based on such principles as (a) providing independent learning and students' autonomy, (b) collective knowledge construction, (c) transformative learning, (d) establishing communities of practice, (e) dialogical learning and (f) self-reflection.

The findings of the case study and suggestions derived from the research are consistent with the studies conducted by Sheena O'Hare (2011), pointing to the problems encountered when switching university instructors from the face-to-face teaching to the online learning environment. Those findings provide evidences that university instructors are required to develop specific competences and abilities in order to conduct online tutoring effectively, which was also stated in the studies by Khan (2005) and Arrizabalaga et al. (2010).

The limitations of the study are conditioned by the specifics and regulations of the venue where the research was conducted. The solutions and suggestions may be reconsidered while implementing online tutoring in other institutions according to their conditions and regulations.

The perspectives of the research are viewed in the development of tools aimed to evaluate online tutors' competences, and effective teaching strategies in ICT-mediated learning environments.

Acknowledgements The research leading to these results has received, within the framework of the IRNet project, funding from the People Programme (Marie Curie Actions) of the European Union's Seventh Framework Programme FP7/2007-2013/under REA grant agreement No. PIRSES-GA-2013-612536.

References

Arrizabalaga, P., Monguet, J. M., & Ferruzca, M. (2010). *Supporting the online tutoring process through a personalized learning environment.* Retrieved from http://pleconference.citilab.eu/wp-content/uploads/2010/07/ple2010_submission_65.pdf. Accessed 20 Jan 2016.
Benson, A. (2002). Using online learning to meet workforce demand: A case study of stakeholder influence. *Quarterly Review of Distance Education, 3*(4), 443–452.
Carliner, S. (2004). *An overview of online learning* (2nd ed.). Armherst: Human Resource Development Press.
Cornelius, S., & Higgison, C. (2001). The tutor's role and effective strategies for online tutoring. In *Online tutoring e-Book*. Retrieved from http://www.fredriley.org.uk/callhull/otis/t2-06.pdf. Accessed 20 Jan 2016.
Davies, C., et al. (2010). *Research and development to support the next stage of the harnessing technology strategy, the learner and their context. The technology-based experiences of*

learners as they approach and enter the world of work: A report for Becta. Oxford: University of Oxford.

Denard, H. (2003). E-tutoring and the transformations in online learning. *Interactions*, 7(2). Retrieved from http://www2.warwick.ac.uk/services/cap/resources/pubs/interactions/archive/issue20/denard. Accessed 3 Sep 2010.

Flowers, A. T. (2007, January 1). NCLB spurs growth in online tutoring options. *School Reform News*. Chicago: The Heartland Institute.

Gray, K., Annabell, L., & Kennedy, G. (2010). Medical students' use of Facebook to support learning: Insights from four case studies. *Medical Teacher*, 32(12), 971–976. https://doi.org/10.3109/0142159X.2010.497826.

Guichon, N. (2009). Training future language teachers to develop online tutors' competence through reflective analysis. *ReCALL*, 21(2), 166–185. https://doi.org/10.1017/S0958344009000214.

Gümüş, S., & Okur, M. R. (2010). Using multimedia objects in online learning environment. *Procedia Social and Behavioral Sciences*, 2(2010), 5157–5161.

Hawkridge, D., & Wheeler, M. (2010). Tutoring at a distance, online tutoring and tutoring in second life. *European Journal of Open, Distance and E-Learning*. Retrieved from http://www.eurodl.org/materials/contrib/2010/Hawkridge_Wheeler.pdf. Accessed 22 Jan 2016.

Khan, B. (2001). *Web-based training*. Englewood Cliffs: Educational Technology Publications.

Khan, B. (Ed.). (2005). *Managing e-learning strategies: Design, delivery, implementation and evaluation*. Hershey: Idea Group Inc.

Marcelo, C., Puente, D., Ballesteros, M. A., & Palazón, A. (2002). *E-Learning, Teleformación: Diseño, Desarrollo y Evaluación de la Formación a Través de Internet*. Barcelona: Ediciones Gestión 2000.

O'Hare, S. (2011). *The role of the tutor in online learning*. Proceedings of Ascilite 2011 Hobart. Retrieved from http://www.leishman-associates.com.au/ascilite2011/downloads/papers/O'Hare-full.pdf. Accessed 20 Jan 2016.

Oblinger, D. G., & Oblinger, J. L. (2005). Educating the next generation. *EDUCAUSE*. Retrieved from http://net.educause.edu/ir/library/pdf/pub7101.pdf. Accessed 15 Dec 2015.

Regan, K., Evmenova, A., Baker, P., .Jerome, M.K., Spencer, V., Lawson, H. & Werner, T. (2012). Experiences of instructors in online learning environments: Identifying and regulating emotions, The Internet and Higher Education, 15 (3), 204-212, https://doi.org/10.1016/j.iheduc.2011.12.001.

Salmon, G., Ross, B., Pechenkina, E., & Chase, A. M. (2015). The space for social media in structured online learning. *Research in Learning Technology*, 23. https://doi.org/10.3402/rlt.v23.28507. Retrieved on January 10, 2016.

Sekret, I. (2012a). Implementing ICT in a higher technical establishment: Institutional level. In *Humanitarian bulletin – Annex 1 to Issue 27. Vol III (36): Thematic issue "Higher Education of Ukraine in the Context of its Integration to the European Educational Space"*, Kyiv (pp. 185–193).

Sekret, I. (2012b). Social media in learning. *Wyższa Szkola Humanistyczna Towarzystwa Wiedzy Powszechnej w Szczecinie/EDUKACJA HUMANISTYCZNA/Półrocznik myśli społeczno-pedagogicznej/Nr*, 2(27), 179–188.

Sekret, I. (2016). Problems, Experiences, and Perspectives of Implementing Social Media in Online Tutoring. In M. Turčáni, Z. Balogh, M. Munk, & Ĺ. Benko (Eds.), *Proceedings "DIVAI 2016 11th International Scientific Conference on Distance Learning in Applied Informatics"* (pp. 407–421). Štúrovo, Slovakia, May 2–4, 2016.

Sekret, I., & Kommers, P. (2014). Conceptual issues of the digital competence development in the framework of the council of the European Union pp, 183–194 DIVAI 2014, *The 10th international scientific conference on distance learning in applied informatics*. ISBN: 978-80-7478-497-2.

Sekret, I., & Williams, P. (2013). Social media in learning: A case of implementing Facebook in undergraduates' learning. In L. Gómez Chova, A. López Martínez, & Candel TorresI (Eds.),

Edulearn 2013: Proceedings of 5th international conference on education and new learning technologies, 1–3 July (pp. 5198–5206), Barcelona, Spain.

Seoane, A. M., García, F. J., Bosom, Á., FernÁndez, E., & HernÁndez, M. J. (2007). Lifelong learning online tutoring methodology approach. *International Journal of Continuing Engineering Education and Life-Long Learning (IJCEELL), 17*(6), 479–492.

Smyrnova-Trybulska, E., Morze, N., Pavlova, T., Kommers, P. A. M., & Sekret, I. (2017). Using effective and adequate IT tools for developing teachers' skills. *International Journal of Continuing Engineering Education and Life-Long Learning (IJCEELL), 27*(3), 219–245.

Tomei, L. A. (2006). The impact of online teaching on faculty load: Computing the ideal class size for online courses. *Journal of Technology and Teacher Education, 14*(3), 531–541.

Veletsianos, G., & Navarrete, C. (2012). Online social networks as formal learning environments: Learner experiences and activities. *The International Review of Research in Open and Distance Learning, 13*(1), 144–166.

Vlachopoulos, P. (2008). *Reconceptualising e-moderation in asynchronous online discussions* (Unpublished doctoral dissertation). Scotland: University of Aberdeen.

Williams, P., & Sekret, I. (2018). Implementation of social media for enhancing learning interactivity in formal education. *Pedagogical Advances in Technology-Mediated Education, 1*(1), 68–83. Retrieved from http://www.patme-iatels.com/index.php/patme/article/view/15.

Yukselturk, E., & Curaoglu, O. (2010). Blended assessment methods in online educational programs in Turkey: Issues and strategies. In S. Mukerji & P. Tripathi (Eds.), *Cases on transnational learning and technologically enabled environments.* https://doi.org/10.4018/978-1-61520-749-7.ch018.

Chapter 11
E-learning Competencies for University and College Staff

Magdalena Roszak, Iwona Mokwa-Tarnowska, and Barbara Kołodziejczak

11.1 Introduction

An interest in enhancing education with online technologies has grown considerably over the last decades (Jump 2011; Kirkwood and Price 2013; Walker et al. 2012). With the emergence of new, more interactive web-based systems, behaviourist ideas, which have substantially affected a face-to-face classroom and virtual learning environments, are being slowly replaced with other paradigms which seem to engage students more effectively in the learning experience. There is a gradual move towards constructivism (Koohang et al. 2009), constructionism (Papert and Harel 1991) and connectivism (Siemens 2005), which can be seen in the affordances of LMS tools and the approach to the instructional design of various new online courses, e.g. MOOCs provided by the UK's Open University (Freitas et al. 2015; Mokwa-Tarnowska 2015b).

The focus on the collaborative nature of knowledge development and the availability of multilayered interactions between and among tutors, course participants, course content as well as course structure allow designing resources and activities which shift control to students and provide them with additional learning opportunities, increasing their engagement (Mokwa-Tarnowska 2015a). New environments structured around learner-centred pedagogies and Web 2.0 technology provide a

---

M. Roszak (✉) · B. Kołodziejczak
Poznan University of Medical Sciences, Poznań, Poland
e-mail: mmr@ump.edu.pl; bkolodziejczak@ump.edu.pl

I. Mokwa-Tarnowska
Gdańsk University of Technology, Gdańsk, Poland
e-mail: imtarn@pg.edu.pl

variety of methods and tools to build mental models in a more effective way than traditional, face-to-face classrooms (Seppälä and Yajima 2017). However, the synergy that can be gained from any use of web-based education can only be attained by staff who are equipped with an appropriate level of knowledge and understanding, as well as pedagogical and ICT skills to supervise the learning process in such an environment.

The chapter aims to show how post-secondary school teachers and academics who are either involved in e-learning or are interested in adding an online component to the curricula of their courses perceive web-enhanced classes and e-learning. Moreover, it tends to analyse whether they can engage their students in an active and collaborative development of knowledge and skills through the use of online tools. The competencies necessary for staff to develop an effective online programme are of utmost importance, and they are also addressed.

The comparative research targeted the staff of Poznan University of Medical Sciences (PUMS), Gdansk University of Technology (GUT) and West College Scotland (WCS) to assess how staff with a varied level of ICT skills, ranging from advanced to basic, are able and willing to work in an online environment. The presented hypotheses are supported by survey results and discussions with the staff. The data were collected from June 2017 to May 2018. The research on teachers and academics competencies required to provide quality online education is in its initial stage. However, its findings have clearly identified a range of areas that must be targeted to make online education a successful endeavour.

11.2 Online Developers' and Tutors' Competencies

11.2.1 Initial Criteria

Online learning requires its participants, course suppliers, instructional designers, online pedagogy specialists and learners (Kołodziejczak and Roszak 2017), to meet certain initial criteria, i.e. to have the competencies necessary to perform their specialised tasks (Morze and Kuzminska 2017; Roszak and Kołodziejczak 2017). This means that every online course developer and tutor must now be able to handle multimedia and interactive components as the majority of web-enhanced materials contain multi-format resources and activities. The areas of special expertise include learning group management, content development, knowledge and skills evaluation, one-to-one and one-to-many communication, support structures and ways to motivate students to work effectively (Mokwa-Tarnowska 2017a, b, Noskova et al. 2017; Roszak et al. 2016). Thus, well-trained staff should possess varied pedagogical and ICT competencies, which, depending on the fields educational institutions specialise in, are often neglected and marginalized.

11.2.2 ICT Competencies

There are a number of ICT competencies which developers of attractive and engaging educational materials should have. They need to be familiar with a broad and continuously expanding set of technologies for streamlining software developers' work and machine communication, as well as for content creation, collaborative work and group management. Technological advances are so broad, rapid and dynamic that educators have to continuously reflect on their teaching in a technology-based environment and their own development in order to identify areas for growth and improvement (Bromer 2017).

11.2.3 Online Publication

To start with, to be able to create effective resources, they should understand the methods of online publication such as embedding in an HTML, inserting a video file as an integral part of an HTML5 file and streaming – playing up-to-date information downloaded through the network to buffer the recipient's computer. What is more, the proper selection of the most appropriate graphics and multimedia tools also requires from online specialists to possess specialised knowledge and considerable experience. Finally, the knowledge of affordances of Internet tools helps prepare various activities that stimulate students to engage in the learning process (Becker et al. 2017; O'Callaghan et al. 2017).

11.2.4 Modifications

Moreover, electronic resources prepared for online classes may and should be modified during the course. Changes in the infrastructure (e.g. purchases of software, literature, hardware) are likely to affect the course content. So if any modifications have to be made, they have to be introduced within a very short time period, and students should be immediately notified about the latest additions and new options available. Thus, being professionally equipped with versatile knowledge about modern technologies and their functionalities, e-learning specialists do not have to use third-party suppliers to assist them in updating and upgrading the learning content.

11.2.5 Community of Learners

In addition, creating a community of learners is very important in e-learning. Course participants can be members of more than one group (at their own faculty or elsewhere), and tutors can teach more than one subject (including interfaculty courses).

Some LMSs allow grouping participants and establishing learning areas (Kołodziejczak et al. 2014). Therefore the tutor's ability to use advanced setting options will result in collaborative opportunities for their students, which result in them being able to develop also a wide variety of soft skills, ranging from communicative, critical thinking to time management and leadership.

11.2.6 Assessment

The assessment of the students' knowledge and skills made during tests and exams and on the basis of their overall performance when preparing projects or performing online tasks requires a significant amount of time and organisation from the tutor (Tobin et al. 2015). If they are trained to effectively use the virtual learning environment that they have chosen for their courses, the available advanced functionalities will allow:

- Preparing a vast number of multiple choice, true/false, matching, short answer, fill-in-the blank and computational questions
- Generating a set of random questions from the course bank
- Organizing and supervising the examination process
- Evaluating hundreds of written works sent to electronic mailboxes or other storage media
- Distributing the results and storing them in the LMS or the faculty data banks

11.2.7 Pedagogical Skills

There are also numerous pedagogical skills that an online tutor should have. Involving course participants in the learning process which takes place in a virtual classroom, i.e. increasing their willingness to actively participate in various course activities as well as motivating them to learn on their own or in a group at a steady pace, is the responsibility of an online tutor. If the learning design of a course with an e-learning component or of a web-enhanced course does not include pre-emptive or responsive tutor support structures, the learning outcomes may not be as assumed during the preliminary development phase (Allen 2016; Kołodziejczak et al. 2015; Krajka 2012). A move from an instructivist online classroom towards a constructivist one which has also activities designed according to constructionist and connectivist principles, that is, towards a more engaging, student-centred educational environment, can only be made by experienced educators who specialise in online pedagogy.

11.2.8 ICT Competencies and Pedagogical Skills

Designing a learning environment which is les instructive in nature is not an easy task. It requires from an educator to acquire a deeper understanding of other pedagogies and the ways of their application to online education. Even the best resources and activities from a technical point of view, prepared by highly qualified ITC specialists who can apply innovative solutions and use modern, state-of-the-art technologies, are likely to be ineffective and cause a number of problems if the pedagogical aspects of instructional materials and course design are not taken into consideration. A lack of pedagogical preparation has been identified as a problem among online course developers with an IT background, and it may contribute to a high drop-out rate and lead to the attendants not meeting the course aims or objectives or both (Mokwa-Tarnowska 2013). On the other hand, the lack of expertise in ICT on the part of course developers may lead to users developing a negative attitude towards e-learning. Thus, instructional designers who specialise in innovative pedagogies, and who do not possess advanced technical skills, should be supported by ITC specialists who are able to develop a well-functioning environment and tailor it to the pedagogical paradigm that will meet the learners' needs (Ren-Kurc et al. 2012:203–207). Therefore a great emphasis should be placed on the continuous improvement of developers' and tutors' qualifications in teaching methods and technologies most effective in e-learning, blended learning and web-enhanced learning (Kołodziejczak and Roszak 2017).

11.2.9 Continuous Training

This means that training courses for university staff should target various fields of expertise, helping their attendees to upgrade their skills and develop professionally to be able to address growing and changing demands. A range of training routes, for advanced professionals, intermediate users and inexperienced staff willing to become online tutors, must emphasise practical training in education, technology and innovation. A vast majority of academic and college staff in Poland and other countries have not yet had the opportunity to participate in any e-learning courses. Thus, for highly qualified experts who deliver classroom-based lectures, tutorials or workshops, it would be a valuable experience to immerse in any educational programmes offered in an online environment (Roszak and Kołodziejczak 2017). By doing it, they could gain hands-on experience and appropriate skills necessary to successfully engage in e-learning as developers and supervisors. Supported by a thorough introduction to established educational theory and thinking and exposed to new solutions and ideas, they will be able to create materials tailored to their students' needs, monitor their progress and stimulate them to learn actively (Mokwa-Tarnowska 2017a). Training programmes run by experienced educators, and ITC specialists can also help e-learning staff become self-directed learners who will be willing to continuously upgrade their skills and knowledge.

11.3 Online Teaching at Poznan University of Medical Sciences, Gdańsk University of Technology and West College Scotland

Poznan University of Medical Sciences (PUMS, Poland) is a leading medical university, and with just under 1500 academics, it is currently recognized as the largest educational, research and clinical centre in Poland. The university's total student enrolment is 7000 students, including nearly 1000 international undergraduates (Centre for Medical Education in English). Following a 1-year project, in February 2010, the Department of Pathophysiology and the Department of Computer Science and Statistics made available an exam platform to deliver online tests in pathophysiology. PUMS's Centre of Innovative Teaching Methods, established in 2011, supports the use of technology for the enhancement of student learning. It assists the four faculties in designing and delivering e-assessment, analysing its results and maintaining the exam standards across the university. In 2014 the Department of Pathophysiology was the first university unit to introduce web-enhanced learning. The department's LMS called ESTUDENT is used for the administration and delivery of multimedia educational materials, as well as student-student and student-tutor communication. It supports learner autonomy and personalisation and provides a new learning experience through interactive digital technologies. Its Medical E-education Lab coordinates all e-learning activities in the pathophysiology area and offers training sessions for all staff involved in online teaching. Since the academic year 2017–2018, 11 staff of the Department of Pathophysiology have been running a number of online lectures and seminars for over 800 students.

Gdańsk University of Technology (GUT, Poland) has a domestic and worldwide reputation of being a significant scientific centre. Its nine faculties give opportunities to create a superior climate for intellectual and personal growth. They provide education for more than 25,000 students offering undergraduate, postgraduate and doctoral courses. The total number of academics amounts to approximately 1200. Lectures, seminars and laboratory workshops that run in a traditional face-to-face environment are a dominant form of teaching, online assignments and courses being a marginal percentage of the workload assigned to the students. Whichever educational paths GUT students are offered depends on the faculty board and the directors of the supportive centres in the case of language, mathematics and physical education, as well as on individual academics. There are no full-time courses run online, and only some include online modules or are enhanced by web-based materials. The latter category could be assumed to be the major field of e-learning activity at GUT. The statistics are difficult to obtain because it is not necessary for the academics to report the exact composition of their courses to the authorities. The syllabus must include a division into traditional and online learning only if the course is provided in a blended format – and such types are infrequently delivered at GUT.

Created on 1 August 2013 by the merger of Clydebank College, Reid Kerr College in Paisley and James Watt College in Greenock, West College Scotland (WCS, United Kingdom) is a further education institution with 30,000 students and

1200 staff, which makes it one of the liveliest educational institutions in Scotland. It offers a wide variety of undergraduate programmes and vocational training, full-time, part-time, evening and distance learning, designed to satisfy varied needs of different-age students and job seekers, including those wanting a career change. The college promotes distance learning and extends course offer by adding web-based components developed by its experienced and devoted staff from the technology and innovation unit. So far some online courses have also been taught, including an optional course on Health and Safety at Work Regulations and compulsory introductory courses such as Copyright Law, Online Searching, Study Skills and Touch Typing Tutor. It is worth adding that Microsoft has accepted West College Scotland as a Microsoft Showcase School.

11.3.1 Research Methods

The qualitative and quantitative research into the nature of web-enhanced classes and blended courses at various educational institutions is in its initial stage. Upon completion the research findings will be published and available to the academic community. Generally, it targets impact on an increase in student competencies, quality of online teaching and learning (Półjanowicz et al. 2014), the tutor's role in a versatile educational environment and an interest in a move towards e-learning and incorporating more Internet technologies into education. Students' and teachers' opinions shown in comments presented in class and outside it, as well as open-ended questions in surveys will help to uncover trends to be further tested using quantitative research, which has just been initiated (Roszak et al. 2018). Two basic tools have been used so far to produce a qualitative analysis: direct observation and group discussions. The quantitative research whose results are presented in this paper involved surveys carried out in June and July 2017 and May 2018. The research questions were as follows:

- How do teachers and academics perceive e-learning and web-based education?
- How do teachers and academics assess their readiness for teaching in online environments?
- Do faculty and college staff understand the difference between teaching in a traditional and online environment?

It can be assumed that the composition of the study group (Table 11.1) is quite homogeneous with respect to many factors: intellectual capacity, interest in innova-

Table 11.1 Respondent distribution by institution

Institution	Count	Cumulative count	Procent	Cumulative procent
PUMS	75	75	60.5	60.5
GUT	44	119	35.5	96.0
WCS	5	124	4.0	100.0

Source: Own work

tive learning and quality teaching and teaching experience. The respondents' ICT skills necessary to develop online materials differ substantially and depend on their qualifications. At Gdańsk University of Technology, 18 respondents are ESP teachers, and 26 academics are science and engineering degree holders. Poznan University of Medical Sciences respondents consist of professors, assistant professors, senior lecturers and assistants, all of them are academic teachers and none of them are clinicians. West College Scotland staff are teachers.

11.3.2 Statistical Analysis

The data are presented as medians, interquartile ranges (lower quartile, upper quartile) and minimum and maximum values or percentage, as appropriate. For comparison of the two groups, the Mann-Whitney U test was applied. For comparison of the three groups, the Kruskal-Wallis test and the Dunn's post hoc test were used. The nominal data were analysed with the chi-square test or the Fisher-Freeman-Halton test. All the results were considered significant at $p < 0.05$. Statistical analyses were performed with STATISTICA 12.0 PL (StatSoft Polska, Kraków, Poland) and StatXact 11.0 (Cytel Inc., Cambridge, MA, USA).

11.4 Findings

A two-stage analysis was conducted to clarify the findings. The first one involved a comparison of all the data collected at the three targeted institutions. The second one focussed on a comparative analysis of the opinions expressed by the staff from the two Polish universities – GUT, which offers courses in science, technology and business, and PUMS, whose course curricula are structured around non-technical and non-ICT subjects. The questionnaire included 15 close-ended and 6 open-ended questions. The analysis provided below is based on the answers to nine close-ended questions which can be divided into three categories, labelled as follows:

- Respondents' participation in courses, training programmes and workshops on e-learning as well as respondents' self-evaluation of knowledge and skills in this area (questions 1, 2, 3 and 4) (Table 11.2, Figs. 11.1 and 11.2)
- Development of online educational materials and frequency of their use in post-secondary school education (questions 8, 9 and 11) (Table 11.3, Fig. 11.3)
- Collaborative work in an online environment and assessment of its effectiveness (questions 14 and 15) (Table 11.4)

Substantial differences can be noticed in the answers provided by the PUMS and GUT staff to question 1 ($p < 0.05$, Fig. 11.1), which focussed on completed courses and workshops on e-learning (Table 11.2), whereas there is virtually no difference between the GUT and WCS respondents ($p > 0.05$). The medical university academ-

Table 11.2 Analysis of the first category: questions 1, 2, 3 and 4

No. question		PUMS	GUT	WCS		
Scale: 0–4	[a]CB	n = 75	n = 44	n = 5	p-value	Interpretation
1. Completed courses/ workshops on e-learning	3	[b]Me = 1	Me = 3	Me = 3	0.003	Difference between PUMS and GUT (p = 0.008)
	2			–	0.002	Difference
4. Willingness to attend courses/workshops on e-learning	3	Me = 4	Me = 3	Me = 3	0.145	No difference
	2			–	0.074	
2. Knowledge about how to teach in an e-learning environment	3	Me = 1	Me = 2.5	Me = 1	0.203	No difference
	2			–	0.096	Difference
3. Skills in developing e-learning materials	3	Me = 2	Me = 2	Me = 2	0.972	No difference
	2			–	0.831	

Source: Own work
[a]CB = comparison between educational institutions
[b]Me = median

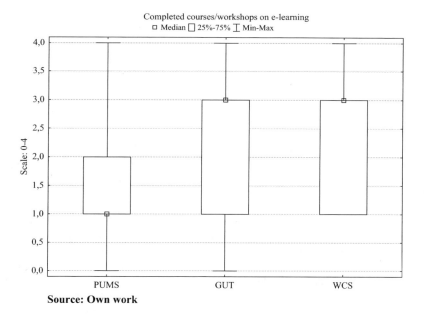

Source: Own work

Fig. 11.1 Respondents' participation in courses, training programmes and workshops on e-learning (question 1). (Source: Own work)

ics rarely participated in training programmes on e-learning (median 1 = no) when compared to the GUT and WCS staff (median 3 = yes, a few). Similar responses are expected from other non-technical higher education institutions which do not provide ICT support or which do not run ICT courses. Universities of science and

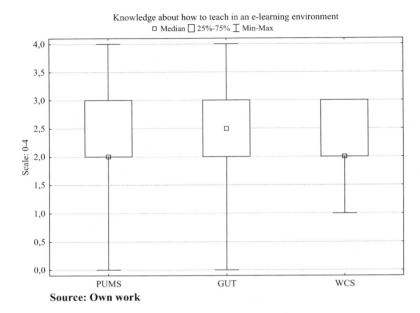

Fig. 11.2 Respondents' self-evaluation of knowledge on e-learning environment (question 2). (Source: Own work)

Table 11.3 Analysis of the second category (questions 8, 9 and 11)

No. question		PUMS	GUT	WCS		
Developing e-learning materials	CB	n = 75	n = 44	n = 5	p-value	Interpretation
8. Have you developed your own e-learning materials?	3	39.2%	79.6%	60%	< 0.001	Difference between PUMS vs GUT (p < 0.001)
YES [%]	2			–	< 0.001	Difference
9. Have you developed your own web-based learning materials for use in class?	3	34.4%	72.7%	25%	< 0.001	Difference between PUMS vs GUT (p < 0.001), GUT vs WCS (p < 0.001)
YES [%]	2			–	< 0.001	Difference
11. Frequency of using e-learning materials	3	Me = 1	Me = 3	Me = 1	< 0.001	Difference between PUMS vs GUT (p < 0.001)
Scale: 0–4	2			–	< 0.001	Difference

Source: Own work

technology are usually better equipped, and their staff are more qualified to deliver training in ICT and online teaching. This results in them being able to support academics and teachers by addressing their ICT needs necessary for e-learning. Other universities assist their employees by establishing e-learning centres or pro-

11 E-learning Competencies for University and College Staff

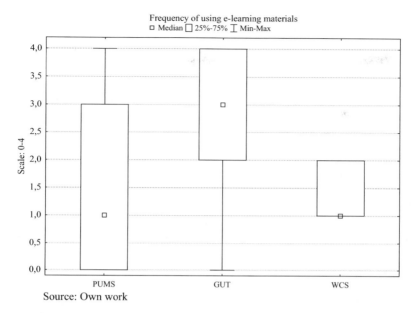

Fig. 11.3 Frequency of using e-learning materials in post-secondary school education (question 11). (Source: Own work)

Table 11.4 Analysis of the third category (questions 14 and 15)

No. question		PUMS	GUT	WCS		
Online collaborative projects	CB	n = 75	n = 44	n = 5	p-value	Interpretation
14. Would you like to supervise online collaborative projects?	3	38.9%*	27.3%*	0%*	0.063	No difference
		54.2%**	50%**	100%**		
YES [%]*, I do not know [%]**	2			–	**0.041**	Difference
15. Do you think that online collaborative projects can be effective? Scale: 0–4	3	Me = 3	Me = 3	Me = 1.5	0.458	No difference
	2			–	0.922	No difference

Source: Own work

vide training through government funding in the form of grants and projects. Commercial workshops are too expensive, so they are rarely offered for academics and teachers. There is no significant difference (p > 0.05) as far as the respondents' willingness to participate in training programmes on e-learning is concerned (Table 11.2, question 4). All the staff would like to improve their knowledge about teaching in an online environment and learn appropriate skills to develop online modules. The median for WCS and GUT is 3 = Probably yes and for PUMS is 4 = Definitely yes.

Assessment of knowledge about how to teach in an e-learning environment shows no significant differences between PUMS and GUT ($p > 0.05$) (Table 11.2: question 2). The technology university staff consider their knowledge in this field to be better than the medical university academics (Fig. 11.2). However, the difference is not substantial because the median for PUMS is 1 = Slightly dissatisfied and for GUT is 2.5 (3 means Moderately satisfied). It must be stressed that the p-value is greater than the significance level but close to 0.05. It seems that the GUT staff should have assessed their knowledge higher than they did in the survey. This shows that the level of understanding how to teach on an online course is still insufficient and needs to be improved through, e.g. workshops. The comparison of the answers (question 2) provided by all the institutions does not show statistically significant differences ($p > 0.05$).

The analysis of the answers to question 3 (on a 0–4 scale), addressing skills needed to develop e-learning materials, does not indicate significant differences between the institutions either ($p > 0.05$, median 2 = Average). It was expected that the technology university staff would regard their competencies as high, and it appears that all the respondents rated them similarly.

The analysis of the data on developing online materials to enhance traditional classes (question 9) and creating stand-alone online modules (question 8) shows significant differences between the three institutions ($p < 0.05$) (Table 11.3). The results are consistent with the findings based on questions 1 and 2 (Table 11.2) and prove that technology and science universities, by their nature, are better prepared to handle e-learning than non-technical ones. The GUT staff that develop their own online materials amount to 70–80%, whereas the percentage of the PUMS academics ranges from 34% to 40%. The structure, content and embedded interactivity of these materials are not known, neither are the tools used to develop them. Further research is going to be carried out into their nature, which may result in reinterpreting the findings.

There is a statistically significant difference ($p < 0.05$) between the answers to question 11 (frequency of using e-learning materials, Fig. 11.3) given by the PUMS and GUT staff, median 1 = Every 2–3 months and median 3 = Every 2–3 weeks, respectively. However, there is no difference between the respondents from PUMS and WCS ($p > 0.05$). This is in line with the answers to questions 8 and 9.

Table 11.4 includes data on the third category (questions 14 and 15), which involves online collaborative work. Taking into account the institutional response, it can be seen that all the three share the same attitude ($p > 0.05$) towards the effectiveness of online projects (question 15). Their staff think that they may be effective (median 3 = Very, 2 = Moderately). The analysis of the responses to question 14 (answer options: Yes, I do not know, No) shows no significant differences between the institutions ($p > 0.05$). However, the p-value is higher than the significance level but close to 0.05. It must be emphasised that a vast number of the respondents chose the I don't know answer (50–100%) when asked to expresses their attitude to engaging students in online collaboration. The comparison of the responses only from the Polish institutions (PUMS and GUT) indicates that the differences between them are significant ($p < 0.05$). The PUMS staff are more willing to supervise online collaborative work than the GUT staff, which is very interesting because online collaborative projects are rarely incorporated into the curricula of medical courses. The PUMS academics see their potential in developing knowledge and skills required from doctors and specialists in health care.

11.4.1 Summary of Results

The research has shown that the surveyed university and college staff see the need to improve their e-learning competencies, including ICT and pedagogical, through attending workshops and courses. Increased knowledge and skills will allow them to meet the requirements of today's students and employers (Roszak et al. 2018). Regardless of the educational institution, the respondents consider their competencies necessary to teach in an e-learning environment to be average. The technology university staff more often participated in training focused on ICT skills, online tools and teaching on an online course. They also developed their own e-learning materials twice as often as the others. A greater experience in creating online modules resulted in them using such resources and activities more regularly. The GUT academics stated that they used online materials at least 2–3 times a month, whereas the PUMS and WCS staff did it once every 2–3 months, which means twice a semester. As was explained in the previous section, university of science and technology employees have more practical experience in the use of ICT. Thus, they have less fear of using new teaching practices in a technology-rich environment. This assumption was verified in this research study. The quality of online modules they had developed was not targeted in the survey, but it is known that quantity has an effect on quality together with knowledge and experience.

The surveyed staff expressed a positive attitude towards online collaborative work, recognising its potential high effectiveness. However, they were reluctant to supervise online group projects in the future. At least half of all the respondents chose the I don't know answer to the question about willingness to be an online tutor assisting students in their collaborative work, which can be attributed to a lack of experience.

11.5 Conclusions and Final Remarks

In order to teach in an e-learning, blended learning or web-enhanced environment, course developers and tutors need to have certain additional competencies based on the nature of the LMS service and the pedagogy around which their teaching is structured. In addition to professional knowledge and organizational skills, which are indispensable for every teacher in a traditional classroom, they must have a number of competencies that merge ITC skills with pedagogical skills and knowledge about legal and ethical issues, e.g. copyright laws, identity verification, and data validity. They are needed to:

- Compile and publish professional materials, including multimedia resources
- Create engaging and effective activities and student-friendly resources to develop various hard and soft skills
- Prepare knowledge assessment, particularly in the form of tests, outcome analysis, stealth learning
- Manage effective student-tutor, tutor-group of students and student-student communication
- Archive learning resources, evaluation results, contents published on the forum

Some developments and activities can be supported by university IT departments or other technology and innovation units, whereas others are the sole responsibilities of online tutors.

The research has shown that there is a great demand for training ranging from online teaching methods, through tools and techniques of creating quality materials, to supervision and group management in an e-learning environment. Many universities and colleges in Poland have not yet introduced uniform regulations concerning funding blended learning and e-learning programmes. Financial support for developing online interactive multimedia resources, which requires a great amount of effort and commitment from authors and tutors, is limited. Pre-emptive and responsive support coming ICT and online pedagogy specialists is insufficient. A lack of knowledge about how to teach online often results in staff perceiving a move towards web-enhanced education as a threat leading to job reduction. University and college authorities sometimes treat e-learning as a possibility to reduce high running costs. Once this belief is eradicated, and various support structures are introduced, universities will not lag behind.

Nowadays students usually treat the Internet as the main source of information and data and knowledge. Thus, if universities and colleges do not equip them with best study opportunities encompassing skills and knowledge development in new technology-enhanced environments, their learning experience will be incomplete, chaotic and devoid of correct reasoning. As the research has shown, teachers are ready for new challenges, but without comprehensive support, they will not be eager to use innovative methods and techniques, and qualitative changes will not be possible.

11.5.1 Final Remarks

Blending and enhancing face-to-face classes with Web 2.0 technologies, as well as converting classroom or instructor-led training to e-learning, can lead to a very successful outcome if the pedagogical approach is based on the principles of constructivism, constructionism and connectivism. These paradigms support learner autonomy and personalisation, community integration and social interactions, cognitive processing strategies, problem-solving through interactive processing of information, peer review and collaborative learning by doing, context-based learning and research- and project-based learning. A carefully structured environment can result in better learning outcomes measured by instruments available through the use of online tools. It is not sufficient to replace some traditional resources and activities that have always taken place in the classroom with their equivalents developed in a new environment, using innovative technologies. An online component for use in class or outside it has to be incorporated into the learning design in a meaningful way so as to enhance and improve the learning experience and achieve a synergistic effect.

References

Adams Becker, S., Cummins, M., Davis, A., Freeman, A., Hall Giesinger, C., & Ananthanarayanan, V. (2017). *NMC horizon report: 2017 higher education edition*. Austin: The New Media Consortium.

Allen, M. (2016). *Guide to e-learning*. Hoboken: Wiley.

Bromer, B. L. (2017). An enhanced role for classroom teachers during student teaching. Effective collaboration within a professional community. In M. D. Crawford & L. D. Hardy (Eds.), *Teacher to teacher mentality. Purposeful practice in teacher education* (pp. 69–83). Lanham: Rowman and Littlefield Publishing Group.

Freitas, S. I., Morgan, J., & Gibson, D. (2015). Will MOOCs transform learning and teaching in higher education? Engagement and course retention in online learning provision. *British Journal of Educational Technology, 46*, 455–471. Retrieved from https://doi.org/10.1111/bjet.12268.

Jump, L. (2011). Why university lecturers enhance their teaching through the use of technology: A systematic review. *Learning, Media and Technology, 36*(1), 55–68. Retrieved from https://doi.org/10.1080/17439884.2010.521509.

Kirkwood, A., & Price, L. (2013). Technology-enhanced learning and teaching in higher education: What is 'enhanced' and how do we know? A critical literature review. *Learning, Media and Technology, 39*(1), 6–36. Retrieved from https://doi.org/10.1080/17439884.2013.770404.

Kołodziejczak, B., & Roszak, M. (2017). ICT competencies for academic e-learning. Preparing students for distance education – authors' proposal. *International Journal of Information and Communication Technologies in Education, 6*(3), 14–25. Retrieved from https://doi.org/10.1515/ijicte-2017-0012.

Kołodziejczak, B., Roszak, M., Ren-Kurc, A., Kowalewski, W., & Bręborowicz, A. (2014). Management of groups in distance education. In E. Smyrnova-Trybulska (Ed.), *E-learning and intercultural competences. Development in different countries* (pp. 423–438). Katowice-Cieszyn: Studio-Noa.

Kołodziejczak, B., Roszak, M., Kowalewski, W., Ren-Kurc, A., & Bręborowicz, A. (2015). Participants academic distance education – case study. *Technics, Technologies, Education, Management, 10*(2), 242–249. e-ISSN 1986-809X.

Koohang, A., Riley, L., & Smith, T. (2009). E-learning and constructivism: From theory to application. *Interdisciplinary Journal of E-Learning and Learning Objects, 5*, 91–109. Retrieved from http://ijello.org/Volume5/IJELLOv5p091-109Koohang655.pdf.

Krajka, J. (2012). *The language teacher in the digital age – towards a systematic approach to digital teacher development*. Lublin: Maria Curie-Skłodowska University Press.

Mokwa-Tarnowska, I. (2013). *Analiza efektów szkoleń z tworzenia kursów oraz materiałów interaktywnych na platformie Moodle* (Analysis of workshops on developing courses and interactive materials on Moodle). Report. Gdansk: Gdansk University of Technology.

Mokwa-Tarnowska, I. (2015a). How to engage students in online learning – web-enhanced and blended ESP classes. In E. Smyrnova-Trybulska (Ed.), *IT tools – good practice of effective use in education* (pp. 81–88). Katowice-Cieszyn: Studio Noa.

Mokwa-Tarnowska, I. (2015b). Motywowanie uczestników MOOC-ów (Motivating MOOC Participants). *Eduakcja, 1*(9), 4–11. ISSN: 2081-8.

Mokwa-Tarnowska, I. (2017a). Higher interest, deeper concentration, more satisfaction – Web 2.0 tools to enhance technical English classes. In M. Sowa, J. Krajka, & P. Lang (Eds.), *Innovations en langues sur objectifs spécifiques: défies actuels et engagements à venir (Innovations in languages for specific purposes: present challenges and future promises)* (pp. 156–167). Frankfurt am Mein: Peter Lang Edition.

Mokwa-Tarnowska, I. (2017b). *E-learning i blended learning w nauczaniu akademickim: Zagadnienia metodyczne (E-learning and blended learning in academic education: Teaching aspects).* Gdansk: GUT Publishing House.

Morze, N., & Kuzminska, O. (2017). Blended learning in practice of e-learning managers training. In M. Hrubý (Ed.), *Proceedings (selected papers) of distance learning, simulation and communication 2017* (pp. 121–126). Brno: University of Defence.

Noskova, T., Pavlova, O., & Yakovleva, T. (2017). Electronic communication in education: A study of new opportunities. In M. Hrubý (Ed.), *Proceedings (selected papers) of distance learning, simulation and communication 2017* (pp. 127–135). Brno: University of Defence.

O'Callaghan, F. V., Neumann, D. L., Jones, L., & Creed, P. A. (2017). The use of lecture recordings in higher education: A review of institutional, student, and lecturer issues. *Education and Information Technologies, 22*(1), 399–415. Retrieved from https://doi.org/10.1007/s10639-015-9451-z.

Papert, P., & Harel, I. (1991). *Situating constructionism.* Retrieved from http://www.papert.org/articles/SituatingConstructionism.html

Półjanowicz, W., Roszak, M., Kołodziejczak, B., & Bręborowicz, A. (2014). An analysis of the effectiveness and quality of e-learning in medical education. In E. Smyrnova-Trybulska (Ed.), *E-learning and intercultural competences development in different countries* (pp. 177–196). Katowice-Cieszyn: Studio-Noa.

Ren-Kurc, A., Kowalewski, W., Roszak, M., & Kołodziejczak, B. (2012). Building digital content for E-learning. Information and communication technologies (ICT) competence. In E. Smyrnova-Trybulska (Ed.), *E-learning for societal needs* (pp. 201–212). Katowice-Cieszyn: Studio-Noa.

Roszak, M., & Kołodziejczak, B. (2017). Teachers' skills and ICT competencies in blended learning. In E. Smyrnova-Trybulska (Ed.), *Effective development of teachers' skills in the area of ICT and E-learning* (pp. 91–103). Katowice-Cieszyn: Studio-Noa.

Roszak, M., Kołodziejczak, B., Kowalewski, W., & Ren-Kurc, A. (2016). Implementation of e-learning portal for academic education and lifelong learning. *International Journal of Continuing Engineering Education and Life-Long Learning, 26*(2), 135–152. Retrieved from https://doi.org/10.1504/IJCEELL.2016.076011.

Roszak, M., Mokwa-Tarnowska, I., & Kołodziejczak, B. (2018). Smarter education - preparing a new generation of university and college teachers. In E. Smyrnova-Trybulska (Ed.), E-learning and smart learning environment for the preparation of new generation specialists (pp. 97–112). Katowice-Cieszyn: Studio-Noa.

Seppälä, J., & Yajima, K. (2017). *Development of student-centred language learning environment.* Paper presented at the 9th International Conference on Information Technology and Electrical Engineering (ICITEE), Phuket, Thailand, 12–13 Oct 2017. Retrieved from https://doi.org/10.1109/ICITEED.2017.8250433

Siemens, G. (2005, April 5). *Connectivism: A learning theory for the digital age.* Retrieved from http://www.elearnspace.org/Articles/connectivism.htm

Tobin, T., Mandernach, B. J., & Taylor, A. H. (2015). *Evaluating online teaching: Implementing best practices.* San Francisco: Jossey-Bass.

Walker, R., Voce, J., & Ahmed, J. (2012). *2012 survey of technology enhanced learning for higher education in the UK.* Oxford: Universities and Colleges Information Systems Association. Retrieved from http://www.ucisa.ac.uk/~/media/groups/ssg/surveys/TEL_survey_2012_with%20Apps_final.

Chapter 12
Approaches to the Development of the ICT Competence Standard in the System of Research-Based Training for the Future Specialist of Social Sphere in Ukraine

Roman O. Pavliuk and Tetiana L. Liakh

12.1 Introduction

Nowadays, the final problem of the newest educational environment in Ukraine is the transition to a new system with an understanding of the transformational processes taking place in the political, economic, educational, scientific, and technical fields. This problem in the system of higher education in Ukraine arises, first of all, through a series of reforms and globalization processes, which, undoubtedly, affect the domination and thinking of the individual.

Reforms in the system of higher education (Law on Higher Education in 2014) and in the scientific and technical sector (Law on Scientific and Scientific and Technical Activities of 2015) provide ample opportunities for the training of highly skilled specialists and clearly regulate the educational and scientific policies of modern universities and research institutions. The changes announced in these laws include the training of specialists in the system of higher education and lifelong education, primarily through research techniques, i.e., research-based education/learning, and active use of IC technologies and tools in educational and professional activities. In particular, these reforms relate to the training of modern specialists in the social sphere, since their activities are directly related to work in a society with different categories of clients, constant monitoring of social transformations, research of basic needs, analysis of social challenges, changes and peculiarities of personality life in society, etc.

In addition to internal state education reforms, the world's trends in updating the educational environment are influenced by the professional training of specialists, in particular the social sphere. So, at the World Economic Forum (Switzerland, Davos, 2016), the experts presented key skills to be mastered by a successful

---

R. O. Pavliuk · T. L. Liakh (✉)
Institute of Human Sciences, Borys Grinchenko Kyiv University, Kiev, Ukraine
e-mail: r.pavliuk@kubg.edu.ua; t.liakh@kubg.edu.ua

specialist in 2020: integrated problem-solving, critical thinking, creativity, human management, coordination with others, emotional intelligence, judgment making and decision-making, service orientation, interaction, negotiation, and cognitive flexibility (10 key skills by 2020). These skills of a new specialist in modern society are organically formed into the structure of a new educational strategy of higher educational institutions of Ukraine related to the active use of IC technologies. However, not all Ukrainian universities are ready to start upgrading their education strategy and developing the ICT competencies of a modern specialist. This is primarily due to many factors: logistics, motivation of administration and faculty, understanding of the need to reform the education system as a whole, taking into account new social challenges, and taking into account the rapid pace of globalization of all social processes.

The ways of using ICT depend on the subject being taught, the learning objectives, and the particularities of the students. However, it is still important to formulate the basic principles of the use of ICT in education, and this is the task of the UNESCO project "Structure of ICT Competence of Teachers." This project draws attention to the many ways in which ICTs can transform education. Information and communication technologies enable the emergence of rapidly developing educational environments, erode the boundaries between formal and informal education, and encourage teachers to develop new ways of transferring knowledge and learning of students. In the end, these technologies require educators to rethink the complex of skills and competences that students need in order to become active citizens and employees and full-fledged members of the knowledge society (Structure of ICT Competence of Teachers 2011).

The UNESCO "Structure of ICT Competence of Teachers" project can be fundamental to specialists from other fields and can serve as a basis for the development of the ICT standard for the training of specialists from different fields, including the social sphere.

The Structure of ICT Skills for Teachers is part of a series of initiatives by the United Nations and its specialized agencies (in particular UNESCO) to promote education reform and sustainable economic development. Goals of initiatives Millennium Development Goals (MDG), Education for All (EFA), UN Literacy Decade (UNLD), and Decade of Education for Sustainable Development (DESD) are to reduce poverty, improve health, and improve quality of life, and education in these initiatives is seen as an important tool for achieving these goals.

At the same time, the modern system of higher education is in the process of updating and restructuring to the best European and world standards. First of all, this is connected with the preparation of a highly skilled specialist who can present himself well to the world and European labor market. The national policy of restructuring the higher education system is also connected with ensuring the participation of Ukrainian universities in joint research programs with European universities. It is no secret that the current state of scientific research in Ukraine is not fully consistent with the world due to the lack of proper academic integrity of the academic community, compliance with European and world trends, low level of interdisciplinary, etc.

Modern universities need to go through a simple way to ensure compliance with European and international standards and the main traditions of Ukrainian education and the deep study of European experience in order to strengthen the practices of the higher educational system.

Another urgent issue for Ukraine today is the provision of an individual trajectory for development and access to all social phenomena of people with special needs and the development of an inclusive environment. Accordingly, there is an urgent problem of training a specialist in the social sphere, which can provide people with special needs and people who are in a difficult life circumstances, full development and participation in public life on an equal footing with others.

Today in Ukraine, social workers, social educators, special teachers (speech therapists, defectologists), and psychologists (practical psychologists) belong to specialists of social sphere. The key person in this list is a social worker, since it provides a link between a person with special needs and people who are in difficult living conditions (DLC) with specialists from other social spheres. However, we tend to use the general term, a social sphere specialist, since each of them must have the basic knowledge and competencies to help people with special needs and people with DLC. In addition, in all European countries, the term "specialist in the social sphere" is used mainly in the competence of which we all have the above. Therefore, the question arises on the analysis of the best European practices of training a specialist in the social sphere for their implementation of the practice of Ukrainian universities.

The peculiarity of the activity of a specialist in the social sphere is not only his participation in providing equal conditions and support for people with special needs and people with DLC but also the ability to conduct various types of research. We mean monitoring and evaluation of social needs and requests, attraction of different capital of foreign funds into the social sphere, which cannot take place without a justified project or grant application, etc. That is, the current issue is the preparation of a future specialist in the social sphere on a research basis in accordance with the best European practices.

12.2 Structure of Training of a Specialist in the Social Sphere in the System of Higher Education of Ukraine

The system of training specialists in the social sphere is quite a new challenge for modern Ukrainian science, but now there are studies that either reflects different aspects of the problem under study. The question of substantiation and the importance of reorienting the domestic system of the world to the best European samples were reflected in the studies of N. Ascheniuk, G. Yelnikova, O. Zubchenko, N. Kosharna, L. Kuzminska, O. Norkhina, M. Leschenko, Yu. Palkevich, L. Petrenko, V. Svystun, and others; the renovation of the system of higher national education, in particular the elements of the implementation of research-based training, is devoted to the works of T. Zhyzhko, L. Pukhovska, V. Proshkin, O. Slyusarenko, and many others; a comparative analysis of foreign educational systems and the practice of their application in Ukraine is highlighted in the works of N. Bidyuk, O. Lokshina, R. Rhodes, C. Torres, O. Romanovsky, and O. Sukhomlynska; and the study of the system of training a specialist in social sphere abroad is devoted to the works of O. Bezpalko, T. Veretenko, S. Dugan, I. Kovchyn, V. Kozubovsky, N. Lavrinenko, T. Lyakh, V. Polischuk, O. Prishlyak, P. Reder, and others.

At the same time, the concept of research-based training acquired its systematic justification in the works of such foreign researchers: P. Hanus, E. C. Lageman, J. Dewey, J. McKinney, J. Green, G. Baldwin, P. Blackmore, M. Fraser, J. W. Thomas, and others.

Although in foreign research, studies on research-based training have their methodological foundations, implementation practices, and positive experimental results, in Ukraine it is considered as a component of the research work of university students. Some aspects of studying on a research basis as a component of research work can be observed in the study of models of preparation of teachers of higher education in the conditions of the master's degree (N. Batechko, T. Fedirchik); designing of systems of open education (S. Priima) and systems of research of students (bachelor/magistracy) (L. Suschenko, N. Bondarenko); and development of student's scientific activity as a component of professional training (I. Lutsenko, V. Proshkin).

Research of Ukrainian scientists L. Sultanova, O. Egorova, M. Kniazian, Ye. Kulyk, G. Klovak, A. Rogozin, A. Yanovski, V. Kuleshova, N. Moskaluk, M. Samoilova, O. Milash, O. Bilostotskaya, S. Launa, and V. Tusheva one or the other way outline the research component and educational work in the process of training specialists in the system of higher education.

In Ukraine, training of specialists in the social sphere (social workers, social pedagogues) is carried out in the system of continuous professional education. Such a system includes the following structural components: preprofessional training (which includes updating self-knowledge and professional self-determination, preprofessional training and professional selection); multilevel professional training in higher educational establishments (carried out by educational qualification levels junior specialist, bachelor, master); and postgraduate training (which involves upgrading skills, retraining, mastering new specializations, professional development, and self-education) (Veretenko and Denysiuk 2011).

The systematic elements of the continuing professional education of social workers are the requirements and needs of society and clients; values, purpose, content, and technology of social and socio-pedagogical activities; the need to form specialists with readiness to perform professional duties; professional competence; and professionally determined personal qualities. The purpose of professional training of social workers in the conditions of continuous education is to form a professionally competent, competitive, and mobile specialist by creating favorable conditions for informed professional self-determination, professional-personal formation in the system of multilevel professional training, and professional growth at all stages of labor activity.

The activities of specialists in the social sphere are aimed at solving social problems of man and society such as social and psychological conflicts, crisis, and stress situations; emotional and psychological problems; need and poverty; alcoholism and drug addiction; violence and discrimination; ethnic and national problems; crimes and offenses; unemployment and professional adaptation; disability and lonely old age; and housing problems. Social work is not limited to providing assistance to people who need it, but is one of the tools of social control.

The main purpose of professional activity of a specialist in the social sphere is welfare care, the disclosure of the capabilities and abilities of the individual, family, and society to normal social functioning.

The functions of a specialist in the social sphere are a substantive and instrumental basis of his professional activities. Professional functions of a specialist in the social sphere allow us to imagine the structure of functional responsibilities as a certain amount of knowledge and skills that provide the professional competence of specialists in practical work.

The model of practical social work includes three basic elements: a client, a specialist, and a social component of the process of change, which, in turn, includes the social component of the client's field, the specialist of the social sphere, as well as the activity or energy of the subjects of interaction and mutual influence participants of professional interaction in social work (Tymoshenko 2014). Scientists distinguish a set of professional functions that are implemented by specialists in social services in the process of assisting different categories of clients.

Let's dwell on the specifics of professional training of specialists in the social sphere of the levels "bachelor" and "master."

The main feature of bachelor's professional readiness is the ability to solve complex specialized problems and practical problems in the field of their own professional activity or in the process of study, which involves the application of certain theories and methods of the corresponding science and is characterized by complexity and uncertainty of the conditions. In the process of training and practical training, students acquire conceptual knowledge (including certain knowledge of the field of modern achievements) and skills in solving complex unpredictable tasks and problems in specialized areas of professional activity and/or training, which involves the collection and interpretation of information (data) selection of methods and tools and application of innovative approaches. The future of social worker tasks is to manage complex projects or actions; it is responsible for decision-making in unpredictable conditions. Regarding the communication component qualification, it should be able to convey to specialist and nonspecialist information, ideas, and proposals to address the problem, based on their knowledge and experience in the profession. Professional types of work requiring a bachelor's qualification, according to the classifier of professions, belong to the section of "specialists."

Currently, in Ukraine, on the basis of many educational institutions, the training of social workers at the educational level "master" is carried out. A specialist who holds a bachelor's degree, if he has discovered a tendency to research and teaching work, may continue his studies at the magistracy. This allows you to achieve a certain degree of completeness of training at each level, helps the specialists of the social sphere to master the new (higher) educational qualification level, promotes professionalism, and expands the range of new opportunities.

From the described characteristics of the activity of a specialist in the social sphere, it follows that the effectiveness of the training of a highly skilled specialist depends to a large extent on the willingness to conduct various kinds of monitoring, that is, conducting social and scientific mini-global studies. Consequently, we can conclude that the effective in this aspect will be the training of a specialist in the educational environment of a modern university on a research basis and with a high standard of ICT competence.

12.3 Characteristics and Attributes of a Research-Based Training System

Leading European and world universities in the middle of the last century have made major reforms on effective integration of research and education including the development of the universities as the main center of the latest research using best research-based training practices.

The system of research-based training has become widely developed in foreign higher educational institutions as a type of active learning (Wildt 2010; Ludwig 2011), which can be implemented through specific forms and has its features and specifications. In addition, research-based training is an unifying concept that covers a range of pedagogical approaches in the process of students' professional training aimed at developing of research skills (formulation and problem-solving) (Aditomo et al. 2013).

Our analysis of foreign researches of research-based training made it possible to isolate its general approaches and concepts of development. Some foreign researchers (Lageman 2002; Dewey 1933) relate the emergence of research-based training with the distinction of pedagogical research from the psychological system. This was preceded by a general scientific study in the system of joint sciences (e.g., the humanities). Such a statement originates from the first half of the twentieth century. In many foreign studies, research-based training is associated with project training – student prepares a graduation work on the basis of a lengthy study on interdisciplinary basis (Abbott and McKinney 2013; Baldwin 2005; Blackmore and Fraser 2007; Thomas 2000, etc.). In addition, it is known from the history of science and education that the views and activities of the German scientist Wilhelm von Humboldt (Humbold 1984) are a classic and the first example of the introduction of a research-based learning system. His ideas about the unity of science and education date back to the beginning of the nineteenth century. American scientist John Dewey more than a hundred years ago expresses a similar view – study through action and verification. The current understanding of research-based training has been developed since the 1970s of the twentieth century (Spoken-Smith and Walker 2010). Due to this, now we have a significant foreign arsenal of researches in the methodology of using of research-based training. Thus, foreign studies have convincingly shown that research-based learning contributes to student-centered learning, aimed at fulfilling of student needs (Justice et al. 2009; Prince and Felder 2006, 2007), and contributes to the implementation of the scientific potential of the teaching staff of a higher educational institution (Healy 2005); research-based training can be realized as a means of understanding of science and as a method of teaching (Spoken-Smith and Walker 2010).

In our research paper, we understand research-based training as a form of learning/training that has its purpose, content, methods, forms of organization, and tools and can be implemented by using a specific set of learning technologies. Confirmation of such an opinion is found in the researches of well-known foreign scientists, whose research were concerned with the methodological basis of research-based training. So, the confirmation that research-based training cannot be a form of organization of training is found in the researches of Prince, M. and Felder, R. (Prince and Felder 2006) and Mills, J. E. and Treagust, D. F. (Mills and Treagust 2003), who argue that research-based learning can be implemented through certain organizational forms: problem-oriented learning, project-oriented learning, and learning based on case techniques/technologies. That is, these forms of organization of teaching contribute to the implementation of research-based training as a type of training. Ifenthaler, D. and Gosper, M. (Ifenthaler and Gosper 2014, p. 74) on the basis of theoretical and empirical research argue that "research-based training is based on a multidisciplinary approach for the application of diverse goals and strategies training for the purpose of interconnected and logical conducting of research and teaching/instruction." Levy, P. and Petrulis, R. (Levy and Petrulis 2012) in many of their writings have repeatedly argued that research-based training embraces a fairly wide range of pedagogical goals. This means that the concept of research-based training is very broad, and according to our deep conviction (and according to research by leading foreign scholars in this field), this is a type of study.

Consequently, according to the results of studies of foreign scientists, we can conclude that research-based learning is a complex of pedagogical goals, which are united with the main tasks in the development of research competence of students (development of skills for setting a research task and finding ways to solve it).

Research-based training is a complex of pedagogical goals which are united with the main tasks in the development of research competence of students (development of skills for setting a research task and finding ways to solve it).

Research-based training as a type of study has the following features:

- A set of student-centered learning and teaching goals that are realized through research.
- Teaching students by setting up specific tasks that involve the interpretation of experimental data, case studies (tasks) for analysis, or a set of real-life situations/problems for solving.
- A set of tasks that contain specific instructions and which promote student-oriented and consulting research (the teacher is a consultant).

- Management of the learning process is done by setting questions and problems/practical tasks.
- Training is based on the search for novelty and its relevance.
- Implication of student-centered learning where the teacher is a facilitator.

Learning objectives of research-based training are:

- Formation of knowledge about science as a holistic and integrated education
- Development of skills for determining the novelty and relevance of the research (through conducting own research and verification of its evidence)

Teaching methods of research-based training are:

- Search/research activities aimed at solving self-identified issues/problems in an unexplored/underdeveloped field
- Search for new knowledge, solving a research problem set by a teacher
- Situational analysis of research results through verification of their evidence using their methodology

Key research-based training elements are the research questions and problem situations that require their pilot testing.

The main subtypes of research-based training are:

- Problem-oriented learning (focused on the process of solving the problem/in the process of research, the main goal is the definition of new, unexplored)
- Project-oriented training (focused on product development; the main goal is to determine the practical use of research results)
- Evidence-based training (can be verified practically)

Forms of study of research-based training are:

- Content-oriented learning (studying the general methodology of science)
- Practically oriented training (participating in short-term or fundamental academic studies)
- Applied research (aimed at solving practical problems or providing practical recommendations)
- Academic comprehensive research
- Simplified research (research by model, algorithm, or methodology developed by others)
- Research on the basis of literature analysis (theoretical research, development)
- Discussion on a specific scientific topic (with the selection of unexplored aspects and when the result is a new knowledge)

Main types of tasks and forms of work of research-based training are case studies, project tasks, problem-search tasks, brainstorming, focus group, polls (surveys, interviews, etc.), press conference, discussion, and presentation (research results).

The role of students in research-based training is characterized as active participants in the research process (producing ideas, determining relevance, engaging in research, developing methodologies, empirical studies, etc.).

12.4 Components of the ICT Competence Standard of the Future Specialist in the Social Sphere

To develop the standard/structure of the ICT competence of the future specialist in the social sphere, we have taken the fundamental principles of the UNESCO project "Structure of ICT Competence of Teachers."

Recommended by UNESCO structure is based on the fact that teachers are not sufficiently competent in the field of ICT and can teach these students. Teachers should help students not only learn from the use of ICT but do so creatively and develop cooperation and problem-solving skills in order to become effective citizens and employees in the future. It closely resembles the activities of the future specialist of the social sphere (social teacher, social worker); only the subject of activity here is not a student, but a client, and the subject is not a teacher, a social worker.

The structure provides three different approaches to learning (three consecutive stages of development of a specialist in the social sphere). The first of these is the "technology literacy" approach, in which future social professionals learn to use ICTs for more effective learning. The second one was called "deepening of knowledge" and allows getting deep knowledge of professional disciplines and applying them to solving complex problems of real life. The third approach, "creating knowledge," ensures that students and future specialists acquire the skills to create the new knowledge necessary for building a more harmonious, perfect, and prosperous society.

By transforming the structure of the ICT competence of teachers into the structure of the ICT competence of the future specialist in the social sphere, the main components of it can be presented as follows (see Table 12.1).

This structure is intended to bring the role of ICTs in educational and social reform to the attention of social specialists (now practitioners), as well as to those

Table 12.1 The structure of the ICT competence of the future specialist in the social sphere

	Technology literacy	Deepening of knowledge	Creating knowledge
Understanding the role of ICTs in education and professional activities	Knowledge of educational and social policy	Understanding educational and social policy	Innovation in education and social policy
Curriculum and evaluation	Basic competencies	Application of competencies	Competence of the knowledge society
Educational and research activities	The use of technology	Use of complex tasks	Self-education
IT	Basic toolkit	Sophisticated toolkit	New technologies
Certification training	Literacy in digital technologies	Management and direction	Specialist in social affairs as a model for imitation

Source: Based on the author's design

who develop educational policy and work in the social, educational, and qualification systems.

The strategic goal of the "technology literacy" approach is the ability of future professionals in the social sphere, citizens and employees, to use ICTs to support social development and increase the efficiency of the economy. Other strategic goals are related to it: raising the level of employment, providing all citizens with access to high-quality resources, and raising the level of literacy and skills. Social professionals need to be aware of these goals and be able to relate them to the relevant components of educational reform programs. Such an approach leads to changes in the curriculum, which should include measures for the improvement and extension of skills that are common technological literacy, and the development of ICT skills in the relevant learning context (Structure of ICT Competence of Teachers 2011).

In the early stages of the approach, "technology literacy" relevant to competence of future specialists provides basic social skills in the civil use of digital technologies and the ability to choose and use prepared educational software, games, training educational software, and web content in computer classes or restricted computer tools of the usual class in order to achieve the objectives of the standard program, the introduction of evaluation strategies, and the implementation of modular plans and methods of training. Also, future social professionals should be able to apply ICTs to manage the data of educational activities and social activities and improve their qualifications.

The purpose of the "deepening of knowledge" approach is to develop the ability of future professionals in the social sphere, clients and employees, to contribute to the development of society and the economy, through the application of knowledge gained during the study of specialized subjects while performing complex high-priority tasks that arise in real life, work, and public relations. Such tasks can be related to the environment, health, and conflict resolution. Under this approach, future social professionals should be aware of their strategic goals and social priorities and be able to identify, develop, and use special educational and social measures to achieve their goals and priorities. Often, such an approach requires the inclusion of a change in the curriculum that reflects the priority of comprehension before the material reach and an appropriate assessment strategy that focuses on understanding the real-life objectives. During the assessment, the analysis of the ability of future social professionals to solve complex problems is carried out, and evaluation procedures are implemented as part of the educational process. The pedagogical techniques associated with this approach include training in collaboration based on the accomplishment of the tasks and projects implemented; students deeply explore the subject and apply their knowledge to find answers to complex daily issues and solve problems (Structure of ICT Competence of Teachers 2011).

The goal of the "creating knowledge" approach is to increase productivity by educating students, clients, and employees who are constantly involved in creating knowledge and innovation, using the results of this process, and studying throughout their lives. According to this approach, future social professionals should not only build their own educational process in accordance with the objectives of such a policy but also participate in the development of educational programs aimed at their achievement. An educational program that implements such an approach should go beyond the mere study of specialized disciplines and involve the development of the skills and knowledge of the society necessary for the creation of new knowledge. These include, in particular, the ability to solve problems, interact, collaborate, experiment, critically think, and apply creative approaches. Such skills become the objectives of the curriculum and the objects of new methods of evaluation (Structure of ICT Competence of Teachers 2011).

The creation of this society is facilitated by a variety of network devices, digital resources, and electronic environments that provide technical support for the process of creating knowledge and for continuous and widespread joint learning.

Each of the identified levels of ICT competence of the future specialist in the social sphere has certain knowledge and skills. Let's dwell in more detail on their description (Tables 12.2, 12.3, and 12.4).

Table 12.2 Knowledge and skills inherent in the level of technological literacy

Activity	Knowledge and understanding, skills and abilities, forming judgments
Understanding the role of ICTs in education and professional activities	Awareness of ICT educational documents
	Understanding of the influence of different approaches to informatization of education on participants in the educational process
	The ability to describe the general purpose of informatization of activities in the social sphere
	The ability to describe the general principles of the use of ICTs in their own activities
	The ability to analyze the barriers that arise when using ICT in their own activities
	The ability to understand the legal norms regarding the protection of information resources as intellectual property
	The ability to describe the educational outcomes that will be obtained in the process of ICT education
Curriculum and evaluation	The ability to use IT in educational and professional activities
	To understand the basics of social policy in the field of development of infra-technology
	Understanding of the economic fundamentals of the use of IC technologies in the social sphere
	Observance of the ethical foundations of the use of IC technologies in the social sphere
	Understanding of sociopsychological peculiarities of different groups of clients in the application of infrared technologies
	The ability to manage ICT in the social sphere

(continued)

Table 12.2 (continued)

Activity	Knowledge and understanding, skills and abilities, forming judgments
Educational and research activities	Knowledge of key concepts and processes in their subject area
	Understanding of the impact of ICT on learning and increasing motivation for learning
	Forecasting of expected results of ICT use in educational and research activities
	Observance of legislation and copyright in the application of ICT in educational and research activities
	Knowledge and compliance with copyright protection provisions when publishing or using e-content
	Ability to determine the effectiveness of ICT when achieving educational and professional goals
	The ability to use electronic dictionaries, encyclopedias, manuals, databases, etc.
	Creation of documents with text, graphic, and tabular data for educational activities and work in the field of social services
	Selecting appropriate ICTs to monitor and disseminate information about work with different categories and groups of clients
	The use of various presentation software, video films, animations, and computer models to support the educational process and the effectiveness of working with different categories and groups of clients
	Use of Internet services and resources for educational and research activity
	The use of postal services
	Possession of methodology of sociological research and methods of statistics with the use of IC technologies
	Ability to assess the needs of individuals and families with the use of IC technologies
	Knowledge of the general principles of the operation of repositories, scientific metric databases, electronic libraries, electronic journals and the ability to use them
	Knowledge of the rules and structure of writing articles about the results of their own research and the peculiarities of their presentation at various conferences, publications in domestic and foreign publications, etc.
IT	Basic knowledge of computer equipment and computer networks and their use (the notion of computer hardware and software, understanding of concepts such as data storage and memory, knowledge of what computer networks and their applications, the ability to bring examples of the use of computers in everyday life; knowledge of the safety requirements and factors of possible harmful effects of the computer on human health)
	Knowledge of the general principles of operation of various operating systems and the ability to work on computers running under the control of various operating systems: running a computer to work, working with a reference system

(continued)

12 Approaches to the Development of the ICT Competence Standard in the System... 213

Table 12.2 (continued)

Activity	Knowledge and understanding, skills and abilities, forming judgments
	Knowledge of the general principles of work with Internet services and their ability to use them for communication, cooperation, search, organization of activity, and publication of results of social and scientific activity
	Understanding the basic principles of safe Internet work and data protection
	Ability to use basic operations with folders and files: creation, deletion, copying, editing, renaming, restoring
	The ability to process data in environments: a word processor, a table processor, a card-knowledge
	Ability to work with antivirus programs
Certification training	Ability to implement and plan professional self-development by means of IT
	Understanding the benefits of using ICTs to improve the quality and efficiency of their own educational and research activities
	Knowledge of the possibilities, advantages, and disadvantages of using ICT in the process of raising their own skills
	Use of ICT for communication with clients, external experts, and colleagues from international social, educational, and scientific institutions
	Use of ICT for the search, organization, analysis, integration, and evaluation of information necessary for professional development
	The ability to carry out online qualification upgrading, including through open distance courses

Source: Based on the author's design

Table 12.3 Knowledge and skills inherent in the level of knowledge deepening

Activity	Knowledge and understanding, skills and abilities, forming judgments
Understanding the role of ICTs in education and professional activities	Awareness of the benefits of informatization of education
	Knowledge of innovative (pedagogical, informational, and social) technologies and their ability to apply them in their own educational, research, and professional activities
	Understanding of the influence of modern technologies on the labor market and changing requirements for the level of professional-pedagogical and social readiness of the graduate
	Understanding the notion of nonformal education and the possibilities of its use in self-education and professional activities
	The ability to explain and analyze the principles of using ICT in its own educational and research activities
	The ability to analyze the barriers that arise when using ICTs in their own educational and research activities and the ability to find effective ways to address them
	Participation in group educational and social initiatives at the regional and national levels

(continued)

Table 12.3 (continued)

Activity	Knowledge and understanding, skills and abilities, forming judgments
Curriculum and evaluation	The ability to plan a system for assessing the needs of social groups by means of IC technologies
	The ability to analyze contemporary social policies and the use of ICTs to plan various social initiatives
	Ability to effectively plan the economic component of the use of IC technologies in the social sphere
	The ability to apply ethical bases of work with different groups of clients using the IC technologies in the social sphere
	The ability to apply ICT in the study of psychic phenomena in the process of interaction between people in large and small groups
	Possession of ICT by means of assessment and measurement of individual psychological characteristics of a person and a social environment
Educational and research activities	Knowledge of the methodology of the introduction of innovative social and information technologies, development of social projects on the application of ICT
	Understanding of the individual-personal trajectory of development based on the use of ICT
	Effective and systematic use of ICTs in educational and research activities
	Knowledge of the use of ICT for group work
	The application of methods of interactive social interaction based on the use of ICT
	The use of educational sites for the organization and conduct of social studies
	The ability to analyze and describe social problems (in their own and professional activities) associated with the peculiarities of using ICT
	An analysis of the effectiveness of using ICTs during social research and the implementation of its own educational and research activities
	Awareness of the need for the use of electronic means of scientific communication: repositories, electronic libraries and open access journals, as well as webinars and online conferences
	Presentation of the results of their own scientific activity on the basis of ICT use: publication of articles in repositories, participation in online conferences, publication in professional electronic journals
IT	Using ICT to develop critical thinking, creativity, and ability to solve problems, make decisions, gain knowledge of your industry, collaborate, search for information, and publish the results of your research
	Use of data visualization software

(continued)

Table 12.3 (continued)

Activity	Knowledge and understanding, skills and abilities, forming judgments
	Use of ICT for the creation of teaching materials, educational resources
	Using ICT to work together with colleagues and clients
Certification training	Knowledge of the criteria for evaluating open electronic educational rewards
	Knowledge of ethical norms of communication on the Internet and their observance in electronic communication
	Ability to find and use electronic resources for their own professional development
	Ability to collaborate on the Internet for personal professional development
	The ability to analyze and summarize data on the advantages and disadvantages of working together with ICTs to provide various social services
	Ability to find and design various innovative methods and forms of improving the quality of the results of providing social services to different groups of clients through ICT

Source: Based on the author's design

Table 12.4 Knowledge and skills inherent in the level of knowledge creation

Activity	Knowledge and understanding, skills and abilities, forming judgments
Understanding the role of ICTs in education and professional activities	Knowledge of successful strategies for providing social services to different groups of clients using ICT
	Participation in collective social initiatives to disseminate information on the effectiveness of ICT in providing social services to different groups of clients
	Develop and implement effective strategies for providing social services to different groups of clients using ICT
Curriculum and evaluation	Knowledge of the methodology of skills development of the XXI century based on the use of ICT in the provision of social services to different groups of clients
	Creation of own professional websites and blogs for the purpose of providing social services to different groups of clients
	Social support, provision of social services, and assessment of the needs of different groups of clients through ICT
Educational and research activities	Establishment of communication, creation of social communities and networks
	Description of the experience in a format that allows obtaining information on innovative ideas and ways of changing social practices using ICT
	Activities on designing and designing a community of practitioners to adapt experience and implement it in mass practice

(continued)

Table 12.4 (continued)

Activity	Knowledge and understanding, skills and abilities, forming judgments
	Consulting of subjects of innovative experience, providing them methodical assistance in the technology of social support of different groups of clients
IT	Knowledge of the features of work with services Web 2.0, Web 3.0
	Development and implementation of various social projects using ICT
	Development and implementation of telecommunication social projects
	Presentation of results of social projects, social studies in the form of diagrams and charts
	Creation and constant support of your own blog, wiki pages, personal educational, social and consulting environment
Certification training	Participation in international distance education courses, qualification projects
	Use of the Internet to find professional courses in the socio-pedagogical field
	Participation in international open courses
	Development and implementation of training programs to enhance the use of ICT in the provision of social services to different groups of clients

Source: Based on the author's design

12.5 Characteristics of the Disciplines of Professional Training of a Specialist in the Social Area on the Formation of ICT Competencies and the Application of a System of Training on a Research Basis

In accordance with the curriculum of educational programs Social Work and Social Pedagogy, students study a wide range of disciplines. The training of such specialists at the master's level takes place through educational and professional programs, but this does not mean that such a program excludes the scientific component. Consistent with the topic of the study – the formation of the ICT competence of the modern specialist in the social sphere with the use of a system of research-based training – there are program results of training. We illustrate the competency and program results of training professionals in the social sphere for educational programs Social Work and Social Pedagogy.

The purpose of the educational program Social Work is to provide academic training of highly skilled social work professionals capable of solving complex specialized tasks and practical problems in professional activities that ensure professionalism and competitiveness in the field of social work. To conduct original independent research and to carry out scientific and pedagogical activities focused on further professional self-education.

Objects of study are to ensure the rights, needs, and interests of man as the highest social value; processes of socialization, social adaptation, and integration (reintegration) of the individual; realization of tasks and functions of social protection of the population; project activity in the social sphere; assistance and support for people in difficult living conditions; and provision of social services, etc.

The theoretical content of the subject area is the concepts, laws, and principles that reveal the development of the individual, social group, community, and society as a whole and form the professional competence of a specialist.

A student of higher education should combine the theory and practice of social work on the basis of an interdisciplinary approach and possess innovative methods of professional activity.

The program is a special one aimed at preparing a teacher of a higher educational institution. The emphasis is on knowledge, skills, and abilities in teaching social work disciplines, organizing and conducting research on topical social issues, introducing innovative social technologies, and managing social work. The emphasis is on leadership, teaching, and technology competencies.

The programmatic competencies of specialist training for the educational program Social Work are integral, general, and professional competencies.

Integral Competence:

1. Ability to solve complex special tasks and practical problems in the field of social work
2. Ability to take appropriate analytical and managerial decisions in the field of implementation of state social policy
3. Ability to realize the tasks of state social programs and projects

General Competencies:

- Communicative. Ability to communicate verbally and in writing in the first language. Possession of basic skills of communication in a foreign language
- Information and communication. Ability to choose and implement IC technologies in professional activity
- Self-education. Ability to study and to pursue a career. Ability to apply modern methods and technologies for personal and professional growth
- Prognostic. Ability to predict the strategy of professional activity. Ability to generate new ideas and nonstandard approaches to their implementation (creativity)
- Analytical. Ability to critical thinking, analysis, and synthesis. Ability to conduct scientific and applied research on a professional level
- Managerial. Ability to initiate, plan, and manage changes to improve existing and develop new social systems
- Scientific research. Ability to implement socio-pedagogical and sociopsychological knowledge in the process of setting research tasks in professional activities

- Deontological. Ability to act on the basis of ethical considerations (motives) in accordance with the principles of deontology

Professional Competencies:

- Moral and ethical. Readiness for absolute observance of moral norms and ethical principles in social work
- Organizational and managerial. Ability to determine problem situations and to simulate possible variants of their transformation and to implement social projects in the activities of social institutions
- Professional diagnostic. Ability to assess critical situations and risks that may arise from clients and provide appropriate assistance. Readiness to monitor and evaluate the effectiveness of individual interventions and programs
- Professional-technological. Readiness to develop and implement social technologies taking into account the specifics of the region, time dynamics, and the peculiarities of the situation
- Social and human rights. Ability to protect, assist, and support the rights and interests of various social groups. Ability to legal protection and representation of clients' social interests
- Professional and teaching staff. Ability to use in its cognitive activity modern pedagogical technologies and techniques. Knowledge about the essence and specificity of teaching activity and about methods of work in the modern pedagogical environment
- Understanding the foundations of social policy. Understanding of social problems, social structure, and processes at the level of society and community. Ability to use knowledge in the field of social policy, relevant social problems, and approaches in the organization of providing assistance to recipients of services
- Understanding the economic foundations of social work. Ability to organize economic activity of social institutions and carry out economic and financial analysis of the activities of social institutions
- Owning a method of sociological research and statistical methods. Operation of basic methods and techniques of sociological research, statistical methods; understanding of social priorities, social processes, and social relations
- Understanding the sociopsychological characteristics of different categories of recipients of services. Ability to use a wide range of methods and means of solving social and psychological problems of recipients of services
- Ability to create a health-preserving space. Ability to form healthcare management at recipients of services
- Ability to plan and carry out professional self-development and improvement. Ability to study throughout life, to increase professional competence, and to plan and carry out professional self-development, self-knowledge, self-determination, and self-organization
- Ability to conduct advocacy and mentoring support. Ability to conduct advocacy and mentoring support and to form a supportive client network

- Ability to perform social therapy. Possession of therapeutic general and specific technologies of social therapy (labor therapy, therapy of self-education, art therapy, game therapy, etc.)
- Ability to develop the implementation of innovative forms and methods of social work. Knowledge of innovative forms and methods of social work with different groups of recipients of services. Ability to adapt innovative forms and methods of work to modern realities

Program Learning Outcomes:

Knowledge and Understanding

Understanding of social problems, social structure, and processes at the level of society and community

Knowledge of innovative forms and methods of social work with different groups of recipients of services and the ability to adapt innovative forms and methods of work to modern realities

Application of Knowledge and Understanding

Ability to use knowledge in the field of social policy, relevant social problems, and approaches in the organization of providing assistance to recipients of services

Readiness for the preparation of analytical research work in the field of social policy; understanding of social priorities, social processes, and social relations; the ability to design sociological research, analyze and interpret their results, and use them in practice

Ability to organize economic activity of social institutions and carry out economic and financial analysis of the activities of social institutions

Ability to analyze the nature and content of legislative acts and other normative documents regulating legal relations in various social spheres

Possession of general therapeutic as well as specific technologies of social therapy

Readiness for absolute observance of moral norms and ethical principles in social work

Ability to communicate in a foreign language, readiness to study, and compilation of scientific and professional texts

Ability to implement IC technologies in professional activities. Readiness to conduct distance education and advisory activity, use computer and multimedia technologies and digital educational resources, and do working documentation on electronic media.

Formation of Judgments

Ability to develop, improve, adapt, and optimally use modern technologies of social work with different categories of recipients of services

Ability to conduct management in the social sphere

Ability to mediation and facilitation of conflict situations of recipients of services

Ability to carry out social expertise and to prepare recommendations for making managerial decisions and social designing in conditions where the research task is difficult to formalize

Ability to teach

Ability to find organizational and managerial decisions in nonstandard situations and be responsible for these decisions

Ability to lead and teamwork (Table 12.5)

Certification of graduates of the educational program of the specialty Social Work is carried out in the form of defense of the qualification work of the master's

Table 12.5 Structural-logical scheme of educational program Social Work

First semester	Second semester	Third semester
Formation of general competencies		
Foreign language professional communication, 2 credits	Foreign language professional communication, 2 credits	
ICT in professional activity, 4 credits		
Formation of special (professional) competencies		
Modern strategies for providing social services, 3 credits	Modern strategies for providing social services, 3 credits	
Management of social work in Ukraine, 3 credits	Management of social work in Ukraine, 3 credits	Management of social work in Ukraine, 1 credit
Social work with special groups of recipients of services, 4 credits	Social work with special groups of recipients of services, 4 credits	
Research of actual social problems, 2 credits	Research of actual social problems, 2 credits	
Practice		
Industrial (trainee), 3 credits		
	Industrial (trainee), 7,5 credits	
		Pre-diploma (research), 16,5 credits
Attestation		
	Writing a master's thesis, 6 credits	Master's degree defense, 1,5 credits
Choice of specialization "Social administration in the community"		
Technology of organization and activation of communities, 4 credits		
Social expert examination and public hearings, 4 credits		
	Social administration, 4,5 credits	
	Marketing in social work, 4 credits	
		Industrial practice in specialization, 6 credits
Choose from a catalogue of courses		
8 credits	8,5 credits	6 credits

Source: Based on the author's design

level and ends with the issuance of a state standard document awarding them a master's degree in qualification: "Master of Social Work in Specialization Social Work" or "Master of Social Work in the field of social administration in the community." The certification is carried out openly and publicly.

12.6 Conclusions

According to the strategy of modern Ukrainian higher education – the transition from the knowledge paradigm of education to the practice-oriented – the question of implementation of foreign effective practices of the training of modern competitive specialists arises more and more. In our theoretical scientific and pedagogical research, we are concerned with the preparation of a modern specialist in the social sphere on a research basis, considering that such a system of training is quite effective because of the practice-oriented future professional activity of such a specialist. In addition, all of the above is reinforced by the need to rebuild the modern society of Ukraine and an understanding of the development of an inclusive educational space.

Of course, the development of the standard of ICT competence of the future specialist in the social sphere in Ukraine, especially with the application of a research-based training system, requires the further development of specific tools for evaluating activities. Further development of the research problem is seen in the development of evaluation tools that will help to study the effectiveness of ICT competency formation for the future social science specialist in Ukraine in the process of a specially organized educational process – in a research-based education system.

References

10 key skills by 2020. Available online https://www.eduget.com/news/10_klyuchovix_navichok_do_2020-go-907
Abbott, M. L., & McKinney, J. (2013). *Understanding and applying research design*. Hoboken: Wiley.
Aditomo, A., Goodyear, P., Bliuc, A.-M., & Ellis, R. A. (2013). Inquiry-based learning in higher education: Principal forms, educational objectives, and disciplinary variations. *Studies in Higher Education., 38*, 1239–1258. https://doi.org/10.1080/03075079.2011.616584.
Baldwin, G. (2005). *The teaching research Nexus: How research informs and enhances learning and teaching in the University of Melbourne*. Melbourne: The University of Melbourne. Available online http://www.canterbury.ac.nz/media/documents/forms/TR_Nexus2005.pdf
Blackmore, P., & Fraser, M. (2007). Researching and teaching: Making the link. In P. Blackmore & R. Blackwell (Eds.). *Towards strategic staff development in higher education*. Maidenhead: McGraw-Hill International.
Dewey, J. (1933). *How we think: A restatement of the relation of reflective thinking to the educative process*. Boston: D.C. Heath.

Healy, M. (2005). Linking research and learning to benefit student learning. *Journal of Geography in Higher Education, 29*(2), 183–201.

Humbold, V. W. (1984). Der Köningsbrger Schulplan, 1809. In A. Flitner (Ed.), *Schriften zur Anthropologie und Bildunslehre*. Frankfurt am main: Ullstein.

Ifenthaler, D., & Gosper, M. (2014). Research-based learning: Connecting research and instructions. In *Curriculum models for the 21st century: Using learning technologies in higher education* (pp. 73–89). New York: Springer. https://doi.org/10.1007/978-1-4614-73-66-4_5.

Justice, C., Rice, J., & Warry, W. (2009). Academic skill development—Inquiry seminars can make a difference: Reflections and directions on course design and teaching methods. *Innovative Higher Education., 3*, 3: Available at: https://doi.org/10.20429/ijsotl.2009.030109.

Lageman, E. C. (2002). Experimenting with education: John Dewey and Ella Flagg Young at the University of Chicago. In C. H. Seigfried (Ed.), *Feminist Interpretations of John Dewey*. University Park: Pennsylvania State University.

Levy, P., & Petrulis, R. (2012). How do first year university students experience inquiry and research, and what are the implications for the practice of inquiry-based learning? *Studies in Higher Education, 37*, 85–101.

Ludwig, J. (2011). *Forschungsbasierte Lehre als Lehre im Format der Forschung*. Available online: http://www.sq-brandenburg.de/files/bbhd03.pdf

Mills, J. E., & Treagust D. F. (2003). Engineering education—Is problem-based or project-based learning the answer? *Australasian Journal of Engineering Education*. Available online: http://citeseerx.ist.psu.edu/viewdoc/download?doi=10.1.1.620.5767&rep=rep1&type=pdf

Prince, M. J., & Felder, R. M. (2006). Inductive teaching and learning methods: Definitions, comparisons, and research bases. *Journal of Engineering Education, 95*, 123–138.

Prince, M. J., & Felder, R. M. (2007). The many faces of inductive teaching and training. *Journal of College Science Teaching, 36*, 14–20.

Spoken-Smith, R., & Walker, R. (2010). Can Inquiry-based Learning Strengthen the Links Teaching and Disciplinary Research? *Studies in Higher Education., 35*, 723–740.

Structure of ICT competence of teachers. Recommendations of UNESCO. (2011).Version 2.0.

Thomas, J. W. (2000). *A review of research on project-based learning. Research review*. California: The Autodesk Foundation.

Tymoshenko, N. Y. (2014). *Introduction to the specialty: Social work. Module 2:* Textbook.

Veretenko, T. G., & Denysiuk, O. M. (2011). *Introduction to the specialty: Social pedagogy. Module 2*. Textbook.

Wildt, J. (2010, October 13). *Forschendes Lernen: Wie und Warum? Presentation at Leibniz University Hannover*. Available online: https://www.zqs.uni-hannover.de/fileadmin/institut/pdf/Forschendes_Lernen_Leibniz_Universitaet_Hannover_Prof._Dr._Dr._Wildt_13.10.2011.pdf

Chapter 13
Modernization of Environmental Education with the Use of Project-Based Learning, Outdoor Education, and Mobile Learning Supported by Information and Communication Technology

Imrich Jakab, Martina Zigová, and Zuzana Pucherová

13.1 Introduction

"Turn off your mobile phones and put them aside, please." This is a usual start of an ordinary lesson in many of European primary and secondary schools. However, current mobile phones have a strong potential to be an effective teaching aid (Motiwalla 2007; Al-Fahad 2009; Ozdamli and Cavus 2011) as they represent complete multimedia centers that combine the capabilities of the still camera, video camera, personal organizer, and web browser into one single device (Marriott 2005). Our aim is to use mobile learning in combination with student projects, outdoor education, and various information and communication technologies (ICTs) to achieve modernization and efficiency of environmental education in secondary education. We have chosen the global environmental problems as a main topic which links abovementioned pedagogical principles and ICT.

Life on Earth is endangered by many environmental threats. Most important are especially the water problems – drinking water and sanitation, air pollution, soil and agricultural problems, natural habitats destruction, loss of biodiversity, solid and hazardous waste disposal, toxic chemicals, the greenhouse warming effect, energy consumption, and ozone depletion. Seriousness of the situation is proved by multiple scientific studies (e.g., Hoel 1991; El-Fadel et al. 1997; Schipper and Pelling 2006), international political and scientific discussions (e.g., Tbilisi 1977, Rio de Janeiro 1992), laws and conventions eliminating the impact of human activities on the environment (e.g., Kyoto Protocol 1997, Paris Agreement 2015, Vienna Convention 1985, Montreal Protocol 1987), global plans for environmental sustainability (Agenda 2030), and also clearly visible global issues and impacts on the

I. Jakab (✉) · M. Zigová · Z. Pucherová
Constantine the Philosopher University in Nitra, Nitra, Slovakia
e-mail: ijakab@ukf.sk; martina.zigova@ukf.sk; zpucherova@ukf.sk

quality of human life. According to McMichael et al. (2008), global problems have a straight impact on human health.

Global problems have become an inseparable part of education content worldwide, and mean of its implementation is the environmental education. Environmental education presents system view of the world that highlights the dynamic interconnectedness between personal, local, regional, national, and global levels of spatial existence of selected environmental problem. The global is ever present in the local; multiple local events flow into, and influence, the global (Selby 2000). According to Stapp (1969), "environmental education is aimed at producing a citizenry that is knowledgeable concerning the biophysical environment and its associated problems, aware of how to help solve these problems, and motivated to work towards their solution." Environmental education also entails practice in decision-making and self-formulation of a code of behavior about issues concerning environmental quality (IUCN 1970).

Global environmental problems and their connection to a local level (problems of surrounding environment) provide the teacher many various topics and options to help develop students' environmental awareness, ecological knowledge, attitudes, values, commitments for actions, and ethical responsibilities for the rational use of resources and for sound and sustainable development (UNESCO-UNEP International Environmental Education Programme 1992). Due that our environment is threatened by multiple environmental hazards, many researches assess students' relationship and awareness to selected global environmental problems and also within the level of the secondary education. Many researches indicate that teachers play a significant role on global environmental problem education (e.g., Shobeiri et al. 2007) and many of them consider the global environmental issues as a topic their students should to know. Most frequent issues are the climate change (Boyes and Stanisstreet 1997; Shepardson et al. 2009; Punter et al. 2011), global warming and energy (Devine-Wright et al. 2004), soil degradation and solid waste disposal (Ramsey et al. 1992; Ivy et al. 1998; Makki et al. 2003; Ifegbesan 2010), and air pollution (Myers et al. 2004; Boyes et al. 2004; Dimitriou and Christidou 2007).

Our proposed model of environmental education moves the educational process outdoors, directly to the sites where the particular environmental problems are present. Model practically connects content of individual subjects with ICT and purposefully selects pedagogical approaches to increase motivation of students to explore environmental issues, engage in problems solving, and take action to improve the quality of environment.

Students get acquainted progressively with global environmental problems issue; gather information from available sources; directly map problems in the field; record, analyze, and evaluate data; create and share valuable outputs; and get involved personally into problem-solving process. Besides the knowledge, students also gain and develop their environmental awareness, attitudes, values, and wide range of soft skills – critical thinking skills, collaboration skills, communication skills, creativity and innovation skills, self-direction skills, global connections, and local connections using technology as a tool for learning, that are, according to Ravitz et al. (2012), the "21st Century Skills."

13.1.1 Environmental Issues Suitable for Education Model Proposed

Using our proposed model in educational process, the teacher must choose proper environmental problem for students to solve. The selected environmental problem must meet these conditions:

1. Relevance – selected problem or its effects must be actual and present in surroundings of school or a place where the educational process takes place.
2. Solvability – possibility for students to cooperate actively on elimination of the selected problem or its effects.
3. Visibility – selected problem or its expressions are visible with a naked eye.
4. Mappability – selected problem or its effects can be mapped (i.e., located using GPS devices for map creation).
5. Availability – optimal is if the selected issue is present in the surroundings of school or students' residence.
6. Safety – students may not be exposed to any risks threatening their health during the fieldwork.

Environmental issues meeting these requirements, which are realizable in the conditions of the Slovak Republic are, e.g., the illegal dumping (fly dumping) and biotic invasions of invasive species.

13.1.1.1 Illegal Dumping and Littering

Illegal dumping is any unauthorized disposal of waste on any public or private property. People usually dispose their waste on illegal places to avoid the disposal fees, and they do not realize that this way of disposal poses a big threat for the environment. The existence of illegal dumps is an environmental problem in the most of countries.

In response to these situations, several countries have begun to reexamine their regulations for illegal dumping and are introducing more stringent rules and/or penalties for waste crimes (Ichinose and Yamamoto 2011). The problem of illegal dumping is also reflected in environmental education, for example, students located piles of illegally dumped tires in Detroit (Lowenstein et al. 2010) or illegal disposal of garbage fashion in Charlottesville, Virginia (Fullerton and Kinnaman 1994). Many studies focus on illegal dumping in relation to students' behavior, e.g., Hungerford and Volk (1990), Kuhlemeier et al. (1999), Jensen (2002), etc.

Littering means tossing, tipping, or depositing waste on the land and in the water, where it pollutes the environment and harms human health. Littering has gone from being viewed primarily as an aesthetic problem to a broader environmental issue and generally involves paper, bottles, and food packaging (Vesilind et al. 2002; New South Wales Environment Protection Authority (NSWEPA) 2018). Littering is generally very mobile and tends to collect in roadside ditches and verges, making accurate assessment difficult (Gray and Gray 2004). The aim of some studies is to assess the current situation regarding littering on the streets, e.g., (Al-Khatib2009) monitor children behavior and attitudes concerning glass littering; evaluate the influence of socioeconomic factors on street litter, for example, the Middle East (Arafat et al. 2007), where main sources of marine and coastal litter of beach users are concerned (Santos et al. 2005) or marine littering (Hartley et al. 2014); and describe the litter deposition on minor rural roads in Ireland (Gray and Gray 2004).

13.1.1.2 Invasive Species and Biotic Invasions

Since the beginning of the Age of Exploration, biogeographic barriers have been drastically breached, and the massive movement of organisms across the world began. This causes unplanned biological experiments which may result into biological invasions of non-native (alien) species (Mooney and Cleland 2001). Consequences are disruptions of ecosystem processes, cultural landscapes, reduction of the land value, etc. The biggest problem is that native species are being replaced by alien species (McKinney and Lockwood 1999; Mooney and Cleland 2001). This may lead to a global homogenization of the biosphere. Lower biological diversity will be a threat for food production, human health, and wealth (Vitousek et al. 1996; Westbrooks 1998; McKinney and Lockwood 1999).

Invasive plants are a subset of non-native plants which produce reproductive offspring in areas distant from sites of introduction and have the potential to spread over long distances. They invade all types of environments and threaten the integrity of ecosystems all over the world (Williamson 1996; Richardson et al. 2000; Pyšek et al. 2002). Invasive plants have important consequences for reducing global biodiversity, disrupting ecosystem stability and the balance of nature (Westbrooks 1998; Daehler 2003). Their impact is probably greater than the more widely known aspects of global environmental change, such as rising CO_2 concentrations or climate change (Vitousek et al. 1996; Westbrooks 1998; Callaway and Aschehoug 2000).

13.2 Material and Methods

Proposed innovative model for realization of environmental education is based on the practical mapping of selected environmental issues or their effects by students of secondary education level using ICT and principles of outdoor education, project-based learning, and mobile learning.

13.2.1 Selected Pedagogical Approaches

Model links principles of three pedagogical approaches:

1. *Project-based learning (PBL)* – project-based learning is a comprehensive approach to classroom teaching and learning that is designed to engage students in investigation of authentic problems (Blumenfeld et al. 1991). It is a student-driven, teacher-facilitated approach to learning – students develop a question and are guided through research under the teacher's supervision (Bell 2010). PBL allows students to investigate questions, propose hypotheses and explanations, discuss their ideas, challenge the ideas of others, and try out new ideas. Students are engaged in real, meaningful problems that are important to them. They gain a deeper understanding of material when they actively construct their understanding by working with and using ideas. One of the benefits is that students can more easily see the value and meaning of the tasks and activities they perform (Krajcik and Blumenfeld 2006).

In the case project-based learning is used in the environmental education, Hungerford and Volk (1990) distinguish two basic curricular strategies: (1) Issue Investigation and Action Model and (2) Extended Case Study Model.

The fundamental difference between these two strategies lies in the definition of the issue that will be addressed by the students. In choosing the extended case study model, students focus on a predetermined issue (an environmental problem), sometimes chosen by the class but most often chosen by the instructor. In the issue investigation and action model strategy, each student chooses a single issue of interest and investigates the issue in depth.

In our case, students address the issue of global environmental problems associated with the practical mapping of these problems in their immediate surroundings. Depending on the selected curricular strategy, the teacher has two options. First is that the teacher defines one environmental problem and students focus on detecting this problem in their surrounding environment, i.e. in their town or village, in the vicinity of their school, in their residence, etc. An example of such a problem is illegal dumping or littering or the presence of invasive plants. In the second option, the teacher selects a certain area – an ecosystem – and students are investigating possible environmental problems that affect this ecosystem on their own. Using this strategy, students have greater possibilities to find and investigate more environmental problems. They are not focused only on one single problem but may discover many others, such as soil erosion, environmental pollution, deforestation, etc.

Both strategies create sufficient scope for building up curriculum interrelationships. The topic is directly linked to the objectives of environmental education as well as the educational content of several secondary education subjects (e.g., geography, search for specific locations in the field and on maps using geographical coordinates; biology, the mutual relationship of man and his environment and ecological conditions of life; ethical education, religious education, and civic doctrine, the personal responsibility of each person for the environment and the importance of ecological thinking in a society-wide context).

2. *Outdoor education (OE)* – is a means of curriculum enrichment (Lappin 1984). According to Priest (1986), the definition of outdoor education is found upon six major points: (1) is a method for learning, (2) is experiential, (3) takes place primarily in the outdoors, (4) requires the use of all senses and domains, (5) is based upon interdisciplinary curriculum matter, and (6) is a matter of relationships involving people and natural resources. The outdoor environment has massive potential for learning. Outdoor experiences are very effective in providing relevance and depth to the curriculum in ways that are difficult to achieve indoors in the classroom (Brown 2010). Various activities in outdoor education can stimulate environmental education and nature studies in suitable ways so that students learn about and experience nature while, at the same time, they learn action strategies to protect it. Experiences in outdoor activities offer great possibilities for the development of a strong empathic relationship to the nature among students (And their teachers!) (Palmberg and Kuru 2000). Potential of outdoor education in relation to the environmental education is confirmed by many published studies aimed at, e.g., investigation of organisms in their natural environment (Pfligersdorffer 1984; Starosta 1990), observation of non-native animals (Braun Buyer and Randler 2010), species conservation (Bogner 1999; Randler et al. 2005), environmental issues and conservation (Bogner and Wiseman 2004), and examination of water quality (Kamarainen et al. 2013).

We use outdoor education as a part of our model for global issues teaching purposes. Through education in the outdoors, we allow students a direct contact with the environment. Students carry out their studies and reveal environmental problems that negatively affect and change the environment.

3. *Mobile learning (ML)* – the term "mobile learning" refers to the use of mobile and handheld IT devices, such as mobile telephones, laptops, and tablet technologies, in teaching, training, and learning (Sarrab et al. 2012). Alsaadat (2017) defines mobile learning as "Learning that happens across locations or that of learning opportunities offered by portable technologies." Advantages of mobile learning are that with the mobility of general portable devices, learner is not fixed at predetermined location, and it is accessible virtually from any place, which provides access to all the different learning materials available (Alsaadat 2017). Mobile learning offers new ways to extend education outside the classroom, into the conversations and interactions of everyday life (Sharples et al. 2009).

Mobile learning is a type of learning which appeared as a conclusion of co-evaluation of "mobile informatics" and e-learning fields and provides accession to e-learning content independently of a specific location, utilization of services created dynamically, and communication with others (Korucu and Alkan 2011).

E-learning allows students to have access to the basic theoretical background necessary for successful realization of their projects at each stage of the educational process (waste issue and illegal dumping, mapping methodology, manuals for work with ICT, etc.). They are able to communicate with each other and with the teacher, share results and outputs, and respond promptly to the current challenges by teachers and classmates.

Nowadays, mobile learning is often linked with fast-developing game-based learning (Admiraal et al. 2007; Guazzaroni 2012; Klopfer et al. 2012). Other studies point out the use of mobile phone for creating and sharing students' own photographs (Marriott 2005; Ekanayake and Wishart 2011), as well as for the localization of selected objects and phenomena using GPS system (McGreen and Arnedillo-Sánchez 2005). Mobile learning also has its purpose in interaction with the environmental education confirmed by many studies. Educational process can be enriched with mobile applications and systems to support observation and investigation of animals and plants outdoors, their interactions in their environment, functions in ecosystem (Chen et al. 2004; Chu et al. 2010; Ruchter et al. 2010; Ekanayake and Wishart 2011), and investigation of various environmental issues, e.g., erosion (Uzunboylu et al. 2009; Bannan et al. 2012).

In our proposed model, the mobile learning is carried out through mobile phones (smartphones), which currently own more and more students. Using smartphones, students can accurately locate the environmental problem, create the necessary documentation, communicate with teacher and classmates, as well as search additional information on the Internet.

13.2.2 *Involvement of Information and Communication Technologies*

Essential part of the model is information and communication technology (ICT) which has the ability to enhance teaching and learning through its dynamic, interactive, and engaging content and it can provide real opportunities for individualized instruction. Information and communication technology can make the school more efficient and productive (Kirschner and Woperies 2003) and have the potential to accelerate, enrich, and deepen skills, motivate and engage students in learning, and help to relate school experiences to work practices (Davis and Tearle 1999).

Our proposed innovative model of environmental education integrates several ICT, which are used at different stages of teaching and in relation to the different pedagogical approaches included in the model (Fig. 13.1).

Most important ICT used in the model are the following:

– *Global navigation satellite system (GNSS)* – constellation of satellites providing signals from space transmitting positioning and timing data. Each satellite transmits a unique signal and orbital parameters that allow GNSS receivers to decode and compute the precise position of the satellite. The receiver measures the distance to each satellite by the amount of time it takes to receive a transmitted signal. This information is used in trilateration to calculate a user's exact location.

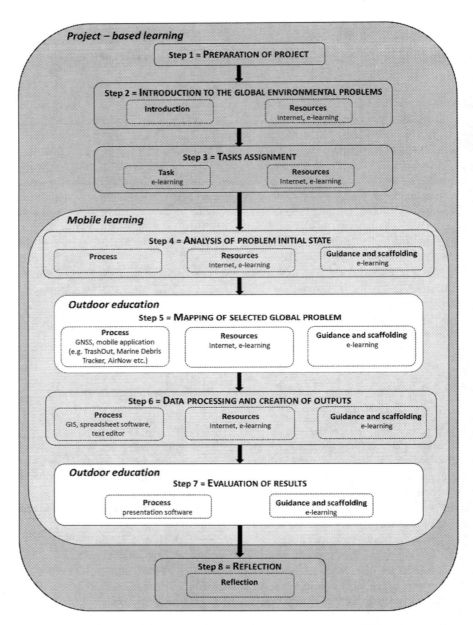

Fig. 13.1 Scheme of educational model steps including selected pedagogical approaches (PBL, OE, and ML), various ICTs, and respect basic features, according to Grant (2002): (1) introduction, (2) task, (3) resources, (4) process, (5) guidance and scaffolding, and (6) reflection

Examples of GNSS are, e.g., the USA's NAVSTAR Global Positioning System (GPS) or Russia's Global'naya Navigatsionnaya Sputnikovaya Sistema (GLONASS) (www.egnos-portal.eu).

There is no need to own a professional GPS device for the localization of environmental problems in the field. The variety of mobile applications that can measure coordinates is available for every mobile phone operating system. Many of them are available for free (e.g., for Android, GPS coordinates, Map coordinates, UTM Geo Map; for iOS, My GPS coordinates, GPS and Maps, GPS data).

– *Geographic information system (GIS)* – the term geographic information system represents an integration of many subject areas. GIS is a system of hardware, software, data, people, organizations, and institutional arrangements for collecting, storing, analyzing, and disseminating information about areas of the Earth (Dueker and Kjerne 1989).

Teaching with the use of GIS provides the opportunity for issues-based, student-centered, standards-based, inquiry-oriented education (Kerski et al. 2013). The educative argument for GIS is that it helps students to learn geography by practicing spatial thinking (Bednarz 2004; Liu and Zhu 2008; Kerski et al. 2013). The argument goes like this: GIS model the processes of spatial thinking. By mirroring these processes, doing GIS (following its procedures and steps to produce maps) demonstrates for students the cognitive strategies used in spatial thinking. Student ability to engage in spatial thinking is then enhanced. Students benefit from using a GIS to produce maps, because it practices and sharpens their cognitive mapping skills, such as assessing similarity and proximity, and their spatial thinking skills, such as associating and correlating spatially distributed phenomena (Bednarz 2004).

Using GIS tools, learners can inactively explore geographic data; manipulate maps, images, graphs, and tables to answer the questions of "What's where?" and "Why is it there?"; and perform "what-if" scenario analyses (Liu and Zhu 2008; Kerski et al. 2013).

The rapid increase in using GIS in secondary education around the world is due mainly to the perceived benefits it provides for teaching and learning, which have been addressed in numerous studies, e.g., Landenberger et al. (2006), Liu et al. (2010), Kerski et al. (2013), and Huizenga et al. (2017).

In our model, we use GIS in the meanings of Wiegand (2001), according who GIS provide technological capability for real-world problem-solving, and, at the same time, they have a potential to facilitate project-based learning (Johansson 2003). Students can process spatial data obtained through GNSS in the environment of GIS, i.e., compute their size and distance from selected objects and phenomena, analyze their relations with the surrounding landscape, and visualize results through map outputs.

In addition to these basic ICTs, a variety of mobile applications can be included in the model depending on currently addressed global environmental problem. Examples of optional applications are depending on the selected environmental problem:

Waste issue:

- *TrashOut* – global environmental project and also available as a mobile application. It allows locating and reporting of illegal dumps anywhere in the world. Reporting is easy – all what have to be done is take a photo of dump, define its size and type, or add a comment. Reports will appear in the TrashMap. TrashOut project also supports local governments, environmental organizations, and waste companies in the region, and this all may lead to solving of fly-dumping problem (www.trashout.ngo).
- *Marine Debris Tracker* – easy way to report marine debris or litter anywhere in the world and then prevent it from impacting oceans (www.marinedebris.engr.uga.edu).
- *Marine LitterWatch* – mobile app to collect information on marine litter and strengthen Europe's knowledge base and thus provide support to European policy making. Marine LitterWatch is a citizen science-based app that aims to help fill data gaps in beach litter monitoring and support voluntary clean-ups (www.eea.europa.eu).

Biotic invasions:

- *Invasive Alien Species Europe* – application helps citizens to capture and share information about 37 invasive alien species of Union concern in Europe. The application contains detailed information and photos of those plants and animals and makes it possible for citizens to use their phones' GPS system and camera to capture images of them (ec.europa.eu).

Quality of the air:

- *AirNow* – providing information about the latest air quality, available for the USA. The application provides an increasingly mobile public with real-time air quality information that people can use to protect their health when planning their daily activities (www.airnow.gov).
- *EuropeAir* – easy way to retrieve instant information about the major components of air pollution, e.g., ozone (O_3), nitrogen dioxide (NO_2), and airborne particulate (PM_{10} and $PM_{2.5}$) for Europe (www.eea.europa.eu).

13.3 Results

Model should be realized in eight successive steps (Fig. 13.1):

1. *Preparation of project*
2. *Introduction to the global environmental problems*
3. *Tasks assignment*
4. *Analysis of problem initial state*
5. *Mapping of selected global problem*

6. *Data processing and creation of outputs*
7. *Evaluation of results*
8. *Reflection*

Steps follow from four phases of project-based learning according to Mergendoller et al. (2006): (1) plan the project, (2) project launch, (3) guided inquiry and product creation, and (4) project conclusion, and respect basic features, according to Grant (2002), that are essential for PBL: (1) introduction, (2) task, (3) resources, (4) process, (5) guidance and scaffolding, and (6) reflection. Model steps also follow five project-learning steps according to Zigová et al. (2018).

13.3.1 Anatomy of Environmental Education Model

1. *Preparation of project*

The first step of the model (Fig. 13.1) takes place even before students begin working on the project. According to Mergendoller et al. (2006), teachers begin planning the project by considering how it will fit within the curriculum and help students attain important content and skill outcomes.

Our model links the issue of global environmental problems with environmental problems on local level. The aim of the model is to discover and map them. We dare to say that the education content directly follows from the curriculum of environmental education on global scale. Educational process is built up on several ICT attractive for students and various pedagogical approaches; thus it has an interdisciplinary character. Besides the knowledge gained, students develop broad spectrum of important soft skills, hard skills, environmental awareness, attitudes, and values.

Within the preparation step, the teacher has to select one of the curricular strategies. According to Hungerford and Volk (1990), there are two options: (1) extended case study model and (2) the issue investigation and action model.

Choosing the extended case study model, the teacher focuses on one particular global environmental problem and its effects on the local level, e.g., the waste issue where students map the presence of illegal dumping or the biotic invasion issue through mapping of invasive plant species. Using this model, attention is aimed on concrete problem only within sites selected by teacher or students.

The issue investigation and action model offers a strategy where first attention is paid to concrete site (ecosystem) and students have the opportunity to investigate, discover, and map all visible environmental problems.

2. *Introduction to the global environmental problems*

Many projects use an introduction "to set the stage" for, or anchor, the project. This often contributes to motivating learners (Mergendoller et al. 2006). Students' motivation plays a crucial role in the educational process. In our model, students have a difficult task to cooperate on process of solving the environmental problem. Since environmental problems are the real-world problems that students may encounter and solve in the real life, the use of real professional tools and scientific methodology enhances the attractiveness of model.

In the introduction step, it is necessary to present sufficiently the issue of global environmental problems (Fig. 13.1). Students acquire information about their causes and impact on life on Earth, as well as the risks they pose to the individual components of our environment and to humans. Simultaneously they recognize the seriousness of the various global problems and the need for finding a solution to their elimination.

In the case where attention is focused on one particular issue (e.g., illegal dumps), it is essential to provide students with a sufficient amount of additional information. The teacher should inform students about the impropriety of illegal dumping in several aspects, e.g., in terms of ecological, environmental, sanitary and hygiene, aesthetic, ethical, cultural, etc. In the case of invasive plants, the teacher should provide information about the causes of biotic invasions and their impact on native species, human, economy, etc.

It's important to mention that in this step, not only should students be sufficiently informed and appropriately motivated, but they also have to receive various sources of basic and supplementary information on selected global issues from the teacher (printed version, web links, videos, etc.) (Fig. 13.1). These resources can help them to understand the issue further and can be helpful in next steps of the model.

3. *Tasks assignment*

According to Mergendoller et al. (2006), the tasks of the student project should be engaging, challenging, and doable. The content of the task depends on the selected curricular strategy by Hungerford and Volk (1990). In the case of the extended case study model, students' mission is to map the selected environmental problem within the chosen site, point out the seriousness of the problem, and take the necessary steps toward its elimination. As we have mentioned before, suitable problem for this strategy is, e.g., illegal dumping, littering, or invasions of alien plants. Suitable research site should be chosen by students or teacher, e.g., a part of the city, town section, cadaster, etc.

Task based on the strategy of issue investigation and action model should consist of investigating, discovering, and mapping of all environmental problems present in the chosen ecosystem. Students are not limited by one particular problem and try to discover all present problems in the area. As well as in the previous strategy, in the next step, students point out the seriousness of these problems and take the necessary steps to achieve their elimination.

Students exposed to such challenging issues see environmental education in a new context. They identify a real problem, hypothesize, collect data, formulate a step-by-step procedure, and come up with workable results (Ramirez and Althouse 1995).

Even at this stage of the project, it is important for students to have all the necessary information available, but the most essential is to give them the exact assignment as well as the proper methodology (Fig. 13.1). Appropriate methods are necessary for successful completion and achievement of requested outcomes. For this purpose, the teacher may create an e-learning course through which students can receive the necessary materials also in time spent outside the classroom. Students have to be aware of the importance of addressing the problem, as well as the fact that they themselves are capable of action to assist in the elimination of problem in the surroundings of their school or residence.

4. *Analysis of problem initial state*

Even before the mapping itself, students have to find out the actual state of the selected problem (Fig. 13.1). That means that is necessary to become acquainted with the research site where the mapping will be carried out, especially in the case of the issue investigation and action model, where students investigate the selected natural environment – an ecosystem.

Students have to understand the importance of the ecosystem for humans and other living organisms and why it is valuable for the surrounding landscape or region. Students should find out the degree of protection of the selected area and know the object of protection, as well as activities prohibited in the area. Students should check available literature to acquire valuable information about animals, plants, and protected species that would be present in the area.

The analysis of the initial state also includes the knowledge of the current state of the map out of the selected environmental problem. There is a probability that someone mapped the area before and the results are available to the public. For this purpose, a variety of mobile applications are available for student smartphones (Fig. 13.1). An example is the TrashOut app (www.trashout.ngo) – world database of illegal dumping. Through the existing mobile application TrashOut, the teacher can make students get acquainted with the status of illegal dumps in the selected area (Fig. 13.2b). The application contains information about illegal dumps that has been discovered, described, and reported previously. The advantage of this application

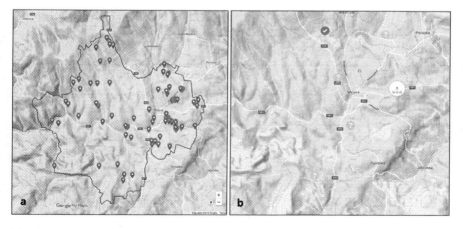

Fig. 13.2 (**a**) Map of illegal dumps localized and mapped by the student in the cadaster of Myjava town (Slovakia) visualized through Google Maps and for comparison (**b**) Map of reported illegal dumps (TrashMap) in Myjava cadaster at the same time

is the resulting map – TrashMap with accurate locations of illegal dumps, according to the period when they were reported. Using this map, students can search for new illegal dumps, look for specific information about the illegal dump, update the status of previously reported dump, as well as monitor the dynamics of illegal dumps in the area. In case of invasive species, students should search for database of biotic invasions, because there is a possibility that the given country gathers reports of their presence.

5. *Mapping of selected global problem*

Investigation phase of project-based learning starts with the mapping of environmental problems (Fig. 13.1). The process and investigation include the steps necessary to complete the task. The process should include activities that require higher-level and critical thinking skills, such as analysis, synthesis, and evaluation of information (Mergendoller et al. 2006).

Mapping of the environmental problem is associated with movement in the external environment; therefore, it's necessary to pay enough attention to the general safety instructions. At the same time, it is very important to set an exact delimitation of the research site which should be closely linked to the students' residence or school. Mapping can be carried out together with the teacher or separately, e.g., during the students' journey to school or during a walk with their parents. Students can work on the task divided into smaller groups or all class together as a one team.

The process of mapping itself is associated with the localization of issues and by recording their basic properties. Students should check for available mobile applications aimed at the selected problem. In the case of illegal dumping, the mapping process can be realized directly through the TrashOut application or GPS/GNSS applications available for free. In the case of invasive plants, available apps are not applicable worldwide, because the list of invasive species varies from country to country and apps are aimed only at individual region (e.g., app for Europe – Invasive Alien Species Europe). If there is no application usable for the selected site, students simply measure location with the use of GNSS/GPS app and record basic information of the problem. Information about invasive plants should include the discovered species, size of the affected area, species ratio in the vegetation, etc. In the case of the illegal dumping, basic attributes for each dump includes a size of dump (in TrashOut app tree categories are available) and type of waste (household, automotive, construction, plastic, etc.). At the same time, it is possible to estimate the percentage of representation of the various materials and describe the place where the waste is stored. Mobile phones can be also used to create photographic documentation, audio or text notes, etc.

In this step it is important that the teacher should be available for guidance and scaffolding (Fig. 13.1). As learners need help, guidance and scaffolding will be needed. These can include student-teacher interactions, practice worksheets, peer counseling, guiding questions, job aides, project templates, etc. Many projects include groups or teams, especially where resources are limited. But, cooperative learning may also employ rounds of peer reviews or group brainstorming sessions (Mergendoller et al. 2006).

6. *Data processing and creation of outputs*

Processing of spatial data (Fig. 13.1) can be carried out directly during lessons of geography (orientation on maps, thematic map creation) and informatics (processing of tables in spreadsheet software, making presentations, working with various ICT, etc.).

For visualization of obtained spatial data, desktop or web-based GIS software can be used. Both options are distinguished by advantages and disadvantages.

Web-based GIS, e.g., Google Maps, is an easy way of disseminating spatial data. Users do not have to purchase and install commercial GIS software. Data can be easily and quickly imported and presented on a map (Fig. 13.2a). Data are accessible anytime and anywhere via the World Wide Web (WWW) or an intranet. Disadvantage of Web GIS is only the basic functionality and need of Internet connection (Verma et al. 2012).

Desktop GIS software programs, e.g., open-source QGIS, have the ability to perform many advanced spatial related operations. It is possible to analyze data to reveal patterns, relationships, and trends and create maps of high quality (Figs. 13.3 and 13.4).

The intensity of the selected phenomena of the environmental problems (e.g., the ratio of the area of illegal dumps in relation to the size of the research site) is possible to convey graphically through cartograms within the process of making the map outputs using the GIS software. It is also possible to use cartodiagram (Fig. 13.3) for graphical representation of statistical data (e.g., the ratio of the waste

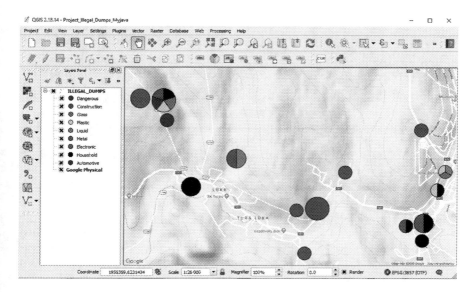

Fig. 13.3 Example of processing acquired illegal dumping spatial data in the environment of open-source GIS software (QGIS) with the use of cartodiagrams as one of the basic expression methods in thematic cartography

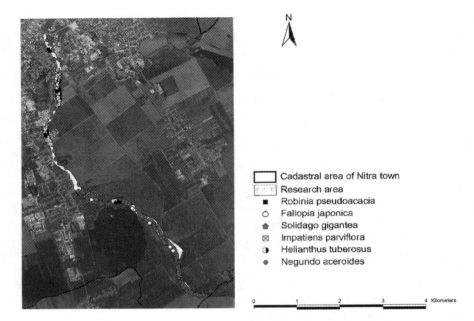

Fig. 13.4 Example of map output created by student of 9th grade of elementary school within students' professional activities. Student has mapped circa 8 km length of Nitra River (Slovakia) and though GPS recorded 715 specimens of 6 selected invasive plant species. Map output was created in the environment of open-source GIS software (QGIS)

composition according to the categories on each of illegal dumps, expressed through the pie charts). Cartogram expresses relative and cartodiagram absolute value of the phenomenon. Students can also process data using basic statistic methods to express the average size of the problem, type of waste or invasive species prevailing, distance of dumps from the nearest settlement, etc.

7. *Evaluation of results*

Completing the investigation, students have to present their project results (Fig. 13.1). The form of presentation should be chosen properly depending on the audience. The good way to present results in class among classmates is an oral presentation. Students can use any available presentation software (PowerPoint, Prezi, etc.) to create the presentation or make a project poster. Environmental problems discovered and examined by students often present new valuable information which is not often known not only by citizens but also the competent authorities, which have the competence to deal with the problem. Illegal dumps are hidden in the vegetation on distant and less frequent locations, and invasive plants are an unknown term for citizens and grown as ornamental plants in gardens that pose a threat to the environment.

Since the global environmental problems are a serious issue for human, as well as for other living organisms, wide range of people should be informed. Students may present results using the media available to the public, e.g., school journal and school web, or create posters and brochures and take steps to achieve solution of the problem – notify competent authorities on the presence of the problem, organize a volunteer brigade, launch an information campaign on the environmental problems of environment, etc. Part of the project can also be rechecking of the status of the problem whether it has been solved and what to extend or if the environmental problems appear again or even grow bigger. This all may lead to the solution of the problem in cooperation with the school, the municipality, and the third sector.

8. *Reflection*

The superior examples of project-based learning offer the opportunity for closure, debriefing, or reflection. These may include relevant in-class discussions, journal entries, or even follow-up questions about what students have taught (Grant 2002).

Successful student projects can be a positive feedback for the teacher, efficient and interesting way to spend time for students, and appropriate advertising for school that is personally engaged in activities aiming at the protection and creation of the environment.

13.4 Discussion

The main objective of proposed model is the modernization of environmental education. Modernization can concern several components of the educational process:

1. *Modernization of the content of environmental education*

In an effort to modernize the content of education, actuality and attractiveness of the main topic play a very important role. We have chosen the issue of global environmental problems as it is a very hot and frequently discussed topic worldwide. Global environmental problems represent a serious threat to the world and affect every living organism on Earth, what also means us, our students, and our immediate environment. In the 1990s, Boh (1994) demanded that it is necessary to include the problem of global environmental problems in the curriculum of secondary education. Topic allows students a direct contact with the contents of education, as it is straight linked to local environmental problems occurring often in the immediate vicinity of the school or residence. An important factor in the modernization of the environmental education content is a cross-curricular character of the selected topic. In conditions of the Slovak school system, global environmental problems issue offers a number of opportunities for cross-curricular relations in secondary education level during stages of model implementation. The very educational content of the model has a strong cross-curricular character, and the topic is the content of the education of the cross-sectional theme of environmental education.

The content of education is directly connected to the lower secondary curriculum of biology (the relationship of man and the environment, the ecological conditions of life) and chemistry (water and soil pollution). Waste issue is also part of the educational content of the history. Students of 6th–9th grade are progressively familiarized with the waste issue of the different historical periods. Within the ethics, religious education, and civics, it should be the endeavor of the teacher to direct the student to the personal responsibility for the environment. The content of the geography is to teach students search for specific locations in the field and on maps with the use of geographical coordinates. Within the informatics, the student has the opportunity to use various ICTs, mainly application software (e.g., spreadsheet, presentation, word processors, GIS software) and mobile devices (e.g., taking photos and video and measure coordinates through GPS/GNSS). Data acquired in the mapping phase can be further processed in the mathematics, where the topic can be applied in any grade of secondary education, e.g., according to the demands of the curriculum, in the case of illegal dumps, students can calculate area and volume of the dumps in the shape of different geometry objects and percentage of waste categories composition or do the basic descriptive statistics. In physical education, students can within the seasonal physical activities undergo a continuous march with overcoming terrain obstacles to the length of 4–8 km, and the teacher might also include the mapping of environmental problems in this activity.

Within the higher secondary education, global environmental problems are directly addressed in the geography in several thematic units, e.g., man in the landscape and its protection, analysis of global problems, causes and effects of nature elements pollution and global impacts of human activities on the ecosystems of Earth, positive examples of international cooperation on global problems elimination, etc. As in the case of lower secondary education, the global environmental problems issue can be implemented directly into subjects of the Mathematics, Informatics, Physical Education, History, etc. (NEP of Slovakia 2015).

According to practical and cross-curricular character of the selected topic and the wide range of involved pedagogical approaches and ICTs, the proposed model of environmental education can develop a wide range of knowledge, attitudes, and skills. However, we agree with So and Kim (2009) that designing and implementing PBL lessons are time-consuming and require IT skills from both students and teachers. Despite this fact, the goals of PBL include helping students develop (1) flexible knowledge, (2) effective problem-solving skills, (3) self-directed learning skills, (4) effective collaboration skills, and (5) intrinsic motivation. Mobile learning, outdoor learning experiences, and ICT offer different opportunities for personal and learning skills development in areas such as communication, problem-solving, working with others, critical thinking, and technological skills. It helps develop the skills of enquiry, critical thinking, and reflection (Graham 2006; So and Brush 2008; Brown 2010).

2. *Modernization of educational process*

According to Marsh (2012), the most effective teaching and learning involve different teaching methods, approaches, and strategies to maximize knowledge acquisition and skills development. Good teachers always use more than one method or approach, and good learners will always combine different strategies of learning.

The proposed model combines selected pedagogical approaches (PBL, OE, and ML) toward one goal – to make teaching of environmental education more efficient and modern (Fig. 13.1). Model design is based on the use of PBL, where students address the real problems working on student projects, OE moves part of the educational process to the exterior, and ML allows the effective use of students' mobile phones (smartphones). Model gives students the opportunity for cooperation and confrontation of their ideas, planning their own activities, mapping, self-learning, dedicated use of smartphones, the use of ICT for the collection and presentation of spatial data, but mainly active participation in solving environmental problems.

3. *Modernization of used teaching aids*

Modernization of the educational process is closely related with the use of modern teaching aids. One of the major educational developments in the past quarter of a century that has potential for fostering project-based education is the creation and expansion of new teaching technology aids that can support students and teachers in obtaining, analyzing, and sharing information and constructing artifacts. Technological power is advancing rapidly. Prices are falling, making sophisticated options affordable for schools. Technology has the potential to sustain student motivation and support student learning and doing during the various phases of projects. It can support teachers in similar ways. Technology can supplement and complement teachers' instructional and managerial roles, relieving teachers of some of the complexities of implementing projects. It also can help sustain teacher involvement in project-based education by enhancing their knowledge and professional competence (Blumenfeld et al. 1991).

ICT contributes to change the overall educational structure (Anderson 2005). We agree with Rose (2009) and Livingstone (2012) that ICT skills are becoming accepted as a third life skill alongside literacy and numeracy. According to Gaible et al. (2011), students are frequently ready to benefit from instructional methods; therefore the use of ICT in the educational process does not present any problem for them. ICT becomes an efficient medium for dissemination of educational content and a convenient way to increase student motivation to learn (Zigová et al. 2018).

In our model, the use of information and communication technology (ICT) in education is represented mainly by means of GIS and GNSS, which provides the students with experience and technical know-how, which may be beneficial for their future job opportunities (Johansson 2003).

4. *Modernization of the role of the teacher*

The teacher's role no longer includes just delivering instruction or expecting students to repeat facts on tests. Instead, the role of the teacher is to offer resources that help students investigate and develop content purposefully and creatively (Solomon 2003). Within our model, the role of the teacher expands depending on the used pedagogical approaches.

In project-based education, as in traditional instruction, teachers need to (a) create opportunities for learning by providing access to information, (b) support learning by scaffolding instruction and modeling and guiding students to make tasks more manageable, (c) encourage students to use learning and metacognitive processes, and (d) assess progress, diagnose problems, provide feedback, and evaluate overall results. In addition, teachers need to create an environment conducive to constructive inquiry and manage the classroom to ensure that work is accomplished in an orderly and efficient fashion (Blumenfeld et al. 1991).

Realization of the proposed model using principles of mobile learning demands the extension of teacher role. Teachers should be qualified to use required mobile tools and technologies, be capable to guide and give advices, determine the strengths and weaknesses of used methods and study to resolve the weaknesses with different methods, have high levels of self-confident about courses, earn with their students, eliminate the barriers, increase motivation of learners, arrange activities to support interactive interactions between collaborative groups, and arrange activities for the evaluation of process (Ozdamli and Cavus 2011).

13.5 Conclusions

Contribution highlights an innovative approach to the teaching of environmental education with the use of project-based learning, outdoor education, mobile learning, and ICT. Students of secondary education level are built into the role of cartographers mapping environmental problems in their surroundings, which also help to solve global problems. Our proposed educational model has the potential to efficiently overlap the contents of individual school subjects and thereby help to build and strengthen the cross-curricular relationships.

However, the realization of the model brings several disadvantages. Gilbertson (2006) points out the general danger that is present during the outdoor education. Preparation and implementation of the teaching through PBL are also very time-consuming (Finucane et al. 1998; So and Kim 2009). The use of mobile phones in teaching brings several constraints, as small screen and associated reading difficulties on such as screen, data storage, multimedia, and battery limitations, and many of the mobile phones are not designed for educational purposes. This means that it is difficult for the learners to use them for the task given by the teachers (Korucu and Alkan 2011; Hashemi et al. 2011; Kukulska-Hulme and Traxler 2005).

Nevertheless, we think that the model can be an effective teaching aid to meet the selected objectives of environmental education according to Tbilisi Report Recommendation 2 (1978): encourage participation in the learning experience; emphasize active responsibility; use and broad range of teaching and learning techniques, with stress on practical activities and firsthand experience; concern with local the global dimensions and past/present/future dimensions; encourage the development of sensitivity, awareness, understanding, critical thinking, and problem-solving skills; and encourage the clarification of values and the development of values sensitive to the environment.

Model uses various ICT to increase students' motivation to learn and support interdisciplinary approach to the student projects. Through the effective combination of different pedagogical approaches, it has a potential to develop wide range of additional knowledge, skills, and attitudes not linked directly to the goals and curriculum of the environmental education.

But the most important fact is that using the proposed model in the school can actively participate in solving specific environmental problems that have not only local but also global character (dimension).

Acknowledgments The research was supported by the projects VEGA 1/0608/16 and KEGA 025UKF-4/2015.

References

Admiraal, W., Raessens, J., & Van Zeijts, H. (2007). Technology enhanced learning through mobile technology in secondary education. *Expanding the knowledge economy. Issues, applications, case studies (Part 2)*, 1241–1248.

AirNow [ONLINE] Available at: https://www.airnow.gov/index.cfm?action=topics.about_airnow [2018-05-10].

Al-Fahad, F. N. (2009). Students' attitudes and perceptions towards the effectiveness of mobile learning in King Saud University, Saudi Arabia. *TOJET: The Turkish Online Journal of Educational Technology, 8*(2), 111–119.

Al-Khatib, I. A. (2009). Children's perceptions and behavior with respect to glass littering in developing countries: A case study in Palestine's Nablus district. *Waste Management, 29*(2009), 1434–1437.

Alsaadat, K. (2017). Mobile learning technologies. *International Journal of Electrical and Computer Engineering (IJECE), 7*(5), 2833–2837.

Anderson, J. (2005). IT, E-learning and teacher development. *International Education Journal, 5*(5), 1–14.

Arafat, H. A., Al-Khatib, I. A., Daoud, R., & Shwahneh, H. (2007). Influence of socioeconomic factors on street litter generation in the Middle East: Effects of education level, age, and type of residence. *Waste Management and Research, 25*, 363–370.

Bannan, B., Peters, E., & Martinez, P. (2012). Mobile, inquiry-based learning and geological observation: An exploratory study. In *Refining current practices in mobile and blended learning: New applications*. Hershey: Information Science Reference,156 p.

Bednarz, S. W. (2004). Geographic information systems: A tool to support geography and environmental education? *GeoJournal, 60*(2), 191–199.

Bell, S. (2010). Project-based learning for the 21st century: Skills for the future. *The Clearing House, 83*(2), 39–43.

Blumenfeld, P. C., Soloway, E., Marx, R. W., Krajcik, J. S., Guzdial, M., & Palincsar, A. (1991). Motivating project-based learning: Sustaining the doing, supporting the learning. *Educational Psychologist, 26*(3–4), 369–398.

Bogner, F. X. (1999). Empirical evaluation of an educational conservation programme introduced in Swiss secondary schools. *International Journal of Science Education, 21*(11), 1169–1185.

Bogner, F. X., & Wiseman, M. (2004). Outdoor ecology education and pupils' environmental perception in preservation and utilization. *Science Education International, 15*(1), 27–48.

Boh, B. (1994). *Environmental issues in secondary education*. World Bank, 122 p. [ONLINE] Available at: http://documents.worldbank.org/curated/en/382181468764386963/pdf/multi-page.pdf

Boyes, E., & Stanisstreet, M. (1997). Children's models of understanding of two major global environmental issues (ozone layer and greenhouse effect). *Research in Science and Technological Education, 15*(1), 19–28.

Boyes, E., Stanisstreet, M., & Pui-ming Yeung, S. (2004). Air pollution: The knowledge and attitudes of secondary school students in Hong Kong. *International Research in Geographical and Environmental Education, 13*(1), 21–37.

Braun, M., Buyer, R., & Randler, C. (2010). Cognitive and emotional evaluation of two educational outdoor programs dealing with non-native bird species. *International Journal of Environmental and Science Education, 5*(2), 151–168.

Brown, K. (2010). Curriculum for excellence through outdoor learning. *Learning and teaching Scotland,* 28 p. [ONLINE] Available at: https://education.gov.scot/Documents/cfe-through-outdoor-learning.pdf

Callaway, R. M., & Aschehoug, E. T. (2000). Invasive plants versus their new and old neighbors: A mechanism for exotic invasion. *Science, 290*(5491), 521–523.

Chen, Y. S., Kao, T. C., Yu, G. J., & Sheu, J. P. (2004). A mobile butterfly-watching learning system for supporting independent learning. In *Proceedings of the 2nd IEEE international workshop on wireless and mobile technologies in education, 2004* (pp. 11–18). IEEE.

Chu, H. C., Hwang, G. J., Tsai, C. C., & Tseng, J. C. (2010). A two-tier test approach to developing location-aware mobile learning systems for natural science courses. *Computers and Education, 55*(4), 1618–1627.

Daehler, C. C. (2003). Performance comparisons of co-occurring native and alien invasive plants: Implications for conservation and restoration. *Annual Review of Ecology, Evolution, and Systematics, 34*(1), 183–211.

Davis, N. E. & Tearle, P. (Eds.) (1999). *A core curriculum for telematics in teacher training. Teleteaching 98 Conference, Vienna (1999)* [ONLINE] Available at: http://www.ex.ac.uk/telematics/T3/corecurr/tteach98.htm. Accessed 23 Nov 2003.

Devine-Wright, P., Devine-Wright, H., & Fleming, P. (2004). Situational influences upon children's beliefs about global warming and energy. *Environmental Education Research, 10*(4), 493–506.

Dimitriou, A., & Christidou, V. (2007). Pupils' understanding of air pollution. *Journal of Biological Education, 42*(1), 24–29.

Dueker, K. J., & Kjerne, D. (1989). Multipurpose cadastre: Terms and definitions. In *Proceedings of the Annual Convention of ACSM-ASPRS, American Congress on Surveying and Mapping, Bethesda, MD,* 5 (pp. 94–103).

Ekanayake, S., & Wishart, J. (2011). Identifying the potential of mobile phone cameras in science teaching and learning: A case study undertaken in Sri Lanka. *International Journal of Mobile and Blended Learning (IJMBL), 3*(2), 16–30.

El-Fadel, M., Findikakis, A. N., & Leckie, J. O. (1997). Environmental impacts of solid waste landfilling. *Journal of Environmental Management, 50*(1), 1–25.

EuropeAir [ONLINE] Available at: https://www.eea.europa.eu/mobile/apps [2018-05-16].

Finucane, P. M., Johnson, S. M., & Prideaux, D. J. (1998). Problem-based learning: Its rationale and efficacy. *Medical Journal of Australia, 168*(9), 445–447.

Fullerton, D. & Kinnaman, T. C. (1994). *Household demand for garbage and recycling collection with the start of a price per bag.* National bureau of economic research, *Working Paper* No. 4670, 43 p. [ONLINE]. Available at: http://www.nber.org/papers/w4670.pdf

Gaible, E., Bloome, T., Schwartz, A., Hoopes, J. & Wayan, P. (2011). *First principles: Designing effective education programs using Information and Communication Technology (ICT).* [pdf] Available at: http://www.equip123.net/docs/E1-FP_ICT_Compendium.pdf. Accessed 02 Jan 2018.

Gilbertson, K. (2006). *Outdoor education: Methods and strategies.* Champaign: Human Kinetics.

GLONASS. https://www.egnos-portal.eu/discover-egnos/about-egnos/what-gnss – [2018-02-14].

Graham, C. R. (2006). Blended learning systems. In *The handbook of blended learning* (pp. 3–21).

Grant, M. M. (2002). Getting a grip on project-based learning: Theory, cases and recommendations. *Meridian: A Middle School Computer Technologies Journal, 5*(1), 83.

Gray, N. F., & Gray, R. O. (2004). Litter deposition on minor rural roads in Ireland. *Municipal Engineer, 157*(3), 185–192.

Guazzaroni, G. (2012). Emotional mapping of museum augmented places. *Archeomatica, 3*(3), 44–46.

Hartley, B. L., Thompson, R. C., & Pahl, S. (2014). Marine litter education boosts children's understanding and self-reported actions. *Marine Pollution Bulletin* (2014). [ONLINE] Available at: https://doi.org/10.1016/j.marpolbul.2014.10.049.

Hashemi, M., Azizinezhad, M., Najafi, V., & Nesari, A. J. (2011). What is mobile learning? Challenges and capabilities. *Procedia-Social and Behavioral Sciences, 30*, 2477–2481.

Hoel, M. (1991). Global environmental problems: The effects of unilateral actions taken by one country. *Journal of Environmental Economics and Management, 20*(1), 55–70.

Huizenga, J. C., ten Dam, G. T. M., Voogt, J. M., & Admiraal, W. F. (2017). Teacher perceptions of the value of game-based learning in secondary education. *Computers and Education, 110*, 105–115.

Hungerford, H. R., & Volk, T. L. (1990). Changing learner behavior through environmental education. *The Journal of Environmental Education, 21*(3), 8–21.

Ichinose, D., & Yamamoto, M. (2011). On the relationship between the provision of waste management service and illegal dumping. *Resource and Energy Economics, 33*(2011), 79–93.

Ifegbesan, A. (2010). Exploring secondary school students' understanding and practices of waste management in Ogun State, Nigeria. *International Journal of Environmental and Science Education, 5*(2), 201–215.

International Union for the Conservation of Nature, IUCN. (1970). *International working meeting on environmental education in the school curriculum*. Paris: UNESCO.

Invasive Alien Species Europe [ONLINE] Available at: https://ec.europa.eu/jrc/en/news/new-application-tracking-invasive-alien-species-your-smartphone [2018-05-14].

Ivy, T. G.-C., Road, K. S., Lee, C. K.-E., & Chuan, G. K. (1998). A survey of environmental knowledge, attitudes and behaviour of students in Singapore. *International Research in Geographical and Environmental Education, 7*(3), 181–202.

Jensen, B. B. (2002). Knowledge, action and pro-environmental behaviour. *Environmental Education Research, 8*(3), 325–334.

Johansson, T. (2003). *GIS in teacher education – Facilitating GIS applications in secondary school geography*. [ONLINE] Available at: https://pdfs.semanticscholar.org/a691/303ad2d0f30ab92d819bd86e113ac5ab20b4.pdf

Kamarainen, A. M., Metcalf, S., Grotzer, T., Browne, A., Mazzuca, D., Tutwiler, M. S., & Dede, C. (2013). EcoMOBILE: Integrating augmented reality and probeware with environmental education field trips. *Computers and Education, 68*, 545–556.

Kerski, J. J., Demirci, A., & Milson, A. J. (2013). The global landscape of GIS in secondary education. *Journal of Geography, 112*(6), 232–247.

Kirschner, P., & Wopereis, I. G. (2003). Mindtools for teacher communities: A European perspective. *Technology, Pedagogy and Education, 12*(1), 105–124.

Klopfer, E., Sheldon, J., Perry, J., & Chen, V. H. (2012). Ubiquitous games for learning (UbiqGames): Weatherlings, a worked example. *Journal of Computer Assisted Learning, 28*(5), 465–476.

Korucu, A. T., & Alkan, A. (2011). Differences between M-learning (mobile learning) and e-learning, basic terminology and usage of M-learning in education. *Procedia-Social and Behavioral Sciences, 15*, 1925–1930.

Krajcik, J. S., & Blumenfeld, P. C. (2006). Project-based learning. In R. Keith Sawyer (Ed.), *The Cambridge handbook of the learning sciences* (pp. 317–333). Cambridge: Cambridge University Press.

Kuhlemeier, H., Van Den Bergh, H., & Lagerweij, N. (1999). Environmental knowledge, attitudes, and behavior in Dutch secondary education. *The Journal of Environmental Education, 30*(2), 4–14.

Kukulska-Hulme, A., & Traxler, J. (Eds.). (2005). *Mobile learning: A handbook for educators and trainers*. London: Routledge.

Landenberger, R. E., Warner, T. A., Ensign, T. I., & Nellis, M. D. (2006). Using remote sensing and GIS to teach inquiry-based spatial thinking skills: An example using the GLOBE program's integrated Earth systems science. *Geocarto International, 21*(3), 61–71.

Lappin, E. (1984). *Outdoor education for behaviour disordered students*. ERIC clearinghouse on rural education and small schools, Las Cruces, N. Mexico, 4 p. [ONLINE] Available at: https://files.eric.ed.gov/fulltext/ED261811.pdf

Liu, S., & Zhu, X. (2008). Designing a structured and interactive learning environment based on GIS for secondary geography education. *Journal of Geography, 107*(1), 12–19.

Liu, Y., Bui, E. N., Chang, C. H., & Lossman, H. G. (2010). PBL-GIS in secondary geography education: Does it result in higher-order learning outcomes? *Journal of Geography, 109*(4), 150–158.

Livingstone, S. (2012). Critical reflections on the benefits of ICT in education. *Oxford Review of Education, 38*(1), 9–24.

Lowenstein, E., Martusewicz, R., & Voelker, L. (2010). Developing teachers' capacity for ecojustice education and community-based learning. *Teacher Education Quarterly, 37*(4), Education and the Environment (Fall 2010), 99–118.

Makki, M. H., Abd-ed-Khalick, F., & Boujaoude, S. (2003). Lebanese secondary school students' environmental knowledge and attitudes. *Environmental Education Research, 9*(1), 21–33.

Marine Debris Tracker [ONLINE] Available at: http://www.marinedebris.engr.uga.edu/ [2018-05-16].

Marine Litter Watch [ONLINE] Available at: https://www.eea.europa.eu/data-and-maps/data/marine-litter [2018-05-08].

Marriott, M. (2005). Use this phone to find a date. Or see videos. Or even talk. *New York Times*, July 4, 2005. [ONLINE] Available at: https://www.nytimes.com/2005/07/04/technology/use-this-phone-to-find-a-date-or-see-videos-or-even-talk.html

Marsh, D. (2012). Blended learning creating learning opportunities for language learners. Retrieved April, 20, p. 2015.

McGreen, N. & Arnedillo-Sánchez, I. (2005). Mapping challenge: A case study in the use of mobile phones in collaborative, contextual learning. *Mobile learning*, 213–217.

McKinney, M. L., & Lockwood, J. L. (1999). Biotic homogenization: A few winners replacing many losers in the next mass extinction. *Trends in Ecology & Evolution, 14*, 450–453.

McMichael, A. J., Friel, S., Nyong, A., & Corvalan, C. (2008). Global environmental change and health: Impacts, inequalities, and the health sector. *BMJ: British Medical Journal, 336*(7637), 191–194.

Mergendoller, J. R., Markham, T., Ravitz, J., & Larmer, J. (2006). Pervasive management of project-based learning: Teachers as guides and facilitators. In *Handbook of classroom management: Research, practice, and contemporary issues* (pp. 583–615). Mahwah: Lawrence Erlbaum, Inc.

Mooney, H. A., & Cleland, E. E. (2001). The evolutionary impact of invasive species. *Proceedings of the National Academy of Sciences, 98*(10), 5446–5451.

Motiwalla, L. F. (2007). Mobile learning: A framework and evaluation. *Computers and Education, 49*(3), 581–596.

Myers, G., Boyes, E., & Stanisstreet, M. (2004). School students' ideas about air pollution: Knowledge and attitudes. *Research in Science and Technological Education, 22*(2), 133–152.

New South Wales Environment Protection Authority (NSWEPA), 2018. [ONLINE] Available at: https://www.epa.nsw.gov.au/

Ozdamli, F., & Cavus, N. (2011). Basic elements and characteristics of mobile learning. *Procedia: Social and Behavioral Sciences, 28*, 937–942.

Palmberg, I. E., & Kuru, J. (2000). Outdoor activities as a basis for environmental responsibility. *The Journal of Environmental Education, 31*(4), 32–36.
Pfligersdorffer, G. (1984). Empirische Untersuchung über Lerneffekte auf Biologieexkursionen. na.
Priest, S. (1986). Redefining outdoor education: A matter of many relationships. *The Journal of Environmental Education, 17*(3), 13–15.
Punter, P., Ochando-Pardo, M., & Garcia, J. (2011). Spanish secondary school students' notions on the causes and consequences of climate change. *International Journal of Science Education, 33*(3), 447–464.
Pyšek, P., Sádlo, J., & Mandák, B. (2002). Catalogue of alien plants of the Czech Republic. *Preslia, 74*(2), 97–186.
Ramirez, M., & Althouse, P. (1995). Fresh thinking: GIS in environmental education. *THE Journal (Technological Horizons In Education), 23*(2), 87.
Ramsey, J. M., Hungerford, H. R., & Volk, T. L. (1992). Environmental education in the K-12 curriculum: Finding a niche. *The Journal of Environmental Education, 23*(2), 35–45.
Randler, C., Ilg, A., & Kern, J. (2005). Cognitive and emotional evaluation of an amphibian conservation program for elementary school students. *The Journal of Environmental Education, 37*(1), 43–52.
Ravitz, J., Hixson, N., English, M., & Megendoller, J. (2012). Using project based learning to teach 21st century skills: Findings from a statewide initiative. PBL and 21st Century Skills, AERA – Vancouver, BC(2012).
Richardson, D. M., Pyšek, P., Rejmánek, M., Barbour, M. G., Panetta, F. D., & West, C. J. (2000). Naturalization and invasion of alien plants: Concepts and definitions. *Diversity and Distributions, 6*(2), 93–107.
Rose, J. (2009). *Identifying and teaching children and young people with dyslexia and literacy difficulties: An independent report*, 214 p. [ONLINE] Available at: http://dera.ioe.ac.uk/14790/7/00659-2009DOM-EN_Redacted.pdf
Ruchter, M., Klar, B., & Geiger, W. (2010). Comparing the effects of mobile computers and traditional approaches in environmental education. *Computers and Education, 54*(4), 1054–1067.
Santos, I. R., Friedrich, A. C., Wallner-Kersanach, M., & Fillmann, G. (2005). Influence of socio-economic characteristics of beach users on litter generation. *Ocean and Coastal Management, 48*(2005), 742–752.
Sarrab, M., Elgamel, L., & Aldabbas, H. (2012). Mobile learning (m-learning) and educational environments. *International Journal of Distributed and Parallel Systems, 3*(4), 31.
Schipper, L., & Pelling, M. (2006). Disaster risk, climate change and international development: Scope for, and challenges to, integration. *Disasters, 30*(1), 19–38.
Selby, D. (2000). Global education as transformative education. *Zeitschrift fuer internationale Bildungsforschung und Entwicklungspaedagogik, 23*(3), 2–10.
Sharples, M., Arnedillo-Sánchez, I., Milrad, M., & Vavoula, G. (2009). Mobile learning. In *Technology-enhanced learning* (pp. 233–249). Dordrecht: Springer.
Shepardson, D. P., Niyogi, D., Choi, S., & Charusombat, U. (2009). Seventh grade students' conceptions of global warming and climate change. *Environmental Education Research, 15*(5), 549–570.
Shobeiri, S. M., Omidvar, B., & Prahallada, N. N. (2007). A comperative study of environmental awareness among secondary school students in Iran and India. *International Journal of Environment Research, 1*(1), 28–34.
So, H. J., & Brush, T. A. (2008). Student perceptions of collaborative learning, social presence and satisfaction in a blended learning environment: Relationships and critical factors. *Computers & Education, 51*(1), 318–336.
So, H. J., & Kim, B. (2009). Learning about problem based learning: Student teachers integrating technology, pedagogy and content knowledge. *Australasian Journal of Educational Technology, 25*(1), 101–116.

Solomon, G. (2003). Project-based learning: A primer. *Technology and Learning-Dayton, 23*(6), 20–20.

Stapp, W. B. (1969). The concept of environmental education. *Environmental Education, 1*(1), 30–31.

Starosta, B. (1990). *"Erkundungen der belebten Natur nach dem Prinzip des entdeckenden Lernens- didaktische Konzepte und Ergebnisse einer empirischen Untersuchung* [Discoveries in living nature according to the principle of learning by discovery: Didactic concepts and results of an empirical study]". In W. Killermann, & L. Staeck (Eds.), *Methoden des Biologieunterrichtes* [Methods of biology education] (pp. 316–326). Köln: Aulis–Verlag.

The National Education Programme of Slovakia. (2015). The National Institute for Education of the Ministry of Education, Science, Research and Sport of the Slovak Republic. [ONLINE] Available at: http://www.statpedu.sk/sk/svp/statny-vzdelavaci-program/statny-vzdelavaci-program-gymnazia/vyssie-sekundarne-vzdelavanie/

Trash Out [ONLINE] Available at: www.trashout.ngo [2018-04-28].

UNESCO-UNEP International Environmental Education Programme. (1992). *Environmental education activities for primary schools*. [ONLINE] Available at: http://unesdoc.unesco.org/images/0009/000963/096345eo.pdf

Uzunboylu, H., Cavus, N., & Ercag, E. (2009). Using mobile learning to increase environmental awareness. *Computers and Education, 52*(2), 381–389.

Verma, S., Verma, R. K., Singh, A., & Naik, N. S. (2012). Web-based GIS and desktop open source GIS software: An emerging innovative approach for water resources management. In *Advances in computer science, engineering & applications* (pp. 1061–1074). Berlin/Heidelberg: Springer.

Vesilind, P. A., Worrell, W. A., & Reinhart, D. R. (2002). *Solid waste engineering*. Forest Loadge Road, Brooks/Cole, Pacific Grove, CA, 428 p.

Vitousek, P. M., Antonio, C. M., Loope, L. L., & Westbrooks, R. (1996). Biological invasions as global environmental change. *American Scientist, 84*(5)., 468 p.

Westbrooks, R. (1998). *Invasive plants, changing the landscape of America: Fact book*. Washington, DC: Federal Interagency Committee for the Management of Noxious and Exotic Weeds (FICMNEW), 109 p.

Wiegand, P. (2001). Geographical information systems (GIS) in education. *International Research in Geographical and Environmental Education, 10*(1), 68–71.

Williamson, M. (1996). *Biological invasions* (Vol. 15). Springer Science and Business Media. 244 p.

Zigová, M., Pucherová, Z. & Jakab, I. (2018). *Innovative model of environmental education in lower secondary education. DIVAI 2018 – The 12th international scientific conference on distance learning in applied informatics*. Conference proceedings Štúrovo, Slovakia May 2–4, 2018, 205–216.

Chapter 14
Collaborative Learning as Learning Based on Cooperation with the Use of New Technologies

Jolanta Szulc

14.1 Introduction

The *collaborative learning* model refers to the concept of Lev Vygotsky, according to which tasks performed by learners are divided into those that can be performed and those that cannot be performed. Between the two areas, there is a so-called zone of proximal development, which includes tasks that the learner cannot do on his own the first time but is able to do it with the support of the council (Chaiklin 2003). The area of the nearest development allows to formulate conclusions on the development of the learner's skills. In his definition, L. Vygotsky stressed the importance of learning through communication and interaction with other people, and not only through independent work ("Lev Vygotsky" 2018).

The term *collaborative learning* means:

- An e-learning method in which one or more students, teachers, and/or people learn together, conduct research, and participate in educational courses. Collaborative learning strengthens the typical educational approach, enabling remotely connected peers and individuals to collaborate in real time through technological aids and resources ("Collaborative Learning," In *Technopedia* 2018a).
- The teaching techniques for student groups that have a positive effect on joint learning can be used for two students or a larger group. These techniques include one-on-one (when students help each other), peer learning (time when one student works with another student), and small group (simple and short activities, such as playing in games, charting, or project-based learning that requires

---

J. Szulc (✉)
Institute of Library and Information Science, University of Silesia in Katowice, Katowice, Poland
e-mail: jolanta.szulc@us.edu.pl

teamwork of students lasting several weeks or longer) ("What Is Collaborative Learning" 2018).
- A situation in which two or more people learn or try to learn something together. In contrast to individual learning, those involved in collaborative learning can use each other's resources and skills (e.g., by asking each other, assessing each other's ideas, monitoring each other's work, etc.) ("Collaborative Learning," In *Wikipedia* 2018b).

In Polish, other terms are also used, such as cooperative teaching, learning in cooperation, and group form of students' work. In English, the term *collaborative learning* is combined with the expression *cooperative learning*; in the first case we are talking about a joint effort of learners and in the second about the systematic division of work in the learning process (Dillenbourg 1999).

The ultimate goal in collaborative learning is building common knowledge among group members. It is achieved in a cooperation system that provides real-time communication and collaboration between users. Each student or teacher can interact with others in real time via instant messengers, voice calls, video, or a combination of these communication solutions. Students can share, collaborate, and act on various tasks and assignments through the online portal ("Collaborative Learning," In *Technopedia* 2018a).

In the wider context, *collaborative learning* is based on the model that knowledge can be created within a population whose members actively interact by exchanging experiences and undertaking different (asymmetric) roles. Moreover, *collaborative learning* involves such issues as cooperative teaching methods (e.g., method of structured collaborative learning, informal learning methods based on cooperation) and its effectiveness (Bobula et al. 2018), teacher's role in cooperative learning (e.g., teacher–planner, teacher–moderator/facilitator, teacher–arbitrator, teacher–evaluator) (Kisner 2018), and the impact of cooperative learning on the motivation of students (Panitz 1999).

14.2 Theoretical Assumptions and Findings/Results

Based on the analysis of the literature, the following assumptions and conclusions were formulated:
- Promoting group awareness is a key challenge for online collaboration. In the research conducted, three categories of group consciousness are distinguished: behavioral, knowledge, and social awareness. Most research concerns awareness of knowledge that can be expressed through technology. Its users can consciously express their current knowledge and feelings or evaluate themselves and others and provide the necessary information. These data can be visualized. *Collaborative learning* environments are supported by the *group awareness tool* (GAT). The subject of the research is the relationship between the use of GAT

and cognitive functions in the group, the quality of interaction, learning achievements, and changes of these data over time (Ghadirian et al. 2016).
- *Computer-supported collaborative learning* (CSCL) is widely used to facilitate learning in classes. The study involved students who used CSCL in single-user mode and in multiuser mode. Research results indicate that students prefer to use the multiuser mode and, moreover, show that the social impact plays an important role in decision-making, (2) training and help in solving problems facilitate the work of students, and (3) strategies for students engaging in mode for many users require further research (each student has the right to edit the shared file, which makes it difficult to reach a consensus) (Wang and Huang 2016).
- Cognitive styles affect student learning preferences, both during individual learning and collaborative learning. It seems necessary to examine how cognitive styles influence the way students relate to these two methods of learning. Special attention was paid to the serialist approach and holistic approach. The research results indicated that heterogeneous groups of students (applying both approaches) obtained the best results in learning using collaborative learning (Chen and Chang 2016).
- *Collaborative project-based learning* (CPBL) has been used in an interdisciplinary research project in which the elements of CPBL influence the way of learning. The study was conducted at the university located in the urban city of Los Angeles. As an institution serving minorities, the university's student body consists of approximately 53% Hispanic, 22% Asian–American, 15.6% White, 9% African–American, and 0.4% American Indian. The research results indicated that significant learning outcomes and higher efficiency in engineering design were directly related to the project experience. In addition, Hispanic students showed the largest growth of self-efficacy through CPBL. In the longer term, it is planned to conduct research on three areas: (1) course related knowledge and skills outcomes, (2) engineering efficacy in relation to the presence of learning, and (3) student engagement (deep vs. surface learning) and team dynamics (Chen et al. 2015).
- Research on interdisciplinary joint learning and its impact on assessment was carried out in the artistic/humanistic school environment. The research concerned the effectiveness of interdisciplinary collaborative student symposium as an assessment task and a practical model for facilitating interdisciplinary collaborative learning. The test results showed that collaborative teaching and learning, coupled with social software tools and associated modes of communication, foster innovative, high-quality interdisciplinary work and offer an adaptable assessment framework for broader application in higher education settings (Miles and Rainbird 2015).
- Research on *social anxiety* (SA) and *foreign language anxiety* (FLA) during online *collaborative learning* sessions showed that among participants who had experience with the Wiki during international cooperation, a level of anxiety (SA and FLA) was reduced. The study involved 49 high school students, aged between 15 and 18, from a private school in Taipei, Taiwan (Ku and Chen, 2015).

- Research on *collaborative learning* and the theory of cultural reproduction in cyberspace takes up the topic of criticism as an integral part of all teaching methods that seek to change society or transform the status quo. The subject of the research is *authoring functions* embedded in some communication technologies. Criticism can serve as an information function in pedagogical practice aimed at social change, instead of cultural reproduction (Payne 2000).
- *Collaborative learning* also requires a "physical" place, which can be a library. In planning and arranging contemporary library spaces, the needs of learners are increasingly taken into account, emphasizing the need for a space of social learning and cooperation as well as traditional places for quiet learning and reflection. Academic library is perceived as a permanent "physical" place, providing a hybrid environment of traditional and electronic services crucial for the future of universities and their communities (Mcdonald 2006).
- The development of new technologies requires changes in the field of teaching styles. The research results suggest that the so-called gray literature and content found in repositories, databases, and training platforms will be more and more common. Diverse teaching methods should take greater account of the environment in which teaching and learning take place in small groups (Gelfand 2006).
- Research shows that various tools and technologies were developed and used to support e-learning communities. Three components and systems have been identified: (1) the document-focused Web-based training tools, (2) tool focused on meetings (such as video conferencing tools, Centra symposium, etc.), and (3) the three-dimensional (3D)-centered multiuser tools which are based on multiuser *virtual reality* (VR) technology. The first system focuses on document management and individual learning. The second system – tools focused on the meeting – uses the approach of virtual representation of the concept of frontal learning. The general problem of these tools is the limited social integration of participants. Therefore, in such e-learning sessions, participants experience a sense of alienation. The third system, VR tools, focuses on the participants to have a sense of interaction and the existence of other participants. Participants of a virtual 3D session are represented by avatars that can move in a 3D environment. They are also able to see the actions of all other chips. In addition, virtual reality technology tools for many users, used in communication media, offer benefits related to the creation of a social presence and thus strengthen communication and interaction among participants. That's why many VR technology users are used to support collaboration (Badawy 2012).

14.3 Application of Modern Technologies

The tools used in collaborative learning include:

- *Internet forums*. In the research, the authors try to indicate what factors determine the use of students from online forums and provide empirical evidence on their impact on learning performance. The results indicate that not the ease of use, but the perceived usability, determines the positive attitude to the forum. The new education system should be seen as a gradual process in which students develop their positive attitude toward the system. Particular attention should be paid not only to the layout of the website supporting the forum but also to its usefulness and ability to stimulate current discussions among students (Camarero et al. 2012).

Interesting results were obtained during the study of the online course discussion forum, which were used to assess students' critical thinking. We measure critical thinking with the help of an appropriate model developed by D. R. Newman, Brian Webb, and Clive Cochrane, who distinguish 40 critical thinking indicators grouped into 10 categories. Calculated critical indicators of thinking for the analyzed two threads of discussion in the forum indicate a strong use of outside knowledge and intensive justification as well as critical assessment of posts by the student. But at the same time, weak points are also repeated. Based on these results, changes were made to the next course cycle to improve students' critical thinking (Beckmann and Weber 2016).

- *Tools shared by Google.* For example, Google apps for education (GAFE), as a Google service, provides independently configurable versions of several Google products, using the domain name provided by the customer. It contains several Web applications with functionality similar to traditional office suites, such as Docs, Drive, Gmail, Google Calendar, Groups, Hangouts, News, Play, Sheets, Sites, Slides, and Vault (Boudreau 2016).

The results suggest that Google Docs is a useful tool for collaborative writing and influenced student learning. The research was about (1) assessing the effectiveness of using Google Docs in an out-of-class collaborative writing activity through measuring the assignment's influence on students' learning experiences, (2) teaching students to work collaboratively, and (3) teaching students to successfully communicate their understanding and application of concepts through writing. Most students were unfamiliar with Google Docs prior to the study. During the study, the results of students working in two teams were compared, one with Google Docs and one without. The following detailed results were obtained: (1) Google Docs changed the means of communication used in collaborative writing, (2) 93% of students considered Google Docs a useful tool for group work, and (3) using Google Docs had no effect on students' paper grades. Half of the students participating in the study reported that they would like to use Google Docs in the future (Zhou et al. 2012).

Another study used a Web-based tool, Google Docs, to determine the effects of Web-based collaboration on vocabulary improvements among learners of English as a foreign language (EFL). The study was attended by 210 students who undertook the designed tasks such as vocabulary pre-/posttests and a self-report questionnaire survey of self-regulated vocabulary strategy use and perceptions of Web-based collaboration (SRvsWBC). The findings of the study suggest that collaboration using a Web-based tool affects knowledge development and strengthens the process of L2/FL learning (Liu et al. 2014).

- *Open access to tutorials*. For example, access to tutorials on information literacy in the InfoSkills database at the University of Technology Sydney (UTS) in Australia. The State Library of New South Wales provided access to an open repository of information literacy materials to enable the reuse of accumulated resources and collaborative learning. This is possible thanks to a combination of metadata and the work of search engines. In its InfoSkills database, the library also has implemented Web 2.0 functions (England 2010).

  Another example is the Configurable Argumentation Support Engine (CASE). The platform was designed in order to reduce the developmental effort and development costs. CASE detects pedagogically relevant patterns in argument diagrams and provides feedback and hints in response. A wide range of patterns are supported, including the ones sensitive to students' understanding of the domain, problem-solving processes, and collaboration processes. Teachers and researchers can configure the behavior of tutorial agents on three levels: patterns, tutorial exercises, and tutorial strategies (Scheuer and McLaren 2013).

  Hidden Markov models (HMMs) can be used to explore the relationship between dialogue structure and learning effectiveness. A model was developed to identify effective tutorial strategies using a machine-learning approach that (1) learns tutorial modes from a corpus of human tutoring and (2) identifies the statistical relationships between student outcomes and the learned modes. Research results suggest that HMMs can learn the structure of hidden tutorial dialogues. More specifically, the results point to specific mechanisms within a task-oriented tutorial that improves student learning (Boyer 2011).

- *Semantic Web*. In practice, there are Semantic Web services (SWS) perceived as a technology that has the chance to change the way of learning. For example, the Design Patterns Teaching Help System (DEPTHS) operating in the interactive personal learning environment was developed as a template for software design (Jeremic et al. 2009).

  The teacher can plan a collaborative learning (CL) scenario that increases the effectiveness of learning to help students properly acquire and develop their knowledge and skills. Such a scenario defines pedagogically structures that prevent non-task activities and involve students in more significant interactions. The main difficulty in designing effective CL scenarios is to change the teacher's intentions into elements constituting a learning scenario. To solve this problem, an intelligent document creation tool called CHOCOLATO was developed, using Semantic Web technologies (e.g., ontologies) to represent knowledge about the various methods and practices involved in collaboration. Through the use of this knowledge, CHOCOLATO can provide smart tips that help teachers create CL scenarios based on theory. The CHOCOLATO project has been verified in several experiments (Isotani et al. 2013). The latest research on collaborative learning uses the term pervasive knowledge. The broad spectrum of acquiring pervasive knowledge enriches the users' experience in learning. The use of online learning resources (OLR) from multichannels in learning activities such as compiling big data, cloud computing, and Semantic Web allows you to learn anywhere, anytime. Researchers propose pervasive knowledge that can meet the need for integration of technologies such as cloud computing, big data, Web 2.0, and Semantic Web. Pervasive knowledge redefines value added, variety, volume, and velocity of OLR (Anshari et al. 2016).

Currently, the e-learning 2.0 model is proposed with social networking features, ubiquitous knowledge management, and the approach to cloud computing. We providing cloud services and we offer specialized service, dedicated personnel for specialized service, fees for use, richness of content and knowledge of Web 2.0 and Semantic Web. Web 2.0 enabled students to dynamically enrich personalized informations. Semantic Web will support the cloud service providers in providing e-learning services to users (Anshari et al. 2015).

- *Virtual technology platforms*. The platform that supports electronic business management section (eBMS) is an example of such a platform. *Collaborative learning* should use a mixed learning strategy in which the "personalization" principle plays a strategic role: A personalized learning model is applied to learning processes and services embedded in the technology platform that support an international community of scientists and learners (Assaf et al. 2009).

Experiences in cooperation in learning in an asynchronous environment through discussion forums on the WebCt platform of the virtual campus of the University of Huelva in Spain in 2007–2008 were subject to analysis. This interesting project describes processes of common knowledge building and meaning multi-to-many communication in solving collective cases in asynchronous writing contexts. Two analytical approaches were adopted: discourse analysis and social network analysis. In case group A, where the occurrence of speech was less widespread, social network analysis markers showed significant coherence and low level of network centrality. However, the occurrence of speech was higher in group B, and network centrality rates were higher, although the group was less coherent. These observations allow to formulate the conclusion that many-to-many communication is more important in collective knowledge generation processes than dyadic or triadic communication (Tirado et al. 2011).

Research in virtual worlds on collaborative learners are gradually gaining importance. Virtual learning environments are active for educational purposes and are often sponsored by academic institutions or nonprofit organizations. Virtual educational environments can use spaces where students can meet for lectures, class activities, group work, discussion, and projects or socialize with their peers. They are used as an addition to traditional classes or as a supplemental mode in distance education delivery programs. It is estimated that over 200 universities and other educational institutions run a virtual class in Second Life. These include the British Open University, MIT, Harvard, and Princeton (Hanewald 2013).

In addition, creating software for 3D simulation and virtual platforms for many users is the scope of activity of many companies that are prospering on the market. This is confirmed by experience in working with Linden Lab in the Second Life education department and neurological research. Its main goal is to learn together and to provide instructional design and cooperation with academic and business clients to create immersive learning environments (Beaubois 2013).

14.4 Original Projects

In practice, numerous activities are undertaken to help in the implementation of collaborative learning. Numerous projects are created, e.g., the international CoLab project "Promoting innovative collaborative teaching and learning," implemented by a consortium of seven European institutions, including the Educational Research Institute. The project concerns, among others, the support of professional development of teachers in the field of innovative methods and forms of teaching in lessons and, above all, the use of group work of students ("Instytut Badań Edukacyjnych" 2018). The home page of the project is available at http://colab.eun.org/home. An example of another project is "Mobile Intercultural Cooperative Learning (MICOOL)," conducted as part of Erasmus + by Dublin City University, in cooperation with the Faculty of Pedagogical Sciences of the Special Education Academy. Maria Grzegorzewska and partners: Agrupamento de Escolas de Figueiró dos Vinhos (Portugal), Pädagogische Hochschule FHNW (Switzerland), Staatliches Schulamt Lörrach (Germany), Osnovna Skola Marsal Tito (Montenegro), and Infocus Training Ltd. (Ireland). The project was being implemented in the period 01/09/2015–1/09/2017 ("Akademia Pedagogiki Specjalnej" 2018).

As part of another concept, a methodology for creating and disseminating audiovisual projects enabling online cooperation has been developed, using new technologies and video tools (*open source*) that can be used in any e-learning environment in higher education. The methodology was developed and applied at the Open University of Catalonia (Universitat Oberta de Catalunya, UOC). It combines three pedagogical strategies in an e-learning environment: project-based learning, computer-supported *collaborative learning*, and participatory culture as a new *literacy* form (Ornellas et al. 2014).

Interesting projects can also include a project implemented by the College of Architecture and Design and the Littman Architecture Library at the New Jersey Institute of Technology for cooperation of the academic community in the field of improving the quality of education (Cays and Gervits 2012) or the space design project of the Hong Kong University of Science and Technology Library (HKUST Library) understood as a platform for various educational activities (Chan and Spodick 2014).

14.5 Conclusion

Collaborative learning has advantages and disadvantages. It allows students to collaborate on the understanding, solution, or creation of an artifact in science. At the same time, it redefines the traditional student–teacher relations in the classroom, which causes controversy as to whether this paradigm is more favorable than harmful (Inaba et al. 2003), (Isotani and Mizoguchi 2006). Undoubtedly, joint educational activities may include joint writing and joint problem-solving as well as joint debates, group projects, research teams, and other ventures. This approach is closely related to *cooperative learning* (Johnson et al. 2008), (Johnson et al. 2018).

Another important issue related to collaborative learning is the impact of new technologies. New media and technologies influence the learning process at every stage (Bowdur and Aptekorz 2014). In addition to traditional training methods and techniques, discussion groups are available on social networks, podcasts, webinars, WebQuests, etc. There are also new – for example, *blended collaborative learning*. All these technological facilities can increase the efficiency of training and education. However, remember that they do not override the most important principles and goals of learning and teaching.

The first step to implementing an effective virtual e-learning environment is to examine its main functions. These functional features should distinguish the e-learning environment from other designs and designed virtual environments commonly used. Research indicates that any virtual environment that integrates certain features can be characterized as *collaborative e-learning* (CEL). The following features of the CEL are listed in the literature on the subject:

- Users who have different roles and permissions can visit the environment.
- Educational interactions in the environment should change the simple virtual space to the communication space.
- Users should be provided with multiple communication channels that allow them to interact with each other in the virtual space.
- The environment should be represented by various representation forms, which can range from simple text to 3D worlds.
- Learners in the environment should not be passive but should be able to interact.
- The system supporting the e-learning environment should be able to integrate various technologies.
- The environment should support various e-learning scenarios.
- The environment should have common features with the physical space.

It seems that these features will have a decisive impact on the development of the CEL.

References

Akademia Pedagogiki Specjalnej im. Marii Grzegorzewskiej. (2018, June 10). Retrieved from http://www.aps.edu.pl/uczelnia/projekty/projekty-w-trakcie-realizacji/mobile-intercultural-cooperative-learning-micool.aspx
Anshari, M., Alas, Y., & Guan, L. S. (2015). Pervasive knowledge, social networks, and cloud computing: E-learning 2.0. *EURASIA Journal of Mathematics, Science & Technology Education, 11*(5), 909–921.
Anshari, M., Alas, Y., & Guan, L. S. (2016). Developing online learning resources: Big data, social networks, and cloud computing to support pervasive knowledge. *Education and Information Technologies, 21*(6), 1663–1677.
Assaf, W., Elia, G., Fayyoumi, A., & Taurino, C. (2009). Virtual eBMS: A virtual learning community supporting personalised learning. *International Journal of Web Based Communities, 5*(2), 6.

Badawy, M. K. (2012). Collaborative E-learning: Towards designing an innovative architecture for an educational virtual environment. In E. Pontes, A. Silva, A. Guelfi, S. T. Kofuji (Eds.), *Methodologies, tools and new developments for E-learning* (pp. 217–240). New York: InTech. (2018, June 10). Retrieved from https://docs.google.com/viewerng/viewer?url=http://cdn.intechopen.com/pdfs/27927.pdf&time=5e5320df6d4216bfef9cfab7c8cdee85

Beaubois, T. (2013). Speaking personally–with John "pathfinder" Lester. *American Journal of Distance Education, 27*(4), 265–268.

Beckmann, J., & Weber, P. (2016). Cognitive presence in virtual collaborative learning: Assessing and improving critical thinking in online discussion forums. *Interactive Technology and Smart Education, 13*(1), 52–70.

Bobula, S., Karaszewski, N., Kołodziejczyk, J., & Salamon-Bobińska, K. (2018, June 10). *Sesja II/9 Nauczanie kooperatywne (nauczanie we współpracy)*. Retrieved from http://www.npseo.pl/data/various/files/Sesja%20II_9%20Jakub%20Ko%C5%82odziejczykpdf

Boudreau, T. (2016). Connected library going Google! *Teaching Librarian, 23*(3), 24–26.

Bowdur, E., & Aptekorz, M. (Eds.). (2014). *Selected issues and trends of contemporary digital education: Wybrane zagadnienia i trendy współczesnej edukacji cyfrowej* (p. 60). Katowice: Stowarzyszenie Komputer i Sprawy Szkoły.

Boyer, K. E., Phillips, R., Ingram, A., Ha, E. Y., Wallis, M., Vouk, M., & Lester, J. (2011). Investigating the relationship between dialogue structure and tutoring effectiveness: A hidden Markov modeling approach. *International Journal of Artificial Intelligence in Education, 21*(1–2), 65–81.

Camarero, C., Javier, R., & José, R. (2012). An exploratory study of online forums as a collaborative learning tool. *Online Information Review, 36*(4), 568–586.

Cays, J., & Gervits, M. (2012). Evolving libraries: People and technology collaborating to build university design communities. *Art Documentation: Bulletin of the Art Libraries Society of North America, 31*(2), 235–244.

Chaiklin, S. (2003). The zone of proximal development in Vygotsky's analysis of learning and instruction. In A. Kozulin, B. Gindis, V. Ageyev, & S. Miller (Eds.), *Vygotsky's educational theory and practice in cultural context* (pp. 39–64). Cambridge: Cambridge University.

Chan, D. L. H., & Spodick, E. (2014). A case study of HKUST library. *New Library World, 115*(5/6), 250–262.

Chen, S. Y., & Chang, L.-P. (2016). The influences of cognitive styles on individual learning and collaborative learning. *Innovations in Education and Teaching International, 53*(4), 458–471.

Chen, P., Hernandez, A., & Dong, J. (2015). Impact of collaborative project-based learning on self-efficacy of urban minority students in engineering. *Journal of Urban Learning, Teaching, and Research, 11*, 26–39.

Collaborative Learning. (2018a, June 10). *Technopedia*. Retrieved from https://www.techopedia.com/definition/2484/collaborative-learning

Collaborative Learning. (2018b, June 10). *Wikipedia. The free encyclopedia*. Retrieved from https://en.wikipedia.org/wiki/Collaborative_learning#Technology

Dillenbourg, P. (1999). What do you mean by 'collaborative learning'? In P. Dillenbourg (Ed.), *Collaborative learning* (pp. 1–19). Oxford: Elsevier.

England, A. (2010). Open content: from walled gardens to collaborative learning. *inCite, 31*(1/2), 10.

Gelfand, J. (2006). Challenges for collections in new collaborative teaching and learning environments: Does grey literature fill a void? *Grey Journal (TGJ), 2*(2), 77–83.

Ghadirian, H., Ayub, A. F. M., Silong, A. D., Bakar, K. B. A., & Hosseinzadeh, M. (2016). Group awareness in computer-supported collaborative learning environments. *International Education Studies, 9*(2), 120–131.

Hanewald, R. (2013). Learners and collaborative learning in virtual worlds: A review of the literature. *Turkish Online Journal of Distance Education, 14*(2), 233–247.

Inaba, A., Ikeda, M., & Mizoguchi, R. (2003). What learning patterns are effective for a learner growth? In *Proceedings of the international conference on artificial intelligence in education* (pp. 219–226). Amsterdam: IOS Press.

Instytut Badań Edukacyjnych. (2018, June 10). Retrieved from http://www.ibe.edu.pl/pl/o-instytucie/aktualnosci/613-innowacyjne-metody-nauczania

Isotani, S., & Mizoguchi, R. (2006). A framework for finegrained analysis and design of group learning activities. In *Proceedings of the international conference on computers in education* (Vol. 151, pp. 193–200). Amsterdam: IOS Press.

Isotani, S., Mizoguchi, R., Isotani, S., Capeli, O. M., Isotani, N., de Albuquerque, A. R. P. L., Bittencourt, I. I., & Jaques, P. (2013). A semantic web-based authoring tool to facilitate the planning of collaborative learning scenarios compliant with learning theories. *Computers & Education, 63*, 267–284.

Jeremic, Z., Jovanovic, J., & Gasevic, D. (2009). Evaluating an intelligent tutoring system for design patterns: The DEPTHS experience. *Educational Technology & Society, 12*(2), 111–130.

Johnson, D. W., Johnson, R. T., & Johnson Holubec, E. (2008). *Cooperation in the classroom* (8th ed.). Edina: Interaction Book Company.

Johnson, D. W., Johnson, R. T., & Smith, K. A. (2018, June 10). *Cooperative learning: Improving university instruction by basing practice on validated theory*. Retrieved from http://personal.cege.umn.edu/~smith/docs/Johnson-Johnson-Smith-Cooperative_Learning-JECT-Small_Group_Learning-draft.pdf

Kisner, M. J. (2018, June 10). *Teaching strategies used in a classroom by teachers*. Retrieved from http://peopleof.oureverydaylife.com/teaching-strategies-used-classroom-teachers9362.html#ixzz2Nk6sNEIG

Ku, T. D., & Chen, N. L. (2015). Influence of wiki participation on transnational collaboration learning anxiety in middle school students. *Internet Research, 25*(5), 794–810.

Liu, S. H.-J., Lan, Y.-J., & Ho, C. Y.-Y. (2014). Exploring the relationship between self regulated vocabulary learning and web-based collaboration. *Educational Technology & Society, 17*(4), 404–419.

Mcdonald, A. (2006). The ten commandments revisited: The qualities of good library space. *Liber Quarterly: The Journal of European Research Libraries, 16*(1–4), 104–119.

Miles, M., & Rainbird, S. (2015). Evaluating interdisciplinary collaborative learning and assesment in the creative arts and humanities. *Arts and Humanities in Higher Education: An International Journal of Theory, Research and Practice, 14*(4), 409–425.

Ornellas, A., Muñoz, C., & Pablo, C. (2014). A methodological approach to support collaborative media creation in an e-learning higher education context. *Open Learning, 29*(1), 59–71.

Panitz, T. (1999). The motivational benefits of cooperative learning. *New Directions for Teaching and Learning, 78*, 59–67.

Payne, D. (2000). Collaborative learning and cultural reproduction in cyberspace: Publishing students in electronic environments. *Journal of Electronic Publishing, 6*(1) (2018, June 10). Retrieved from http://quod.lib.umich.edu/j/jep/3336451.0006.109?view=text;rgn=main

Scheuer, O., & McLaren, B. M. (2013). CASE: A configurable argumentation support engine. *IEEE Transactions on Learning Technologies, 6*(2), 144–157.

Tirado, R., Aguaded, I., & Hernando, A. (2011). Collaborative learning processes in an asynchrnous environment: An analysis through discourse and social networks. *Journal of Latin American Communication Research, 2*(1), 115–146.

Vygotsky, L. (2018, June 10). *Wikipedia. The free encyclopedia*. Retrieved from https://en.wikipedia.org/wiki/Lev_Vygotsky

Wang, C.-S., & Huang, Y.-M. (2016). Acceptance of cloud services in face-to-face computer supported collaborative learning: A comparison single-user mode and multi-user mode. *Innovations in Education and Teaching International, 53*(6), 637–648.

What Is Collaborative Learning? – Benefits, Theory & Definition. (2018, June 10). *Study.com. Foundtions of Education: Help and Review*. Retrieved from http://study.com/academy/lesson/what-is-collaborative-learning-benefits-theorydefinition.html

Zhou, W., Simpson, E., & Domizi, D. P. (2012). Google docs in an out-of-class collaborative writing activity. *International Journal of Teaching and Learning in Higher Education, 24*(3), 359–375.

Chapter 15
Possible Cultural Diversity and Digital Competences: Retrospection from Mathematical Textbooks for Lower Secondary Level

Ján Gunčaga, Matthias Brandl, and Péter Körtesi

15.1 Introduction

UNESCO declares in its declaration (see UNESCO (2002)) that important factors of cultural diversity are an adaptive process in the society and have a big capacity for expression, creation and innovation. Expression, creation and innovation are important also in education process in our schools. If we have interest to access them, then we must start in the teacher training at universities.

The development of teacher training in Europe is a good example of cultural diversity and cultural exchange between countries, which brings implementation of best practice in solving many problems in preparing future teachers. Institutionalization of teacher training study was started in the primary level for preparing teachers in village schools. The first teacher institute in Europe was established by Saint John de la Salle (1651–1719) in Rems (France) in the year 1685. It was good example for institutional teacher training in other European countries, and these countries follow this example.

Another example of applying of cultural diversity is the field of mathematics education. According to Kántor (2013), it is good to know in mathematics education about mathematical concepts, theorems and proofs, but it is even better to know where they came from and why they are studied. Some inspirations are possible to find in historical mathematical textbooks or in mathematical books from known

---

J. Gunčaga (✉)
Faculty of Education, Comenius University in Bratislava, Bratislava, Slovakia
e-mail: guncaga@fedu.uniba.sk

M. Brandl
Faculty of Computer Science and Mathematics, University of Passau, Passau, Germany
e-mail: matthias.brandl@uni-passau.de

P. Körtesi
Faculty of Materials Science and Engineering, University of Miskolc, Miskolc, Hungary

© Springer Nature Switzerland AG 2019
E. Smyrnova-Trybulska et al. (eds.), *Universities in the Networked Society*,
Critical Studies of Education 10, https://doi.org/10.1007/978-3-030-05026-9_15

mathematicians in the past. These authors are from different countries, and they represent different cultural and schooling background.

The process of digitalization in libraries and archives makes historical mathematical textbooks more accessible for using in the teaching process. Different suitable educational software brings possibility to interpret and to use them in the new way, which can support digital and mathematical competences by students and pupils.

According to the document of the European Union Recommendation of the European Parliament and of the Council on 18 December 2006 on key competences for lifelong learning (2006), digital competence involves the confident and critical use of Information Society Technology (IST) for work, leisure and communication. It is underpinned by basic skills in information and communications technologies (ICT): the use of computers to retrieve, assess, store, produce, present and exchange information and to communicate and participate in collaborative networks via the Internet.

Digital competence requires a sound understanding and knowledge of the nature, role and opportunities of IST in everyday contexts: in personal and social life as well as at work. This includes main computer applications such as word processing, spreadsheets, databases and information storage and management and an understanding of the opportunities and potential risks of the Internet and communication via electronic media (e-mail, network tools) for work, leisure, information sharing and collaborative networking, learning and research.

Similar role in the document of the European Parliament play mathematical competence. This is the ability to develop and apply mathematical thinking in order to solve a range of problems in everyday situations. Building on a sound mastery of numeracy, the emphasis is on process and activity, as well as knowledge. Mathematical competence involves, to different degrees, the ability and willingness to use mathematical modes of thought (logical and spatial thinking) and presentation (formulas, models, constructs, graphs, charts). Necessary knowledge in mathematics includes a sound knowledge of numbers, measures and structures, basic operations and basic mathematical presentations, an understanding of mathematical terms and concepts, and an awareness of the questions to which mathematics can offer answers.

Digital competences have now big place in mathematics education. According to Oldknow and Taylor (2003), we can identify at least three reasons to promote an integration of Information and Communications Technologies (ICT) in the teaching process of mathematics at schools.

- **Desirability:** The use of ICT may stimulate pupils' motivation and curiosity and encourage them to develop their problem-solving strategies. Regarding teachers, the use of ICT can improve their efficiency, provide more time to address students individually or stimulate rethinking of their approach to teaching and understanding.
- **Inevitability:** Many fields of publishing have moved from a printed to an electronic form. This fact applies to conference proceedings and reference works such as encyclopaedias, small-circulation textbooks, special journals, etc.

- **Public policy:** Slovak National Curriculum ISCED 1, 2 and 3 classifies mathematics as a school subject, which is a part of the group called mathematics and working with information.

During the teaching process, ICT support the development and implementation of high-quality teaching and assessment materials. An important aspect of ICT-aided education is visualization. Within the framework of mathematics education, ICT promotes mathematical communication among teachers and students in the following ways.

- ICT provides an effective medium for communicating one's method for solving mathematics problems and discovering/communicating structures of various mathematical models.
- ICT promotes the visualization of relationships within and among various mathematical models, enabling students and teachers to develop new results and new connections in other fields within and outside of mathematics.
- ICT supports the building of various mathematical competences, including basic science, communication, and digital competences.

The educational software GeoGebra supports the realization of the above concerns. This software connects features of computer algebra system (CAS), interactive geometric software (IGS) and spreadsheet. GeoGebra provides this functionality within an intuitive, user-friendly interface. The software provides teachers and students with a method for authoring dynamic HTML websites with interactive pictures (see Hohenwarter and Lavicza 2010).

We will present in this chapter some concepts for school mathematics via materials from historical mathematical books and textbooks. We choose software GeoGebra for them, because this software is used in 62 languages. Using of ICT in mathematics education has influence to the process of gaining knowledge. We present in the following chapter the stages of gaining knowledge using GeoGebra.

15.2 The Process of Gaining Knowledge and GeoGebra

The process of gaining knowledge in mathematics education by Hejný and Littler (2006) is based on stages. It starts with motivation and its cores are two mental lifts: the first leads from concrete knowledge to generic knowledge and the second from generic to abstract knowledge. The permanent part of the gaining of knowledge process is crystallization, i.e. inserting new knowledge into the already existing mathematical structure. The whole process has following stages:

1. Motivation
2. Isolated models
3. Generic model(s)
4. Abstract knowledge
5. Crystallization
6. Automation

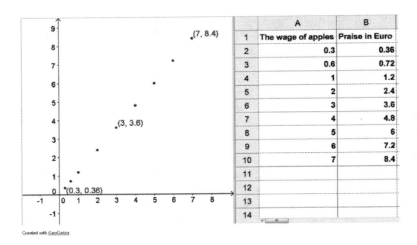

Fig. 15.1 Relationship wage of apples and price

Motivation is the tension which occurs in a person's mind as a result of the discrepancy between the existing and desired states of knowledge. The discrepancy comes from the difference between "I do not know" and "I need to know", or "I cannot do that" and "I want to be able to do that", sometimes from other needs and discrepancies, too. GeoGebra can be used an effective motivational tool because this software can represent a lot of mathematical notions and their relationship more visible in a dynamical way.

The pupils' experiences about some mathematical notions are possible to use as an isolated model. We can represent in the next example the price of apples according the wage of apples by the following table and graph prepared in GeoGebra. (1 kg apple ~ 1.20 Euro). First, in this case we can represent a function as a set of isolated points (see Fig. 15.1).

It is similar to the old Babylonian mathematicians, who studied the position of planets and represent their movement with the set of isolated points (picture of the positions of planets). In this stage (isolated models) the pupils in the school can measure the temperature, the high of the water level of the river during some time period. Their measurements were written in the table, which GeoGebra can represent very easily graphically.

In the third stage (generic models), we can try to find the curve which obtain the points and can lead to the graph of the function, which represent the concrete relationship. Abstract knowledge can be in this case the definition of the function, which we received in spontaneous and natural way from the previous isolated and generic models. Crystallization and automation work with concrete functions and also with functions which are not continuous and have more complicated shape (Fig. 15.2).

Fig. 15.2 An example of the graph of the function, which is not linear

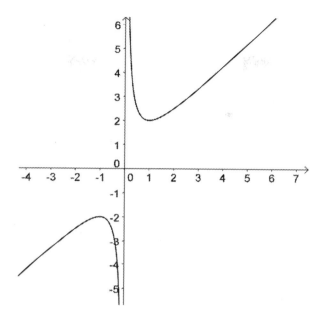

15.3 The Method of Generating Problems

There is often used in historical mathematical textbooks the method of generating problems (see Wittman (2001)). The aim of this method is to create areas in which pupil may – using the result of guided teaching – move as independently as possible and in which he/she may develop his/her own initiatives. The pupil is considering his own problem, and he could ask for help as far as it is necessary.

By this way he can obtain the basis for further work. After a problem has been completely solved and clarified, the teacher together with the students is thinking about further questions and generated problems which are related to the problem, which was just solved. Thus the original problem acts as a generating problem; we will call it generator problem (GP). Related problems are obtained by analogy, variation, generalization, specialization, etc. The group of all new problems together with their GP will be called the set of generated problems of the GP or the problem domain of GP.

The idea of generating new problems related to a given problem is also often used in the context of a specific educational focus on fostering a child's mathematical creativity. As described in Singer et al. (2016), the research team of Mihaela Singer took an approach to foster the so-called cognitive flexibility (which is described by cognitive variety, cognitive novelty and changes in cognitive framing) by the method of problem posing. Especially cognitive variety "manifests in the formulation of different new problems/properties from an input stimulus" (ibid., p. 15). Singer et al. (2013) explain further that the "problem-posing research is an emerging force within mathematics education, which offers a variety of contexts for studying and developing abilities in mathematically promising students" (Singer et al. 2016, p. 18).

Another big theory in didactics of mathematics and especially when it comes to aspects of fostering mathematical giftedness and creativity (but not only there) is the idea of multiple-solution tasks (MST) as suggested by Leikin (2009, 2013), for example, where MSTs are used as a lens to observe creativity in a problem-solving context.

In the context of historical approaches, authentic parts from history of mathematics can help to bring it "back to life". As mentioned in Klassen (2006), the "humanizing and clarifying influence of history of science brings the science to life and enables the student to construct relationships that would have been impossible in the traditional decontextualized manner in which science has been taught" (p. 48).

Whereas a direct use of original historical artefacts may be problematic, Kubli (2002, 2005) reports that students react more positively to historical materials when it is prepared in a narrative form. Bruner (1986) opposes the "logico-scientific mode" to the "narrative mode", too. An emotional engagement of the learners by an application of a so-called narrative didactic in mathematics education is, for example, intended in Brandl (2010, 2016).

15.4 Historical Background of the Mathematics Education in Textbook from René Descartes (1596–1650)

Arithmetic in the seventeenth century used geometrical representation. René Descartes (1596–1650) wrote in his textbook *La Geometrie* that "Any problem in geometry can easily be reduced to such terms that a knowledge of the lengths of certain straight lines is sufficient for its construction. Just as arithmetic consists of only four or five operations namely, addition, subtraction, multiplication, division and the extraction of roots" (see Descartes (1954)). We present now his approach, which can be presented in dynamical form via software GeoGebra.

Now let *AB* taken as a unity and let be done the triangles *ABC* and *DBE* (the lines *AC* and *DE* are parallel, see Fig. 15.3) and let be required to multiply *BD* by *BC*. Descartes argue that "I have only join the points *A* and *C*, and draw *DE* parallel to *CA*, then *BE* is the product of *BD* and *BC*. If it be required to divide *BE* by *BD*, I join *E* and *D*, and draw *AC* parallel to *DE*; then *BC* is the result of the division". Descartes used here similar triangles *ABC* and *DBE* (Fig. 15.4):

$$\frac{|BE|}{|BC|} = \frac{|BD|}{|BA|} = \frac{|BD|}{1}$$

Fig. 15.3 Similar triangles ABC and DBE. (See Descartes 1954)

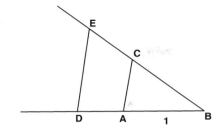

Fig. 15.4 Similar triangles ABC and DBE presented in dynamical form via software GeoGebra

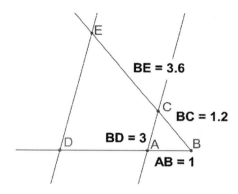

$$|BE| = |BD| \cdot |BC|$$

$$\frac{|BE|}{|BD|} = |BC|$$

Now, he used the theorem of Euclid (see Fig. 15.5) about height: "If the square root of *GH* is desired, I add, along the same straight line *FG* equal to unity, then bisecting *FH* at *K*, I describe the circle *FIH* about *K* as a centre, and draw from G a perpendicular and extended it to *I*, and *GI* is the required root" (Fig. 15.6).

$$|IG|^2 = |FG| \cdot |GH|$$

$$|IG|^2 = 1 \cdot x$$

$$|IG| = \sqrt{x}$$

Fig. 15.5 Using the theorem of Euclid about high. (See Descartes 1954)

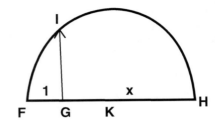

Fig. 15.6 Using the theorem of Euclid about high in dynamical form via software GeoGebra

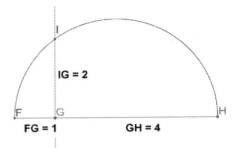

15.5 Visualization of Three-Dimensional Constructions in Farkas Bolyai's Tentamen

We present in this part the possible interpretation of historical mathematical textbooks written by Farkas Bolyai in the eighteenth century in Romania via software GeoGebra.

Farkas Bolyai was born on 9 February 1775 in Bolya (near Nagyszeben (Sibiu), now Romania (Transylvania)), and died on 20 November 1856 in Maros-Vásárhely (Targu Mures), now Romania (Transylvania). A detailed biography of his life can be found in Bolyai (2017). He studied since the age of 6 years in the Calvinist school in Nagyszeben. When finishing his studies here at the age of 12 years, he became the tutor of the 8-year son of Baron Kemény, Simon. Farkas was treated as a family member, the two young men became close friends, and they followed studies together from 1790 in the Calvinist College in Kolozsvár.

The time spent in Kolozsvár was a very good start in the development of Farkas Bolyai, and he decided to accompany Simon Kemény in his studies abroad. The two young men went first to Jena in 1796 for about 6 months, where Bolyai started his systematic mathematical studies, and then they moved to Göttingen, where they were taught by Kästner and became close friends with Gauss.

In 1799 Bolyai returned to Transylvania, and become a tutor in Kolozsvár, where he married Zsuzsanna Benkő, and their son János Bolyai was born in 1802. Soon after Farkas was appointed as the chair in the Calvinist College of Marosváráhely, where he was teaching for almost 50 years. His mathematics masterpiece Tentamen written in Latin language, published in 1832, was a rigorous and systematic

15 Possible Cultural Diversity and Digital Competences: Retrospection... 269

foundation of geometry, arithmetic, algebra and analysis, but is not as well-known as the famous Appendix of this volumes, written by his son János Bolyai. We would like to mention some nice examples from Farkas Bolyai's Tentamen in which one of the authors included visualization of three-dimensional examples by some special annexes, special figures which can be manipulated in space.

These ideas and the method itself can be considered as an important contribution expressing his pedagogical views, his way of teaching and his efforts to make the best visualization, as the annexes had to be produced by hand and introduced separately in the volumes by hand.

Let us include some photos of some pages of Bolyai de Bolya (2017) to illustrate the given examples (Figs. 15.7, 15.8 and 15.9).

These figures above are possible to represent via the software GeoGebra.

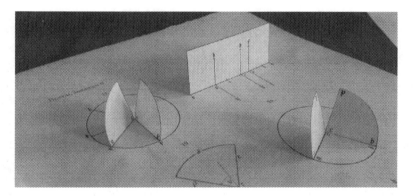

Fig. 15.7 Three-dimensional figures in Farkas Bolyai's Tentamen. (Photo was made in the library of Miskolc University by Péter Körtesi)

Fig. 15.8 Another three-dimensional figures in Farkas Bolyai's Tentamen. (Photo was made in the library of Miskolc University by Péter Körtesi)

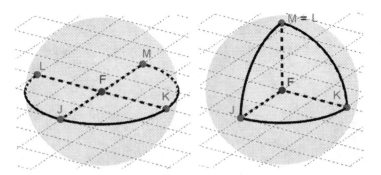

Fig. 15.9 Three-dimensional figures from Farkas Bolyai's Tentamen prepared in GeoGebra

15.6 Establishing of Teacher Training Institutes in Hungary and Slovakia: Background for Mathematics Educators

There were no specialized colleges in Slovakia and Hungary for the preparation of primary school teachers up to the modern times. The situation changed only during the reign of Maria Theresia (1740–1780). Her education reform was based on the idea of Frederick II, the Great, the King of Prussia (1712–1786), that people have to take their part in the building of the state by enhancing education and the state should ensure that the investments in education will be returned many times over (see Schubring and Karp (2014)).

In 1777 Maria Theresia issued a basic document for education reform Ratio educationis that was amended in 1806. This document also created the conditions for the institutional training of teachers in the so-called normal school courses. In 1775 the first normal school in Hungary was opened in Bratislava. In this school, students learned, inter alia, methodology of teaching elementary subjects, and its graduates could become teachers in the village schools (Fig. 15.10).

According Gunčaga (2014) the founder of the training of primary school teachers in Hungary is regarded to be Bishop Johann Ladislaus Pyrker (1772–1847). Pyrker was appointed a Bishop of the Spis Diocese on 18 August 1818. He soon started with his preparatory visit for the oncoming canonical visitation, which was made on 21 July 1819. The result of his visitation proved low education level of teachers in the parishes and villages. It is evident from his letter to the Austrian Emperor on 24 August 1819, in which he writes:

"As for schools, high schools perform education on a good level; however, there is a poor quality of education at schools in the villages because they lack qualified teachers. For this reason, I suggest to form a preparatory training school for the village school teachers".

He founded the first teacher institute in Hungary in Spišská Kapitula (1819). Later in the year 1827, he became an Archbishop in Eger and the established second teacher institute in Eger (1828). There were many active mathematics educators and

Fig. 15.10 Johann Ladislaus Pyrker (1772–1847, see Gunčaga (2014))

educators of other subjects, who prepared many methodological books. In the following part, we will describe the most important author of mathematical textbooks in Austrian-Ugrian monarchy, Franz Močnik (1814–1892).

15.7 Franz Močnik (1814–1892): The Author of the Central Austrian-Hungarian Math Textbooks

In 2014 we commemorated the 200th anniversary of the birth of the significant personality in the field of principal mathematical textbooks of the Austro-Hungarian monarchy in the second half of the nineteenth century, Dr. Franc Močnik.

Franc Močnik was born on 1 October 1814 in Cerkno, Slovenia, as a son of Slovenian peasant parents, Andrej and Marjana Močnik (see Povsic (1966)). He attended the primary school in the town of Idrija and the secondary grammar school in Ljubljana. Later he studied at the Faculty of Theology in Gorica (today a town on the Italian-Slovenian border), but he did not become a priest. In 1836–1846 he worked as a teacher at the normal school in Gorica.

At that time he personally met the French mathematician Augustin-Louis Cauchy (1787–1857) who was living in this area for political reasons. Močnik presented his method of numerical solutions of equations in German language in his work *Theorie der numerischen Gleichungen mit einer Unbekannten* that was published in 1839. Meeting Cauchy motivated him to study mathematics at the university in Graz from which he graduated in 1840 with a doctorate in philosophy.

In 1846 Močnik became a professor of elementary mathematics at the Technical Academy in Lviv (today Ukraine). In 1849–1851 he was a professor of mathematics at the University in Olomouc (today Czech Republic, see Jeraj (1995)).

In 1851–1860 he worked as an inspector of primary schools in Ljubljana. In 1861 he was appointed an inspector of primary and secondary schools (Realschule) in Graz for Styria and Carinthia. In 1869 Močnik became a provincial inspector of the first class for Styria. He retired for medical reasons in 1871. Literary active, he lived in Graz until he passed away on 30 November 1892.

Močnik's mathematical textbooks are very numerous. According to Branko Sustar (see Sustar (2014)), his last bibliography was compiled by Jose Povsic. Močnik's textbooks were originally published in German (148 textbooks in 980 editions), and they were translated to 14 other languages: 39 Slovenian textbooks (174 editions), 29 Croatian textbooks (132 editions), 32 Serbian textbooks (77 editions), 4 textbooks for Bosnia and Herzegovina (36 editions), 9 Albanian textbooks (13 editions), 9 Bulgarian textbooks (23 editions), 39 Czech textbooks (109 editions), 46 Italian textbooks (130 editions), 38 Hungarian textbooks (185 editions), 4 Greek textbooks (4 editions), 39 Polish textbooks (86 editions), 20 Romanian (36 editions), 5 Slovak (5 editions) and 40 Ukrainian textbooks (74 editions). That shows practical application of cultural diversity at that time.

We will now turn to three examples from a Močnik textbook on visual geometry. This textbook was a Hungarian translation and was published in Budapest in 1856 (see Fig. 15.11 and Močnik and Szabóky (1856)) (Fig. 15.12).

These examples are in the exercise part of the book after the chapter "The Positions of Circles in the Plane". In this part the method of generating problem was used.

Example 15.1 Construct three circles with the radii m, n and p where each circle touches the other from the outside.

Solution: We construct the triangle ABC with sides $AB = m + n$, $AC = m + p$ and $BC = n + p$. Now we construct the circle with centre A and radius m, circle with centre B and radius n and circle with centre C and radius p. The circles fulfilled the objective of the task (see also Figs. 15.13 and 15.14).

Example 15.2 We have done three circles of the same size, e, f and g, which touch each other outside. We must now circumscribe fourth the circle k, which touches previous three circles inside.

Solution: Example 15.2 is a continuation of Example 15.1 and has a logical connection to it. First we construct three circles of the same size, e, f and g, in a similar way as to Example 15.1. The circle k has its centre in the orthocentre of the triangle ABC (see also Fig. 15.15).

Fig. 15.11 Franc Močnik (1814–1892, see Povsic (1966))

Fig. 15.12 Textbook Močnik-Szabóky: Mértani nézlettan. (Visual Geometry)

Fig. 15.13 Figure from the textbook Močnik and Szabóky: Mértani nézlettan (1856)

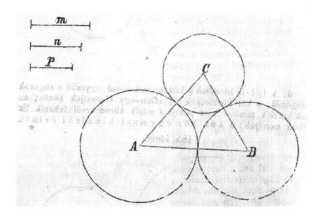

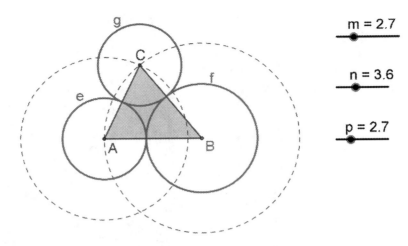

Fig. 15.14 Construction for Example 15.1 prepared in GeoGebra

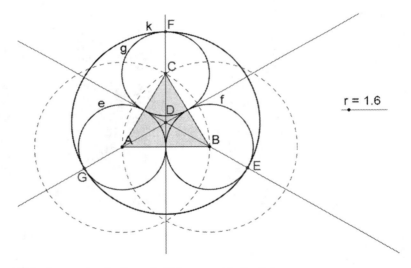

Fig. 15.15 Construction for Example 15.2 prepared in GeoGebra

Example 15.3 We have done two different circles *k* and *l* with the common centre *S*. On the small circle is given the point A. Draw another circle, which obtains the point A and touches the circles *k* and *l*.

Remark: It is possible to draw some circle, which touches the small circle from inside or outside.

Solution: Let the radius of the small circle *k* be *s* and the bigger circle *l* be *r*. The line *SA* has two common points *X* and *Y* with the bigger circle *l*. Now we can draw circles m_1 and m_2 with diameter *XA* and *YA* (they have radius $\frac{r+s}{2}, \frac{r-s}{2}$; see also Fig. 15.16).

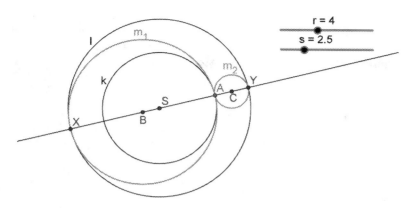

Fig. 15.16 Construction for Example 15.3 prepared in GeoGebra

15.8 Possible Student Projects in GeoGebra

There was realized some successful student projects for implementing historical mathematical textbooks into school education. One of them was at the Liceo Scientifico Isaac Newton in Rome. This project in the years 2010–2012 for students was devoted to the Italian mathematician Lorenzo Mascheroni (1750–1800). The results of the project were successful monograph of the two students of this secondary school, Federico Fabrizi and Pietro Pennestri (see Fig. 15.17), and other results are on the webpage (http://www.liceonewtonroma.gov.it/).

We were inspired by this project that can present now some students' works prepared for different topics from the actual curriculum in mathematics education. We collect some works of students in GeoGebra since 2013. The examples were prepared by students – future mathematics teachers for lower and upper secondary level in Slovakia. Some of them are on the webpage of the Slovak GeoGebra Institute http://geogebra.ssgg.sk/. The first example is for the topic "The set of the points in the plane". We see on the Fig. 15.16 an applet for the construction of the set of points with the property that every point has the same distance k from the given line a. Parameter k is possible to change with slider (Fig. 15.18).

The second example describes how to draw a cube in the plain using the rule that the side edges have the half-length compared to the front edges (Fig. 15.19). Playing the construction is an important advantage in this teaching unit (Bayerl and Žilková (2016)).

In Fig. 15.20 we present the representation of a composition of non-parallel forces (notice here a connection to pupils' knowledge of mathematics). Consequently this composition is used in Fig. 15.21 to illustrate a motion on the inclined plane (available at https://archive.geogebra.org/en/wiki/index.php/Materiály_pre_vyučovanie_fyziky).

The last example describes how to draw a graph of the function in the coordinating system via searching the properties of function such as first and second deriva-

Fig. 15.17 Monograph of the students Frederico Fabrizi and Pietro Pennestri published in 2012

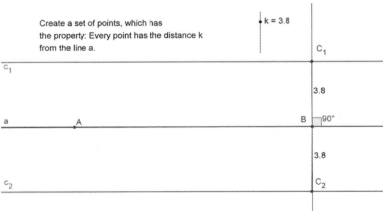

Fig. 15.18 Example with construction

Fig. 15.19 Cube construction sketch

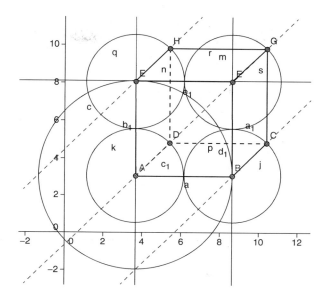

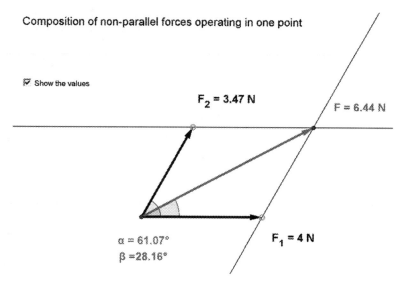

Fig. 15.20 Composition of forces

tive. These properties have dominant connection to the visualization, which is represented by the graph of the function. These student projects are possible not only for mathematics and physics but also for other science education for different kinds of pupils and students (see Vančová and Šulovská (2016)) (Fig. 15.22).

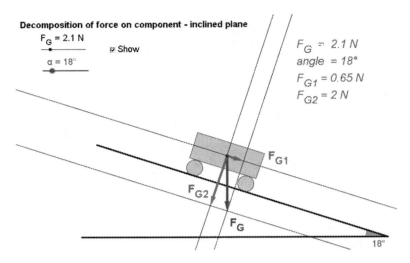

Fig. 15.21 Motion on the inclined plane

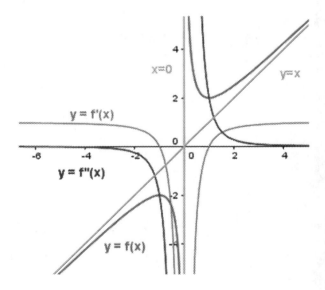

Fig. 15.22 Graph of the function with his first and second derivative

15.9 Conclusions

The use of technology is slowly becoming a substantial part of today's education (Hohenwarter and Lavicza (2010)). Although due to the increased accessibility of affordable computing technologies in the 1980s and 1990s it was predicted that computers would become rapidly integrated into mathematics teaching and learning (Kaput 1992), technology uptake in schools has been considerably slow. The current expansion of technology use took a new unconventional direction: a bottom-up, community-based collaborative development, catalysed by Internet-based communities and increasingly available community-developed software packages. During the past decades, it has been demonstrated that a large number of enthusiasts can alter conventional thinking and models of development and innovation. The success of open source projects like Linux, Firefox, Moodle and Wikipedia shows that collaboration and sharing can produce valuable resources in a variety of areas of life.

The teaching of mathematics based on historical mathematical textbooks is also relevant today because the methodological framework of the curriculum is based on the models and tasks from the cultural environment of the children and their parents. Use of these textbooks in Central Europe is practical application of the cultural diversity, which is an essential part of the school tradition of the Austrian-Ugrian monarchy.

Establishing of teacher training institutes in Europe in the beginning of the nineteenth century brought big progression in the development of methodology of mathematics teaching at that time. It supports creating of mathematical textbooks and also methodological books for teachers. Austrian-Ugrian monarchy was an example of territory with cultural diversity dimension in schooling, because many textbooks were translated into languages used in the monarchy.

These textbooks can help both current and future teachers of mathematics. A great number of materials in these textbooks can be used in the modern e-learning courses by the use of appropriate educational software. This can be an incentive for student scientific work of students of teacher training programs, as well as for the professional projects of primary and secondary school students (see Koreňová (2016), Partová (2002)).

Educational software GeoGebra offers innovative ideas for teaching space geometry, especially to contribute to the formation of space perception of pupils. Nowadays some similar possibility is offered by the 3D version of GeoGebra; we can mention some nice results obtained by László Budai in his PhD thesis Budai (2016) and some of his publications related to the subject – see Budai (2013) and Budai (2015). Is it possible to find another application in the field of financial mathematics in Simonka (2016). Teachers and students develop their digital and mathematical competences, when they use the appropriate educational software..

It is very important nowadays mathematical education in schools and also in math teacher training programs that students develop their ability to explain every problem in more ways, they need to find also other solution than their teacher. Franz Močnik (1814–1892) solved in their works mostly practical problems and tried to explain their findings to people, who didn't have any studies of mathematics. His textbooks are example of cultural diversity, because his textbooks originally written in German were translated into 14 languages.

In the future it will be possible that parts of mathematics by different historical authors can be presented in modern form through ICT tools and educational software, because a lot of original historical mathematical works is possible to find in electronic form in the Internet or in electronical libraries of archives. An example serves the project of digitalization of historical textbooks from Austrian National Library in Vienna by Google. For this reason some textbooks is possible to find in the google e-book form. These activities can help in popularization and teaching of mathematics in every kind of schools.

Acknowledgements The research was supported by the scholarship of the Catholic Academic Exchange Service (KAAD) and project APVV-15-0378 "Optimisation of the mathematic educational materials on the base of needs analysis by younger school age pupils".

References

Bayerl, E., & Žilková, K. (2016). Interactive textbooks in mathematics education – What does it mean for students? In L. Balko et al. (Eds.), *Aplimat 2016 – 15th conference on applied mathematics* (pp. 56–65). Bratislava: Slovak University of Technology in Bratislava.

Bolyai, F. (2017). *Farkas Bolyai in the MacTutor history of mathematics database*. Retrieved from http://www-groups.dcs.st-and.ac.uk/history/Biographies/Bolyai_Farkas.html

Bolyai de Bolya, W. (2017). *Wolfgangi Bolyai de Bolya: Tentamen*. Retrieved from http://mek.oszk.hu/06500/06507/

Brandl, M. (2016). Narrative Mathematik-Didaktik mittels Elementen bildender Kunst. In S. Kaufmann et al. (Eds.), *Beiträge zum Mathematikunterricht* (pp. 1415–1418). Münster: WTM-Verlag.

Brandl, M. (2010). Narrative didactics in mathematical education: An innovative didactical concept. In T. Bianco & V. Ulm (Eds.), *Mathematics education with technology – Experiences in Europe* (pp. 103–110). Augsburg: University of Augsburg.

Bruner, J. (1986). *Actual minds, possible worlds*. Cambridge, MA: Harvard University Press.

Budai, L. (2016). *Téri képességek mérése és fejlesztése GeoGebrával a középiskolákban*. PhD dissertation. Debrecen: University of Debrecen.

Budai, L. (2013). Development of spatial perception in high school with GoeGebra. *Teaching Mathematics and Compuer Science, 11*(2), 211–230.

Budai, L. (2015). Interactive dynamical tests for evaluating the development of spatial abilities in high school. *Creative Mathematics and Informatics, 24*(2), 12–136.

Descartes, R. (1954). *La Geometrie (The Geometry of René Descartes) Translated from French and Latin by David Eugene Smith and Marcia L. Latham*. Retrieved from http://isites.harvard.edu/fs/docs/icb.topic1062138.files/Geometry_of_Rene_Descartes_rev2.pdf

Gunčaga, J. (2014). Teachers Institute in Spisska Kapitula. The first teachers Institute in the Area of Slovakia. *History of Education & Children's Literature, 9*(1), 409–429.

Hejný, M., & Littler, G. (2006). Transmissive and constructivist approaches to teaching. In Hejný et al. (Eds.), *Creative teaching in mathematics* (pp. 11–34). Prague: Charles University.

Hohenwarter, M., & Lavicza, Z. (2010). Gaining momentum: GeoGebra inspires educators and students around the world. *GeoGebra The New Language for the Third Millennium, 1*(1), 1–6.

Jeraj, S. (1995). *Franc Močnik Osnovni življenski podatki*. Retrieved from http://vlado.fmf.uni-lj.si/sola/1995/mocnik/PODATKI.HTM#Gorica

Kaput, J. (1992). Technology and mathematics education. In D. A. Grouws (Ed.), *Handbook of research on mathematics teaching and learning* (pp. 515–556). New York: Macmillan.

Kántor, T. (2013). Historical aspects in teaching mathematics. In A. Ambrus & É. Vásárhelyi (Eds.), *Problem solving in mathematics education* (pp. 80–94). Eger-Budapest: Eötvös Loránd University-Eszterházy Károly College.

Klassen, S. (2006). A theoretical framework for contextual science teaching. *Interchange, 37*(1–2), 31–61.

Koreňová, L. (2016). Digital technologies in teaching mathematics on the faculty of education of the Comenius University in Bratislava. In L. Balko et al. (Eds.), *Aplimat 2016 – 15th conference on applied mathematics* (pp. 690–699). Bratislava: Slovak University of Technology in Bratislava.

Kubli, F. (2005). *Mit Geschichten und Erzählungen motivieren: Beispiele für den mathematisch-naturwissenschaftlichen Unterricht*. Cologne: Aulis Deubner.

Kubli, F. (2002). *Plädoyer für Erzählungen im Physikunterricht: Geschichte und Geschichten als Verstehenshilfen – Ergebnisse einer Untersuchung* (2nd ed.). Cologne: Aulis Deubner.

Leikin, R. (2013). Evaluating mathematical creativity: The interplay between multiplicity and insight. *Psychological Test and Assessment Modeling, 55*(4), 385–400.

Leikin, R. (2009). Exploring mathematical creativity using multiple solution tasks. In R. Leikin, A. Berman, & B. Koichu (Eds.), *Creativity in mathematics and the education of gifted students* (pp. 129–145). Rotterdam: Sense Publishers.

Močnik, F., & Szabóky, A. (1856). *Mértani nézlettan*. Budapest: Lampel Róbert Sajátja.

Oldknow, A., & Taylor, R. (2003). *Teaching mathematics using information and communications technology*. London/New York: Continuum.

Partová, E. (2002). *Prirodzené čísla*. Bratislava: ASCO Art & Science.

Povsic, J. (1966). *Bibliographie von Franc Močnik*. Ljubljana: Academia Scientarium et Artium Slovenica.

Recommendation of the European Parliament and of the Council of 18 December 2006 on key competences for lifelong learning (2006/962/EC). (2006). Retrieved from https://eur-lex.europa.eu/legal-content/EN/TXT/PDF/?uri=CELEX:32006H0962&from=EN

Schubring, K., & Karp, A. (2014). *Handbook on the history of mathematics education*. New York/Heidelberg/Dordrecht/London: Springer.

Simonka, Z. (2016). Kresliče grafov – možnosti zobrazenia a ich použitie (online aplety). In M. Hrubý & P. Račková (Eds.), *Matematika, informační technologie a aplikované vědy (MITAV)* (pp. 1–8). Brno: Univerzita Obrany.

Singer, F. M., Sheffield, L. J., Freiman, V., & Brandl, M. (2016). Research on and activities for mathematically gifted students. In G. Kaiser (Ed.), *ICME-13 topical surveys* (pp. 1–41). New York/Heidelberg/Dordrecht/London: Springer.

Singer, F. M., Ellerton, N., & Cai, J. (2013). Problem-posing research in mathematics education: New questions and directions. *Educational Studies in Mathematics, 83*(1), 1–7.

Sustar, B. (2014). Pogledi na Mocnikove matematicne ucbenike v prevodih na stevilne jezike. In M. Magajne (Ed.), *Z Vrlino in Delom* (pp. 41–51). Ljubljana: Narodna in univerzitetna knjiznica.

UNESCO Universal Declaration on Cultural Diversity. (2002). Retrieved from http://unesdoc.unesco.org/images/0012/001271/127160m.pdf

Vančová, A., & Šulovská, M. (2016). Innovative trends in geography for pupils with mild intellectual disability. In P. Hajek, T. Sahota, & T. Jones (Eds.), *CBU international conference on innovations in science and education (CBUIC)* (pp. 392–398). Prague: Central Bohemia University, Unicorn College.

Wittman, C. E. (2001). The alpha and omega of teacher education: Organizing mathematical activities. In D. Holton (Ed.), *The teaching and learning of mathematics at university level: An ICMI study* (pp. 539–552). Dordrecht: Kluwer Academic Publishers.

Chapter 16
Reinforcement of Logical and Mathematical Competences Using a Didactic Aid Based on the Theory of Constructivism

Tomasz Kopczyński and Anna Gałuszka

16.1 Introduction

Mathematics, like other products of culture, is a creation of the human mind. Logic and mathematics is the basis of the learning society's pyramid; without this competence, the participant is not able to consciously and creatively participate in the learning society. From the evolutionary point of view, its development is legitimized by the fact that it was more practical for one to formalize certain matters by means of a universal system of recording quantity, volume or other measures that were to serve this purpose. In order to function in the world, one needs a certain set of mathematical skills to be able to distinguish one object from several others. What is more, the ability to manipulate them by means of arithmetic calculation not only provides one with the ability to classify objects in a logical way, but above all, to solve specific problems in an abstract manner.

The aim of the article is to present the results of a study utilizing the EduMata didactic aid, which has been developed on the basis of Jean Piaget's constructivism theory and enables a problem-based approach to working on numerals/objects. The aid may also be used to carry out similar work in fields other than mathematics.

Currently, three main concepts are used to try to explain the processes of teaching and using mathematical operations: developmental and cognitive concepts related to the biological development of a child (Piaget 1966; Snow et al. 1989), neuropsychological and cognitive concepts based on the neuroimaging of brain structures and functions (Piazza et al. 2007; Piazza 2011) and linguistic concepts explained in relation to social interactions (Spelke 2005; Pinker 1995). As describ-

---

T. Kopczyński (✉)
University of Silesia in Katowice, Katowice, Poland

A. Gałuszka
University of Bielsko-Biala, Bielsko-Biała, Poland

ing all three concepts would significantly extend and go beyond the framework of this article, the author will venture to focus only on presenting the developmental and cognitive concept employed by him and then proceed to make a methodological description of the presented research.

16.2 Theoretical Background for Selecting the Subject

There are four large studies being conducted in Poland to help diagnose mathematical education in the country. Two deal with measuring overall class competences of primary school students. The third is focussed on teachers while the last one on the general characteristics of the school and activities (e.g. extracurricular activities). The first three are carried out by the Educational Research Institute (IBE), which include the OBUT/K3 nationwide survey of the skills of grade three students (2015 Report), the DUMa diagnosis of mathematical skills of primary school students (2014 Report) and a survey of the needs of teachers of early childhood education and mathematics in the scope of professional development (2015 Report). The fourth survey is carried out by the Central Statistical Office (GUS) (2016/2017 Report) entitled "Education" and consists of regularly published reports on the general characteristics of educational institutions in the country. All of them provide a very concise characterization of the teaching process. The conclusion drawn from the research is that the level of mathematical competence in Poland is unsatisfactory and, what is more, its quality has a significant influence on the later educational choices of students and their chances on the labour market. The most important conclusions from the above reports are as follows: too little emphasis on developing reasoning, lack of variety during math lessons, blocking of original solutions put forward by students, lack of teamwork in lessons and training for teachers that does not meet their practical expectations.

A large part of the above statements leads to the conclusion that there is a lack of universal educational support allowing for a practical presentation of the problem in the scope of mathematical tasks, providing variety in lessons, conducting lessons and tasks in a team manner and developing a coherent system of good practices between teachers and schools. Therefore, it was necessary to develop the aid, implement it and evaluate it in accordance with methodological standards.

The theoretical foundation adopted for the study is based on the developmental and cognitive approach created by such researchers as J. Piaget, J. S. Bruner and L. Wygotski (1966, 1987, 1989). According to them, mathematical knowledge is actively created by the learner. The learner's knowledge and cognitive structures are developed in his or her mind. J. Piaget noticed that the child produces personal concepts of the reality being discovered. They are created by confronting concepts belonging to the system of knowledge of the individual with visions offered by the environment, especially by educational institutions. As a result, the child's mental structures (schema) undergo constant transformation, which is done through assimilation (i.e. adaptation) and accommodation of meanings through the creation of new structures (Piaget 1966; Bruner and Haste 1987; Wygotski 1989). Thus, the child's development must complete its particular cycles, i.e. certain functions must first mature before the school can begin to teach the child with certain knowledge and habits. Therefore, the child's development must somehow precede teaching; otherwise the transfer of knowledge will be ineffective or will be conveyed in an insufficiently comprehensible way. It must be conveyed in a way that matches the child's intellectual capacity (Piaget, Inhelder 1970).

The concept developed by constructivists sets a child's mathematical skills in the context of one's overall cognitive development. Knowledge of this subject is the result of numerous studies conducted in a single paradigm, thanks to which it is coherent and organized. Both supporters and opponents of Piaget's concept use a common language of concepts, which enables a constructive discussion in the field of the undertaken research.

16.3 Introduction to Methodology of Research

The collected data was subjected to statistical analysis in the SPSS Statistics 23.0 program in order to demonstrate the significance of the EduMata didactic aid in improving third grade primary school children's logical and mathematical proficiency. The theoretical foundation of the experiment is based on the cognitive theory of Jean Piaget, which speaks of the legitimacy of building mathematical concepts on the basis of particulars. The test for mathematical competence K3 2015 version M1 was used for both groups in the pretest, and for the post-test the mathematical competence test K3 2015 version M2 was tested. The lessons were taught by several designated teachers who had previously been trained on how they could teach the lesson (limiting the method, limiting the scope of the material) to exclude additional independent variables.

The said objective was reached using *ANOVA* two-factor variance analysis in a mixed scheme: 2 (time of measurement: initial vs. final) x 2 (use of the EduMata didactic aid: control vs. experimental). The dependant variable consisted of the total result of mathematical competence in the K3 (version M1 for the pretest and version M2 for the post-test) test and the result in three areas of competence, i.e. calculation skills, geometry skills and the ability to solve word problems. Care was taken to ensure uniformity of research by drawing attention to the most important disruptive factors. This was done thanks to the instruction for teachers including choosing a homogeneous teaching material, time devoted to its implementation (which results come from the plan of school hours) and strict transfer of procedures (methods and forms) to teachers in both groups.

The level of significance of differences (level of mathematical competence) that is received is much higher than the standard accepted as acceptable ($p < 0.05$), which indicates a very small probability of the significance of random factors as the causes of the detected differences between the studied groups.

Lack of statistically significant differences between the dependent variable in the pretest in both randomly selected groups indicates the high reliability of the obtained results (Fig. 16.4).

The distribution was found to conform with normal distribution as demonstrated by skewness and kurtosis values that did not exceed the $<-1,1>$ range significantly. The homogeneity of variance of the groups compared was also confirmed on the basis of statistically insignificant Levene test results. The statistical significance of the results was established at $p < 0.05$.

16.4 Sample Characteristics

The study was conducted on a sample of 469 pupils from 9 third grade classes. The experimental group consisted of 239 students aged 7–11 years ($M = 8.35$; $SD = 0.63$), including 51.1% girls and 48.9% boys. The control group consisted of 230 students aged 7–11 years ($M = 8.44$; $SD = 0.64$), including 50.2% girls and 49.8% boys.

16.5 Descriptive Statistics

The main descriptive statistics measure values are presented, i.e. central tendency measures (average, median, mode), dispersion measures (minimum, maximum, standard deviation, dispersion) and dispersion shape measures (skewness, kurtosis).

Table 16.1 shows the descriptive statistics of the K3 M1 mathematical competence test results of the experimental group in the initial and final measurement.

In the overall result of the K3 M1 test, the experimental group scored between 0 and 16 points in the initial measurement, averaging 7.46 points (SD = 4.15) out of 16 points possible, usually 5 points. In the final measurement, the group scored 0–16 points, averaging 10.33 points (SD = 3.87), usually 11 points.

In the field of calculation skills, the experimental group achieved scores in a range of 0–4 points in the initial measurement, averaging 2.08 points (SD = 1.15) out of 4 points possible, usually 3 points. In the final measurement, the group scored 0–4 points, averaging 2.87 points (SD = 1.06), usually 3 points.

In the area of geometry skills, in the initial measurement, the experimental group achieved scores in the range of 0–6 points, averaging 2.46 points (SD = 1.67) out of 6 points possible, usually 2 points. In the final measurement, the group scored 0–6 points, averaging 3.55 points (SD = 1.80), usually 3 points.

In the initial measurement of the word problem-solving skills area, the experimental group achieved scores in the range of 0–6 points, averaging 2.94 points (SD = 2.08) out of 6 possible points, usually 1 point. In the final measurement, the group scored 0–6 points, averaging 3.93 points (SD = 1.73), usually 5 points.

Table 16.1 Main descriptive statistics of the K3 M1 mathematical competence test results of the experimental group in the initial and final measurement

	Measurement	N	M	Me	D	SD	Skewness	Kurtosis	Min	Max	V
Total result	Initial	239	7.46	8	5	4.15	0.05	−0.89	0	16	56%
	Final	239	10.33	11	11	3.87	−0.64	−0.38	0	16	37%
Calculation skills	Initial	239	2.08	2	3	1.15	−0.06	−0.94	0	4	55%
	Final	238	2.87	3	3	1.06	−1.03	0.72	0	4	37%
Geometry skills	Initial	239	2.46	2	2	1.67	0.53	−0.55	0	6	68%
	Final	239	3.55	4	3	1.80	−0.28	−0.89	0	6	51%
Word problem-solving skills	Initial	239	2.94	3	1	2.08	0.03	−1.09	0	6	71%
	Final	239	3.93	4	5	1.73	−0.56	−0.67	0	6	44%

Legend: *N* size of group, *M* average, *Me* median (middle value), *D* mode (most frequent value), *SD* standard deviation, *Skewness* skewness value, *Kurtosis* kurtosis value, *Min* minimum value, *Max* maximum value, *V* dispersion coefficient

Table 16.2 Main descriptive statistics of the K3 M1 mathematical competence test results of the control group in the initial and final measurement

	Measurement	N	M	Me	D	SD	Skewness	Kurtosis	Min	Max	V
Total result	Initial	230	6.88	6	5	4.41	0.28	−1.09	0	16	64%
	Final	230	8.40	9	13	4.19	−0.12	−1.10	0	16	50%
Calculation skills	Initial	230	2.00	2	1	1.29	0.00	−1.14	0	4	65%
	Final	230	2.53	3	3	1.20	−0.63	−0.51	0	4	47%
Geometry skills	Initial	230	2.20	2	1	1.65	0.49	−0.56	0	6	75%
	Final	230	2.74	2	2	1.88	0.24	−1.07	0	6	69%
Word problem-solving skills	Initial	230	2.66	2	0	2.14	0.28	−1.02	0	6	80%
	Final	228	3.18	3	3	1.81	−0.06	−1.12	0	6	57%

Legend: *N* size of group, *M* average, *Me* median (middle value), *D* mode (most frequent value), *SD* standard deviation, *Skewness* skewness value, *Kurtosis* kurtosis value, *Min* minimum value, *Max* maximum value, *V* dispersion coefficient

For all areas of mathematical competence, skewness and kurtosis values did not significantly exceed <−1.1> in the initial and final measurement. The dispersion of the results was greater in the initial than in the final measurement, which indicates a reduction of results differentiation in the experimental group in the final measurement.

Table 16.2 shows the descriptive statistics of the K3 M1 mathematical competence test results of the control group in the initial and final measurement.

The overall result of the K3 M1 test showed that the control group scored between 0 and 16 points in the initial measurement, averaging 6,88 points (SD = 4.41), usually 5 points. In the final measurement, the group scored 0–16 points, averaging 8.40 points (SD = 4.19), usually 13 points.

In the field of calculation skills, in the initial results, the control group achieved scores in a range of 0–4 points, averaging 2 points (SD = 1.29), usually 1 point. In the final measurement, the group scored 0–4 points, averaging 2.53 points (SD = 1.20), usually 3 points.

In the area of geometry skills, the control group achieved scores in a range of 0–6 points in the initial measurement, averaging 2.20 points (SD = 1.65), usually 1 point. In the final measurement, the group scored 0–6 points, averaging 2.74 points (SD = 1.88), usually 2 points.

In the word problem-solving skills area, the control group achieved scores in the range of 0–6 points in the initial measurement, averaging 2.66 points (SD = 2.14), usually 0 points. In the final measurement, the group scored 0–6 points, averaging 3.18 points (SD = 1.81), usually 3 points.

For all areas of mathematical competence, skewness and kurtosis values did not significantly exceed <−1.1> in the initial and final measurement. The dispersion of the results was greater in the initial than in the final measurement, which indicates a reduction of results differentiation in the control group in the final measurement.

16.6 Results

Table 16.3 presents ANOVA variation analysis statistics for the influence of the interaction between the measurement time and EduMata didactic aid use on the results of the K3 mathematical competence test.

A statistically significant influence of the interaction between the time of measurement and application of the EduMata didactic aid on the overall result of the K3 mathematical competence test as well as on the results in the areas of calculation, geometry and word problem-solving skills was found. In order to learn the structure of the said influence of interaction, pairwise comparisons were made. Table 16.4 presents pairwise comparison statistics between the initial and final measurement in the control and experimental group.

In the experimental group, a statistically significant increase in mathematical competence was found between the initial and final measurement in the areas of general mathematical competences (by 38.4%), calculation skills (38.1%), geometry skills (44%) and word problem-solving skills (33.8%) (Fig. 16.1).

Table 16.3 ANOVA variation analysis statistics for the influence of the interaction between measurement time and EduMata didactic aid use on the results of the K3 mathematical competence test

	Type III sum of squares	Average square	$F(1, 464)$	p	η^2
Total result	100.16	100.16	9.66	**0.001**	0.02
Calculation skills	4.18	4.18	3.85	**0.05**	0.01
Geometry skills	17.25	17.25	9.12	**0.001**	0.02
Word problem-solving skills	12.11	12.11	4.60	**0.03**	0.01

16 Reinforcement of Logical and Mathematical Competences Using a Didactic Aid...

Table 16.4 Pairwise comparison statistics between the initial and final measurements of the K3 M1 mathematical competence test results in the control and experimental group

	Group	Initial measurement M	SD	Final measurement M	SD	Difference in average values	*p* of the difference
Total result	Control	6.88	4.41	8.40	4.19	22.0%	**0.001**
	Experimental	7.46	4.15	10.33	3.87	38.4%	**0.001**
Calculation skills	Control	2.00	1.29	2.53	1.20	26.0%	**0.001**
	Experimental	2.08	1.15	2.87	1.06	38.1%	**0.001**
Geometry skills	Control	2.20	1.65	2.74	1.88	24.3%	**0.001**
	Experimental	2.46	1.67	3.55	1.80	44.0%	**0.001**
Word problem-solving skills	Control	2.66	2.14	3.18	1.81	19.3%	**0.001**
	Experimental	2.94	2.08	3.93	1.73	33.8%	**0.001**

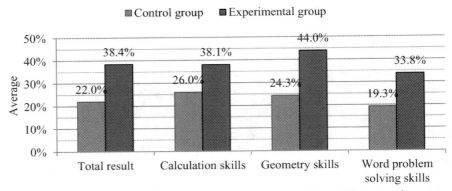

Fig. 16.1 Comparison of the K3 mathematical competence test results of the experimental group between the initial and final measurement

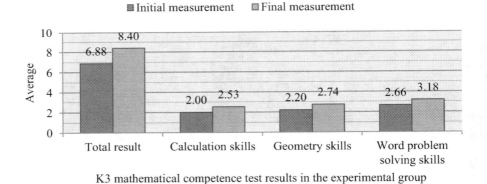

Fig. 16.2 Comparison of the K3 mathematical competence test results of the control group between the initial and final measurement

A statistically significant increase in mathematical competences was also found in the control group between the initial and final measurement in the area of general mathematical competences (by 22%), calculation skills (26%), geometry skills (24.3%) and word problem-solving skills (19.3%) (Fig. 16.2).

It is worth noting that the increase in the K3 mathematical competence test results between the initial and final measurement was greater in the experimental group than in the control group in the area of general mathematical competences, as well as calculation skills, geometry skills and word problem-solving skills (Fig. 16.3).

Table 16.5 presents pairwise comparison statistics between the K3 mathematical competence test results of the control and experimental group in the initial and final measurements.

16 Reinforcement of Logical and Mathematical Competences Using a Didactic Aid... 291

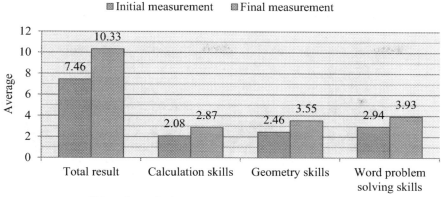

Fig. 16.3 Comparison of the K3 mathematical competence test results of the experimental and control group between the initial and final measurement

Table 16.5 Pairwise comparison statistics between the K3 mathematical competence test results of the control and experimental group in the initial and final measurements

		Control group		Experimental group		Difference in average values	p of the difference
	Measurement	M	SD	M	SD		
Total result	Initial	6.88	4.41	7.46	4.15	7.8%	0.13
	Final	8.40	4.19	10.33	3.87	18.7%	**0.001**
Calculation skills	Initial	2.00	1.29	2.08	1.15	3.4%	0.48
	Final	2.53	1.20	2.87	1.06	11.8%	**0.001**
Geometry skills	Initial	2.20	1.65	2.46	1.67	10.6%	0.09
	Final	2.74	1.88	3.55	1.80	22.8%	**0.001**
Word problem-solving skills	Initial	2.66	2.14	2.94	2.08	9.4%	0.13
	Final	3.18	1.81	3.93	1.73	19.2%	**0.001**

In the initial measurement, there were no statistically significant differences between the control and experimental group in terms of general mathematical competences, calculation skills, geometry skills and word problem-solving skills (Fig. 16.4).

In contrast, in the final measurement, statistically significant differences were found in the K3 M2 mathematical competence test results between the control and experimental groups. The experimental group, compared to the control group, achieved a higher score for general mathematical competences (by 18.7%), calculation skills (by 11.8%), geometry skills (by 22.8%) and word problem-solving skills (by 19,2%) (Fig. 16.5).

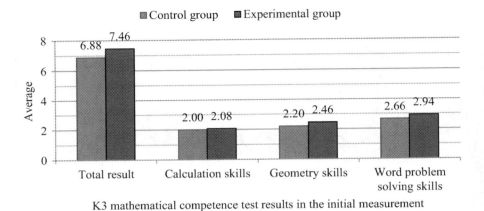

Fig. 16.4 Comparison between the K3 M1 mathematical competence test results of the control and experimental group in the initial measurement

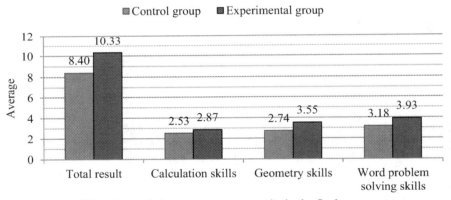

Fig. 16.5 Comparison between the K3 M2 mathematical competence test results of the control and experimental group in the final measurement

16.7 Conclusion

Research carried out by researchers (Semadeni 2016; Majewska 2014; Gruszczyk-Kolczyńska 2015, 2012; Siwek 2011; Raszka 2011) in the use of additional forms of verbalization of content have shown that using them causes a better understanding and remembering content that is related to both the learning environment and sensory materials. Extensive research in this area was carried out in 2007–2010 by Gruszczyk-Kolczyńska, showing a positive relationship between the verbalization of mathematical operations carried out and their lack in the form of negative effects. Lack of verbalization in the process of understanding the tasks of the mathematician was called "paper math" because it did not involve the role of verbal learning of children. Gruszczyk-Kolczyńska and Semadeni in their research refer to a more broad and general context of the constructivist approach in teaching mathematics; however, they do not provide any specific didactic help that could be the implementation of these tasks and give a ready solution to teachers wanting to teach in this way. Therefore, the authors of this article deepened the research issues of the constructivist approach by introducing a specific solution in the form of using EduMat's didactic help.

Researchers in this area (Semadeni 2016; Majewska 2014; Grusczyk-Kolczyńska 2015, 2012; Siwek 2011; Raszka 2011) write about creating and organizing an educational space in the field of observing, manipulating and collecting experiences. However, in the final conclusion they do not give a name or a specific didactic tool that would modify the educational environment.

The authors of the article see a multitude of various didactic aids that could support a constructivist approach. However, without distinguishing a given element through which this concept is practiced, it is difficult to conclude on the validity of a given concept.

It is difficult to conclude on effectiveness in teaching based only on a given method without providing specific tools. It is true that Piaget in his research introduced a very wide spectrum of various types of help, puzzles, levers and vessels that were verbal in nature.

However, in the educational reality of at least Polish, this element (a constructivist approach) is rarely introduced in the teaching of mathematics. This is evidenced by numerous studies recalled at the beginning of the article.

Researcher Diallio Sessoms (2008) says that the teaching process is more often discussed in the context of a broad spectrum of concepts, theories and methodologies. On the other hand, research on specific didactic tools is rarely undertaken (multimedia boards, educational works, educational mats, counters, etc.). Therefore, the authors of this article made efforts to explore the last link of almost every educational concept.

The presented results show a significant statistical significance of the EduMata didactic aid on the results achieved in the area of logical-mathematical thinking among third grade primary school children. There was a significant increase in general mathematical competences and a significant increase in calculation skills, geometry skills and word problem-solving skills in the final measurement. The increase occurred both in the experimental group and in the control group. The improvement in mathematical competence, however, was greater in the experimental group.

There was no significant difference in mathematical competence between the control group and the experimental group in the initial measurement. However, in the final measurement, the experimental group achieved significantly higher general mathematical competence results and significantly improved calculation skills, geometry skills and word problem-solving skills than the control group. In conclusion, the use of the EduMata didactic aid in improving logical-mathematical thinking among grade 3 primary school children was proven to be effective.

References

Bruner, J., & Haste, H. (1987). Making sense. In *The child's construction of the world*. New York: Methuen.
Grusczyk-Kolczyńska, E. (2012). O dzieciach matematycznie uzdolnionych. [ang. About mathematically gifted children]. Red. E. Gruszczyk-Kolczyńska, Wyd. Nowa Era. Chapter: *Wnioskowanie uzdolnieniach matematycznych. Wyniki badań, interpretacje i wnioski*. [ang. Infering mathematical aptitudes. Research results, interpretations and conclusions] (pp. 340–365), Warszawa.
Grusczyk-Kolczyńska, E. (2015). *O kryzysie edukacji matematycznej na przykładzie pierwszego roku nauki szkolnej. Co trzeba zmienić, żeby dzieci mogły odnosić sukcesy w nauce matematyki*. [ang. On the crisis of mathematical education on the example of the first year of schooling. What you need to change so that your children can succeed in learning math.] *In Uczenie się dzieci. Myślenie i działanie*. [ang. Learning children. Thinking and acting.] red. J. Malinowska i T. Neckar-Ilnicka, Wydawnictwo EPIDEIXIS.
Majewska, K. (2014). *Efektywność interaktywnej formy nauczania z użyciem tablicy multimedialnej. (ang. Efficiency of the interactive form of teaching with the use of a multimedia board)*. Wyd. *E-mentor, 1*(63), 31–40.
Piaget, J. (1966). *Studies on child psychology*. Warszawa: PWN.
Piaget, J., & Inhelder, B. (1970). *From the logic of a child to the logic of adolescents. A discussion on the development of formal operating structures*. Wyd. PWN.
Piazza, M. (2011). Neurocognitive start-up tools for symbolic number representations. In *Time and number in the brain by Stanislas Dehaene and Elizabeth Brannon* (pp. 267–286). London: Elsevier.
Piazza, M., Pinel, P., Le Bihan, D., & Dehaene, S. (2007). A magnitude code common to numerosities and number symbols in human intraparietal cortex. *Neuron, 53*(2), 293–305.
Pinker, S. (1995). *Language Instynkt*. New York: Peungwin Books.
Raszka, R. (2011). *Integrowanie matematyki z innymi obszarami dziecięcego poznawania*. [ang. Integrating mathematics with other areas of childhood learning]. Wyd. TWP, Warszawa, In *An integral system in child's education: contexts and consequences of changes* (pp. 255–266).
Report. (2014). *Research report: A diagnosis of mathematical skills*. Retrieved from http://eduentuzjasci.pl/.../ibe-raport-diagnoza-umiejetnosci-matematycznych-DUMa.pdf [25.03.2018].
Report. (2015a). *Research report: Mathematical competences of third grade pupils*. Retrieved from http://eduentuzjasci.pl/publikacje-ee-lista/raporty/258-raport-z-badania/ibe-ee-raport-k3-mat/1269-ibe-ee-raport-k3-mat.html [25.03.2018].
Report. (2015b). *Research report: Needs of teachers of early education and mathematics in terms of professional development*. Retrieved from http://eduentuzjasci.pl/publikacje-ee-lista/raporty/239-raport-z-badania/badania-potrzeb-nauczycieli-edukacji-wczesnoszkolnej-i-nauczycieli-matematyki-w-zakresie-rozwoju-zawodowego-bpn/1241-badania-potrzeb-nauczycieli-edukacji-wczesnoszkolnej-i-nauczycieli-matematyki-w-zakresie-rozwoju-zawodowego-bpn.html [25.03.2018].
Report. (2016/2017). Research report: Education. Retrieved from https://stat.gov.pl/obszary-tematyczne/edukacja/edukacja/oswiata-i-wychowanie-w-roku-szkolnym-20162017,1,12.html
Semadeni, Z. (2016). *Podejście konstruktywistyczne do matematycznej edukacji wczesnoszkolnej. (ang. Constructivist approach to mathematical early childhood education)*. Wyd. ORE, Warszawa 2016.
Sessoms, D. (2008). Interactive instruction: Creating interactive learning environments through tomorrow's teachers. *International Journal of Technology in Teaching and Learning, 4*(2), 86–96.
Siwek, H. (2011). *System integralny w edukacji dziecka: konteksty i konsekwencje zmian*. [ang. An integral system in child's education: contexts and consequences of changes]. Wyd. TWP, Warszawa.
Snow, C., Bornstein, M. H., & Bruner, J. S. (1989). Interaction in human development.
Spelke, E. (2005). Differences in intrinsic aptitude for mathematics and science. *American Psychologist, 60*(9), 950–958.
Wygotski, L. S. (1989). *Thinking and speech*. Wyd. PWN.

Author Index

A
Al-Khatib, I.A., 226
Alonso-Díaz, L., 133–152
Alsaadat, K., 228
Altınpulluk, H., 105
Anderson, L.W., 115
Annabell, L., 174
Arías Masa, J., 133–152
Arrizabalaga, P., 173, 181
Ascheniuk, N., 203
Aydin, C.H., 104, 112

B
Balaji, V., 128
Baldwin, G., 204
Bassi, R., 119
Bezpalko, O., 204
Bidyuk, N., 204
Bilostotskaya, O., 204
Blackmore, P., 204
Boh, B., 239
Bolyai de Bolya, W., 269
Bolyai, F., 268
Brandl, M., 261–280
Brown, M., 112
Bruner, J., 266, 284
Budai, L., 279
Buinytska, O., 19–36

C
Caballe, S., 119
Cochrane, C., 253
Cornelius, S., 172
Costello, E., 112
Cubo Delgado, S., 133–152
Curaoglu, O., 171–181

D
Dalsgaard, C., 112
Daradoumis, T., 119
Descartes, R., 266, 268
Dewey, J., 204
Dugan, S., 204

E
Egorova, O., 204
Esteban, G., 140

F
Felder, R., 207
Ferruzca, M., 173
Fraser, M., 204

G
Gaible, E., 241
Gałuszka, A., 283–293
Garrido, C.C., 118
Gilbertson, K., 242
Gil-Jaurena, I., 112
Gosper, M., 207
Grant, M.M., 233
Gray, K., 174
Green, J., 204
Guichon, N., 173

Gunčaga, J., 261–280
Gurba, K., 119

H
Hanus, P., 204
Hawkridge, D., 173
Hejný, M., 263
Higgison, C., 172
Huizenga, J.C., 231
Hungerford, H.R., 225, 227, 234

I
Ifenthaler, D., 207
Issa, Theodora, 89–99, 103–129
Issa, Tomayess, 89–99, 103–129

J
Jakab, I., 223–243
Jansen, D., 104, 112, 155–169
Jensen, B.B., 225

K
Kántor, T., 261
Kennedy, G., 174
Kerski, J.J., 231
Kesim, M., 105
Khan, B., 172, 173, 181
Kim, B., 240
Klassen, S., 266
Klovak, G., 204
Kniazian, M., 204
Kołodziejczak, B., 185–199
Kommers, P., vii, 1, 6, 171
Kopczyński, T., 283–293
Körtesi, P., 261–280
Kosharna, N., 203
Kovchyn, I., 204
Kozubovsky, V., 204
Krathwohl, D.R., 115
Kubli, F., 266
Kuhlemeier, H., 225
Kuleshova, V., 204
Kulyk, Ye., 204
Kuzminska, L., 203
Kuzminska, O., 71–85

L
Lageman, E.C., 204
Landenberger, R.E., 231

Launa, S., 204
Lavrinenko, N., 204
Leikin, R., 266
Leschenko, M., 203
Levy, P., 207
Liakh, T.L., 204, 220
Littler, G., 263
Liu, Y., 231
Livingstone, S., 241
Lokshina, O., 204

M
Marcelo, C., 173
Marsh, D., 240
Martin-Espada, R., 133–152
McKay, E., 103–129
McKinney, J., 204
McMichael, A.J., 224
Mergendoller, J.R., 233, 234
Milash, O., 204
Mills, J.E., 207
Močnik, F., 271, 274, 279
Mokwa-Tarnowska, I., 185–199
Monguet, J. M., 173
Morze, N., vii, 1–17, 19–36, 49–68, 71–85, 103–129
Moskaluk, N., 204

N
Negroponte, N., 39
Newman, D.R., 253
Norkhina, O., 203
Noskova, T., 39–47

O
O'Hare, S., 172, 181
Olazabalaga, I.M., 118
Oldknow, A., 262

P
Palkevich, Yu., 203
Patru, M., 128
Pavliuk, R.O., 201–221
Pavlova, T., 39–47
Petrenko, L., 203
Petrulis, R., 207
Piaget, J., 284
Polischuk, V., 204
Priest, S., 228
Prince, M., 207

Author Index

Prishlyak, O., 204
Proshkin, V., 204
Pucherová, Z., 223–243
Pukhovska, L., 204

R
Ravitz, J., 224
Reder, P., 204
Rhodes, R., 204
Rogozin, A., 204
Romanovsky, O., 204
Rose, J., 241
Roszak, M., 185–199
Ruiz, U.G., 118

S
Salmon, G., 173
Samoilova, M., 204
Santos, I.R., 226
Schuwer, R., 104, 112
Sekret, I., 155–169, 171–181
Semadeni Z., 293
Seoane, A.M., 173
Sessoms, D., 293
Simonka, Zs., 279
Singer, F.M., 265
Slyusarenko, O., 204
Smyrnova-Trybulska, E., vii, 1–17, 71–85, 103–129
So, H.J., 240
Stapp, W.B., 224
Sukhomlynska, O., 204
Sultanova, L., 204
Svystun, V., 203
Szulc, J., 249–257

T
Taylor, R., 262
Teixeira, A., 104, 112

Theresia, M., 270
Thomas, J.W., 204
Tomei, L.A., 172
Torres, C., 204
Treagust, D.F., 207
Tusheva, V., 204

U
Umryk, M., 49–68

V
Varchenko-Trotsenko, L., 110
Veretenko, T., 204
Vlachopoulos, P., 172
Volk, T.L., 225, 227, 234
Vygotsky, L., 249, 284

W
Webb, B., 253
Wheeler, M., 173
Wiegand, P., 231

X
Xhafa, F., 119

Y
Yakovleva, O., 39–47, 103–129
Yanovski, A., 204
Yelnikova, G., 203
Yousef, A.M.F., 119

Z
Zhyzhko, T., 204
Zigová, M., 223–243
Zubchenko, O., 203

Subject Index

A
Adobe Connect, 136, 138, 140, 144, 150

B
Blended learning, 4, 6, 114, 117, 126, 127, 129, 189, 197, 198

C
Communication, 7, 8, 14–16, 19–21, 25, 34, 35, 43–46, 91, 97, 106, 108, 112, 117, 135, 136, 141, 157, 173, 174, 176, 178, 179, 186, 190, 202, 205, 213, 215, 217, 220, 237, 249–253, 255, 257, 262, 263
Computer science and STEM subjects, 3
Connectivist massive open online courses (cMOOCs), 106, 107
Contents, 4, 6–8, 20, 21, 25, 42–45, 62, 64, 77, 90, 91, 95, 106, 109, 110, 113, 115, 118, 125, 126, 134, 144, 145, 150, 152, 158, 168, 169, 173, 174, 176, 178–180, 185–187, 196, 198, 204, 207, 210, 217, 219, 224, 227–229, 233, 234, 239, 241, 242, 252, 255, 292
Cultural diversity, 1, 156, 275

D
Development of distance courses, 14
Digital competences, 19, 59, 60, 63, 262, 268
Digital competences of teachers, 19
Digital humanities, 108

Digital learning environment, 22, 45, 47
Digitally-competent teacher, 19

E
Educational institutions, 8, 14, 34, 43, 44, 74, 117, 156, 162, 186, 191, 193, 197, 202, 205–207, 217, 255, 284
Educational space of the University, 27
E-learning, vii, 27, 34, 42, 76, 78, 105, 110, 112–115, 118, 119, 128, 173, 199, 228, 235, 249, 252, 254–257, 279
Electronic training courses, 29, 79
E-portfolio system, 29
European standards of quality, 32

F
Field of pedagogic, 8, 13, 76, 186

H
Higher education (HE), 1, 5, 9, 17, 22, 29, 60, 79, 85, 90, 103–112, 115, 128, 149, 155–169, 193, 201–204, 217, 221, 256

I
ICT applications, vii, 44, 114
ICT-competence of university teachers, 23, 25, 202, 209, 210
ICT-mediated learning environment, 171, 172, 174, 178, 181

ICT tools, vii, 40, 42, 44, 113, 115, 118, 128, 171, 174, 178, 180, 279
ICT tools for e-learning, 113
Implementation, vii, 6, 8–12, 14, 17, 21, 30, 36, 40, 43, 71, 72, 74, 77, 80, 83, 85, 89, 99, 105, 112–127, 145, 158, 159, 163, 164, 169, 171, 173, 181, 203, 204, 207, 210, 214, 216, 217, 219, 221, 224, 239, 242, 256, 261, 263, 285, 293
Implementation of e-learning, 14
Information Technology (IT), 4, 8, 15, 44, 52, 60, 61, 91–93, 95, 96, 198, 213, 228, 240
In-service teachers, 112, 113
Intercultural learning environment, 13, 14, 16
Interdisciplinary knowledge, 146
IRNet, vii, 1, 8, 9, 17, 76, 78, 81, 82, 105, 119, 121

K
Key competences, 20, 262

L
Leadership in ICT, 33
Learning environment, 6, 22, 23, 43, 45, 62, 106, 110, 171, 172, 174, 176, 181, 188, 189, 196, 250, 254–257, 292
Learning management systems (LMS), vii, 34, 35, 42, 45, 115, 116, 126, 141, 174, 175, 180, 185, 188, 190, 197

M
MA course degree, 17, 113, 114
MA programme, 1
Management, 10, 16, 20, 29, 34, 43, 45, 63, 79, 91, 93–95, 97, 98, 106, 111, 114, 135, 138, 143, 152, 186, 187, 198, 202, 208, 219, 255
Mapping, 106, 226, 227, 229, 231–236, 240–242
Massive open online courses (MOOCs), vii, 42, 51, 56, 59, 68, 78, 129, 157–169, 185
Modern society, 202, 221
Modernization of the educational process, 241
MOODLE system, 4

N
Networking, 1, 63, 85, 173, 255

O
Online learning, 108, 114, 159, 161–163, 167, 169, 171–173, 175–178, 181, 186, 190, 254
Online teaching strategies, 171, 181
Online tutoring, 118, 171–181
Open and distance learning (ODL), 104, 106, 163

P
Primary school, 58, 270, 271, 284, 285, 293
Problem-based learning, 143
Professional and personal skills, 90
Professional competences of teachers, 22, 218, 219
Programming and Algorithmic Competencies, 50

Q
Quality, 10, 16, 19, 23, 27, 30–32, 34, 40, 41, 47, 58, 71, 78, 83, 85, 98, 105, 108, 110, 111, 119, 128, 149–151, 157, 158, 169, 172, 173, 176, 181, 191, 192, 197, 202, 215, 224, 228, 232, 237, 251, 256, 270, 284
Quality of higher education, 29

R
Refugee adaptation, 156, 161, 165
Refugee crisis, 155
Refugee education, 161, 166, 169
Refugee employment, 161, 168
Report writing, 89

S
Scientific communication of researchers, 79, 80, 83
Secondary schools, 192, 195, 223, 271, 275, 279
Securing of quality of education, 256
Social competences, 4, 16

Subject Index

Standards, 4, 14, 15, 22–25, 32, 60–63, 65, 79, 109, 128, 163, 190, 202, 284
Structure, 23, 63, 65, 89, 95, 115, 118–120, 124, 185, 196, 202–205, 209, 210, 212, 218, 219, 241, 254, 288
Syllabus of an advanced training program, 33
Synchronous Virtual Classrooms (SVC), 133–152

T
Technology, 3, 7, 8, 15, 20–23, 36, 40, 41, 59–61, 79, 89, 90, 106–108, 110, 128, 134, 161, 172, 175, 185–187, 189–192, 194, 196–198, 204, 209, 210, 217, 223–243, 250, 252, 254–256, 262, 278

Telematics Engineering, 148
Transformation of the educational system, 201

U
University education, 152, 158, 175

V
Validation, 128
Visualization, 27, 214, 231, 235, 237, 250, 263, 268–270, 277

X
xMOOCs, 106, 107

Printed in the United States
By Bookmasters